CAMBRIDGE STUDIES IN EARLY MODERN HISTORY

Editors

J. H. ELLIOTT   H. G. KOENIGSBERGER

FRENCH FINANCES, 1770–1795

CAMBRIDGE STUDIES IN EARLY MODERN HISTORY

Edited by Professor J. H. Elliott, King's College, University of London, and Professor H. G. Koenigsberger, Cornell University

The idea of an 'Early Modern' period of European history from the fifteenth to the late eighteenth century is now finding wide acceptance among historians. The purpose of Cambridge Studies in Early Modern History is to publish monographs and studies which will help to illuminate the character of the period as a whole, and in particular to focus attention on a dominant theme within it— the interplay of continuity (the continuity of medieval ideas, and forms of political and social organization) and change (the impact of new ideas, new methods and new demands on the traditional structures).

FRENCH FINANCES
1770–1795

FROM BUSINESS TO BUREAUCRACY

J.F.BOSHER

Professor of History
York University, Toronto

CAMBRIDGE
AT THE UNIVERSITY PRESS
1970

Published by the Syndics of the Cambridge University Press
Bentley House, 200 Euston Road, London N.W.1
American Branch: 32 East 57th Street, New York, N.Y.10022

© Cambridge University Press 1970

Library of Congress Catalogue Card Number: 73–111124

Standard Book Number: 521 07764 8

Printed in Great Britain
at the University Printing House, Cambridge
(Brooke Crutchley, University Printer)

TO
MY MOTHER AND FATHER

CONTENTS

ILLUSTRATIONS

TABLES

PREFACE

This is a financial history with most of the figures left out, and with only passing mention of taxes. The infamous *gabelle, taille* and the rest have already found their historians; most books on the financial history of the eighteenth century are filled with discussion of taxes and with estimates of revenue and expenditure. Such masters as Réné Stourm, Marcel Marion, Edmond Esmonin, and Frédéric Braesch have developed those aspects of the subject. Instead of following in their footsteps in the hope of adding something useful to their work, I have pursued a different inquiry. Who collected, held and spent government funds in the reign of Louis XVI? How was the central administration of finance arranged and how did it function? What was the Royal Treasury? These are some of the questions I have tried to answer. Others have touched upon them already, of course, and I have relied on their work a good deal. If this book can pretend to any originality, it is perhaps in trying to interpret the financial history of the ancien régime in terms of the administration rather than the budget and the taxes. We have usually been led to believe that Louis XVI was short of funds because he could not tax privileged classes, whereas it is very probable that even if he had taxed the privileged he would still have been in difficulties. The financial system seems to me to have been a bottomless pit capable of absorbing almost any amount of revenue. The Finance Ministers of Louis XVI were facing fundamental problems of public administration and the search for funds and the growing deficits of the reign were only symptoms of those problems: this is the underlying theme of the following chapters.

How could the Minister of Finance and his department manage the royal finances efficiently when nearly all the collecting and spending was in the hands of accountants who were independent of administrative control because they owned their offices? Here was the main problem. Several hundred venal accountants (if we may adapt the French word *vénal-e* to avoid awkward and inexact English expressions such as 'holding purchasable or saleable offices') held practically all government funds and behaved more like private businessmen than public officials. They were usually called *comptables* or *financiers* to distinguish them from bankers. A *financier* was defined in the dictionaries of the eighteenth century as someone who received, held or spent government funds, and this definition is a clue to another problem in administration: there was little practical distinction between private and public funds or between private businessmen and public officials. For all practical purposes the accountants were private businessmen, and the Crown could control them only by occasional legal process, not by continuous administrative direction. It follows that the financial administration was not a bureaucracy even in the loosest sense of that abused term. Bureaucracy began in the reign of Louis XVI and in the course of the French revolution it superseded the private enterprise of the financiers. In the realm of government finance, the French revolution was a triumph of bureaucracy as a method of public control. Here, in summary, is the main thesis of this volume.

The term 'bureaucracy' I have tried to use in a neutral sense, with none of its usual unpleasant connotations, not because I think a bureaucracy is always a desirable form of organization but because I take a certain detachment to be part of a scientific attitude. Thus, when I write of the revolutionary bureaucracy as being formed in the public interest, I am thinking of it merely as an instrument of public policy. The question of whose interests that policy expressed and of whose purposes were served by the machinery of the central administration—these are very different questions and have little place in this book. I have preferred to think of the bureaucracy simply as a neutral executive force ready to serve any government, democratic, royal, dictatorial or parliamentary. If this is not strictly accurate, it is true enough for this book which hardly touches upon the uses of bureaucracy but deals mainly with a stage in its growth.

To that special reader, the learned reviewer, whom the writer of today may perhaps be excused for presuming to single out, I must explain that I intended this book as a rather nubbly study with a special thesis and in no sense a complete or balanced financial history of the period. Had I tried to achieve the completeness of the encyclopedia or the balanced narrative of the survey, these chapters would have been very different. As they are, they hardly *cover* anything. Indeed, they omit a great deal of information which I feared might obscure their particular thesis. If some of the great themes and people are missed, if page after page is given over to lowly men, flitting in and out with little shape or colour, 'political and literary mushrooms' in Rivarol's phrase, this deformity—as it may appear to the learned reviewer—is essential to my argument about the administrative system which is itself, after all, the main subject of the book.

Many people have helped me in my research and writing these past few years and I am very grateful to them. For criticizing parts of the text at various stages, I wish to thank Jean Laponce, John Norris, Mack Walker and my colleagues in the history colloquium at the University of British

Columbia. The final version owes a great deal to the willing and careful attention of H. G. Koenigsberger, joint editor of the series, and my colleague at Cornell University. I have to thank Emmanuel Le Roy Ladurie for the sub-title that I finally adopted. To Geoffrey Mead I owe the stimulating suggestion that the Royal Treasury never existed and I am also indebted to Henry Roseveare for interesting conversations about financial history. I have often received special assistance from librarians at Cornell, the University of British Columbia, the British Museum, the Bibliothèque Nationale and the Archives Nationales in Paris. Many of the months I have spent at the British and French libraries were paid for by the generosity of the Canada Council. My research trips were a pleasure, thanks to the inexhaustible hospitality of Hubert and Mayence Mondor in Paris and of other friends at Marden Hill, Hertford. For all this aid, however, I should never have been able to finish the book without the encouragement and help of my wife, Cecil. I should not have begun it, may I add, without the assistance of Professor S. T. Bindoff and the guidance of the late Professor Alfred Cobban during my first years of research in London and Paris.

J.F.B.
Toronto

FRENCH TERMS

As in every field of foreign history, certain terms of French administration are difficult to translate. I have used English cognates as much as possible, but I have not hesitated to slip into French when the exact sense of a term seemed pertinent. Common words with technical meanings, such as 'financier,' 'accountant,' 'magistrate,' or 'bureau,' I have defined as necessary and the definitions may be found through the index. Wherever the title *Receveur particulier*, or *Receveur des tailles* appeared often on the same page, I have translated it as Receiver intending it to be distinguished from Receiver General, and to avoid having a page full of italics. Eight of the most common French terms, with no useful translations, I have simply used in the text as though they were English words: ancien régime, arrêt, caisse, livre, parlement, rentes, rescriptions, and venal. Some of these, too, have definitions and appear in the index. Many terms and titles have inevitably been rendered in French and for the reader unfamiliar with them, the best book of reference is Marcel Marion, *Dictionnaire des institutions françaises aux XVIIe et XVIIIe siècles* (Paris, 1923). Some of the more common terms are the following:

arrêt: official resolution or decision, usually having the force of law.

assignation: a payment order, not unlike the rescription, but drawn on a particular revenue and 'assigned' to it.

cahier: register of petitions or requests which a provincial Estates or other body might send to the King.

état au vrai: the accountant's report on his receipts and expenditures.

état du Roi: table of receipts and expenditures which the Crown sent to each accountant; it was binding on him.

caisse: a fund independently managed by an accountant; roughly the equivalent of 'chest' as in 'community chest' etc.

caissier: the clerical manager of a caisse; might be translated as 'cashier' except that the link with the word caisse ought not to be obscured.

exercice: the business of one year, the normal accounting unit; a fiscal year.

livre: the common unit of money, divided into 20 *sols*; the *sol* was in turn divided into 12 *deniers*.

Ponts et Chaussées: the royal administration of bridges and roads.

rapporteur: the member of a council charged with preparing and presenting the business to the other councillors.

régie: a government administrative body responsible to the Royal Council rather than to the Chamber of Accounts.

rente: as used in this book, it is a bond or debenture, but named for the regular income it afforded rather than for the investment capital.

rescription: a kind of cheque, loosely speaking, usually drawn by an accountant on his clerk or *caissier*.

soumission: legal instrument listing the Farmers General's commitments to the Crown.

traitant: a businessman who undertook by a contract (*traité*) to perform some business for the Crown.

vénal: purchasable, saleable, or holding a purchasable office. Hence, *venalité* refers to the system of selling royal offices.

PART 1

THE CENTRAL ADMINISTRATION OF FINANCE AND HOW IT WORKED

I

INTRODUCTION

THE FRENCH monarchy of the Valois and Bourbon kings was continually in financial difficulties. From the Middle Ages it suffered a long series of crises growing like cacti in a desert of confusion, waste and fraud, with only rare oases of plenty and security. In this the French monarchy might appear no different from most other régimes in most periods of history, except that one of its crises developed into the French revolution. That last crisis appears to have been unique by its consequences. Though we may well wonder whether it was really any different from the earlier ones, coming as it did in a long series, that famous crisis in the reign of Louis XVI lends a special interest to the entire series. A study of the financial troubles facing Louis XVI may therefore usefully begin with a bird's eye view of similar troubles over the previous two centuries.

François I began his reign (1515–47) with a legacy of debt and by 1523 was facing a serious crisis which he ultimately resolved by selling offices and borrowing heavily from Lyon bankers.[1] Henri II (1547–59) inherited this system of borrowing and ended his reign in a grand financial crash.[2] Unable to depend thereafter upon the ruined and disappointed merchant bankers, Catherine de Medici and her three reigning sons (1559–89) were chronically short of funds, and that shortage was one reason why they called three meetings of the Estates General (1560, 1576, 1588) and two Assemblies of Notables (1560, 1583) in thirty years. Of the Bourbon kings who ruled for the two hundred years from 1589 to 1789, all except the first of them, Henri IV (1589–1610), struggled unsuccessfully to make ends meet and all financed their governments by emergency measures. Louis XIV managed very well, it is true, for the first decade of his personal rule (1661–72), the years of Colbert's ascendancy, but in the course of the next forty years the royal government sank deeper and deeper into difficulties. The long crisis during the last decades of the seventeenth century and the first decades of the eighteenth has impressed many historians as being the

---

[1] Roger Doucet, *Etudes*, p. 175; Doucet, 'Le grand parti', *Revue historique*, vol. 171 (1933), pp. 473–513; vol. 172 (1933), pp. 1–41
[2] Hauser, 'The European Financial Crisis of 1559'.

beginning of the monarchy's fall.[1] Looking back rather than forward, however, we might just as easily compare the financial crisis of the years between the treaties of Ryswick (1697) and Utrecht (1713) with the earlier crisis between the treaties of Westphalia (1648) and the Pyrenees (1659). Deep financial trouble was normal throughout the life of the French monarchy. It was the times of relief, not the continual difficulties, which were abnormal.

Kings, ministers and people tended in every age to look for the causes of financial trouble in the misdeeds of individuals, and as the trouble was always there, so accusing fingers were forever pointing out certain individuals responsible for it. Again and again royal tribunals punished men for financial crimes, and most writers and statesmen of those early centuries believed fraud to be the cause of the shortage of royal funds. A rogues gallery of French public finance might show in the front rank such high officials as Enguerrand de Marigny, minister of Philippe le Bel (1285–1314), hanged in 1315; Jean de Montargis executed in 1409 by Charles VI; Pierre des Essarts in 1413; Jacques Coeur banished by Charles VII on 29 May 1453. The series continues in modern times with Beaune de Semblançay hanged on 11 August 1527; Benoît Milon, seigneur de Videville, who fled from the wrath of Henri III in 1583; Charles, marquis de la Vieuville, Superintendent of Finance, arrested and disgraced on 13 August 1624; Nicolas Fouquet, another Superintendent, imprisoned for life on 21 December 1664 after a long and famous trial; John Law, who fled in disgrace in 1721; François Bigot, the last Intendant of New France, condemned to death in August 1763 with the sentence commuted to banishment for life. In the middle ranks, a large number of men in nearly every reign were fined or stripped of their property, imprisoned or executed by the royal courts.

Another persistent and widespread opinion imputed the Crown's financial troubles to foreign bankers, Italian until the reign of Louis XIV and then Swiss, Huguenot and Belgian. But whether foreign or French, individuals were always found to be the main cause of the recurring crises in government finance. How could people in the ancien régime think otherwise when even a royal edict inspired by Colbert could thunder against 'the enormous crimes of peculation which have exhausted our finances and impoverished our provinces...'?[2]

These opinions were not lost on the historians who, after the French revolution, tried to explain the finances of the ancien régime. The best of

---

[1] Legohérel, Les Trésoriers généraux, p. 228; Marion, Histoire financière, vol. 1; Martin and Besançon, L'Histoire du crédit, p. 1; Sagnac, 'Le crédit de l'état'.

[2] Clément, Lettres, instructions, vol. 2, pp. 751–3. Edict of November 1661.

them, Auguste Bailly,[1] Dareste de la Chavanne,[2] René Stourm,[3] Marcel Marion,[4] and others, wrote a great deal about the evil effects of fraud committed by greedy and faithless royal servants; but their books also show folly, as well as crime, to have been a fatal flaw in the monarchy. Weakness of character and deficiencies of policy appear again and again as explanations of the Crown's difficulties. To open almost any history book on the subject of finance is to discover François I mistakenly selling royal offices, Richelieu neglecting financial matters, Mazarin enriching himself and giving way to financial interests, the regent Duke of Orléans naïvely listening to John Law, nearly all the Bourbons spending too much on wars and the great majority of their finance ministers foolishly running the monarchy into debt. The heroes of the story are the few who succeeded in reducing expenditures and increasing revenues—'balancing the budget'— or in convincing historians of their ability and good intentions: men like Sully, Colbert and the tragic hero, Turgot. In greater or lesser degree, most of the other policy makers and administrators still appear in history books either as fools or as villains, and the financial history of the ancien régime seems to be a record of their folly and villainy. In most essentials, we still tend to see the financial history of the Bourbon monarchy through the eyes of the eighteenth and nineteenth centuries.

That approach, in however subtle a form (and my description above is a caricature), will not do today. Looking for scapegoats and following heroes was all very well for the men in the Bourbon monarchy who faced the problems of their time as practical issues. But it no longer seems very useful to deal with those problems in the terms of old questions like, 'What did the leading statesmen do, and what should they have done?' To answer such questions is to deal with public affairs in the manner of a political party out of office, pretending to know how the men in power ought to have acted. Such questions encourage the unwarranted assumption that the Bourbons and their servants, by taking certain steps prescribed in retrospect, might have overcome their financial difficulties. Perhaps the present-day historian may be excused for refusing to make that assumption and for shirking the distasteful and unprofitable duties of a magistrate engaged in trying the leading men of the eighteenth century *ex post facto* and assigning responsibility for the financial problems of the monarchy.

'How did the financial system work, and what problems did it pose for the statesmen of the time?' These questions have the merit of turning our attention to the institutions of the monarchy. To seek faults in these

[1] *Histoire financière* (1830).   [2] *Histoire de l'administration* (1848).
[3] *Les Finances* (1885).   [4] *Histoire financière* (1914).

5

institutions is surely as reasonable as to look for them in the actions of statesmen and officials, for it is easy to suspect after Marx and Freud that men are formed by the social and political systems in which they grow and are partly prisoners of underlying forces in society and in their own minds. However that may be, systems tend to perpetuate themselves. One way of avoiding the unsatisfactory conclusion that most of the financial officials of the ancien régime were either fools or rogues, as the standard histories would have us believe, is to inquire into the social and political conditions in which they lived. We shall discover, I think, that the financial system was not theirs to change. Until the French revolution, the system had certain enduring features which stand out in the vast literature on the ancien régime as fundamental causes of the monarchy's financial ills.

The Crown practically always relied upon the services of intermediaries to manage its financial business. Large though the royal administration was, it was never equipped to collect taxes, to borrow, to hold royal funds or to spend them, and this was one of its most persistent and striking deficiencies. All financial operations were in the hands of municipal governments, the clergy, provincial estates, tax farms and, most of all, a great many financiers, private or semi-private. These agents and agencies were largely independent and often engaged in profit-making enterprises, and there were very few phases in the management of government funds which could be properly described as *public* finance.

Nearly all the Crown's long-term borrowing from 1522 until the revolution was managed by city governments, especially by the Hôtel de Ville of Paris.[1] Medieval kings had created rentes (debentures) of various types, but in modern times the royal government made continuous use of municipal credit, founded upon the investors' confidence in the Hôtel de Ville; and thus large numbers of merchants and magistrates became *rentiers* through the agency of a city government in which they had great power. They were more willing to lend when they controlled the borrowing process. The city turned the capital investments over to the Crown and in return took certain royal tax revenues assigned to the Paris Receiver General so that he could pay the rentes. In these arrangements, the Crown was relying on the business management of the Hôtel de Ville as well as its credit. When in 1561 the assembled clergy of France agreed to pay the arrears on the rentes, they paid this new revenue over to the city. The venal offices for Payers of the rentes, established in April 1594, hardly increased royal control over the management of this debt. The Payers and the Paris Hôtel de Ville remained permanently in this powerful intermediary position, for all the world like an

---

[1] Schnapper, *Les Rentes*, p. 153

independent financial syndicate, subject to the King's orders but not to his continuous supervision. They and not he took the regular profits of the lending business.

Municipal tax-collecting services, also, were useful to kings at various times. By seizing the municipal *octrois* (taxes on commodities) in an act of 1647, Mazarin was not merely diverting municipal revenues from the towns to the uses of the central government but also depending on the towns to collect these revenues.[1] This arrangement did not last long; in 1663 the Crown leased the collection of *octrois* to another intermediary, the tax farms of the *aides* (excise taxes).

The clergy and the provincial estates, however, performed the same function of tax-collecting on an even greater scale than the cities. Beginning with the *contrat de Poissy* in 1561, the clergy periodically granted subsidies (*dons gratuits*) to the Crown and in the time of Louis XIV these became a regular though variable part of royal revenues. The Receiver General for the clergy paid the Crown its share of clerical revenues, yet the tithe collectors worked for the clergy. In much the same way the provincial estates of Brittany, Languedoc, Burgundy, Artois, Provence and other former domains made arrangements to collect most of the taxes in their own provinces (*pay d'états*) and at their periodic meetings voted subsidies to the Crown. Irregular in the sixteenth century, though more and more frequent in response to royal pressure, these subsidies, like the *don gratuit* of the clergy, took the form of an annual Crown revenue in the time of Colbert and so remained until the revolution. Each of the estates appointed a Treasurer to manage provincial finances and to pay the *don gratuit* to the Crown. These revenues and the excellent credit of the provincial estates were obviously useful as security for loans, and beginning in 1742 the royal government was able to mortgage them, using royal power and persuasion in time of need to win the acquiescence of the estates. 'The Estates were only playing the role of intermediary,' writes an historian of Brittany, 'their treasurer withholding the sums necessary for the payments of interest and principal from the total of subscribed taxes.'[2] Revenues from the clergy offered the same possibilities and from the very beginning of clerical contributions the Crown secured certain rentes on them.[3] Other corporate bodies, such as the Ordre du Saint Esprit and the postal farms, served the same purpose.

The royal government was always ready to employ business organizations

[1] Matthews, *The Royal General Farms*, p. 166.
[2] Rébillon, *Les Etats*, p. 730.
[3] Schnapper, *Les Rentes*, p. 155; Martin and Besançon, *L'Histoire du crédit*, p. 96. In the reign of Louis XVI the clergy were paying 1,300,000 livres a year in rentes on the Hôtel de Ville, still under protest. (*Encyclopédie méthodique. Finance*, vol. 1, p. 306.)

whenever their services were convenient. For about a century beginning in the reign of Louis VII (1137–80) French kings left the Royal Treasury in the care of the Knights Templar who managed royal finances as one account among many in their keeping.[1] In modern times, the most usual and characteristic business groups serving the monarchy were the tax farmers. These worked in enormous numbers of small groups during the fifteenth and sixteenth centuries, leasing the *aides* (excise taxes mainly on alcohol) from the *élus* town by town and even parish by parish.[2] Many more contracted with the bailiffs and seneschals to collect the various taxes attached to the royal domains, and still others leased parts of the *gabelle* (salt monopoly) and the many provincial and local systems of customs duties and tolls. From the middle of the sixteenth century the royal government had some success in consolidating these infinitely various tax farms and in 1578 one group of capitalists undertook to manage the salt monopoly throughout a large group of provinces, the *pays de la grande gabelle*; in 1584 Henri III gathered many of the customs duties into five great farms (*cinq grosses fermes*) and in May 1604 Sully was for a time able to incorporate more than half of the *aides* in one large lease. Most of these consolidated tax farms disintegrated during the reign of Louis XIII and the regency that followed. When Colbert took up the work again, he had only modest success in unifying these various taxes on commodities, but in 1681 he managed to incorporate them, together with the new tobacco monopoly of 1674, in one comprehensive lease to a large syndicate of forty tax farmers, the famous Farmers General, and this arrangement continued with only minor or temporary changes until the revolution. Large or small, in monopoly or in competition, the groups of tax farmers were private entrepreneurs making profits in collecting taxes, selling salt and tobacco, arranging payments and money transfers, lending larger and larger sums to the Crown. Would-be reformers like François I and John Law failed utterly in their attempts to 'nationalize' tax-collection. The tax farmer was perhaps the most typical and successful of businessmen in the ancien régime.

Until the reign of Louis XV tax farmers were an indistinguishable part of a large, fluctuating group of businessmen, variously called *traitants, partisans, financiers* or *gens d'affaires*. These continued to flourish until the revolution, but in the reign of Louis XV (1723–74) the Farmers General became a group apart, wealthier and more firmly established, monopolizing official business which had earlier fallen to various *traitants* and *partisans*. These latter terms began to fall out of use after the organizing of the Far-

[1] Lot and Fawtier, *Histoire des institutions*, vol. 2, p. 188.
[2] Doucet, *Les Institutions*, vol. 2, pp. 559–61.

mers General as a quasi-monopoly in 1726. But this change made little fundamental difference to the system. Until the revolution the various groups of *gens d'affaires* performed a great many different services. Practically any matter which entailed handling money went beyond the capacity or inclination of the royal administration and, more important, offered the possibility of immediate cash advances. Business for the Crown was therefore let out to private businessmen by means of a *traité* or *parti* (contract) supplying the army, purchasing and transporting grain, selling offices, managing the postal and public transport services, collecting all the various taxes and so on. In the sixteenth and seventeenth centuries *traitants* commonly proposed new sources of revenue to the ministers of the Crown. Methods varied, but in the time of Richelieu and Mazarin, once the Crown and the *traitants* had agreed in principle, the contract passed before the royal *Conseil d'état et des finances* which drew up a formal resolution setting forth the names and titles of the *traitants*, the subject and terms of the agreement.[1] In the case of new taxes the arrêt stipulated that the King would propose an edict or declaration and have it registered by the sovereign courts. The *traité* also stated the business expenses—clerks' wages, cost of accounting, etc.—and the *traitants'* profit of 10%, 25% or more of the sums to be collected. As a general rule, the *traitants* undertook to advance the revenue in question and for the royal government this was the most attractive feature of the arrangement. The system was flexible and made way for men too highly placed to appear as *traitants* themselves to have their servants or others sign the *traité* for them. The *traité* lent itself to all manner of business transactions, for it passed as a form of wealth which a *traitant* might give to his creditors or use as security for a loan or for setting up a system of sub-leasing to *sous-traitants*.

The tax farmers and the *traitants* in general were evidently engaged in private enterprise and bound to the royal service only by leases and contracts. They were not officials, but there was a third group of financiers, often included in the meaning of the term *traitants*, who appear superficially to have been government officials. These were the royal accountants (*officiers comptables*), chiefly the Receivers General and ordinary Receivers who collected the *taille*, the *vingtième*, the *capitation*, and the Treasurers General who managed most of the Crown's spending. The greatest of these in modern times were the two or three Treasurers General of the Epargne (Royal Treasury) from 1523 to 1661, and then, after Colbert and Louis XIV had abolished these offices, the two or three Keepers of the Royal Treasury (*Gardes du trésor royal*). In spite of appearances to the contrary,

[1] Chauleur, 'Le rôle des traitants', p. 21; Ranum, *Richelieu*, p. 129.

9

these accounting officers were not officials at all, not civil servants in any modern sense of the term.

One of the two acts in creating an accountant was the *provision* by royal letters which made him 'lord (*seigneur*) of the office', Charles Loyseau tells us. This lordship carried with it the rights of office, including the right to collect fees *jure dominii*.[1] The royal letters of *provision* had more in common with letters conferring nobility than with the royal commissions naming officials such as Intendants. Such commissions named their bearers to perform certain tasks in the King's name and were revocable, whereas letters of *provision* conferred honour and rights, status and a permanent title to the office. The second act in creating an accountant was the *reception* by an appropriate sovereign court, and it conferred on the accountant 'l'effet et l'exercice, la qualité et le rang'. In using such language, the jurists showed the accountant to be almost a kind of lower nobleman, lord of his office, bearer of its quality and rank, entitled thereby to certain rights and privileges.

The legal character of an office was not altogether clear either in the court decisions or in opinions based on the *coûtume de Paris*, but no one doubted that an office was a form of property, a kind of fief. French kings had sold offices since the Middle Ages, and in 1522 François I set up an agency 'to serve as a shop for that new merchandise', as Loyseau bluntly observed.[2] Whether an office was real estate (*immobilier*) or moveable goods (*mobilier*) or 'metoyenne entre les meubles et les immeubles' was a difficult question for jurists and full of consequences for an accountant's heirs, creditors and debtors in case of his bankruptcy, arrest or death.[3] Different courts had jurisdiction over different kinds of property and different laws applied. However that might be, Loyseau believed an *officier comptable* to be no [civil] servant, but 'propriétaire et possesseur'.[4] After 1604 the notorious *droit annuel* or *paulette* confirmed the practice of treating offices not merely as the property of one man but as the patrimony of his family from generation to generation. To raise the lords of certain offices to noble rank was then only a short step and the needy Bourbons took it in the seventeenth century.

The practice of selling offices, which we may most conveniently call 'venality', adapting the French term *vénalité*, had social consequences which were clear from the beginning. After the reign of François I, protests

---

[1] Claude de Ferrière, *Corps et compilation*, vol. 1, p. 1470.
[2] Loyseau, *Œuvres*, p. 144; Mousnier, *La Vénalité*, p. xxix. This agency was called 'La partie casuelle'.
[3] Loyseau, *Œuvres*, p. 1; Claude de Ferrière, *Corps et compilation*, vol. 4, p. 393.
[4] Loyseau, *Œuvres*, p. 14.

came from all sides against the swelling class of venal office-holders, a new fourth estate.[1] But few observers, if any, perceived the administrative consequences of venality. Not until the French revolution did most Frenchmen see clearly that the administrative system of the monarchy was founded upon the confusion of public power and private property;[2] that office-holders acquired private rights in the royal administration and so escaped the control of the Crown; that the government sold off its power over many vital processes of justice and finance thereby reducing or inhibiting its own force of action. As owner of his office, a royal accountant was independent of all direct supervision and responsibility of the bureaucratic kind which he might impose on his own employees. Charles Loyseau may seem to have hinted at these effects in complaining that the King 'sells dearly the public authority, the rank and honour that derive from offices', but he was not suggesting that the Crown should have a bureaucratic relationship with its officers.[3] In his eyes the accountants managing royal finances need not have a status any different from that of the magistrates in sovereign courts and he was not interested in the question of whether accountants should be organized in a hierarchy of constant supervision and inspection. Loyseau was only complaining that wealth had become practically the sole road to royal office and had nearly closed 'the two other roads of virtue and favour', or merit and patronage. The method of appointment was what interested him, not the structure and functioning of the administrative system. This was the common seventeenth-century view. Even Richelieu, the architect of what Lavisse has christened 'the administrative monarchy', was thinking only of the method of appointment when he defended venality as better than the system of patronage and argued that patronage would always determine appointments if offices were not sold.[4]

A royal office was an honour and a fief conferred by the King, but it was also a business investment to be exploited for maximum profit at the expense of the Crown and the general public. No cynicism and no exaggeration are necessary to draw the conclusion that in practice a royal accountant was engaged in a private enterprise, dealing in 'public' finances much as he dealt in the funds of his own family or of private clients. His business was neither inspected nor supervised and as long as he continued to make pay-

---

[1] Lucien Romier, *Le Royaume de Catherine de Médicis*, vol. 2, pp. 21–3.
[2] Mousnier, *La Vénalité*, pp. xxix, 63, and 622. Even after the revolution neither A. Bailly nor C. Dareste de. la Chavanne showed any knowledge of the administrative consequences.
[3] Loyseau, *Œuvres*, pp. 144 and 245, and p. 1.
[4] Dareste de la Chavanne, *Histoire de l'administration*, vol. 1, p. 303; Ernest Lavisse, *Histoire de France*, vol. 7, *Le Règne de Louis XIV*.

ments on royal *ordonnances*, to redeem his own notes and to meet his other commitments of collection and expenditure, only he and his clerks need know the extent of his debts or the range of his investments. His annual accounts to the Chamber of Accounts were records only of his business for the Crown, a sort of banker's statement to a client, and gave no information about his other business. Nor did these accounts show what the officer had done with royal funds between the time of receipt and the time of expenditure. The affairs of an accountant only became public if he went bankrupt or was arrested and tried on suspicion of fraud. Little wonder that in the minds of Richelieu, Colbert and others of the ancien régime, the accountants were hardly different from *traitants*.[1]

The independence of accountants was visible in another way. Their clerks were their own and in no sense employees of the Crown. An *ordonnance* of 1550, which first recognized the right of accountants to have employees (though, of course, they had always had them) declared that such clerks could have nothing of the authority or status of royal officers and need not take any oath. The clerk was merely a private person bound to his employer by a private contract.[2]

Accountants, like other *traitants*, were intermediaries on whom the Crown relied to manage funds; but they not only collected and spent, they also lent heavily to the Crown. Their lending is neither so famous nor so well known as that of the merchant bankers, domestic and foreign, who served many kings, especially François I and Henri II. Borrowing from bankers became much more difficult after the great crisis and crash of 1559, when the 'Grand Parti' of Lyon collapsed, and the Crown turned more and more to the intermediary services of its own accountants. There was nothing new about this practice, however; it is reported by students of every century. Maurice Rey explains how the fourteenth-century kings forced their accountants to advance funds.[3] Henri Jassemin and Gustave Dupont-Ferrier tell us that in the fifteenth century 'all the accountants were obliged to become bankers to the King and to advance him sums, often considerable'.[4] A sixteenth-century writer explains how merchant bankers collaborated with royal accountants in lending funds to princes, often

---

[1] *Mémoires du Cardinal de Richelieu*, Paris (Société de l'Histoire de France), 1920, vol. 4, pp. 133–56; Pierre Clément, *Lettres, instructions et mémoires de Colbert*, vol. 2, pp. 54–60.

[2] Gustave Dupont-Ferrier, *Etudes sur les institutions financières de la France* (Paris, 1930), vol. 1, pp. 118 and 121; Loyseau, *Œuvres*, p. 33.

[3] *Le Domaine du Roi* (Paris, 1965), p. 276.

[4] Jassemin, 'La chambre des comptes et la gestion des deniers publics au XVe siècle', *Bibliothèque de l'Ecole des Chartes*, vol. 93 (1932), p. 120; Dupont-Ferrier, *Etudes sur les institutions*, vol. 1, p. 117.

lending the Crown its own money at high interest.[1] 'The King had to borrow', writes Roland Mousnier, taking up this theme in the reigns of Henri IV and Louis XIII. 'His receivers lent him his own money at high interest.'[2] Of the early eighteenth century, too, Philippe Sagnac has written, 'Each receiver, each treasurer, became for the state a banker to whom it could appeal and who issued, on its guarantee, notes secured on the funds of the Treasury.'[3]

An accountant's advances of money were characteristically a form of short-term credit and therefore different from the long-term loans secured on the credit of the Hôtel de Ville, the estates and the clergy. That is, an accountant advanced money which he expected to receive in taxes collected, or from other regular sources, within a few months, and he usually made the loan in the course of his ordinary business by merely honouring the Crown's payment orders drawn on his caisse, even when there was no money in the royal account. The King and those he authorized to issue *ordonnances* in his name usually made them out—rescriptions, *mandements*, *ordonnances*, *acquits*, etc.—like cheques drawn on specified accountants; and orders made out for sums above and beyond official annual collections were, in effect, overdrawing the accountant's royal accounts. In the mid-seventeenth century Colbert reckoned that the Crown paid for such advances at the rate of about 15% annually and that advances by accountants and other *traitants* had cumulated to an enormous total of 170 million livres by the time of the general bankruptcy in August 1648.[4] If, as on that occasion, the accountants could find no more cash with which to meet the claims on themselves, and for lack of public confidence could issue no more paper promissory notes of their own, then they were bankrupt and the whole system of royal short-term credit collapsed. This occurred again at the end of Louis XIV's reign and once more in 1770. Clearly the Crown depended on the credit of its own accountants. Of course, they in turn were able to borrow individually from private sources partly because of the confidence which their royal offices inspired, and offices were thus assets bolstering up the personal credit of the accountants. This was evidently not a system of public credit in any modern sense of the term, for the accountants

[1] Albert Chamberland and Henri Hauser, 'La banque et les changes au temps de Henri II', *Revue historique*, vol. 160 (1929), p. 283. Cf. Romier, *Le Royaume de Catherine de Médicis*, vol. 2, p. 37.

[2] *La Vénalité*, p. 415; Jean-Paul Charmeil, *Les Trésoriers de France à l'époque de la Fronde* (Paris, 1964), p. 410.

[3] Philippe Sagnac, 'Le crédit de l'état...'. *Revue d'histoire moderne et contemporaine*, vol. IX (1908), p. 265; Henri Legohérel, *Les Trésoriers généraux de la Marine*, pp. 175 and 251.

[4] Clément, *Lettres, instructions et mémoires de Colbert*, vol. 2, pp. 23–4.

contracted debts on the Crown's behalf, usually by issuing their own credit notes, rescriptions, which circulated as a kind of currency.[1]

Rescriptions were only a part of a vast quantity and variety of paper currency circulating during the ancien régime, mainly among the business, official, legal and propertied classes. The short-term debt was entirely in this form, and without paper currencies this part of the debt could hardly have existed. Exact descriptions of the various types and precise estimates of the sums in circulation would be difficult or impossible to establish, but they are not needed to affirm that all paper notes were issued either by *ordonnateurs* who made out payment orders or by *traitants*, accountants, *gens d'affaires*, etc. who were supposed to redeem these orders by actually cashing them. The first category included royal *mandements* and *ordonnances* calling for payment at the Royal Treasury; *assignations* assigning payments to certain revenue funds; *acquits de comptant* for payments which the King or his Superintendent of Finance wished to conceal from the Chamber of Accounts, and others; various *récépissés*, *acquits* and other receipts or certificates for supplies and services purchased for the Crown; and finally, the 'playing-cards' which the Intendants and Governors of New France issued in 1686 and from time to time until the conquest in 1759.

All these bore the signature of the King or of his Superintendent of Finances or another *ordonnateur* authorized to make out payment orders. In New France both Governors and Intendants signed the card money.[2] The royal signature, or its equivalent, may have induced people to accept all these in payment, but the royal fiat was largely illusory because all these paper notes could ultimately be cashed only by accountants or other *traitants*, people on the accounting side of the system. In other words, royal payment orders had to be redeemed by men engaged in private enterprise. The card money in New France, for example, could ultimately be cashed only by the Treasurers General for the Marine. A royal authority who issued payment orders could never be quite certain of having them honoured, for all were essentially like orders to a private banker who, at best, was free from any continuous administrative supervision and, at worst, could go bankrupt.[3] In other words, the Crown used its authority to give its notes currency

---

[1] A rescription was something like a cheque: the accountant drew it on his own clerk or cashier in favour of a drawee, but it was unlike a cheque in that it could be discounted like a 'sight bill'.

[2] Adam Shortt, ed., *Documents Relating to Canadian Currency, Exchange and Finance during the French Period* (Ottawa, 1925), p. 768.

[3] Throughout the history of the monarchy, a great many accountants and other *traitants* were continually going bankrupt, especially in times of financial crisis. References to bankruptcies are in the works of Andrée Chauleur; Germain Martin; Julian Dent, 'An Aspect of the Crisis of the Seventeenth Century: The Collapse of the Financial Adminis-

but not to arrange for payment by truly public agencies. The paper signed by *ordonnateurs* was half private and half public, unless we regard royal business as the King's own, in which case such paper was wholly private.

No such ambiguity affected the notes issued by accountants, tax farmers and other *traitants*. The rescriptions of Receivers General and the notes (*billets*) and bills of exchange of Treasurers General, Treasurers of the Epargne and tax farmers were all virtually private notes backed by the fiat and credit of the individuals who issued them. There were two serious drawbacks in having short-term debt held in the form of these notes: the Crown had to pay the issuing financiers handsome interest on loans, and at the same times ran the risk of loss by the bankruptcies of these creditors.

Both kinds of notes, those issued by accountants and other financiers and those issued by the King and other *ordonnateurs*, played great parts in royal finance throughout the history of the monarchy, but they were circulating in unprecedented amounts during the last years of Louis XIV. They were, indeed, evidence of his prestige. After 1704 nearly all government payments were being made in notes, and by the end of 1707 notes of all kinds totalled at least 413 million livres.[1] In 1710 alone over 182 million livres worth of new paper instruments were put into circulation, over 13 millions of them in Receiver General's notes and another 27 millions in notes of the Farmers General.[2] In the same year the Intendant at Québec issued 244,000 livres in card money, thus adding to a total that was to reach 3,355,115 livres before it could be redeemed in bills of exchange drawn on the Marine Treasurers in Paris by their agents in the colony.[3] During the months following the death of Louis XIV in September 1715, the government called for all notes issued in its service and registered nearly 600 million livres worth.[4] Rescriptions were then circulating to the amount of over 60 millions, and the War and Marine Treasurers had issued notes in about the same quantity.[5] Uncashed *ordonnances* on the Keepers of the Royal Treasury represented about 230 millions and *assignations* on various revenues another 82 millions. Most of the rest was in the form of promissory notes issued either by the

---

tration of the French Monarchy (1653–61)', *Economic History Review* (August 1967), pp. 241–56; A. M. de Boislisle, *Correspondance des contrôleurs généraux des finances avec les intendants des provinces* (Paris, 1874), 3 vols., and many other writings.

[1] Armand Seligmann, *La Première Tentative d'emission fiduciaire en France* (Paris, 1925), pp. 69 and 98.

[2] J. R. Mallet, *Comptes rendus de l'administration des finances du royaume de France* (London, 1789) (written early in the century), pp. 136–7.

[3] Guy Frégault, 'Essai sur les finances canadiennes (1700–1750)', *Revue d'histoire de l'Amérique française*, vol. 12 (1959), pp. 472–80.

[4] Mallet, *Comptes rendus*, p. 154; Seligmann, *La Première Tentative*, pp. 130–1.

[5] Martin and Besançon, *L'Histoire du crédit*, p. 161.

Directors of the Mints or by organizations which the Controller General, Nicolas Desmarets, had created in desperation. Nearly every war caused financial crisis, but none more badly than the War of the League of Augsburg (1688–97) and the War of the Spanish Succession (1701–13), occurring as they did during the first twenty-five years of a cycle of economic depression which did not end until the 1730s.[1]

During the bad years, and more particularly the first two decades of the eighteenth century, a pressing need for more and firmer credit drove the government to consider projects for a royal central bank. The Controller General's department and a royal council examined many proposals, inquired about the success of central banks in foreign countries, and in 1709 even went so far as to adopt the scheme put forward by a famous and powerful financier, Samuel Bernard, who had already lent the Crown much money.[2] Even at that advanced stage—new bank notes had been printed—powerful financial interests prevailed on the royal council to abandon the scheme. The furthest the ministers would go was to authorize accountants to band together in the form of a Caisse des Emprunts (1702–15) on a model devised earlier by Colbert, and another grouping of twelve Receivers General called the Caisse Legendre (1709–15). The accountants, Farmers General and other financiers would not tolerate a public bank because it would have cut down their profits to a fraction. As John Law observed shortly afterwards, since the time of Colbert the ministers of the Crown had been governing the finances only in appearance; 'at bottom it is the businessmen (le corps de gens d'affaires) who have been conducting them...'[3]

Law understood and argued at length that the French monarchy was a victim of private enterprise in royal finance. He proposed to equip the monarchy with institutions which could remove the short-term debt, and indeed the entire management of royal finances, out of the hands of private businessmen—to 'nationalize' them. From 1715 when he won the trust of the regent Duke of Orléans, until 1721 when his scheme collapsed, Law took giant strides towards this goal, suppressing the Receivers General, the Farmers General and many other groups. His new organizations had rendered them all unnecessary, he explained. And as for the paper short-term debt, he 'nationalized' that, too, by substituting the notes of the new central bank:

[1] C. E. Labrousse, *La Crise de l'économie française*; Emmanuel Le Roy Ladurie, *Les Paysans de Languedoc*; Pierre Goubert, *Beauvais et le Beauvaisis*.

[2] Colonel Herlaut, 'Projets de création d'une banque royale en France à la fin du règne de Louis XIV (1702–1712)', *Revue d'histoire moderne*, N.S., no. 6 (March–April 1933), pp. 143–60.

[3] John Law, *Œuvres complètes* (Paris, 1934), vol. 3, p. 282.

The use of the paper [notes] established in France [he wrote] only confirms, by public credit, what the private bankers formerly did by their private credit, which was nevertheless variable, uncertain and exposed to a thousand damaging accidents. It is by public credit that the republics of Holland, Venice, Genoa, the kingdom of England and all the other trading states have made up for the lack of specie for more than a century.[1]

Law's brilliant and precocious schemes were soon wrecked on the stubborn opposition of the financial interests they had threatened, and thereafter no minister seriously tried to remove the royal finances from the rapacious hands of private enterprise until the first ministry of Jacques Necker (1776–81). Law's scheme (and Necker's) ultimately only proved the power and endurance of the private interests of their day. Not until the French revolution was a system of financial administration devised to protect the national interest.

The activities of all these lenders, collectors and spenders appeared to be very damaging and expensive in the eyes of kings, ministers and people. A deep hatred of financiers and *gens d'affaires*, etc., by whatever name they were called, was one of the most general and enduring features of the monarchy. Apart from the endless flow of pamphlets, and the satirical plays after the middle of the seventeenth century, the most striking expression of hatred for financiers was the royal practice of establishing temporary tribunals called *Chambres de Justice*. These were a form of extraordinary commission set up from time to time expressly to inquire into the affairs of all who managed royal funds and to punish those found guilty of extortion, fraud, embezzlement and other such crimes. Little is known of these Chambers of Justice, though all financial histories mention them. In one form or another the medieval kings used them, and in modern times there were at least fourteen: eight in the sixteenth century, five in the seventeenth and one soon after Louis XIV died.[2] The writings of statesmen and others show that whatever efforts the Chambers may have made to distinguish the guilty from the innocent, they were a method of striking at financiers as a group. 'The immense and sudden fortunes of those who have grown rich in criminal ways,' said the edict which set up a Chamber of Justice in March 1716, 'their excessive luxury and pomp, which seems to insult the misery of the majority of our subjects, are already in advance a manifest proof of their misdeeds (*malversations*).'[3] According to the judicial practice of the monarchy, all were believed guilty until proven innocent.

[1] *Ibid.*, p. 79.
[2] These were established in 1523, 1524, 1527–36, 1561–2, 1581, 1583–4, 1584–7, 1596, 1601, 1604, 1607, 1624–5, 1661–9 and 1716–17. The Crown threatened to set up many others.
[3] Quoted in Véron de Forbonnais, *Recherches sur les finances*, vol. 2, p. 399. Cf. *Mémoires du Cardinal de Richelieu*, pp. 133–57.

The Chambers of Justice had certain advantages over the Chambers of Accounts, Parlements, Bureaux of Finance and other sovereign courts. Because they took precedence over those courts, they avoided the usual struggles over jurisdiction and could therefore pursue their investigations with the vigour of royal commissions. The processes of the Chambers of Justice therefore threatened financiers much more than did the normal procedures of the sovereign courts. The courts were naturally hostile to the Chambers, but that hostility was mitigated by the Crown's habit of choosing the members of the Chambers from among the magistrates of the courts as well as from the royal councils. In any event, one of the Chamber's purposes was to satisfy opinion among the populace and the nobility, always indignant about the wealth and the misdeeds of financiers. The Chamber of Justice was in part a purge to satisfy public opinion, and indeed Richelieu described the one of 1625 as a 'saignée'.[1]

It was also a source of financial relief for the government. Again and again the Crown used this device to reduce the burden of debt contracted with financiers in wartime. To take only the most obvious examples, Chambers of Justice sought out war profiteers in 1523–4 after the Peace of Cambrai (1517); in 1563 after the Peace of Cateau-Cambrésis (1559); in the reign of Henri IV after the civil and religious wars; in 1648 after the Peace of Westphalia; again after the Peace of the Pyrenees (1659) in 1661; and yet again in 1716 after the Peace of Utrecht (1713). Although they varied a good deal in procedure and severity, they were usually more interested in recovering money or removing an embarrassing creditor than in meting out justice. Even the most famous and powerful victims appear to have been scapegoats, perhaps no guiltier than others around them: Jacques Coeur, Semblançay, Vieuville and even Fouquet, 'little more than a cipher for the faceless ones behind him'[2]—all these appear to have been victims of royal policy or of the ambitions of others at court. Some Chambers of Justice commenced bravely by hanging one or two lesser financiers as examples to the rest who then, fearing for their own lives, paid over large sums of money or cancelled debts. Henri III, Sully and Henri IV were willing to make business arrangements with the financiers even without any hanging and sometimes dismissed a Chamber even before it had begun its hearings.[3] The Chamber of 1607 hanged no one, mainly because of obstruction by Henri IV and Sully, but compiled a list of 220 names to be taxed a total of

---

[1] *Ibid.*, p. 135. Richelieu also spoke of pressing financiers 'like sponges'.

[2] For Fouquet, Julian Dent, 'An Aspect of the Crisis...', *Economic History Review* (August 1967), p. 250. For Vieuville see Lublinskaya, *French Absolutism*, pp. 264–70.

[3] David Buisseret, *Sully* (London, 1968), p. 91; Gaston Zeller, *Les Institutions de la France au XVIe siècle* (Paris, 1948), p. 275.

1,133,000 livres.[1] Richelieu did the same in 1624–5, and in 1635 appears to have allowed himself to be bought off even before naming the Chamber. More stringent and methodical, the Chamber of 1661–9 pronounced several death sentences and taxed some 500 individuals.[2] The Chamber of 1716–17 condemned no one to death but taxed as many as 4,410 people for a total of 220 millions.[3]

Pursuing financiers for their profits after a war was somewhat like hunting wild bees for their honey at the end of a summer. There was certainly honey to be found, but it was not always accessible and, worse still, it could only be had by uncertain, violent and disruptive methods. Yet so long as *traitants* or *gens d'affaires* were allowed to manage royal business and finance as private enterprises by contract, escaping all continuous supervision and inspection, getting rich or going bankrupt at the expense of King and country, building up fortunes real or only rumoured, so long was it necessary to bring them to account by a Chamber of Justice or by the threat of it. The Chamber was an integral part of the financial system. The central government could not dispense with it until the French revolution had produced a class of domesticated bees properly gathered into hives, inspected, supervised and arranged in a modern bureaucratic hierarchy. True, neither Louis XV nor Louis XVI established a Chamber of Justice, unless we count the rather specialized commission of the Châtelet which tried François Bigot and other officials from Canada after the Seven Years War, but then the monarchy was in decline and the businessmen triumphant behind their 'mur d'argent'.[4] Their long summer eventually came to an end in the revolution, and in 1793–4 the committees of the National Convention and the revolutionary tribunals did the work of a Chamber of Justice. Soon after the Estates-General met in 1614–15, Jean Bourgoin had recommended hanging all the financiers;[5] shortly after the next meeting of that body in 1789, revolutionaries made earnest efforts to do so. Their efforts were part of an administrative revolution as well as a social one.

Until then the financial administration was characterized by what historians are inclined to call 'corruption', as though it were the moral turpitude of individuals, but which was a normal feature of the system and

---

[1] Alfred des Cilleuls, 'Henri IV et la Chambre de Justice de 1607', *Séances et travaux de l'Académie des Sciences morales et politiques*, vol. 165 (1906), p. 286.

[2] Chauleur, 'Le rôle des traitants', *Le XVIIe Siècle*, no. 65 (1964), pp. 41–2; Pierre Ravel, *La Chambre de Justice de 1716* (Paris, 1928), p. 9.

[3] Pierre Ravel, *op. cit.*, p. 117.

[4] Lemay, *Le Mur d'argent*.

[5] Jean Bourgoin, *La Chasse aux larrons* (Paris, 1618); *Anti-Péculat* (1620); *Le Pressoir des éponges* (1624). H. Luthy, *La Banque protestante* (p. 729) likens the revolutionary tribunals to Chambers of Justice.

is better described as private enterprise. The activities of financiers were common to all periods of French history. Julian Dent finds the years 1653–61 to be an especially bad time; there were about four thousand financiers by 1660, he tells us, and more powerful than ever.[1] Andrée Chauleur finds the years 1643–53 significant as the period in which the ordinary taxes were turned over to the *traitants*.[2] To Mariéjol, it was under Richelieu that 'une nouvelle puissance est constituée, celle des hommes d'argent',[3] whereas A. D. Lublinskaya draws our attention to the special importance of financiers in the government of the 1620s.[4] Long before Richelieu came to power, Jean Bourgoin was publishing impressive lists of names and other details to show that the King was 'vassal and tributary of the financiers'.[5] Lucien Romier found a vast, fatal growth of financial office-holders in the sixteenth century and Mariéjol, too, wrote of 'the poverty of the people and the wealth of the *traitants*', in the reign of Henri III (1574–89).[6] And so on back even to the reign of Philippe le Bel (1285–1314) which so distinguished an historian as Germain Martin has described as 'the golden age of the financiers'.[7] Most periods, perhaps all, might be so described; we find that even Sully and Colbert depended upon the services of *traitants*. The truth seems to be that a large number of private profit-seeking financiers were a necessary part of the Valois-Bourbon financial administration. Whatever the fortunes of the individual financiers, whether they made large profits or went bankrupt, they were caught up in a system which was not of their own making. The real culprit was the system itself.

Whether the efforts of reforming kings and ministers in French history were directed fundamentally towards defending the money, men and processes of the Crown from private exploitation is a question no one has answered and it is far beyond the scope of this study. Such may well have been the significance of certain attempts at reform by Charles VII, François I, the last two Valois, Charles IX and Henri III, Sully, Colbert and the regent Duke of Orléans. Such was certainly the significance of Jacques Necker's work, as the following chapters will endeavour to make clear. Was it only accidental that almost all the earlier reformers mounted great assaults on the accountants, tax farmers and other *traitants* before or during reforms? Were these reforms attempts to defend and increase royal

---

[1] Julian Dent, 'An Aspect of the Crisis...', *Economic History Review* (August 1967), p. 256.

[2] Andrée Chauleur,'Le rôle des traitants', *Le XVIIe Siècle*, no. 65 (1964), pp. 16, 44 and 47.

[3] Mariéjol, *Henri IV*, p. 430. [4] Lublinskaya, *French Absolutism*, p. 224.

[5] Bourgoin, *La Chasse*; Dent, 'An Aspect of the Crisis', p. 256.

[6] Romier, *Le Royaume*, vol. 2, ch. 1; Mariéjol, *La Réforme*, p. 233.

[7] Martin, *Histoire économique*, p. 157.

revenues at the expense of the financiers and therefore necessarily done under the cover of Chambers of Justice? In the same period that Charles VII promoted several special commissions to prosecute financiers, he reorganized the administration in two main parts: one, the royal domain or *finances ordinaires* directed by four Treasurers of France, and the other, the major tax revenues or *finances extraordinaires* under the direction of four *Généraux des finances*. So the system remained until François I, irritated by large-scale fraud among his financial personnel, prosecuted them in several extraordinary commissions and in 1523 organized a central fund, the *Epargne*, to receive the net revenues from both the ordinary and extraordinary sources.[1] At first sight the reigns of the last two Valois kings, Charles IX and Henri III, hardly seem like an era of reform. Nevertheless they witnessed the firm and regular establishment of Superintendents of Finance (from 1564), Intendants of Finance, roving commissioners later to become resident Intendants in the Generalities, Secretaries of State and Bureaux of Finance (from 1577), all controlling or directing the finances in some way.[2] Throughout this same period Michel de l'Hôpital set up a Chamber of Justice in 1561–2, Henri III another in 1584–5, and there may have been others. The later reformers from Sully to the regent Duke of Orléans made efforts to protect royal finances and each also established a Chamber of Justice. Administrative reform and the prosecution of financiers seem to have been complementary endeavours.

If, indeed, some of these reformers were working towards a truly public system of government financing, none of their efforts had more than a temporary or slight effect. The habit of resorting to *traitants* was not a personal moral failing of kings and ministers, but a necessary and inevitable part of the financial system. When the Crown established Chambers of Justice in 1607 and 1661, these Chambers themselves became subjects for contracts with *traitants*! That of 1607 was financed by a Receiver of *tailles*, Jean Daneau, a bourgeois of Paris, Pierre Nivelle, and a provincial war controller, Claude de Beaufort, through a *traité* signed by a front man. According to its terms they advanced Henri IV some 400,000 livres in six monthly payments and paid the Chamber's expenses and fees of the magistrates in it. In return they were to keep half of the proceeds from any fines imposed by the Chamber and were to name the receiver-of-fines and to supervise the process of collection. A similar contract was signed with Pierre de Champagne for the Chamber of 1661.[3] Until the administrative

---

[1] Jacqueton, *Documents, passim*; Jacqueton, 'Le trésor de l'Epargne'.
[2] Zeller, *Les Institutions*; Doucet, *Les Institutions, passim*.
[3] Chauleur, 'Le rôle des traitants', p. 42.

organization was fundamentally changed, *traitants* and other financiers were necessary, and not until the reign of Louis XVI was the administration basically altered.

When change came it did so in the course of a revolution and this fact may well lead us to think the financial administration an intrinsic and inevitable feature of the monarchy. Perhaps an efficient system of public finance was possible only in conjunction with other fundamental changes in the régime. It may well be that a republic, in the eighteenth-century sense of the rule of law, was necessary to bring about the administrative reforms which eventually came in the French revolution. This thought gains support from a comparison with British financial history, for it was the parliamentary governments of the limited monarchy which developed national institutions of public finance. In the monarchy of the Tudors and Stuarts there was a shadowy borderland between public and private finance, and the Crown depended upon the services and loans of tax farmers, venal office-holders and the City of London.[1] From early in the reign of James I (1603–25) the Crown fell into debt on a growing scale, borrowing heavily from the Customs Farmers and resorting to expedients not unlike those of France in the eighteenth century, after the General Farm of Taxes had been formed. With no system of public debt, short-term or long-term, and no state organization for collecting taxes, the borrowings and revenues of the English absolute monarchy were uncertain, expensive, politically dangerous —and largely private enterprises.[2]

The first major changes came after the Civil War and Commonwealth when Charles II, no longer so absolute as his Bourbon cousins, brought farming in the Customs (1671) and the Excise (1683) to an end in favour of Crown Commissions. But after the Glorious Revolution of 1688–9, the financial system of the now-limited monarchy rapidly developed into a truly public administration. Public finance ceased to be royal and became parliamentary, as Richard Pares has put it.[3] The Bank of England, formed in 1694, took over the management of the debt, long-term and short-term, before the middle of the eighteenth century.[4] In 1714 the office of Lord Treasurer gave way to a permanent Board of Treasury Commissioners to supervise revenue in transit to the Exchequer and to exercise general authority over subsidiary revenue boards and a growing number of other matters of financial administration. At the outbreak of the War of American Independence, J. E. D. Binney tells us, the expressions public revenue and

---

[1] Ashton, *The Crown*, p. xvi; Aylmer, *The King's Servants*, pp. 40 and 201.
[2] Dickson, *The Financial Revolution*, ch. 3.
[3] Pares, *Limited Monarchy*, p. 11. [4] Dickson, *The Financial Revolution, passim.*

public expenditure already covered virtually the whole of the receiving and spending transactions of the state.[1] Government borrowing, too, was no longer a haphazard private enterprise. And by means of an annual budget, the government was charting the course of national finances more and more accurately.

In the century beginning with the Glorious Revolution of 1688-9, while England was engaged in a long struggle with France for overseas empire, the British parliamentary government was taking steps to organize a system of public finance. During that century no less than five wars strained the resources of both governments for a total of more than forty years. For most of that time the British government enjoyed the enormous advantage of having adequate supplies of money for the fleet and the armies, thanks to a superior system of credit.[2] When the last of these wars ended in 1782, the Prime Minister, Lord Shelburne, had to contemplate debts of some 220 million pounds, but he knew that most of the long-term debt was funded, the short-term paper was in the form of Exchequer Bills, the whole was publicly managed and the total annual charges were 7,335,543 pounds sterling.[3] The British government had been borrowing enormous sums at costs of little more than 3 % interest. Over the next ten years, Parliament improved the administration still further with a debt sinking fund, a consolidated revenue fund, a better system of public accounts and a replacement of many venal offices with appointments on fixed salaries paid by the Treasury.

Meanwhile French governments had continued to borrow, to receive and to spend, through the agency of provincial estates, the clergy, the city of Paris, the General Farm of Taxes and a host of venal accountants. After the American War no one knew how much the debt amounted to, but the very idea that they ought to know was itself something of a novelty. Necker estimated annual charges of 207 million livres on rentes amounting to a capital debt of something over 3,400,000,000 livres, and he put the outstanding short-term paper at 27 millions.[4] He thought this burden almost exactly the same as the annual charges on the British debt which (reckoning the pound sterling at 23 livres, 3 sols and 6 deniers) he worked out at about 207 million livres. Less complacent than the physiocratic writers who believed that the English government must collapse under such a burden, England being roughly one-third the size of France in area and population, Necker nevertheless miscalculated in comparing the two debts. According

---

[1] Binney, *British Public Finance*, pp. 168 ff.
[2] Baugh, *British Naval Administration*, p. 18.
[3] Norris, *Shelburne*, p. 230; Binney, *British Public Finance*, appendices; Watson, *The Reign of George III*, pp. 283 and 292.
[4] Necker, *De l'administration*, vol. 2, ch. 11.

to the best scholarly study of figures for the year 1787, the servicing of the French debt came to more than 318 million livres a year, and the capital to perhaps five billions.[1] The capital was therefore the equivalent of about 215 million pounds sterling—almost as much as the English capital debt— but that sum was costing the French government 6% or more in annual interest: nearly twice as much as the English government was paying. Still, in both countries the debt servicing absorbed approximately half of the government's annual expenditures. The greatest differences between the two countries were in their administrative systems and their political constitutions. The most significant thing about Necker's errors is that they demonstrate the impossibility of finding out the answers to questions of government finances. Necker may have been at fault, but his shortcomings were as nothing compared to the faults inherent in the system. The high rate of interest on the French debt was another clue to the fundamental differences between the administrative systems of the two countries. Those differences were sufficient to determine that in the decade between the peace of 1783 and the war of 1793, England would take one road to stronger public finances and France would take another.

In that critical decade the political leaders of the French nation undertook administrative reforms which had been evolving in England for more than a century. English business and financial interests had come gradually to exercise more influence in Parliament and parliamentary politics and less influence in administration. The meeting of private interests in Parliament had fostered a sense of the general interest which more and more strictly marked off the revenue departments, Exchequer, Treasury and the rest of the financial administration as out of bounds to the enterprise of those very private interests. What private business interests lost in the gradual disappearance of offices, tax farms, floating debt and other such opportunities, they more than made up in trade and industry. At the same time the evolving right and responsibility to scrutinize the budget and to find ways and means to implement it had made every parliament face debt and deficit year after year. In this respect every parliamentary session had been like April 1787 in the Assembly of Notables. Those pressures had led to 'economical reform', to the gradual building of a system of public administration and finance whereby the British government could marshal funds enough to face and defeat imperial enemies. After 1782 the process went on with the assistance of some very remarkable parliamentary committees and commissions. Their work and the work of their successors enabled the British government to pay for another twenty years of war beginning in 1793.

[1] Braesch, *Finances et monnaies*, fasc. 2, p. 202.

By that year France, too, was equipped with a system of parliamentary government in which private interests met, and a system of public administration from which they were excluded. Venal offices, tax farmers, *traitants*, accountants, short-term advances—all these had gone and the debt was about to be properly consolidated. True, there was a severe inflation of paper *assignats*, but for the first time in French history such paper notes were being issued by a national government rather than by a private profit-seeking concern. The depreciating *assignats* were a form of national taxation made possible by a revolution in state financing. Inflation and other costs in money are hardly to be measured against the blood shed in defence of the republic during 1793-5, but still that magnificent and astonishing defence owed a great deal to national expenditures and so did the less glorious victories of Napoleon. The ancien régime could not have fought those wars; nor could unorganized, unfed, unpaid or unarmed soldiers of the republic, no matter what their national spirit. 'Without public revenue, there can be no nation', Lebrun, the future duc de Plaisance, reminded the legislature in 1796. 'There can be no liberty if the public revenue approved by the nation does not come to be deposited in a fund subject to the inspection, to the active, regular and permanent supervision of its representatives.'[1] Lebrun, conservative though he was, knew as well as anyone that whatever else had happened in the French revolution, the administration of government finances was on its way to becoming organized, efficient, bureaucratic and protected from the interference and exploitation of private interests. As a protégé of the reforming Chancellor Maupéou, he also must have known that these great changes had begun under the ancien régime.

[1] Lebrun, *Rapport fait sur la résolution* (17 April 1796).

2

KING AND COUNCIL

To all appearances Louis XVI governed the finances of his kingdom no less than his royal ancestors had done before him. The fifteen years of his rule from 1774 to 1789 saw no limitation of his sovereignty, and he was still answerable only to the 'supreme Administrator' (to use Necker's sanctimonious phrase) just as Louis XV had been.[1] If he was ill-prepared for the tasks of government and had none of the despotic genius so fashionable among the rulers of his generation, Louis XVI was a man of his time all the same: humane, conscientious, modest and with good intentions enough to consent to banishing torture from the judicial process (1780 and 1788) and to easing the disabilities imposed on Protestants (1787). He knew very little about financial matters, but few kings did. There had always been councils and ministers to prepare decisions and to implement them. No abdication of royal authority appeared after 1774 either in the flow of edicts, ordinances, arrêts and letters patent, which bore witness to the industry of king and council, or in the list of councils and their meetings printed each year in the *Almanach royal*.[2] From 1774 to 1787 these documents made it clear to the ordinary subjects of Louis XVI that on Tuesdays the King held a meeting with the members of his Royal Council on Finance.

During the eighteenth century the Royal Council on Finance was a symbol of royal authority in financial matters. This was because Louis XIV had created it, on 15 September 1661, for the express purpose of assisting him to rule personally over all matters hitherto governed for the Crown by a Superintendent of Finance with ministerial powers. Part of a royal *coup d'état*, the new council was established only ten days after the arrest of the Superintendent, the unfortunate Fouquet, in order that the very post of Superintendent might be done away with. The founding act of 15 September 1661 pronounced the suppression of the Superintendent in its first article, declared in its second that the King would henceforth 'take upon himself the task of administering his finances' together with a new council,

---

[1] Chapuisat, *Necker*, p. 61.
[2] Louis XVI inherited four councils which his predecessors had presided over: the *Conseil d'en-haut* for foreign affairs; the *Conseil des dépêches* for internal matters; the *Conseil royal du commerce* and the *Conseil royal des finances*.

and in the remaining fifteen articles defined the council's duties and membership.[1]

The statements of duties confirm the impression that the King intended to act as his own Minister of Finance. By article 4, he reserved for his own signature all royal payment orders (*ordonnances*) of all kinds. Article 5 stipulated that all the tables of revenue (*états de distribution* or *états du Roi*) designating funds in advance for specific purposes, were to be brought before the King in the Royal Council on Finance. The Intendant of Finance who supervised the *Epargne* or Royal Treasury was ordered in articles 6, 7 and 8 to show the official registers of receipts and expenditures to no one except on the King's orders and to bring all Treasury payment orders and all schedules of expenditure for the royal signature. As for the complicated business of authorizing all the taxes, leasing the duties on commodities to the tax farmers, approving the accounts of tax receipts, and negotiating *traités* and *partis*, this business too was subject to royal approval and signature in this council. The act of 15 September 1661 leaves no doubt of direct royal command over the entire financial system.

According to this founding act the council was to meet in the King's presence and to consist of the Chancellor or his deputy, the Keeper of the Seals, whenever the King wished him to attend; a *Chef du conseil* 'to take the place [in Council meetings] which the Superintendent had been accustomed to take', that is, next in rank to the Chancellor; and three councillors, one of them to be chosen from among the six venal officers called Intendants of Finance. Louis XIV could normally dominate this group because none of them had *ex officio* a minister's or Superintendent's grasp of the royal financial administration. Even Jean-Baptiste Colbert who had helped Louis XIV to carry out the *coup d'état* sat on the Council only on invitation as its first Intendant of Finances. When he became Controller General of Finance in 1665, he was still not entitled to sit on the Council *ex officio* but only at the King's invitation. From the time of Colbert until the revolution the Controller General acted as a Minister of Finance for most practical purposes, but still he could never claim to sit on the Royal Council of Finance by right; some sat on it and some did not. Strictly speaking, the King continued to govern without a Minister of Finance, according to the original intention of Louis XIV.

In 1774, when Louis XVI began to rule, the Royal Council on Finance had nine members. The highest in rank, next to the King himself, was the Keeper of the Seals (*Garde des sceaux*), because one of Louis' first acts was

---

[1] There is an annotated copy of the founding act appended to M. Antoine, 'Les Conseils', *R.H.M.C.* (1958), p. 188.

to disgrace the Chancellor, Maupéou.[1] Even though a Chancellor in disgrace kept his office for life—until 1792 in Maupéou's case—the usual practice was for the Keeper of the Seals to perform his duties as the chief judicial officer of the realm, and in this case the Keeper, Hue de Miromesnil, was not much interested in financial matters.[2] Next in rank was the *Chef du conseil*, customarily a prominent nobleman with power at court. From 1774 to 1781 this was the comte de Maurepas who enjoyed both the powers of a principal royal adviser and the title of Minister of State, conferred only on members of the senior and most select council, the *Conseil d'en-haut*.[3] The only other Minister of State on the Council in 1774 had been admitted to membership by virtue of that very title, conferred upon him for that precise purpose; the Controller General of Finance, Turgot.[4] Whether or not his many successors as Controller General were admitted to the Royal Council on Finance, there were always a number of Councillors of State with experience in financial administration. In 1774, and until 1777, three of these were also Intendants of Finance and therefore senior magistrates at the heads of divisions in the Controller General's department. These three and the Controller General were the only members with responsibilities in the Finance Department and were therefore the experts in financial business, but their practical functions and knowledge were no measure of their rank in the Council. All members except the Keeper of the Seals and the *Chef du conseil* were ranked in order of their seniority or reception as Councillors of State, not as members of this particular council. Thus, in 1774 they ranked almost in inverse order of their administrative responsibilities: d'Ormesson (1744, Intendant of Finance), Feydeau de Marville (1747), Moreau de Beaumont (1756, Intendant of Finance), Trudaine de Montigny (1757, Intendant of Finance), de Boullongne (1757, Intendant of Finance), Bertin (1759, Secretary of State), and Turgot (1774, Controller General of Finance).[5] As this curious system of ranking suggests, the Royal Council on Finance drew its Councillors of State from a larger group of them which was fixed at thirty during most of the eighteenth century,

[1] René-Nicolas-Charles Augustin de Maupéou (1714–92) actually succeeded in persuading Louis XV to abolish the Parlements in 1771. Maupéou had to be sacrificed when Louis XVI decided to begin his reign with the conciliatory act of restoring the Parlements.

[2] Armand-Thomas Hue de Miromesnil (1723–96) held the office of *Garde des sceaux* from 24 Aug. 1774 until 8 April 1787 and again after the fall of his successor, Lamoignon, in Aug. 1788.

[3] Jean-Frédéric Phélipeaux de Maurepas (1701–81), one of the most powerful figures in the government during the first seven years of the reign.

[4] Anne-Robert-Jacques Turgot, baron de l'Aulne (1727–81), had made a mark as Intendant of Limoges and as a cultivated and thoughtful economist. Louis XVI appointed him in 1774 and he remained in office only two years.

[5] Their full names and dates are in the index.

increased by six supernumerary positions in 1766, and totalling no less than forty-four in the list for 1775.[1] These were the professional members of another and larger council, the *Conseil d'état privé finance et direction*.

The *Conseil d'état privé finance et direction* was the oldest surviving council, the direct descendant of the medieval undifferentiated *Conseil du Roi* which none of the later councils had ever entirely superseded. True to an age-old practice, when Louis XIV created the Royal Council on Finance in 1661 he did not suppress the older council but left it to deal with certain specified parts of conciliar work. The act of 15 September 1661, article 10, referred to it specifically as the *Conseil ordinaire des finances* and set it to receiving tenders for tax farms and awarding contracts. The King presided over it in theory but in fact Louis XIV attended it no more than a few times, Louis XV only twice and Louis XVI never at all. In practice, the Chancellor or the Keeper of the Seals presided over it, and this was one of his principal duties. It had a very large membership and had therefore to meet in a spacious chamber, the *Salle du conseil*, which at Versailles was on the ground floor of the left wing between the royal courtyard and the prince's courtyard. There were *ex-officio* members besides the Chancellor: the dukes and peers of the realm (who seldom came because the business was too technical), the Ministers of State, the Secretaries of State and the Controller General. The professional members, the Councillors of State, never attended council meetings all at once because like the members of the twentieth-century *grands corps de l'état* some of them were posted as Intendants in the provinces, ambassadors abroad or on other service. These Councillors of State ranked very high in governing circles, immediately after the dukes and peers, and were carefully chosen to include at least three from the Church, three from the *noblesse d'épée* and twenty-four from the ranks of the higher magistrates, *la robe longue*.

In the *Conseil d'état privé finance et direction*, the oldest group of members were the *Maîtres des requêtes ordinaires de l'hôtel* who, though not high in rank, had sat in it since the end of the thirteenth century. There were eighty of them in 1673, increased to eighty-eight in 1689, reduced to eighty-five in 1752 and again to sixty-seven by an edict of November 1787.[2] They held venal offices, but it was from this corps that the Crown usually chose the commissioned Intendants of the provinces, the Intendants of Finance, the Intendants of Commerce, the Councillors of State, the Lieutenants General of Police, the *Prévôts des marchands de Paris* and other high officials. When the Royal Council on Finance appointed a commission to study some difficult or

---

[1] *Almanach royal* (1775), p. 177; Antoine, *Le Fonds du conseil*, p. 12.
[2] Their names were listed in the *Almanach royal* (1775), p. 202.

complex matter, a Master of Requests usually put the commission's report before the Council. Unless chosen for such posts, the Master of Requests served the Council, a quarter of them for each quarter of the year, by preparing matters for council meetings, studying files and drafting recommendations.

When a clerical matter was under discussion, the Agents General for the Clergy were allowed to attend and to present their case, but they had to withdraw before the Council discussed the matter.

In addition to its large body of members, the *Conseil d'état privé finance et direction* had three groups of auxiliary personnel. First, all the legal work in the Council and its dependent commissions fell to the corps of *Avocats au conseil* numbering 170 from 1673, but fixed at 70 by an edict of September 1738 and then at 73 in 1783. They held venal offices which they were allowed to purchase only after first acquiring the venal offices of *Avocat au parlement*. Secondly, there were ten ushers (*Huissiers du conseil*) who not only guarded the doors of the chamber during sessions, but kept watch over Council procedures and also had the responsibility of seeing that decisions and judgements went through the proper channels in order to be put into effect. Thirdly, there were groups of secretaries.

This Council was long supposed to have met in two quite different weekly sessions, one on Monday morning called the *Conseil d'état privé* or the *Conseil des parties*, and the other on Tuesday morning under the title of *Conseil d'état et des finances*. This latter session, however, appears to have died out early in the eighteenth century, never to meet at all in the reign of Louis XVI.[1] The *Conseil d'état privé* met, however, to deal with all sorts of matters arising in the administration of justice, such as requests for review of criminal trials, petitions against court decisions, the regulation of judges, appeals against the judgements of Intendants or other Council commissioners, and disputes over jurisdictions.

Most councils, and not least those for financial business, needed subcommittees. These grew up in the sixteenth and seventeenth centuries and from the reign of Louis XIV they were of three kinds, for which the descriptive term 'sub-committee' is accurate enough but was never used in the ancien régime: *commissions extraordinaires*, *commissions ordinaires*, and *bureaux*. The *commissions extraordinaires* were temporary bodies, variously composed, which any of the councils might appoint to take over particular cases of such magnitude that the council could not conveniently deal with

---

[1] For this and most other information about these councils, I am indebted to M. Antoine, 'Les Conseils', *R.H.M.C.* (1958), and to his invaluable inventory, *Le Fonds du conseil*.

them in its regular meetings. In 1775 the *Almanach royal* listed twelve *commissions extraordinaires*, most of them concerned with matters of finance. One, for instance, had been appointed to examine disputes over bank accounts, bank notes and other such matters. Another was to judge cases arising out of the infamous Canadian debts after the Seven Years War as well as legal conflicts over shares in the Indies Company and over land grants in Louisiana dating from the days of John Law. Still another was for the accounts of the *Œconomats*, or agency for supervising revenues from vacant bishoprics, and the accounts of the officials administering the confiscated property of Huguenots and other religious fugitives. Better known than these were the *Commission des péages* appointed in 1724 to examine legal titles to bridge, ferry and road tolls held by private individuals, municipalities, religious orders and the like; the *Commission des prises* which made all official decisions about enemy ships captured or wrecked on the coast in wartime; and the *Commission des postes et messageries* first appointed in 1676 for the settlement of claims by former owners of the *messageries*, a private coach service which little by little over the years the Crown endeavoured to control and then to expropriate.[1]

Such were the *commissions extraordinaires*. The bureaux and *commissions ordinaires* were permanent sub-committees of the *Conseil d'état privé finance et direction*. In eighteenth-century records they are sometimes confused because the actual meeting or session of a *commission* was called a *bureau*. There was a real difference, however, between the two kinds of sub-committee. The *commission* had power to recommend decisions on certain matters, whereas the business of the *bureau* was merely to prepare dossiers for the parent council. Every year the Chancellor prepared a new list of Councillors of State for each *bureau* and for each item of business he appointed a Master of Requests to put it before the *bureau* to which it was destined. The eleven or twelve bureaux at the accession of Louis XVI prepared dossiers on any matter requiring extensive preparations before the *Conseil d'état privé finance et direction* could arrive at its decisions, one specializing in ecclesiastical business, another in cases concerning the *librairie* or censorship and control of publications, but most of them apparently not specializing.[2]

Of all these sub-committees, the *commissions ordinaires* played the largest role in financial administration. There were four of these and the first in importance was the *Grande direction des finances*, sometimes called the *Conseil de direction* and regarded as a third session of its parent council. The

[1] Phytilis, 'Une commission extraordinaire', in *Questions administratives* (1965), pp. 1–155.   [2] Antoine, *Le Fonds du conseil*, pp. 15–16.

Grande direction met under the chairmanship of the Chancellor, every second Monday after the meeting of the *Conseil privé* and in the same room. In 1775 it had twenty members besides the Chancellor and the *Chef du conseil royal des finances*: seven Intendants of Finance and the Intendant of the Generality of Paris (who were also Councillors of State); twelve other Councillors of State; and the Controller General of Finance. All the Masters of Requests could attend its meetings and speak. This commission judged many important cases of individuals versus the state and of litigants opposed to one another over matters in which the state had a financial interest. It also prepared replies to *cahiers* from the provincial estates, but for such business it included only certain members chosen by the Chancellor together with the Governor of the province concerned and the Secretary of State under whose jurisdiction the province fell.

The second of the four *commissions ordinaires*, the *Petite direction des finances*, took lesser cases of much the same kind, and therefore served as a supplement to the *Grande direction*. The *Chef du conseil royal des finances* presided over its meetings in his own room at the château wherever the King was staying, and in 1775 there were fourteen other members of it: the seven Intendants of Finance, three other Councillors of State, the Controller General (all members of the *Grande direction* as well), and the three Keepers of the Royal Treasury. For all this brave listing in the *Almanach royal*, the *Petite direction* probably did very little and held few meetings. 'Those held at present in the apartment of the *Chef du conseil* are so rare,' an official wrote in 1769 or 1770, 'that the matters dealt with in them must not be very interesting to the administration.'[1]

These two *commissions ordinaires* were assisted by the other two, much as the bureaux served the *Conseil d'état privé finance et direction*, even though they often borrowed the powers of *commissions extraordinaires* for special purposes. These were the *Bureau concernant les affaires des domaines et aides* and the *Bureau pour les affaires des gabelles, cinq grosses fermes, tailles et autres affaires des finances*. They both included nearly all the members of the *Grande direction* together with certain designated Masters of Requests and, in the former, with Inspectors General of the Domains.

Anyone might be excused for concluding from the description of these councils and their sub-committees that Louis XVI governed royal finance somewhat the way Louis XIV had set out to do in 1661. Allowing for the modesty and notorious mediocrity of Louis XVI, one might suppose that stronger men in the Royal Council on Finance determined financial policy,

---

[1] Antoine, 'Les Conseils', *R.H.M.C.* (1958), pp. 195 and 199. The *Petite direction* was suppressed by a règlement of 27 October 1787.

thereby preserving the rule of King and council over the vital budgetary affairs of the Crown. This does not seem to have been the case. There is much evidence to suggest that the Royal Council on Finance was losing its control when Louis XVI came to the throne and continued to wane until summer 1787 when the *Chef du conseil*, Loménie de Brienne, made a last vain effort to revive it. What precisely did the decline entail, and why did it take place?

One of the great weaknesses of the French councils at the time Louis XVI ascended the throne was that they were encumbered with a great deal of work which Montesquieu and others in the eighteenth century had identified as judicial process and had marked for separation from the administrative and budgetary work. This was not a matter of constitutional principle, but of rational division of labour. According to the ancient practice, virtually all of the councils and commissions were in one way or another concerned with judicial work, *le contentieux*, as it was called. The *Conseil d'état privé* or *des parties* was a tribunal entirely given over to hearing and judging private cases, and the four *commissions ordinaires* and several of the *commissions extraordinaires* spent much of their time dealing with cases of dispute between the Crown and private parties. So did the Royal Council on Finance, if we may judge from the work of the bureaux 'pour la communication des instances'.[1] The double burden on the King and council was reflected in the use of two types of royal arrêts (resolutions). Those passed at the request of private parties or in judgement of a conflict between private parties were said to be *arrêts simples* rendered by *le Roi en son conseil*, and the original copy was sent to the secretariat of the Royal Council on Finance which dispatched the necessary printed copies to courts, individuals and so on. These were the arrêts embodying decisions arrived at in legal cases. They were different from the arrêts prepared by the government for its own purposes of administration, for the regulation of the various corps of officials and dignitaries, or for settling any matters in which the Crown had a direct interest. Such were called *arrêts en commandement*, rendered by *le Roi étant en son conseil*, and they were sent to the Secretary of State who supervised the business of the province concerned.[2]

There was nothing anomalous or unusual about this confusion of judicial and administrative functions (as it seems to us) in a kingdom where

---

[1] Antoine, *Le Fonds du conseil*, p. 15.

[2] There being no Ministry of the Interior, no Home Office, much royal business in the provinces was assigned to the four Secretaries of State, for War, Marine, Foreign Affairs and the Royal Household, as well as to the Controller General of Finance. In the *Almanach royal* (1775), p. 178, each Secretary of State has a list of provinces and generalities in his jurisdiction.

the monarch was both supreme judge and chief administrator. Indeed, not only the councils but their *commissaires départis*, the famous Intendants in the provinces, sat in judgement on a great many legal cases; and the Crown reserved for the councils all litigation arising out of appeals against the judgements of Intendants. Royal authority implied a unity of government which discouraged any systematic division or separation of powers. In eighteenth-century statements about royal finance, it is often far from clear whether a reference is to a litigious issue or to a matter of pure administration. When the King in his sovereign majesty delegated power to a court or individual, he did not delegate a function classifiable as judicial, executive or legislative; he delegated an undifferentiated bit of sovereignty. Hence officials whom we are tempted to think of as administrative officers—such as the Intendants of Finance at the head of executive divisions—turn out to have been called 'magistrates' and to have spent much of their time in councils which sometimes framed laws and sometimes sat in judgement on legal cases resulting from those laws.

Legal cases, whether of private individuals or of corporate bodies, kept the judicial work of the royal councils before the public gaze and also brought the councils into conflict with the sovereign courts. Undaunted by exile and the suspension of their functions during the last years of Louis XV, the Parlements and the *Cours des aides* once more took up their critical scrutiny of the royal government soon after Louis XVI reinstated them. The *Cour des aides* for Paris was particularly outspoken about the judicial work of the royal councils which often interfered with its own work, or so it believed, and it was attacking the financial councils as tribunals when it made a sharp complaint to Louis XVI on 10 April 1775. At the same time, the main object of the complaint was another and more controversial weakness in the royal councils:

Your Majesty ought to know [the *Cour des aides* declared] that for more than a hundred years what is called his council in financial matters has consisted of the Controller General and one single *rapporteur* who has been for a long time an Intendant of Finance. It is in this tribunal of two men that all the decisions of the *Cour des aides* are over-ruled; and it should not be said that it is Your Majesty himself who renders these *arrêts*: 1º because too many of them are rendered, and the Royal Councils on Finance are too rare for all these matters to be brought before them; 2º because it is not possible for Your Majesty to pronounce personally with the necessary knowledge on all these details of financial procedure. It cannot be said that it is the council of Your Majesty itself which renders such *arrêts*, for we affirm a notorious fact in saying that the council never hears them mentioned. And if it were not true that by this word, *le Conseil*, is meant the Controller General alone, in all matters within the jurisdiction of the *Cour des aides*, then charges of falsifying would have to be brought against all the Controllers General who, during their administrations, have continually signed these *arrêts* not deliberated in the council.[1]

Whether or not Louis XVI was prepared to accept this statement from the *Cour des aides*, always so jealous of its own privileges, the statement was substantially true for the judicial work of the councils and much other work besides. Jacques Necker admitted as much in 1781.[2] Ever since the time of Colbert, the Controller General had been the principal *rapporteur* in the Royal Council on Finance and the most powerful individual in it by virtue of his position at the head of the *Contrôle général des finances*. He had always worked together with the King in preparing some matters for council meetings and in settling other business not important enough for the council. By the end of Louis XV's reign, the King and the Controller General both found it more convenient to do more and more business outside the council. This seemed all the more appropriate because four of the councillors, and the ones most directly concerned with finance, were the Intendants of Finance, all colleagues of the Controller General.

The six Intendants of Finance were the heads of divisions in the Controller General's department, but as venal officials who had purchased their offices they were not subordinate to him in the modern administrative sense. They were *magistrats* with substantial authority over their divisions, 'little ministers', as one official described them, 'disposing more or less despotically of all the financial enterprises of the kingdom'.[3] As each Intendant of Finance was master of his part of official business, he was also the judge of cases arising out of that business, or was powerful enough to guide as he wished the council's judgements in such cases. By the time Louis XVI was crowned, they had begun to hold weekly meetings to settle in common matters which they preferred not to deal with individually.[4] These meetings were in some degree usurping the functions of the royal councils, and the proposals of the Intendants of Finance were put before the King by the Controller General in his frequent working sessions in the royal presence. Thus many important decisions supposed to have been taken in council were in fact taken by the Intendants of Finance, alone or assembled, or by the Controller General alone or in his meetings with the

[1] Quoted by Antoine, 'Les Conseils', *R.H.M.C.* (1958), p. 182 and by M. Marion, *Dictionnaire des institutions*, p. 134.
[2] Necker, *Compte rendu*, p. 59.
[3] A.N., F³⁰ 110ᴬ, *Note*, dated 22 June 1777.
[4] Antoine, 'Les Conseils', *R.H.M.C.* (1958), pp. 195 and 200.

King. In 1787 Calonne's meetings with the Intendants of Finance were so well established as to be scheduled in the *Almanach Royal*.[1]

These decisions were nevertheless incorporated in laws or arrêts ostensibly rendered by the King and his council. Thus did the government maintain a fiction that decisions were being made in the councils. As part of this façade all arrêts in matters of finance were carefully dated Tuesday, the day the Royal Council on Finance was supposed to meet. The arrêts were normally drafted by the clerks of the Department of Finance, who prepared the dossiers for whatever meeting was to review them and to take a decision. When the Controller General returned from his meeting with the King (or, more rarely, with a council), he returned the drafts of the arrêts with the decisions or other notes written on them to these clerks so that they could draw up the final arrêts in the appropriate form. The recommendations of each Intendant of Finance, either alone or after the weekly assemblies of Intendants of Finance, were likewise proposed by his clerks for the meetings of the Controller General and the King. These procedures were for questions arising in the General Control of Finance. When an individual or private agency wished to put a matter before the Royal Council, they had to do so through the intermediary services of an *Avocat au conseil*. The corps of these officials had the privilege of preparing and presenting all cases for the Royal Council and they never ceased to do this even though they obtained decisions more and more directly from the Controller General in his meetings with the King and less and less from the councils.[2] It was alleged that clerks and other subordinate staff had many opportunities for dishonest power and profit in the course of dealing with the litigious work of the councils.

The official who made this allegation also laid bare a trend of thought in high government circles about the judicial work of the councils and also about the danger of having it thus managed by officials. 'It has long been felt', he wrote on 22 June 1777, 'that the litigious part of the finances (*le contentieux*) is a thing apart in the general administration of finance.'[3] It should not be in the hands of individuals, he went on, because it cannot be sufficiently and legally supervised except by a permanent committee (*comité*) or commission or some sort of financial assembly. The members of such a body should not divide up the work among them but judge all cases in common. These magistrates ought not to hold venal offices, like the Intendants of Finance, he thought, but ought instead to be appointed by

---

[1] *Almanach royal* (1786), p. 219; (1787), p. 220. The Intendants of Finance had been restored in 1781, after Necker's fall.

[2] Antoine, 'Les Conseils', *R.H.M.C.* (1958), p. 170.   [3] A.N., F^{30} 110^A, *Note*.

revocable commission so that they might be removed if necessary. Further to prevent private interests from corrupting the judgement process, each case should be put before the magistrates by a different Master of Requests rather than a specialized group known to the public and to the lower employees of the Crown. From such an agency, he asserted, 'would stem the possibility of guaranteeing at once all judgements in matters of finance from arbitrary decisions, of establishing at the same time the liveliest emulation in all members of the council, and of constituting in some fashion a real school for statesmen'. He recommended the suppression of the offices of Intendant of Finance and the nomination of two of the best among the Intendants as magistrates on such a committee.[1]

All this was in a note of 22 June 1777 to the comte de Maurepas, and it helps to explain why a royal edict published in the next few days announced the suppression of the offices of Intendant of Finance and the formation of a *Comité contentieux des finances*, composed of three judges (increased to four in 1781).[2] It would be interesting to discover how much of the judicial work of the financial councils fell to this *Comité contentieux* in the ensuing years, but this is unknown.[3] Certainly all the judgements formerly passed or prepared by the Controller General and the Intendants of Finance devolved upon the new committee and its work remained closely linked with the activities of the Finance Department. Formally subordinated to the Controller General, to whom it was supposed to submit its opinion on each case, the *Comité contentieux* in fact rendered judgements which appeared in the guise of *arrêts du Conseil*. It appears to have behaved as an agency of the Royal Council on Finance as well as of the Finance Department.[4] Acting as a kind of lower court or clearing agency for financial cases, it would sometimes recommend to municipalities, private individuals or other plaintiffs that they take their cases to the *Conseil d'état privé*, and it would send very important cases to the Royal Council itself. Its influence was considerable, until it was suppressed in 1791 with the councils themselves, and in a famous statement, the Keeper of the Seals, Champion de Cicé, reported of it to Louis XVI, 'It must be admitted that the real council on finance is the

[1] Bouvard de Fourqueux and Moreau de Beaumont, together with a third member to be chosen from among the four Councillors of State: Boullongne, Vidaud de la Tour, Auget de Montyon and Dufour de Villeneuve.

[2] The first three judges were Bouvard de Fourqueux, Moreau de Beaumont and Dufour de Villeneuve. See the royal edict, *Portant suppression des six offices d'intendans des finances* (June 1777), reproduced in Isambert, *Recueil des anciennes lois*, vol. 25, p. 51. The names of the committee members are listed in the *Almanach royal* (1778), p. 189.

[3] A useful study of this committee, however, is Aline Logette, *Le Comité contentieux des finances près le Conseil du Roi (1777–91)* (1964).

[4] Logette, *Le Comité contentieux*, p. 248.

Comité contentieux which reviews and discusses all the affairs which used to be brought to the Royal Council and were later reserved by the Controllers General for judgement in their own cabinets on the advice of the Intendants of Finance or the *premiers commis* of the General Control'.[1] Perhaps the greatest tribute to its success appeared in a *règlement* of 9 August 1789 which created in its image a *Comité contentieux des départements* to deal with judicial work of councils other than financial.[2]

The appointment of the *Comité contentieux des finances* was a step in the adoption of a new institution for assisting in the work of the financial councils and their subsidiaries. The word 'comité' had been taken from English in the time of the Regency and had gradually gained currency as a term for the meetings of ministers during the reign of Louis XV and perhaps for other meetings.[3] It had no precise or technical meaning. In a brief definition of the term, the *Encyclopédie méthodique. Jurisprudence* (1783) wrote, 'Committees are especially necessary in republics and in monarchies which, by the balancing of powers, partake of republican government... In France, we may regard as committees the different commissions among which the Councillors of State are divided.' In 1788 Calonne referred to the bureaux of the Assembly of Notables as committees.[4] The Crown probably used the term in 1777 for its very imprecision because the small, business-like *Comité contentieux* was something new among the official conciliar appendages. There were to be more of them, however: the *Comité contentieux* proved to be only the first of at least six committees on finance established in the reign of Louis XVI.

The second of them was a *comité des finances* organized by Necker's successor, Joly de Fleury, on 26 February 1783, only a month before his resignation, for the liquidation of the War of American Independence.[5] Composed of the Keeper of the Seals, the *Chef du conseil royal des finances* and the Controller General, who was to serve as the *rapporteur* and secretary, it was to meet at least once a week ostensibly in an endeavour to reduce the debts and expenditures of the war and marine departments in particular and of the royal government in general, but really in a factious effort by Joly de Fleury and the *Chef du conseil*, Vergennes, to force the resignation of two Secretaries of State, de Castries and Ségur.[6] This 'avorton de

---

[1] Antoine, 'Le Conseils', *R.H.M.C.* (1958), p. 185.

[2] *Ibid.* p. 183 and Logette, *Le Comité contentieux*, p. 13.

[3] Antoine, 'Les comités de ministres', *R.H.D.F.E.* (1951), pp. 193–230.

[4] Calonne, *Réponse de Monsieur Calonne à l'écrit de Monsieur Necker* (London, January 1788), p. 126.

[5] For this and some of the following committees, see Logette, *Le Comité contentieux*, pp. 5–13.

[6] Besenval, *Mémoires* (Paris, 1821), vol. II, pp. 114 ff.

Comité', as one observer called it, aroused hostility in court circles by its efforts and its political intentions miscarried.[1] Calonne let it die out after only a few months of activity.

A third committee was announced on 5 June 1787, soon after the Assembly of Notables had disbanded, as part of a set of administrative changes by Calonne's successor, Loménie de Brienne. The principal change was the union of the Royal Council on Finance with that of Commerce to form a *Conseil royal des finances et du commerce*, and the new committee was intended to act as a sort of steering committee for it. It was to meet every fortnight or more often if desirable at the residence of Loménie de Brienne, the new *Chef du conseil*, and was to include the Controller General, two other councillors from the Royal Council on Finance and such temporary members as they wished to call from the councillors and administrative ranks, especially the Intendants of Finance, who had been restored in 1781, and the Intendants of Commerce. It was mainly intended to prepare work for the council, but it may also have done some judicial work, for five months later a *règlement* of 27 October 1787 announced the suppression of a great many bureaux and commissions of the council, including the *Petite direction des finances*, to be replaced by the new committee.

Loménie de Brienne established at least two other committees for more precise purposes. One established on 15 March 1788 was the *Comité consultatif* 'for the discussion of plans relative to the improvement of the finances, and the order of the Royal Treasury service', that is, to assist in a fundamental reform of the Royal Treasury. The other committee was set up in September 1788 to study the single duty or tariff reform project, and it was composed of four Farmers General and an unstated number of Deputies of Commerce under the chairmanship of an Intendant of Finance.[2]

A sixth committee, 'pour les affaires administratives', appeared in the *Almanach royal* for the first time in 1789 but probably existed for some years previously. Composed of the Controller General and five Intendants in his department, it had purposes which can only be surmised; it, too, may have been concerned with the single duty project. These were years of feverish administrative activity and there were probably other committees dealing with financial matters.

All these committees, particularly the *Comité contentieux*, might conceivably have freed the Royal Council on Finance for attention to the most pressing problems in government finance, problems of a budgetary nature,

[1] Carra, *Un petit mot de réponse* (1787), p. 56.
[2] Douet de la Boullaye. See my *The Single Duty Project* (London, 1964), p. 124.

but this does not seem to have been the case. At no stage do the royal financial councils appear to have been doing much of the general financial administration. A pamphleteer wrote in 1787, with evident knowledge of his subject:

> *Pure administration.* Since the abbé Terray all is concentrated in the will of the Controller General alone. There is no longer a Council on Finance: the names of its members exist only in the *Almanach* and on the registers of the Royal Treasury which pays them. Never these days do they examine, discuss, regulate or correct in council either receipts or expenditures or accounts. The people concerned do them, the clerks verify them, the Controller puts them in his brief-case, has them signed by the King; they are then taken to the Chancellor and to the other ministers who sign where they find *ad relationem*, by virtue of the modern principle, so convenient and so dangerous: 'that the signature of the Minister of Finance for the things of his department presumes all the other signatures'. Thus, never does the King do anything but what the Controller General is pleased to tell him in his work *tête-à-tête*.[1]

Certainly the *brevets* authorizing the collection of the *taille* were brought to the councillors only after the King had signed them; likewise the leases of the tax farms.[2] Many loans and other financial transactions, and many negotiations with local or provincial authorities for reductions of taxes were likewise authorized outside the Royal Council, notwithstanding the original intention to put them before the council first. The accounts of the tax farms, of the domains and forests, of the Receivers General and other financial services were received in the Controller General's department and the Controller General brought them to the King for his signature. The Controller General also put the weekly, monthly, quarterly and annual financial statements from the Royal Treasury before the King, and by no means all of these can have appeared in council meetings. On the spending side, the annual tables of receipts and expenditures prescribed for each of the royal accountants, the *états du Roi*, and the *états au vrai* in which the accountants explained how they had carried out these orders, all these, by an arrêt of 30 October 1767, were put in the charge of one of the Intendants of Finance. He was therefore admitted to the council, but it is not clear whether he brought the tables to be aired in the council meetings or merely to be signed by the King. At any rate, the *ordonnances* authorizing payment were signed by the King in sessions with the Controller General. As for the

---

[1] Carra, *Un petit mot de réponse*, appendix III, 'Mémoire envoyé en manuscrit à plusieurs membres de l'Assemblée des Notables', p. 48. This does not appear to have been written by Carra himself.

[2] Much of this information is in the comments on the *Règlement* of 15 Sept. 1661, apparently written in 1777 and reproduced by Antoine in 'Les Conseils', *R.H.M.C.* (1958), pp. 188–97.

fortnightly or monthly tables of distribution—payments listed with a specific assignment of revenue to each—they were said to be *arrêté au conseil*, signed by the Minister of Finance, and sent to the Keepers of the Royal Treasury, but it is virtually certain that the council never saw them, the Finance Minister signed them as a matter of routine, and the highest official to think about them seriously was his assistant, the *Premier commis des finances*.[1]

It was thus that a council supposed to meet every Tuesday in fact assembled much less often. 'The Royal Council on Finance was held seven or eight times a year,' the Keeper of the Seals reminded Louis XVI in 1789, 'principally to approve the accounts of the Royal Treasury, to prepare replies to petitions (*cahiers*) from the *pays d'état* or to judge some litigious matters brought before the council because of their importance or other considerations.'[2] The stability of this council's membership, in sharp contrast with the rapidly changing Finance Ministers, also suggests that it had become a backwater in the government of finance. From 1774 to 1787 there were eight Ministers of Finance, but a total of only fourteen members of the Royal Council on Finance, even though eight members had died during that period. Of the seven members in 1787 (besides the Keeper of the Seals), two had attended since the previous reign, and two more since 1779. Not until the revolutionary year of 1787 was this council reformed; and then, by an edict of 5 June, Loménie de Brienne not only changed its entire membership but also combined it with another moribund council to form a single *Conseil royal des finances et du commerce*. But not even this change revived the council. One of its best members, Lamoignon de Malesherbes, believed that the real work of the government was being done in 'comités particuliers'.[3] Meanwhile, the *Conseil d'état et des finances* had long since disappeared altogether; the *Petite direction* had died out and was to be suppressed in October 1787; the *Conseil d'état privé* and the *Grande direction* were entirely taken up with judicial work.

Where, we may ask, were the budgets of the ancien régime prepared and the budgetary collection and expenditure supervised? After all, the financial history of the ancien régime as we have come to know it consists mainly of a series of budgetary difficulties, expenditures outrunning revenues and revenues falling short of expenditures. When and where did the King and his councillors do their budgetary work? The answer is that there never was

[1] See my 'The Premiers Commis des Finances', *French Hist. St.* (Fall 1964). B.N., Collection Joly de Fleury, MS 1435, fols. 208–11, a document of 16 October 1781 showing that these tables and other financial papers were of the greatest concern to him.
[2] Antoine, 'Les Conseils', *R.H.M.C.* (1958), p. 184.
[3] Grosclaudes, *Malesherbes*, p. 654.

a budget at all. 'It cannot be said too often,' writes Marcel Marion, 'that the ancien régime never had a budget, never a legislative act foreseeing and authorizing the total receipts and expenditures for a certain lapse of time, never an exact and complete account of the receipts and expenditures of a fiscal year, something of which even the name and the idea are not to be found in the financial documents of the time.'[1] True, Frédéric Braesch has made an analysis of what he calls 'the last budget of the ancien régime', better known as the *Compte rendu* of March 1788, but he declares it to be the first budget as well as the last.[2] He proceeds to show that in order to make sense as a budget it must be totally re-arranged, and much of his re-arrangement of it is hypothetical. Finally, he tells us that it was never put into effect and in the circumstances could not have been. Similarly, in his study, *Les Exercices budgétaires 1790 et 1791*, Braesch declares that there was no real budget for those two fiscal years; he is merely endeavouring to construct a hypothetical budget out of figures given in accounts of the time.[3] Even the word 'budget' was foreign to the ancien régime. The *Encyclo-pédie methodique. Finance* (1784) describes it as 'an English word which means, properly speaking, a bag', and goes on to define it entirely as an English parliamentary term.[4]

Until the revolution, the Controller General and the King scrutinized financial instruments which required the royal signature for their legality, and these instruments conferred an illusion of royal and ministerial control. For each of the spending departments, a table of funds-required was drawn up for the King to sign at the beginning of each year. Likewise, fortnightly or monthly tables of distribution, specifying an assignment of revenue to each item of expenditure, were put before him.[5] Each of the payments listed in these tables, like each of the tax revenues to which they were to be assigned, had been authorized by individual royal acts, but not in any budgetary ensemble. True, there could be no doubt of the royal responsibility for these and any additional payments. The Duc de Choiseul, Secretary of State for many years, spelled out carefully to Louis XV at a council meeting of 6 March 1770:

The administrators [Secretaries of State] are not responsible for the expenditures of their departments. They cannot be, even when they would like to be, for the

---

[1] Marion, *Histoire financière*, vol. I, p.448; also his *Dictionnaire des institutions*, 'Budget', p. 58. [2] Braesch, *Finances et monnaies*, 2e fasc., pp. 59 ff., 189–247.
[3] Braesch, *Finances et monnaies*, 1er fasc., p. 61.
[4] Calonne referred to the English 'budget', putting the word in italics as though it were a foreign word. (*Réponse à l'écrit de Monsieur Necker* (Jan. 1788), p. 22). Loménie de Brienne used the word 'Aperçu' in his *Compte rendu* (1788) but meant budget.
[5] Calonne, *Requête au Roi*, p. 85.

Treasurers cannot give a *sol* without an *ordonnance*, there cannot be any *ordonnance* without it being signed by Your Majesty, and no one can present an *ordonnance* for Your Majesty to sign without first having taken his [the King's] *bon*. So that when someone denounces, or has denounced, in public the expenditures of a department, people do not perceive that it is not the administrators who are being attacked, but rather Your Majesty, since the administrator can do nothing without an order written twice in the hand of Your Majesty.[1]

For payments in the provinces, also, the King signed the *état du Roi* of which there was at least one for each of the accountants.[2] The *états du Roi* were proper little budgets, for the receipts and expenditures balanced exactly and were calculated for one fiscal year only. The balance in the individual *état du Roi*, as in a modern budget, was achieved by listing the expenditures first and then assigning the appropriate funds from tax revenues etc., to meet them; and the document legally bound the accountant to spend exactly and only the specified sums. But what the King and his ministers thus imposed on each accountant they did not impose on themselves.

The famous *comptes rendus au Roi*, what Calonne called 'comptes de situation,' were little more than random personal reports of Controllers General to the King, particularly required at the time a Controller General resigned.[3] Drawn up irregularly, each one different in form, arrangement and scope according to the fancy of the Minister, they defy any but the roughest comparisons, and in any case they reported mainly on the business life of the Keepers of the Royal Treasury and a few other major accountants, and not on the state of government finances. The *comptes de prévoyance* or *aperçus* which Sully describes in his memoirs of 1601 and Mathon de la Cour in his book of 1788 were only estimates of the revenue at the Crown's disposal and not reasoned plans for expenditure.[4] As the following chapters will, I trust, make clear, the system in its very nature defied central planning and control. Such able ministers as Necker and Calonne failed in the attempt to see clearly enough to plan properly, and they revealed the shortcomings of the system incidentally in their writings, especially in the course of their public quarrel in 1787 and the years following. One of the few sound conclusions to be drawn from that quarrel is that neither had been able to get a grip on the financial administration—'cette

[1] Archives de l'Assistance publique, Paris, Papers of Auget de Montyon, *Mémoire de Monsieur le Duc de Choiseul lu au Conseil le 6 Mars 1770* MS 15 pp. in 4°.
[2] *Loc. cit.*, '...on compte 150 états du Roy', not counting those for the Royal Households, the *Parties casuelles*, the Postes and the Royal Treasury.
[3] Calonne, *Réponse de Monsieur de Calonne à l'écrit de Monsieur Necker* (Jan. 1788), p. 29; Mathon de la Cour, *Collection de comptes-rendus* (1788).
[4] Mathon de la Cour, *Collection de comptes-rendus*, p. viii.

immense machine', as they both described it with awe.[1] But those were years of fundamental change in French financial administration. The idea of a budget, like other ideas in public finance, burst upon many Frenchmen as a great discovery in the 1780s and 1790s. Pierre-Louis Roederer, member of the Constituent Assembly, declared that until the revolutionary era writers on government finances had thought only about the public revenues and loans, never about the institutions and principles of expenditure. 'Until the present, they have reduced the whole theory of public expenditure to this adage: *il faut mettre de l'économie dans les dépenses.*'[2]

Certain terms current in the ancien régime can easily create the impression that a budget existed. For instance, the words 'ordinaire' and 'extraordinaire', so common in financial documents of early modern times, look as though they might be budgetary categories. In the reign of Louis XVI, however, they were nothing more than traditional terms with meanings so vague that they served no clear purpose and only confused the accounts. Originally used in the Middle Ages to distinguish the revenues of the royal domains (*ordinaire*) from the revenues of the *aides, tailles, gabelles* and other taxes (*extraordinaire*), these terms were put to a very different use during the sixteenth and seventeenth centuries. Vincent Gelée, writing in 1594, first explains the medieval meanings and then goes on to say: 'by the *deniers ordinaires* are also understood those which are entered as receipts in the general table of finances made at the beginning of the year, and by the *deniers extraordinaires* those which are levied during the year above and beyond the table'.[3] Here was a clear use of the terms to mean 'foreseen' and 'unforeseen'; but there were to be further changes in their meaning. Throughout the eighteenth century, writers commonly referred to the *finances ordinaires* as the fixed and regular revenues and expenditures, and to the *finances extraordinaires* as the accidental and irregular ones, very often foreseen but their exact sums not fixed.[4] Necker added that in his view, the *ordinaires* were those authorized by 'laws emanating from the sovereign authority', and this was the main principle on which he drew up his ill-fated *Compte rendu au Roi* (1781).[5] His critics then and since did not

[1] Calonne, *Requête au Roi* (1787), p. 185; and Calonne quoted in Marion, *Dictionnaire des institutions*, p. 58; Necker, *Compte rendu*, p. 59; Necker, *Sur le compte rendu... nouveaux éclaircissements*, p. 200.

[2] Roederer, *Oeuvres*, vol. VI, p. 2, 'Système général des finances de France', prospectus published on 4 Nov. 1791. To give free rein to his thoughts on the subject, he wrote a play entitled, *Le Budget de Henri III*.

[3] Vincent Gelée, *Annotation de Vincent Gelée* (1594), 71 fols.; for the Middle Ages, M. Rey, *Le Domaine du Roi* (Paris, 1965).

[4] E.g. Bonvalet Desbrosses, *Moyens de simplifier la perception* (1789), p. 8; cf. Ranum, *Richelieu*, p. 138. [5] Necker, *Sur le compte rendu* (1788), p. 22.

understand his purpose, which was merely to compile what Mathon de la Cour called 'un compte de revenus et de dépenses ordinaires'. This kind of account, Mathon wrote, 'by its nature does not offer positive facts: it offers only conjectures and more or less probable estimates'.[1] If some of Necker's estimates were improbable, they stemmed partly from the failings of the royal administration; for the regular, legal, foreseeable body of revenues and expenditures could not be distinguished from the rest without making a false picture of the financial situation.

The editor of the *Compte rendu* of 1788 believed that there was no clear or useful difference between *ordinaire* and *extraordinaire*, and Frédéric Braesch has brought the weight of his scholarly authority to a criticism of the terms as being only inventions of the bureaux, designed to conceal the financial burden on the taxpayers.[2] In 1790 the Constituent Assembly added to this confusion by applying the term *extraordinaire* to its processes and institutions for liquidating the ancien régime. The *finances ordinaires* in the language of the Assembly designated all other legal, annual receipts and payment. Even in this new usage, the terms soon lost their sense because the Treasury drew more and more upon the resources of the *Caisse de l'extraordinaire*, the famous *assignats*: and when the difference between the *ordinaire* and the *extraordinaire* disappeared, then the verbal distinction became artificial.[3]

The councils of Louis XVI, with little or no budgetary control, with committees tending to perform some of their functions, with individual cases absorbing their attention, and with fewer and fewer meetings, were no longer the centres of power in the financial administration of Louis XVI. The Royal Council on Finance seemed important to Jacques Necker, who was excluded from it during his first term as the Minister of Finance (1777–81), yet his accomplishments during that remarkable administration throw doubt upon the importance he attached to membership in the council. A great deal of power lay with the Finance Minister and his department. One observer of Necker's activities wrote, 'the circumstances have given to the place of Controller General a power all the more formidable because it depends solely on opinion, and on events which increase the power of that place to the extent that they shake the whole administration'.[4] Another wrote of the General Control of Finance, 'The clerks do everything and give a twist to everything according to whether they are honest or paid by

---

[1] Mathon de la Cour, *Collection des comptes-rendus*, p. ix and p. 178.
[2] Braesch, *Finances et monnaies*, fasc. II, p. 185 note.
[3] Braesch, *Finances et monnaies*, fasc. I, p. 89.
[4] *Mémoire sur les finances de la France et leur administration par Monsieur Necker* (Amsterdam, 28 October 1788), 98 pp., p. 10.

interested parties. From this, the frightful *Bureaucratie* which exists and which is such that what made seven or eight departments under abbé Terray now makes twenty-seven or thirty.'[1] The word 'bureaucracy' first began to appear in the 1780s, with its modern meaning at least, and it was invented to describe a new development already visible in those years. 'I change my Ministers,' Louis XV is reported to have said, 'but the bureaux remain.'[2] As early as 1777 a high official had complained to Maurepas, with names and other details, about the power of the bureaux and the clerks in the Controller General's department.[3] To this department we must now turn.

[1] Carra, *Un petit mot de réponse*, p. 48.

[2] Lamy, *Opinion sur l'importance de décréter la responsabilité des chefs de bureaux...* (1790), p. 5; A.N., 144 AP 131, Fonds d'Ormesson, *Fragment d'un mémoire sur les secrétaires des finances*, in which d'Ormesson referred to 'l'accroissement effrayant de la bureaucratie depuis quelques siècles'; Jean Blondel, *Introduction à l'ouvrage intitulé de l'administration des finances* (1785), p. 57. The best explanation of the word bureaucracy is in Mercier, *Tableau de Paris* (1789), vol. IX, p. 57.

[3] A.N., F^{30} 110^{A} *Note*, dated 22 June 1777.

3

THE MINISTER AND HIS DEPARTMENT

THE TITLE usually conferred upon Ministers of Finance in the eighteenth century was *Contrôleur général des finances*, but in the reign of Louis XVI three of the most eminent of them were not Controllers General: Jacques Necker was *Directeur général* (1777–81) and, in his second ministry, *Ministre d'état* (1788–90); Joly de Fleury was *Ministre d'état et des finances* (1781–3), sometimes called *Administrateur général*; and Loménie de Brienne was *Chef du conseil royal des finances* and then *Ministre principal* (1787–8). These changes in title were signs of life and change in the administration as the Crown struggled to overcome its financial difficulties. They showed, furthermore, a growth of the Finance Minister's power. Louis XIV had defined the post of Controller General as something much less than that of the Superintendents which he had abolished, and something lower even than the posts of Secretary of State. Only a century earlier the word *contrerolle* had still meant duplicate records, and the *Contrerolleur général* (as Jean Hennequin spelt the title in 1585) had been a kind of auditor-general with no initiative or command in financial policy or administration.[1] With a title still smacking of ledgers and account books, the Controller General of the eighteenth century had no right to sit in the *Conseil d'en-haut*, the highest council, nor in the Royal Council on Finance, unless the King invited him especially, and he could not sign *arrêts en commandement* which were those arrêts about matters of government policy. His first and basic task was 'to verify [contrôler] and register all the acts bearing upon the finances of the King',[2] that is, to see that payments and collections authorized by royal order were duly made and to match the proper receipts with the original orders, this in a set of registers kept for the purpose.

How far the functions of Controller General grew beyond these original duties of 'contrôle' we may judge from the fact that in the years 1715–23 and again in 1777–83 these duties were passed down to two *Gardes des*

[1] Hennequin, *Le Guidon général*, pp. 108 and 117.
[2] *Encyclopédie méthodique. Jurisprudence*, vol. III, p. 307.

47

registres du contrôle général des finances,[1] as though trivial in the practical affairs of the Department; and in 1787–90 the Controller General was himself appointed as a subordinate acting under the orders of a Finance Minister. Furthermore, the activities of the three Ministers who were not Controllers General, Necker, Joly de Fleury and Loménie de Brienne, show that the finances were becoming ministerial and that Louis XIV's original idea of acting as his own Minister of Finance held no sway at the court of Louis XVI. Even some of the Controllers General, Turgot and Calonne, for instance, played roles as Ministers of Finance with policies and programmes to carry out. Strictly speaking, a Controller General of Finance was a Minister only if the King called him to sit in the *Conseil d'en-haut*, otherwise he was called Minister only by courtesy; but Turgot, Joly de Fleury, Calonne and Loménie de Brienne all sat in the *Conseil d'en-haut* and so did Necker during his second ministry. For ten years out of the first fifteen in the reign, therefore, there was a Minister of Finance even in the strictest sense of the term.

Eighteenth-century writings convey an impression that the Minister of Finance was in command of the financial administration. Even if he only assisted the King and councils in making policy, though most Ministers did more, he alone was in a position to implement policy—or so observers of the time would lead us to believe. By later standards, however, the Minister was in a weak position. He was hampered a great deal by the extraordinarily wide range of his responsibilities. As Tocqueville remarked, 'he acted in turn as Minister of Finance, Minister of the Interior, Minister of Public Works, Minister of Commerce' and, we might now add, Minister of Health and Welfare, Minister of Supply, Minister of Economic Development and others.[2] His colleagues, the four Secretaries of State for Foreign Affairs, War, Navy and Royal Household, had more homogeneous functions and so did the Keeper of the Seals, even though they shared in the work of internal administration. Unlike them, the Minister of Finance gained authority over more and more fields of administration as the Crown added to its paternal activities, partly because the Crown seldom drew a distinction between financing an activity and directing it, and partly because the economy of the paternal monarchy, in the eyes of the great kings and ministers of the past, had always embraced national production and distribution, and state taxation and expenditure, in one continuous process. The Department of Finance had grown large and complex.

---

[1] By laws of 25 September 1715; 12 December 1722; 29 June 1777; and 30 March 1783 (B.N., F 21207 (89)).

[2] Tocqueville, *L'Ancien Régime*, vol. i, p. 109.

It neither collected nor spent any money, except for its own working expenses. Government funds were collected and spent by corps of accountants, such as Receivers, Treasurers and Payers, all with clerks and other assistants, and by agencies such as the General Farm of Taxes, the General Administration of the Royal Domains and the *Régie générale* for excise taxes (*aides*). The task of the Department of Finance was to prepare the Crown's business for these agents and agencies; that is, to draw up tax rolls, tables of payments authorized for the spending departments, lists of pensions and rentes for payment, *états du Roi* for each accountant, and such like. The Department also had to keep records of royal business done, based on receipts, *états au vrai* and other returns from the accountants and agencies. These latter being more or less private enterprises, with a business relationship with the government, much like that of a present-day munitions supplier or road-builder, the bureaux of the Department had grown up to assist the Minister in his task of general supervision. Therefore, the basic unit of the Department was the bureau created to prepare business for a certain agency or for a certain corps of accountants, and to see that the business was done, much as a customer of a bank or trust company might see to the business he left in their hands.

In 1788, when the Department was at a mature stage of its development, approximately thirty-eight bureaux, employing about 256 men, dealt with matters arising in the work of financial agencies or corps of accountants.[1] For the General Farm of Taxes there were four bureaux with a total of twenty-one employees and for the *Régie générale* a bureau of six, those for each agency being under an Intendant of Finance. For the General Administration of the Royal Domains there were seven bureaux of forty-four employees under an Intendant of Finance, and for the Royal Lottery a bureau of four men. The Receivers General of Finance, who collected the *tailles*, the *capitation* and the *vingtième*, preoccupied no less than twelve bureaux of ninety-four men under an Intendant of Finance (including the Director of Paris Impositions and his twenty-one Controllers). There was a bureau of three men for the Payers of the rentes, another of five men for the *liquidation* or settlement of repaid rentes and venal offices, a bureau of six

---

[1] These and other figures on employees and bureaux I have compiled from many manuscript sources, but principally the following: A.N., D VI 8, 'Traitements à diverses personnes occupées pour le service de l'administration', signed by Dufresne, 3 Aug. 1789; A.N., D X 3, 'Etat général des traitements des bureaux de l'administration des finances à compter du premier janvier 1788 (cet état a été dressé quelques jours avant la retraite de l'archevêque de Toulouse)'; A.N., F¹ᴬ 565, 'Bureaux de l'administration générale des finances', for 1788, 1789 and 1790; a great number of fugitive papers in A.N., F⁴ 1032²; and *Bureaux de l'administration générale imprimé par ordre de l'assemblée nationale* (Paris, 1790), 15 pp.; and finally, the *Almanach royal*.

for the mints (also supposed to examine financial projects sent in to the Department by the King's loyal subjects), and a bureau of five for the Receiver General of *Revenus casuels* and other accountants. Two bureaux employing seventeen men dealt with the Crown's financial relations with the *pays d'état*. The final item in this list is the seven bureaux of the *Premier commis des finances*, with a total of forty-six employees, for the Keepers of the Royal Treasury and the Treasurers of the major spending departments.

I have reserved these for the end of the list in order to emphasize the relatively modest numbers of men and bureaux, approximately 18%, working on treasury matters. The bureaux of the *Premier commis des finances*, a well-paid and powerful official who worked closely with the Minister, were supposed to compile tables of all the revenues and expenditures of the Royal Treasury, and to follow daily so far as possible the financial situation of each of the funds or caisses.[1] On the payments side, where most of their work lay, they were to follow in detail the processes of payment, especially of the large spending departments of War and Marine, so as to be able to know at any time what remained to be paid. They were supposed to record whether payments were made in cash or in notes in anticipation of revenue, and to verify the title or authority of each claim on the Treasury. In times of financial difficulty, especially in wartime, the *Premier commis des finances* was expected to know where funds could be found to tide the Treasury over and to sustain its credit in case of emergency, and at all times he served as the Minister's chief adviser in Treasury matters. The Treasury preoccupied only a small part, however, of the Department of Finance.

When we turn to those bureaux at work on matters not purely financial, we find that they number approximately twenty-five, in addition to some of those in the foregoing list partly engaged in non-financial business and in addition to an uncertain number of individuals—perhaps twenty—attached to the Department for special purposes. If we group their concerns under the functional heads of our time, we shall find that for Public Works there were bureaux busy with work being done at Cherbourg, for roads and bridges in many parts of the country, for dykes, the streets of Paris and the repair of buildings on the royal domains. Work which might properly fall to a Ministry of the Interior included municipalities, royal domains, waters and forests, salt marshes and mines, the postal and transport services, the provincial estates and in time provincial assemblies, the Royal Veterinary

---

[1] B.N., Joly de Fleury papers, 1435, fols. 208–11, 'Idées générales sur les fonctions du premier commis des finances' (16 Oct. 1781); also my article, 'The Premiers Commis des Finances in the reign of Louis XVI', *French Hist. St.*, vol. III (1964), pp. 475–94.

School at Charenton and the control of animal diseases, the military school at Saint Cyr, statistics of population, the island of Corsica, the royal stud farms. Several bureaux dealt with matters which today would be those of a Ministry of Trade and Industry: mines and minerals, the balance of trade, the reform of the customs, fisheries, foreign tariffs and industrial inspection. As for Health and Welfare, there were bureaux concerned with hospitals, the provisions for paupers and the prisons (closely connected in the eighteenth century) and a certain Jean Colombier served as Inspector General for Hospitals and Prisons from 17 January 1781, and a certain Joseph Bannefroy as Inspector General of the *dépôts de mendicité*. The food provisions (*subsistances*) especially for Paris, and the fuel supplies of that city, were also the concern of bureaux in the Department of Finance. Few of these bureaux were intended actually to carry out the operations for which they were named. Exercising the control which royal power and finance conferred, they corresponded with the men actually doing the work of buying up grain, building roads, inspecting industries and so on. They drew up budgetary tables and supervised expenditures, compiled information and accounts, planned projects and prepared questions for decision at higher levels. They were the eyes and ears of the Minister as well as his secretariat.

A number of employees were attached to the Department to collect information or to compile treatises on certain subjects. Bréquigny collected royal edicts and declarations; Dupont de Nemours and his bureau collected the tariffs and commercial laws of foreign countries; Le Quesne made studies of the population of France, probably under the direction of Jean-Baptiste-François de la Michodière, a Councillor of State in charge of the Bureau of Population Tables. They were reported to be working out the average annual births of every town and village and marking the figures on Cassini's map of France. 'Your Majesty has for a long time known this work and its usefulness', the new Minister of the Interior wrote to the King in October 1791.[1] Isaac Potier headed the bureau for calculating the balance of trade with foreign countries, and abbé André Morellet had a salary for many years and at least one salaried clerk for the purpose of compiling a dictionary of trade which he never finished. Abbé Pernon was at work on mortgage legislation.[2]

Very similar to the work of these scholars and specialists was the task of keeping deposits of papers. Boyetet des Bordes and Coquelay served throughout the reign as the keepers of the *dépôt des minutes et expéditions extraordinaires des finances*. Jacob-Nicolas Moreau, historiographer royal,

---

[1] A.N., F^{IA} I. [2] A.N., AB xix 327, 28e conference.

was in charge of the papers of the financial administration; a certain Laurent kept all the *minutes d'arrêts au Conseil privé*; Villiers du Terrage directed the *dépôt des papiers concernant les pays d'état, des eaux et forêts et autres*; and there were two Keepers of the Registers of the General Control, Perrotin de Barmond and Fougeray de Launay, with clerks out in the provinces.

Another category of official not engaged in strictly financial matters looked after the internal affairs or 'housekeeping' of the Department. The *Bureau des dépêches* consisting of a *premier commis*, a *chef* and six or seven clerks sorted incoming letters and parcels and dispatched outgoing mail, maintaining at the same time a link between the various bureaux. Villiers de Terrage headed another bureau of five who dispatched edicts, declarations and other official decisions to those officially supposed to receive them, and otherwise served as a bureaucratic link with the Royal Council on Finance. Several messengers plied between Versailles and Paris, for the most part. There was a *concierge du Roi* and at least two guards or *suisses* at the *Hôtel du Contrôle général* in Paris; a departmental surgeon and a translator at Versailles; and an almoner in Paris. It is perhaps in this category that the private secretaries of the Ministers belong.[1]

Summarizing the personnel of the Department, we may say that there were altogether some 360 employees, including about 30 *premiers commis*, about the same number of *chefs* under them, approximately 205 *commis* and about 30 office-boys (*garçons de bureau*), the rest with miscellaneous titles or none at all. These employees were certainly more numerous than at the beginning of the reign, but not so much as complaints in those disturbed years might suggest. If salaries increased a little over the reign, and if certain bureaux hired a few more employees, most expansion of the Department was in the form of new bureaux to cope with new duties: a bureau for the Royal Lottery founded in 1776; the *Bureau de la balance du commerce* taken over from the General Farm in 1781; the Bureau of Mines and the supervision of land-clearing and the enclosures of common land taken over from the department of Henri Bertin when it dissolved in 1781;[2] Mahy de

---

[1] Some of the private secretaries were: Louis-François-André Denaux (Turgot), Jean Duclerc (Clugny), Charles Vian and Nicolas de Saint Aubin (Joly de Fleury), Pierre-Joseph Ferrand (d'Ormesson), Jean-Jacques Accarias de Serionne, Jean-Daniel La Garde (Calonne), François Coindet (Necker), Pierre Soufflot de Mérey with a staff of eight *commis* and two office-boys (Loménie de Brienne), Gatty (Laurent de Villedeuil), and Lenfant (Lambert).

[2] Bertin's post of Secretary of State was suppressed by an Edict of Nov. 1780 (A.N., P 2519, fol. 248). The Mines Bureau, formerly under Advenier and others, was reformed under Douet de la Boullaye, Master of Requests, beginning in June 1782, and was functioning under a new *premier commis*, Bergon, by November (A.N., F⁴ 1032²). The super-

Cormeré's bureau for reforming the customs duties, set up during Necker's first ministry;[1] bureaux for the Estates-General set up in 1788 under Joseph-François Coster; a bureau for the provincial assemblies under Tarbé and then Dailly; and other new bureaux.

The size of the Department and the variety of its business do not alone convey any fair idea of the Minister's task. The Department was incoherent to a degree not easy to grasp in the twentieth century, and its incoherence was deeply rooted in the aristocratic society of the ancien régime. Unconsciously holding the ideas of authority which prevailed at court, each Intendant or *Maître des requêtes* with responsibilities in the Department, and each *premier commis* at the head of one or two bureaux, wanted to have his own quarters where he could live, work and have his being as a personnage much as the King did, though naturally on a scale suitable to his social rank. Each *premier commis* normally rented his own premises, established and furnished his bureaux and then applied to the Minister for reimbursement. We catch glimpses of such departmental practices in accounts of the time and in memoranda such as this one which Mathieu-Gaspard Fieux, *premier commis*, sent to the Minister for approval in April 1781:

The lease for the bureaux of the division of cities, hospitals, etc., being due to expire on 1 July next, the Director General [i.e. the Minister] has approved that Monsieur Fieux, in charge of this division, live with his bureaux and that therefore he lease or otherwise take a place sufficient for this double purpose. The rent of it is to be paid entirely by the general administration.

Monsieur Fieux has found an apartment with attached rooms in a house at number sixteen, rue de Gaillon. The owner asks for a lease of three years which will be jointly underwritten by Monsieur Fieux and his wife for 3,600 livres in rent.

Monsieur Fieux begs the Director General to authorize him to sign this lease, and to order that with effect from 1 July next the said sum of 3,600 livres, the amount of the rent, will be paid in quarterly instalments on the fund of the *partie casuelle* together with the salaries of Monsieur Fieux and his employees in this division.[2]

[approved]

The tone of this letter seems, perhaps, to hint that there was something special about Fieux living with his bureaux but there is much evidence to suggest that most *premiers commis* did so unless they were wealthy enough to own houses. For the twenty-six names listed with addresses under the

vision of land-clearing (*défrichement*) and of enclosures fell to the *Bureaux des impositions*, according to Lefèvre d'Ormesson, 'Mémoire sur le département des impositions' (June 1781; B.N., Joly de Fleury papers 1443).

[1] See my book, *The Single Duty Project*, p. 108.
[2] A.N., F[4] 1032[2].

53

head *Département des finances* in the *Almanach royal* for 1788, seventeen different addresses are given, and the address for all the rest except one was *l'Hôtel du Contrôle général.* Under the head, *Ponts et Chaussées de France* were listed fifteen men with fourteen different addresses; and for the Mines and Minerals service there was a listing of thirteen names with ten different addresses, although these last two lists contained the names of some men not in the department of Finance. It is true that the seven *chefs* under the direction of the *Premier commis des finances* were all listed at the same address, and three of the bureaux for the General Farms were likewise together. On the whole, nevertheless, the bureaux of the Department were scattered about the centre of Paris and at least three of them were at Versailles.[1]

In other ways, too, the Department was incoherent. Each bureau was separately paid according to a negotiation between the *premier commis* and the Minister. The bureaux were not paid at the same source, but usually at the agency for which they worked: the bureau for the *Régie générale* was thus paid by the *Régie*, the various bureaux for the domains by the Domains administration, and so on, all such payments for the Crown being marked down on royal accounts and charged to the Crown in the accounting process. If there was no such obvious source of payment, then a bureau was usually paid by the Treasurer of the *partie casuelle*, but in each case the source of payment was specified in the Minister's *bon*. Further to confuse the system of payment, some bureaux were paid monthly and some quarterly; in either case nearly all employees received a gratuity at the end of each year. Thus, out of a total annual payment of 1,403,967 livres for the Department in 1788, some 388,760 livres were paid on a monthly basis, 924,157 livres quarterly, and 91,050 livres annually.[2] As these irregularities suggest, the Department does not appear to have been identified as a whole in any budgetary list or category, until 1788 at any rate, and the various *Comptes rendus* before that year give no figures for its total costs.[3] It was paid as a collection of separate bureaux, not as a Department.

Little wonder, then, that the Department was called by various descriptive titles as though its identity and its limits were uncertain: *Départements des finances*, in the plural; *Département des finances*, in the singular; *Administration des finances*, and *Contrôle général des finances*.[4] One official

---

[1] *Almanach royal* (1788), pp. 227, 569, 574–7; *Almanach de Versailles, passim*. This was common practice, and the clerks of the Payers of the rentes—about 200 altogether—usually lived in the bureaux of their masters (*De l'acquittement des intérêts de la dette publique* (1792), p. 9).
[2] A.N., D x 3, 'Etat général des traitements...'
[3] Mathon de la Cour, *Collection des comptes-rendus*, p. 231.
[4] *Almanach royal* (1786), p. 219; (1787), p. 219; (1788), p. 227; A.N., D x 3, 'Etat général des traitements'.

list of 1790 included the financial bureaux, the bureaux of the Secretary of State for the *Maison du Roi* and those of the Chancellor in one continuous series under the title, *Bureaux de l'administration générale*.[1] Little wonder, too, that the *Almanach royal* never listed the bureaux of the Department all together but instead scattered them through its pages sometimes in five or six different places, usually together with the agencies whose work they followed. It is hardly too much to suggest that the Ministers, with the possible exception of Necker, thought of their various bureaux as their representatives posted to the various agencies and corps of accountants somewhat the way their Intendants were posted out in the provinces. Indeed, the departmental Intendants of Finance, once they were no longer venal after the reform of June 1777, were drawn from the main body of the Masters of Requests and commissioned much in the same way as the Intendants in the provinces.[2] Of course, the provincial Intendants were not really subordinate to the Minister of Finance, at least not in the modern administrative sense, but neither were the Intendants and other Masters of Requests within the Department of Finance. Therein lay a great weakening of the Minister's power.

The grouping of the bureaux in the Department was a problem to any Minister who wanted to make the Department responsive to his wishes, or so we may judge from the changes which occurred. The Minister, with his private secretaries, had somehow to bend the whole Department to serve his purposes. Before the reforms of June 1777, six Intendants of Finance with venal offices directed the work of about thirty *premiers commis* and *chefs* with their bureaux, and the Minister himself directed the work of only about ten in matters of finance. There were also venal offices for the four Intendants of Commerce. These and the Intendants of Finance had the power and independence which venal offices conferred and several of them sat in the Royal Council on Finance. One of the reasons for their dismissal in June 1777 was to prepare the way for Necker, a mere Director General with no seat in any council, to command the work of his Department.

After the reform the four Intendants of Commerce held their posts by revocable commissions,[3] four Masters of Requests were commissioned to supervise groups of financial bureaux under the command of the Director General, Necker, but he still found it convenient to take six key bureaux under his own direct supervision, besides the ones which Turgot had

---

[1] B.N., Lf⁹⁹ 6.

[2] The Minister of Finance named the Intendants to the *pays d'élection*, and those for the *pays d'état* were named by the Secretary of State for War.

[3] A.N., P 2513 fol. 441: An Edict of June 1777 suppressed the four offices of Intendant of Commerce created in June 1724 and substituted four commissions.

supervised, and to create a seventh, with no magistrate intervening between him and the *premiers commis* of these bureaux. They were the four *Bureaux des impositions* which he put under Dailly, the *Bureau des Fermes* which he put under a certain Couturier,[1] the *Bureau des Ponts et Chaussées* which he directed through a *premier commis*, Joseph-François Coster and then Cadet de Chambine, and the bureau of Marie-Romain Hamelin which he set up to deal with the new *Régie générale*. Necker took more bureaux under his own supervision than did any other Minister because he found it so difficult to work through Masters of Requests, who tended to regard him as socially inferior. Even one with a reputation for being enlightened and intelligent, Trudaine de Montigny, refused to supervise the *Ponts et Chaussées* under Necker's direction.[2] In thus struggling to overcome the power of these magistrates, Necker foreshadowed, indeed began, the revolutionary reforms of the financial administration, but there was to be a period of reaction before such reforms became permanent. The first reactionary Minister was his successor, Joly de Fleury.

Joly de Fleury replaced three *premiers commis* with three new Masters of Requests whom he commissioned as Intendants to take charge of certain divisions: Chaumont de la Millière for the *Ponts et Chaussées*, Douet de la Boullaye for the Mines and Minerals and Louis-Guillaume de Villevault for the General Farms. Taking this trend even further, Calonne soon had a total of nine *Intendants des départements*, and at least seven other Masters of Requests in charge of various bureaux, not counting two of the four Intendants of Commerce who were not at the same time Intendants of Finance.[3] It was after counting the nine Intendants and the seven other

[1] It is significant of Necker's conscious intention to make this change that the previous *premier commis* of that bureau, Georges Passelaigue, retired on 1 July 1777, almost as soon as Necker became Director General. Passelaigue had held that bureau under the Intendant of Finance, Trudaine de Montigny. (A.N., F⁴ 1032²; and *Etat général des pensions sur le trésor public.*)

[2] Turgot reported this to Dupont, 10 July 1777 (*Œuvres*, vol. 5, p. 524). One of Necker's clerks later reported that the Intendants of Finance had 'refused to work with a Minister who had no entry into any council. They had to be suppressed and replaced by *premiers commis*' (Hennet, *Théorie du crédit public* (Paris, 1816), p. 270 and p. 587).

[3] These were the *Intendants des départements* for *péages* (Doublet de Persan), municipalities (Valdec de Lessart), *domaines et bois* (de Bonnaire de Forges), *régie générale* (Raillard de Granvelle), impositions (Gravier de Vergennes), the island of Corsica (Blondel), the General Farms (de Colonia), the bridges, roads, hospitals and prisons (Chaumont de la Millière), the mines and *droits domainiaux* (Douet de la Boullaye). The other seven Masters of Requests were de Boulongne, Boutin, Pajot de Marcheval, Bertier, Chardon, Michodière and de Montaran. The four Intendants of Commerce were Blondel and de Montaran (named already among the above), de Tolozan and de Vin de Gallande. Gaudin, duc de Gaëte, writes in his memoirs, 'Monsieur Necker fut remplacé par Joly de Fleury. L'une des premières opérations du nouveau ministre fut de remettre à la tête des divers départements les magistrats que son prédécesseur en avait éloigné...' (vol. 1, p. 6).

Masters of Requests together with the Minister, doubtless as listed in the *Almanach royal*, that a committee of the Assembly of Notables complained in 1787, 'there are seventeen bureaux or departments of the *Contrôle général*, and of these seventeen...eleven have been created since 1783'.[1] This conveyed a false impression, however, because there had been very little increase in the numbers of bureaux or employees; the increase had been merely in the number of magistrates put in charge of them. With so many dividing the work of the Department among them, Calonne endeavoured to achieve a sort of coherence by calling them to meet at an *Assemblée des départements* held every Wednesday at the residence of a Councillor of State, Lenoir, and under his chairmanship.[2] By later standards, Calonne presided over not one Department, but a number of separate ones.

When Loménie de Brienne took charge of the finances as *Ministre principal*, he revoked the commissions of these Intendants and Masters of Requests and issued new commissions to four of them to head large divisions for Domains (de Bonnaire de Forges), Bridges and Roads, Hospitals and Prisons (Chaumont de la Millière), Impositions (Blondel), and the General Farm and *Régie générale* (Douet de la Boullaye). At the same time he consolidated the bureaux of the four Intendants of Commerce under one Intendant, Tolozan. Necker left these largely unchanged during his second and third periods as Minister. The subdivision of the Department of Finance thus reached its final and most logical form in 1788. The Department changed very little thereafter except as bureaux were removed one by one in the rearrangements of 1790 and 1791 which ultimately dissolved it.

The way each Minister subdivided the Department reveals something of his methods and policies. Viewing the reign as a whole, we may say that Turgot, Joly de Fleury, Lefèvre d'Ormesson and Calonne made little or no attempt to reduce the aristocratic, personal power of magistrates and worked with the Department organized around magistrates and referred to in the plural as 'les départements'.[3] According to this organization, the common clerks were in inferior positions, rather like domestic servants, and listed as appendages to their masters, the magistrates, for such clerks no matter what their responsibilities, could not have dignity or authority in the eyes of the higher orders. Not for nothing was the *Almanach royal* arranged fundamentally according to the social order of the realm, beginning with a list of

---

[1] B.N., Nouv. acq. fr., 23617, fol. 264, dated 7 May 1787.
[2] Jean-Charles-Pierre Le Noir (1732–1807) was also a personal friend of Calonne. *Almanach royal* (1786), p. 219; (1787), p. 220.
[3] *Almanach royal* (1776), p. 221; (1786), p. 219, and all other years except 1788 and 1789.

royalty and proceeding to lists of the three estates, clergy, nobility and bourgeoisie. Bureaucratic organizations did not fit easily into this arrangement, however, and the *premiers commis* were in the ambiguous position of holding much administrative power and high salaries, and yet risking the jealous contempt of the magistrates. The appointment of *premiers commis*— Dailly, Coster, Hamelin—to positions of authority normally occupied by magistrates was one of the innovations which brought about Necker's downfall in 1781, for Necker seemed to be undermining the aristocratic control over the Department.[1] He integrated in bureaucratic fashion the Department left him by Turgot, and after Calonne had divided it again among many magistrates Loménie de Brienne began once more in 1787 the work of consolidation. In 1788 and 1789 the *Almanach royal* referred to the Department in the singular. In this matter of organization, the revolution brought a victory of bureaucracy over aristocracy, as I hope to show in later chapters of this book.

Closely connected with changes in departmental organization, and sometimes indistinguishable, were the Ministers' appointments of friends or 'clients' willing to support their policies. Such appointees became involved thereby in the politics of the Minister and liable to discharge with him. Some of these were brought into the Department from outside and others were found already at work and were merely transferred and paid more. Conversely, most Ministers removed men who had been personally devoted to their predecessors. Biographers of a Minister usually pretend that those removed had somehow compromised themselves morally or professionally, that those appointed in their places were superior—or the converse if the biography is unfavourable—but if we look beyond the gossip of the time we see that Ministers made some such changes in order to have men in the Department sympathetic to them and their policies. It is impossible to know in every case whether a change was for such political reasons or merely to have a more able man in place, or to remove a dishonest official.

The most obviously political appointment was that of the *Premier commis des finances*, the Minister's man in charge of the bureaux working with the Royal Treasury. Turgot removed Terray's *Premier commis des finances*, Armand Le Clerc, in order to appoint his own friend, Jean de Vaines; Necker removed de Vaines in favour of Bertrand Dufresne; Joly de Fleury replaced Dufresne with Achille-Joseph Gojard, who remained in place until August 1788 when Necker, in his second ministry, brought back

[1] See my paper, 'Jacques Necker et l'état moderne', *Rapport de la société historique du Canada* (1963), pp. 162–75.

Dufresne, assisted by Cornu de la Fontaine. On the other hand, the many changes in the bureaux of the *Premier commis de finances* do not appear to have been made directly by Ministers, and it seems that the *chefs* of those bureaux were not touched by the politics of ministerial change.[1]

Several Ministers made changes among other *premiers commis* and *chefs*, which seem to have been for the purpose of placing friends in office. Turgot replaced Destouches and Dupuy, a relation of Terray's, with Le Seur and Charles de la Croix, the latter having been one of his secretaries at the Intendancy of Limoges. Necker appointed at least three whom his successors removed: Dailly, who disappeared almost as soon as Necker himself fell, and Hamelin and Coster whom Calonne removed probably for political reasons. Calonne's appointments included at least two *premiers commis* who were immediately removed when he fell: Joseph le Rat, at the head of his *Bureau des dépêches*, and Jean-Baptiste-Bertrand Durban, head of the *Bureau des projets* which one writer described as 'a gulf in which all projects and their authors are swallowed up and drowned'.[2] It is probable that Bruys de Vaudran was a friend of either Loménie de Brienne or Laurent de Villedeuil, for he was appointed on 1 June 1787, soon after their ministries began, to head a bureau for the *partie casuelle*, the Indies Company, the veterinary school and the fuel provisioning of Paris.[3] When Necker took control again in August 1788, he left Bruys de Vaudran in place, but brought back with him his former *premiers commis*, Coster and Dailly.

For all this we should not imagine the Department to have been entirely unstable even during the last decade of the ancien régime. The list of *premiers commis* who remained in service throughout the reign, often longer, includes Mélin, Cadet de Chambine, Duclaud, Bruté de Nierville, Mutel, de Busserole and the de Villiers father and son. Three generations of the de Villiers family served as head of the same bureaux from 1726 to 13 April 1794, and such long service was not uncommon.[4] True, there were certain periods of unusual change, such as Necker's first ministry (1777–81) when about twelve *premiers commis*, half of those employed by the venal Intendants of Finance, disappeared with their masters. But three of them whose fate I was able to trace, Jean-Ambroise Choderlos de Laclos, Pierre Bruyard and Georges Passelaigue, were over seventy years old and retired on pensions; another, Louis-Henri Duchesne, soon became Intendant General

---

[1] See my paper, 'The Premiers Commis des Finances in the reign of Louis XVI', *French Hist. St.*, vol. III (1964), pp. 475–94.
[2] Bonvallet Desbrosses, in A.N., T 1270–1.
[3] A.N., F4 1032².
[4] A.N., F1A 568, papers on pensions for de Villiers de Terrage.

of the Household of *Madame*; the two Desprez de Boissy, 'born gentlemen and belonging to substantial houses', d'Ormesson wrote, 'feared as is only natural with these personal advantages, the humiliation of finding themselves subordinated to *commis des finances* personally inferior to them';[1] and another, Dureau de Blancourt, died either then or shortly afterwards. Few, indeed, ever retired at any time without alternative employment or pensions 'réversibles' to their wives and children in case of death. Writing to the Minister on behalf of Armand Leclerc, Terray's *premier commis des finances*, an official remarked that after more than thirty years of service, Leclerc had obtained no pension when Turgot had discharged him, 'which is without precedent'.[2] It is hardly too much to say that the Department had some of the characteristics of a career service. Many employees and even their bureaux remained unchanged in the early revolutionary years and were merely transferred elsewhere when the Department dissolved. For example, Noel-François-Mathieu Angot des Rotours remained at the head of the bureaux for the mints which was in the Ministry of Public Contributions in July 1792; Joseph-Alexandre Bergon never ceased to head bureaux for the administration of lands and forests until Napoleon called him to the Council of State in the First Empire; and in April 1796 the National Treasury was employing at the head of various bureaux such men as Beckvelt, Vauguyon, Gurber, and Guillaume from the former Finance Department.[3] It was not at the level of the *premiers commis* that the revolution brought sweeping changes, but rather among the magistrates in the administration, who practically all disappeared in the course of 1790 and 1791.

Already under the ancien régime many changes among the Masters of Requests were political. When Turgot came to power in 1774, he immediately removed two of the Intendants of Finance, Foullon and Cochin, because of their association with Terray, and put de Boullongne and Boutin in their places. He also replaced two Intendants of Commerce one of whom, Brochet de Saint-Prest, had been head of the *Bureau des subsistances* supervising grain purchases under Terray. Turgot put that bureau under his physiocratic friend, Albert.[4] Necker removed all the Intendants of Finance; and of the four Masters of Requests whom he commissioned instead, only

---

[1] B.N., Joly de Fleury 1448, fols. 55 ff. Choderlos de Laclos was the father of the famous author of *Liaisons dangereuses*.

[2] B.N., Joly de Fleury papers 1440, fol. 88, dated 19 Dec. 1782. He had in fact secured an *acquit patent* of 3,000 livres in 1775, but this was not comparable with the 23,000 livres granted to de Vaines or the 15,000 livres granted to Dufresne.

[3] A.N., AF III 28; AF II 21^B (pl. 163); AF III 130; and Charles Durand, *Etudes sur le conseil d'état napoléonien* (1949), p. 314, and p. 449.

[4] Faure, *La Disgrâce de Turgot*, pp. 68 ff.

one, Michau de Montaran, had held office under Turgot. Joly de Fleury appears to have left those whom Necker appointed and made three additional appointments. Calonne issued four commissions which did not survive his own downfall, and at least one of them was to a personal friend, de Colonia.[1] After that, Loménie de Brienne and Necker left four commissioned Intendants in place until the revolutionary changes.[2]

In view of the way systems of patronage and clientage flourished in the ancien régime, the wonder is that Ministers made so few changes in the Department. Wisps of evidence show that appointments and promotions were much affected, and often entirely made, by personal or family influence. Many people of high birth, wealth or power busied themselves with the 'protection' of young men in various bureaux. The magistrates and *premiers commis* sometimes brought in friends and relations. Mathieu Gurber and his two sons made up the entire *Bureau des rentes* for many years, and the two Vauguyon brothers likewise headed one of the *Bureaux des impositions*.[3] By way of example, let us explore the patronage brought to bear in one bureau, that of *dépêches* under Charles Hersemulle de la Roche whose family had been in the royal civil service since 1712, and who himself served as *premier commis* from 1778.[4] In his bureau were his son-in-law, Etienne-Marie Denois, who was also the son of a *premier commis* of a Secretary of State for War; de Bouconvilliers, a nephew of de la Roche; Pardon, whose name was linked with that of de la Roche in a marriage of the previous generation, making them probably cousins; Meslin, in whom one of the King's aunts, Madame Victoire, took a patronizing interest; Vassal, son-in-law of a *premier commis*, Cochereau, and with two 'protectors', Madame Adelaide, another royal aunt, and de Villevault, a Master of Requests; de Glatigny, whose father was *valet de chambre* to the Queen; Nay, a nephew of Cadet de Chambine, *premier commis* of the Bridges and Roads; François Delorme, a relation of a *premier commis* in the War Department; and Charles Coster, from a large and powerful family with several members in royal service. It would be surprising if the remaining two employees, Nicolas Gautry and Joseph Perneron de Pradtz, were not likewise assisted, although I have found no evidence to prove it. In any event, the case of this bureau shows how the administration was open to the social struggles of that time, struggles for family advancement in an aristo-

---

[1] The three others were Chardon, Charles Gravier de Vergennes and Raillard de Granvelle.

[2] These were Blondel, de Colonia, Douet de la Boullaye and de Bonnaire de Forges.

[3] Jean-Nicolas-François Vauguyon, l'aîné; and Nicolas-Sophie Vauguyon des Essarts.

[4] The information in this paragraph comes mainly from A.N., F⁴ 1032² and from the *Etat des pensions sur le trésor royal* (Paris, 1789).

cratic society where posts in the royal service, like wealth and high connections, were openly used as a kind of power by everyone from the royal family downward.

The post of Minister was itself political to a degree, and this was one of its most striking features. The King named each new Minister, and eventually discharged him, in a complicated and subtle political process. A Minister had therefore to be a politician, because however good his ideas and however original his plans, they were of little use unless he could stay in power long enough to put them into effect. Turgot (1774–6) is a striking example of the intellectual civil servant with no inclination to trim his plans to match his power and little talent for winning the support he needed. We need not agree with the journalist Linguet, who in 1788 described Turgot as having 'a very limited mind and great obstinacy', to see that Turgot's political support and devoted following were small in his own lifetime and only grew very large in the course of the nineteenth century![1] It is true that none of his successors proved to be a Sully or a Colbert, but at least three of them were *politically* more astute than he and so were able to accomplish more of what they set out to do. One of them, Calonne (1783–7), wrote political tracts, brought the influence of his numerous friends and relatives to bear upon the court, and tried to avoid reforms which, like Turgot's six edicts, might antagonize many powerful groups at once. He also conceived of the Assembly of Notables which, although it did not approve of his plans as he hoped, was at any rate the fruit of considerable political reflection on his part. In extremity, he seems to have tried to gain the royal ear even by writing to the King's confessor, Jean-Jacques Poupart, and when discharged on 8 April 1787 he went on for some days trying to regain credit at court and to improve his public standing.[2] Loménie de Brienne (1787–8) was a leader of the strong clerical opposition to Calonne in the Assembly of Notables and he was therefore Calonne's political opponent as well as his successor. Loménie de Brienne admired Necker and tried to persuade Louis XVI to recall him as Controller General before accepting an alternative choice, Laurent de Villedeuil, and this admiration was perhaps one of the fruits of Necker's work as a politician.[3]

Necker was without a doubt the most skilful politician of the reign, perhaps of the century. His genius was in going beyond the narrow world of the court, the privileged orders and the corporate powers in order to cultivate popularity. As Lord Acton said, 'He was the earliest foreign

---

[1] S. N. F. Linguet, *Annales politiques*, vol. XIV (1788), pp. 416–17.
[2] Chevallier, ed., *Journal de l'Assemblée des Notables*, pp. 61–2.
[3] *Ibid.* p.58.

statesman who studied and understood the modern force of opinion'.[1] His *Compte rendu au Roi* (1781), accurate or not, put government accounts before the reading public for the first time in French history and the public were flattered. 'His *Compte rendu* is a pure appeal to the people', Vergennes wrote to Louis XVI. 'For a long time Your Majesty will not close the wound done to the dignity of the throne.'[2] Necker put himself in a favourable light in his books which enormous numbers of people bought and read; he and his wife took great interest in hospitals and in all aspects of popular welfare; his policy on the controversial matter of the grain trade was to favour the consumers and not (like Turgot) the producers; and he even published engravings of himself like political fly-sheets to keep himself before the public eye,[3] and in many matters of policy he was seen to stand for the general good against private interests. The result was a popularity, a charismatic image which made him a candidate for appointment in every financial crisis and which eventually led to his recall to office in August 1788 and again in July 1789. The influential *Encyclopédie méthodique. Finance* quoted him at length on every possible subject and declared him 'worthy of a place between Colbert and Sully'.[4] In the words of a popular jingle of 1788,

Necker par ses beaux écrits
Enchanta la France.[5]

Even Marat and Robespierre, who later learned to detest Necker, almost adored him in 1788–9. 'Thou, generous citizen,' wrote Robespierre, 'take care not to despair of the French and to abandon on a stormy sea the rudder of this superb vessel, loaded with the destinies of a great empire, which thou art to steer into port...'[6] Necker may well have been vain, hypocritical and slightly ridiculous, as historians are never tired of remarking, but he was certainly neither the first nor the last French statesman to be so and he was better able than any other French Minister of his century

[1] Acton, *Lectures on the French Revolution* (1910), p. 46.
[2] Lavaquéry, *Necker, Fourrier de la révolution*, p. 193. 'Edited with more simplicity and modesty, more details and figures', one of Necker's clerks wrote in retrospect, 'this *Compte rendu* would have been more useful; but only financiers would have read it. There never would have been 20,000 copies of it printed; it never would have found its way onto ladies' dressing tables and into their boudoirs' (Hennet, *Théorie du crédit public* (1816), p. 281).
[3] Lavaquéry, *Necker*, p. 197; Bachaumont, *Mémoires secrets*, vol. 17, pp. 210–13; Barnave, *Œuvres*, vol. II, p. 110, 'Necker es le premier qui, de notre temps, en France, ait joui de ce qu'on appelle popularité'.
[4] (Paris, 1783), vol. I, p. 391.
[5] Recueil Clairambault-Maurepas, *Chansonnier historique du XVIIIe siècle* (Paris, 1884), vol. 10, p. 194.
[6] Gérard Walter, *Robespierre*, vol. I, p. 77 and vol. II, p. 157. Gottschalk, *Jean-Paul Marat*, p. 37.

to marshal popular opinion in his favour. It was in some small measure for Necker's sake that the Paris crowd stormed the Bastille on 14 July 1789. When news of that event reached the National Assembly, it caused only apprehension and what the minutes of the meeting described as a 'mournful silence'. But the prospect of Necker's return to office, which they learned soon afterwards, filled them with delight.

Long before that eventful year, the influence of opinions, events and pressure-groups on the court was visible, yet it is difficult to define. Eighteenth-century memorialists and other observers, great and small, followed court politics with keen interest but little hard fact, speculating on rumours and the meaning of events, and historians of the period have done the same, with the result that we have no thorough study of political life at the court of Louis XVI. But we are not lacking in good studies of the political circumstances in which Turgot found himself. Reflecting on those circumstances with a politician's insight, Edgar Faure described what was in fact the predicament of every Minister:

The influence of lobbies is not negligible, as we know, in a democracy. Imagine what their unanimous confluence would do in a régime of personal power with commanding oligarchies, where the organization which called itself Parlement was itself a lobby. Against that coalition of privilege and prejudice, of profit and routine, against that league of *vested interests*, to use Dakin's expression, what could Turgot bring to bear? The affection of the King of Sweden, the hyperboles of Voltaire, the town councillors of Gex, the liberals of Bristol? The whisperings of sympathy in the markets of small towns?[1]

All Ministers, like Turgot, won and lost their power at the court which was sensitive to the petitions, remonstrances and other expressions of estates, sovereign courts, noblemen, bishops, guilds, financiers, towns and any number of corporate groups. Turgot made enemies by the Flour War of 1775 and the famous Six Edicts. Necker, Loménie de Brienne and even d'Ormesson incurred the hatred of the powerful corps of venal office-holders and semi-official financiers. Calonne suffered political reverses by the efforts of enemies such as the baron de Breteuil and by the inopportune death of an ally, the comte de Vergennes, just as the Assembly of Notables was gathering. The parlements opposed most Ministers but developed a special loathing for Calonne and even tried to bring him to trial in August 1787. Turgot, Joly de Fleury and Necker ran afoul of courtiers and others receiving pensions and favours from the court. The Paris *bourse* tended to rise and fall according to the attitudes of certain groups of investors

[1] Faure, *La Disgrâce de Turgot*, p. 461; Dakin, *Turgot*, p. 361.

and speculators towards a Minister and so to influence his fate.[1] These examples illustrate the complexity of politics at the court of Louis XVI. To perceive the general interest in such a welter of special interests, in matters of appointment as in all others, was the duty and prerogative of the Crown.

Louis XVI was capable of taking an independent stand or decision but not an intelligent one. Therefore, whenever he acted independently his behaviour savoured of stubbornness or of a desire to prove himself independent. The ideas on which he acted practically always came from those around him, especially those who had daily access to him: the Queen throughout the reign, and Maurepas until he died in 1781. Their disfavour was the immediate cause of Turgot's fall, Marie-Antoinette blaming the Minister for steps he took against an ambassador, the comte des Guines, and Maurepas feeling threatened when Louis XVI ignored his advice in order to support Turgot in proceedings againt the Parlement of Paris.[2] Necker had a special disadvantage in that his work with the King was always in Maurepas' presence; Necker was not a member of any of the councils, being protestant, foreign and common; and it was Maurepas supported by Vergennes and Miromesnil who urged Louis XVI to accept Necker's resignation on 19 May 1781.[3] Necker did not lose the sympathy of the Queen, however, and it was she who first wrote to recall him to the court in August 1788.[4] Later, it was the Queen in alliance with the Polignac family, the baron de Breteuil and the comte d'Artois who secured Necker's discharge on 11 July 1789. The Queen also had decisive influence in the decisions to discharge Joly de Fleury (30 March 1783), Calonne (8 April 1787) and Loménie de Brienne (25 August 1788).[5] On the other hand, Louis XVI himself may have chosen Lefèvre d'Ormesson (April 1783), a man of some character but little intelligence, very much like himself.[6] The fate of a Minister depended more upon the politics of influencing the King's decision than upon any intrinsic quality of his programme. For this

[1] Jean-Baptiste-Louis Coquereau, *Mémoires concernant l'administration des finances sous le ministère de Monsieur l'abbé Terray* (1776), p. 213; Chevallier, *Journal de l'Assemblée des Notables*, p. 62. When de Fourqueux became Controller General 'les effets ont baissé'. But when Necker replaced de Brienne on 25 August 1789 certain royal 'effets' rose by 30% on the *bourse*. (Bouchary, *Les Manieurs*, vol. II, p. 45.)
[2] Faure, *La Disgrâce de Turgot*, pp. 464 ff.
[3] Lavaquéry, *Necker*, p. 198. A memorandum dated June 1781 which Coster passed on to Auget de Montyon read, 'Le *Compte rendu* a probablement décidé dans le cabinet la chûte de Monsieur Necker'. Choiseul thought it should be published; Maurepas disagreed. (Montyon papers, carton 19.)
[4] Egret, *La Pré-révolution française*, p. 317.
[5] Marion, *Histoire financière*, vol. I, p. 346; Egret, *La Pré-révolution*, p. 317.
[6] Marion, *Histoire financière*, vol. I, p. 347.

very reason the revolutionary National Assembly did away with the post of Minister of Finance in 1791 and broke up the Department of Finance.

The political and personal influences on the financial bureaux were branded as 'corruption' by the National Assembly, and the Assembly's committees therefore reorganized the bureaux in an effort to protect them. The effect of that reorganization was bureaucratic; that is, the Finance Minister and all the powerful, venal, noble, independent magistrates disappeared leaving the bureaux directed by salaried *premiers commis*, and lodged in other executive departments. An explanation of these changes will have its place in later chapters concerning the French revolution, and this brief glimpse into revolutionary history is only to show that the Department of Finance felt some of the effects of revolutionary bureaucracy early in the reign of Louis XVI, when Necker promoted the *premiers commis* and removed the venal Intendants of Finance during his first ministry.

Incoherent though the Department was, and subject to many personal influences, it was still far from being the most corrupt part of the financial system. In the revolutionary sense of corruption, meaning in the service of private interests rather than the general interest, the corps of accountants and other financial agencies such as the tax farms were much worse. They had contractual relations with the Crown in the form of venal offices, leases, *soumissions* and other such legal contracts, which afforded them great privacy and independence. They were not very effectively supervised by the Department of Finance. The *Bureaux des impositions*, for example, had the task of supervising the work of the Receivers General, and under *premiers commis* like Gaudin and Fieux these bureaux were as efficient as any in the Department. Yet an official from the Department later remembered these bureaux rather scornfully as 'la très-futile intendance des impositions'.[1] Try as they would, Ministers like Necker and Loménie de Brienne could not impose the bureaucratic control of the Finance Department on more than a few of the accountants and other agents. The revolutionary governments completed the Ministers' task by more radical means when they 'nationalized' the various agencies and corps of accountants by incorporating them in the new civil service. Who were these agents and accountants who for so long managed the finances of the kingdom?

[1] Burté, *Pour la convention nationale, des moyens de rectifier l'organisation du département des contributions publiques*, p. 20 (B.N., Lf¹⁹¹ 3).

4

THE ACCOUNTANTS AND
THEIR CAISSES

I

BEFORE the French revolution the Royal Treasury neither held nor managed all the funds of the state. It was not even the centre of the financial system but only part of a loose network of independent financiers, each with his own fund or caisse.[1] In a system with no centre, no consolidated revenue fund, the moneys of the Crown were gathered and spent in various caisses and never found their way into the treasury at all. The two Keepers of the Royal Treasury, each with his caisse, were equipped to deal with only a part of the state revenues. This remained true even in 1787, ten years after Jacques Necker had tried to make the Treasury the accounting centre of the system. The Keepers of the Royal Treasury then still accounted for little more than a half of the Crown's revenues.[2] The Treasury did not gain control over public funds until the revolution, which abolished the caisse system and destroyed the accountants who defended it.

The accountants (*comptables*) were financiers accountable to one of the Chambers of Accounts by virtue of an oath sworn before it. They accounted to the Chamber for public funds received and spent in their own private caisses. Like chartered bankers or financial agents, they were authorized to do certain business for the Crown according to contracts and instructions; but they were in no sense salaried officials and they were subject to no continuous inspection or control. A very few of them were merely commissioned to manage their caisses on behalf of the Crown and held no offices. For example, it was as the administrator (*régisseur*) of the Œconomats that Marchal de Sainscy collected all the funds from vacant benefices, from the property of the suppressed Jesuit order and from other ecclesiastical pro-

---

[1] The term 'caisse' survives in English only in the term 'community chest' and other such antique expressions. The terms 'cash-box' or 'till' convey much of its meaning but are too precise to stand in phrases like, *la caisse d'escompte* or *la caisse de commerce*. 'Fund' is perhaps the closest translation of 'caisse', but alas! it is bound to cause confusion if used in the plural. It seems best, therefore, to leave this vital word in the original French.

[2] Frédéric Braesch, *Finances et monnaie révolutionnaires*, deuxième fasc. (Paris, 1936), p. 105.

perty in the Crown's possession. But such cases were rare. Most accountants held venal offices of *trésorier*, *receveur* or *payeur* for which they had paid several hundred thousand livres. Each holding letters of provision in which the King had granted him his office, the accountant had no administrative superiors. He was part of no administrative organization. The Royal Government, half patron and half client, observed his activities through the Controller General's department and controlled him from a distance through the decisions of the Royal Council and through the jurisdiction of the Chambers of Accounts. An accountant suspected of wrong-doing suffered the legal action of the Chambers or other sovereign courts. A reforming ministry could abolish an office and repay the purchase-price to the owner. Apart from these two contingencies, the accountant was inviolate and he was master of his caisse.

Though confined in no administrative hierarchy, the accountant was very much a part of a social hierarchy. He and his family were engaged in a struggle for the wealth and position which more and better offices afforded. Like the places in the sovereign courts belonging to the *noblesse de la robe*, the financial offices had become the dynastic property of rising and proliferating families of accountants. Calonne once said to Madame Harvoin, the wife of a would-be Receiver General, 'financial offices are made neither to create nor to restore the fortunes of individuals',[1] but the facts belied his words. He was not making a true statement. He was criticizing this prominent feature of the system. Families of *parlementaires* such as Nau, Marquet, Pajot and Radix owed a part of their fortunes to members who had become accountants. Mere clerks such as Armand Le Clerc, Jean de Vaine, Bertrand Dufresne, Pierre-Hubert Anson, Achilles-Joseph Gojard, Jean-Antoine Philippe, entered the ranks of the office-holders—or their sons did—as rewards for faithful service. Calonne himself created the fortunes of several, such as for example Marie-Romain Hamelin, former clerk to a notary and a Neckerite *premier commis* in the Department of Finance. He got in Calonne's way and had to be promoted out of the Department. 'I propose to Your Majesty,' Calonne wrote on 16 November 1783, 'to give him the *survivance* of the first charge of Receiver General of Finance which becomes vacant. Your Majesty has granted places of Farmer General and charges of Receiver General as retirement pensions to several of his colleagues who have done much less service.'[2]

Ambitious clerks with friends in high places used offices like stepping-stones. Witness the rise of René-Augustin Marigner, born in 1731, who

---

[1] Harvoin *fils*, *Journal de tous les evènements* (1787), in A.N., T* 594.
[2] Calonne to the King, A.N., F⁴ 1957.

served for eighteen years as clerk and then *premier commis* in the bureaux of one of the Keepers of the Royal Treasury, Savalette de Magnanville. Very early, he took advantage of Savalette's protection to gather crumbs from financial offices. In 1764 he was appointed to finish the accounts of a Treasurer for the Colonies.[1] Then he acquired an office of *Payeur des rentes* which he held until 1785 and became Treasurer General of the Household of the comtesse de Provence, sister-in-law of Louis XVI. Finally, on 30 September 1789, just as the Constituent Assembly was beginning its work of reform, he wàs received into the office of Receiver General of Finance for Paris.[2] Already his son was associated with him under the weightier name of Marigner de la Creuzardière.

How such families would have spread and flowered in the next generation we know from the development of older families. For example, Charles-Jacques-Louis Meulan inherited his father's (and grandfather's) office of Receiver-General of Finance; and he had one uncle, Meulan de la Sourdière, who was a *Payeur des rentes* and another, Guy-Martin Terré du Petitval, a Receiver-General of Domains and Forests. Guillaume Tavernier de Boullogne, a Payer of the Fees of the Officers in the Bureau of Finance of Orléans, 'secrétaire contrôleur en la Chancellerie près la Cour des Comptes aides et finances de Franche-comté' and also a Farmer General, had two sons of whom the younger, Philippe-Guillaume (born 1712) became Receiver General of Finance for Poitou in 1749 and a Farmer General in 1780 and again in 1786; and the elder, Guillaume-Pierre (born 1710), was a Treasurer General for the French Colonies in America and then Treasurer General *de l'extraordinaire des guerres*. Antoine-Jean-François Mégret de Serilly, was the son of a distinguished Intendant, Antoine Mégret d'Etigny, and the nephew of another Intendant bearing his own name and also of a *Trésorier de l'extraordinaire des guerres*, Thomas de Pange. In 1778, he himself acquired the office of Treasurer General for the War Department and about the same time married his cousin, Anne-Marie-Louise Thomas de Pange. In June 1785 he got royal assurance, through Calonne, that their young sons would succeed him in his office when they grew up and in the meantime would share the *survivance* of the office with their godfather, Jean-Baptiste Chastel de Boinville.[3] In the reigns of Louis XV and XVI, we count no less than ten accountants with the family name of Randon, and ramifying still further by relationship to the families of Millon d'Ainval and Bureau de Serandey.[4]

---

[1] Noel-Mathurin-Etienne Périchon, by an *arrêt du Conseil* 28 March 1764.
[2] A.N., VI 538 and VI 523.   [3] A.N., F4 1935.
[4] Louis Randon (*Receveur des tailles*) and his elder brother, Elie-Pierre-Joseph Randon de la Rochebeleau (*Receveur des tailles*); for the rest of them see Appendix.

There were many routes to the higher places of Receiver General, Treasurer General or Farmer General. Many men began as Receivers (*Receveurs particuliers*) others as *Payeurs des rentes*; and a great number rose rapidly from clerk or *premier commis* into the charmed circles of the highest purchasable offices. Until 1777 the offices of Receiver General of Domains and Forests offered another office of medium value for men who might move on to the more expensive offices.[1] Needless to say, the movement upwards was a process of buying and selling combined with a delicate and difficult accumulation of the influence necessary to gain access to the coveted offices.

For men rising in the world of accountants one of the prizes was noble rank, and all the indications are that it was an easy prize in the eighteenth century. Precise knowledge in this difficult field has always been more plentiful for judicial offices than for financial ones; Necker said nothing about financiers in his chapter on the nobility conferred by offices.[2] Marion and Bluche, too, have worked on the judicial offices.[3] Much patient labour in the archives would be required to discover the rank of every accountant, to show the exact proportion of nobles among them, and to determine the 'frontier', so to speak, between nobles and commoners. Interesting though this knowledge would be, it is not necessary for the purpose of affirming that most Receivers General, Treasurers General and Farmers General were already noble in some degree or were confident of obtaining noble rank either for themselves or for their sons. Many lower accountants were in the same case as the men above them. So also were a number of *premiers commis*, such as Armand Le Clerc, ennobled by royal letters in August 1770, and Angot des Rotours, son of a family in the Grand Conseil. The thousand offices of *Secrétaire du Roi* were the principal avenue into the nobility, as we are told on good authority, and certainly many accountants travelled by that road.[4] Many others were sons of families

---

[1] *Receveurs particuliers* who moved up included Claude Desbrets, Hugues-Eustache Chanorier, Jean-Baptiste Darney, Jean-Lafon Ducluzeau. *Payeurs des rentes* more seldom moved on, but an example is René-Baltazard Alissande de Chazet. Among the *premiers commis* who acquired offices of Receiver General or Treasurer General were Barthélemy-Pierre Drouet de Santerre, Marie-Romain Hamelin, Pierre-Hubert Anson, Achille-Joseph Gojard, and Bertrand Dufresne. Among the Receivers General of Domains and Forests who acquired higher offices were Jacques-Mathieu Augéard, Pierre Rousseau and Nicolas-Marcellin Bréard.

[2] Necker, *De l'administration*, vol. III, ch. 14.

[3] Marion, *Dictionnaire*, 'noblesse'; and Bluche's various genealogical compilations.

[4] A.N., P 3417 contains a list of the *Secrétaires du Roi* for 1770, with full names, allowing us to identify such accountants as Jean-Marie Darjuson (Receiver General), Nicolas Beaujon, François-Abraham-Marie Mouchard, Elie Randon de Massanne, Pierre Delaunay (Receivers General); and Gabriel Prévost, Arnauld-Philippe Le Seurre, Philippe Lemarchand, Jacques-Joseph Le Noir and Claude Darras (Treasurers General); along with a great variety of others, such as Henri-Marie-Alexandre Foacier (*caissier-général des*

already noble, in some degree, by virtue of offices in one of the sovereign courts. As a group, the financial nobility were relatively recent and making their way up the social scale more or less as the *noblesse de la robe* had done a century before.

Even though our knowledge of nobility among accountants is uncertain, we may confidently depict the accountants as a group with the characteristics of a rising social class. They inherited, bought, sold and cumulated offices, received them as favours and rewards for service in a process of dynastic growth and social advancement. The Crown accepted and approved of this process. On the one hand, letters of provision, which bestowed an office, recorded as a matter of royal pleasure the service of a father, uncle or other relation, the patronage of a prince, or the promise of a forthcoming marriage. On the other hand, nothing in the letters of provision required an accountant to confine himself to the royal service and stay out of private business and finance. Nothing suggested that he might not use his office for his own private advantage. He received fees (*gages*), a proportion of the funds he handled (*taxation*), gratuities, pensions and other emoluments, but not a salary (*traitement*) such as clerks received. Nowhere was there a hint that he was entering an administrative organization in which he might be subject to subordination, supervision or inspection. He was required to submit accounts, to be Catholic in religion, to be over twenty-five years of age for many offices, and to give loyal, honest and willing service; but nothing restricted his independence. He was not an official in the modern sense of the term. In short, the accountant lived in a world which assumed that private business and royal service were perfectly compatible and saw no need for an administrative hierarchy of men already part of the social hierarchy.

The employees who worked under an accountant were his own and not those of the Crown. Their numbers and selection, their salaries and other terms of employment, their promotion or discharge, were all matters for the accountant alone to decide. The only way the Crown recognized their existence was in providing for the payment of a fixed sum to certain accountants, such as the Keepers of the Royal Treasury, for office expenses. In 1773 a clerk indirectly challenged the system by resisting his employer with every means at his disposal. The case is interesting for what it reveals of the system.

Jacques-Léon Guimard was a man in his early forties who for twenty-five years had served as a clerk in the bureaux of one of the Keepers of the

Fermiers généraux), and the famous *philosophe* Paul Thiry d'Holbach. These names by no means exhaust the list of accountants ennobled in this way.

71

Royal Treasury, Joseph Micault d'Harvelay. Guimard's salary was 1,900 livres and had remained at this figure even after the Crown had increased d'Harvelay's expense budget by 25,000 livres with effect from 1 January 1771; and in addition, Guimard had received no share of a gratuity which d'Harvelay had distributed among nine other clerks. Guimard had claimed both an increase in salary and a part of the gratuity and had pressed these claims so persistently that d'Harvelay had discharged him on 7 April 1773. However, Guimard had an uncle (of the same name) who, as Master of Requests, was influential enough to have the duc de Noailles ask d'Harvelay to reconsider the matter and, when d'Harvelay replied that he would never re-hire a troublesome clerk, to arrange for a pension of 2,300 livres on the Royal Treasury.[1] Not content with this, Guimard went to law and took his case to the *Cour des Aides*. A letter from a lawyer, Jean-Baptiste Darigrand, only provoked d'Harvelay to write a sharp note to the effect that he was master in his own house. D'Harvelay then appealed to the Royal Council of State which stopped the legal case and sought the advice of one of its own lawyers, Paul-Augustin Moreau de Vormes, who expressed the view that if the Council allowed the case to continue d'Harvelay would certainly win it. His written opinion on the case begins:

The Keeper of the Royal Treasury is always master to choose his own clerks, to keep them or to dismiss them according to their merits or demerits. It is he who pays them from his funds (*ses deniers*), according to the price which their labour requires, of which he is the sole judge. It is he who distributes the *gratifications* as he sees fit and his conduct in that respect has never been, nor should be, submitted to the criticism or praise of the said clerks. This assertion is founded on a point of fact that the clerks owe their condition ('tiennent absolument leur sort') entirely to the Keeper of the Royal Treasury, and that he alone is accountable to the King and to the Chamber of Accounts for His Majesty's service because the clerks cannot be judges in their own cause, and finally on order and good administration which would otherwise be impossible.[2]

On this and on Turgot's opinion, the Council of State formally suppressed Guimard's printed plea and declared his claim to be 'non-recevable et mal fondé'.

The accountant, thus all-powerful, usually organized his employees in a hierarchy, a pyramid of subordination rising from the many office-boys and common clerks to a single *premier commis* at the top enjoying the most

---

[1] Beginning on 25 July 1773 (*Etat des pensions sur le trésor royal* (Paris, 1789), vol. i, p. 456).

[2] A.N., T 200⁷, article 1 dated 2 March 1775. The *arrêt du Conseil* stopping the case was dated 22 January 1775, and the final decision of the *Conseil d'état* dated 11 April 1775 (no. 18), 8 pp.

authority and the highest salary. These bureaux varied radically in size but in the bureaucratic form of their organization they resembled those of the Department of Finance, the General Farm of Taxes and every other organization. Such bureaux were the raw material to be woven into the royal and national civil service in the 1780s and 1790s by a process of organization and reorganization. Already modern in structure, they would survive the revolution which would do away with the *comptables* and unify the caisses.

By destroying the aristocratic privilege which characterized the ancien régime the French Revolution made way for large and imposing systems of administrative inequality. The privilege of the accountant, low in the social pyramid but high in the financial system, was the privilege to remain independent and unorganized; to have contractual and not bureaucratic relations to the Crown; the privilege to engage in a wide range of private and public ventures for personal and family advancement; and the privilege to manage his own caisse. Thus, the accountants and their friends stood as a bulwark against rational—indeed, almost any—organization of the financial system. In its administrative aspect, the French revolution was a major victory in a movement for public financial organization which began in the ancien régime and went on into the nineteenth century; but it was neither the first victory nor the last. Colbert had won a mighty victory when he had organized the General Farm of Taxes. In 1781 Necker was to have a brief triumph in organizing the Receivers General of Finance bureaucratically, and in 1788 Loménie de Brienne was to organize the independent *Trésoriers des deniers royaux* as the Royal Treasury, thus creating the first permanent organ of the French financial administration and the heart of the modern civil service. This event marked the beginning of the end of the Bourbon system of caisses and accountants.

II

The major caisses and accountants appear to modern eyes to fall into two groups, one concerned with the collection of revenue and the other with its expenditure, but this division is somewhat artificial and even misleading. The collecting caisses of the Receivers General, the Farmers General and others also spent the revenues they collected. They paid the operating expenses, salaries and some pensions of the bureaux attached to them, and they held their deposits of Crown revenues at the disposal of the government which drew on them like bank accounts. To be sure, the collecting caisses spent most of their funds in large sums sent to the paying caisses of the Payers of the rentes and the Treasurers of the spending departments, but most of them also made a great many payments for the Crown. Then there were certain accountants such as the Receiver General of *revenus casuels*, the *Trésorier du marc d'or* and the Treasurers of certain *pays d'état*, whose caisses hardly fit into either group. With these reservations, however, a brief introduction to caisses and accountants may still usefully divide them into a collecting group and a spending group.

By far the largest and most highly evolved of all the agencies in the financial system was the organization of the Farmers General who collected the 'indirect' taxes. The General Farm provoked a good deal of popular criticism, mainly because it collected an antiquated array of taxes with modern efficiency. The injustices and inequalities of the customs duties, the royal tolls or *péages*, the *gabelles* salt taxes, the *tabac* tobacco monopoly, the *aides* excise taxes, the taxes at the entrance of Paris, the feudal dues in the royal domains and others—all the anomalies and inequalities of these taxes were made clear and painful to the populace by the professional thoroughness of the General Farm. From their headquarters in Paris near the Louvre, and on the Isle Saint Louis, housing a staff of approximately 200, the Farmers General maintained a continuous bureaucratic control over some 15,000 guards and perhaps 20,000 clerks, accountants *caissiers* and inspectors. With their personnel records, printed forms, graduated salaries and contributory pension scheme, their provisions for a career service up to the level of Director, and their concern for profits, the Farmers General were in almost every respect a modern capitalistic company.

The collective or bureaucratic structure of the General Farm distinguished it from other financial agencies. Bureaucratic organization began at the very top among the Farmers General themselves. Whereas the Keepers of the Royal Treasury and other accountants remained personally and individually responsible for the funds in their caisses, the Farmers General were collectively accountable for the funds managed in one central caisse and in a great many provincial sub-caisses.[1] Their *caissier-général*, Henri-Marie-Alexandre Foacier, and their provincial *caissiers* were responsible to the Company as a whole. Legally, the structure of the company (referred to at the time as 'la compagnie') rested upon a contract by act in private law between each Farmer General and the adjudicator-general of the company. The contract made the Farmers General legal guarantors (*cautions*) of the adjudicator-general who gave his name to the company, signed the lease with the Crown and was therefore the only person in the company directly

---

[1] 181 in 1763 according to G. T. Matthews, *The Royal General Farms in the Eighteenth Century* (New York, 1958), p. 219.

responsible to the Crown in public law. The company normally reformed in this way every six years with a different adjudicator-general in order to negotiate a new lease with the Crown and a new contract among themselves.

The company maintained their collective organization in practice by dividing executive duties among themselves and by making all important decisions in a number of committees. The adjudicator-general was not himself a Farmer General, but merely 'straw man' who received a salary from the company for his services. In his name the forty Farmers General (sixty from 1756 to 1780) issued instructions to the company directors out in the provinces and carried on business with accountants and with the Controller General of Finance and his department. The General Farm was more than a mere caisse with appendages. The caisses and the accountants in charge of them were subservient to the organization as a whole. The Farmers General transmitted their decisions through their Directors, and customarily took turns travelling through the provinces on tours of inspection. The caisses, embedded as they were in the administrative hierarchy, had none of the influential independence of other caisses but were always at the service of the Farmers General. By instructions and cheques or rescriptions, the Farmers General sent money easily and safely from one caisse to another and made payments for the Crown and for the company nearly anywhere in France. They even advertised such banking services for the convenience of the general public. As unspent residues of cash accumulated in the provincial caisses, they were sent together with vouchers for money spent to the main caisses in Paris.

The General Farm served the Crown as much more than a tax-collecting agency. Holding funds which it owed the Crown in its caisse, the company performed a great many banking services for the government. From the royal accounts in the caisses of the General Farm comparatively little money was ever paid directly into the caisses of the Royal Treasury. According to its most careful budget, that for 1788 when many reforms had already altered the system, the royal government expected the General Farm to collect about 150 million livres in the government account and to send only 17,801,218 livres of that to the Treasury. The General Farm was to spend all the rest on behalf of the Crown: 96 millions to the Payers of the rentes and smaller sums to officers in the administration and others.[1]

The General Farm also offered the Crown credit in a number of ways. To begin with, each lease provided for an immediate advance of half the sum which the Farmers General contracted to collect. But the rescriptions, with which the Crown made payments on this account, were based on the

---

[1] Braesch, *Finances et monnaie*, deuxième fasc., pp. 71 ff.

very substantial credit of the Farmers General and could therefore be issued in amounts far exceeding the sums stated in the leases. If the royal government could draw on its accounts with the General Farm, it could also overdraw and did so in ever-increasing amounts. Finally, each Farmer General deposited the purchase price of his place in the government account, as a capital fund on which the Crown authorized the company to pay interest. The price of a place of Farmer General was 1,560,000 livres throughout the reign of Louis XVI so that in 1780, for example, the total capital fund stood at 62,400,000 livres for the forty places and by 1787 the number of places had risen to forty-four, making a capital fund of 68,840,000 livres.[1]

It is the nature of the company's connection with the Crown which permits us to treat it as part of the system of caisses and accountants, for its internal organization seems to set it apart as a precocious, almost anachronistic body resembling administrative departments of the nineteenth century. The Farmers General signed a *soumission* or contract by which they undertook legal responsibility, just as every individual accountant did, for the public funds it was to manage. Thus, their relationship with the Crown was essentially no different from that of other accountants, and in the same way they were obliged to submit accounts to the Chamber of Accounts. True, their responsibility was a collective one, but otherwise it was contractual rather than bureaucratic responsibility, not subject to continuous inspection and control but maintained only through legal enforcement of the contract. A second document linking them with the Crown was also contractual; this was the lease, a formal statement of the terms on which the Farmers General held and used the property and organization of the General Farm. Both documents were renewed every six years and it was in the negotiations for each new lease that the Crown normally imposed its demands upon the Farmers General. Otherwise, as G. T. Matthews observed, 'for most of the 18th century, the General Farm was regarded as an autonomous province in the internal affairs of which the monarchy could not intervene except on invitation. The relation of the government to the company of the General Farm, unlike the relation of the company to the General Farm itself, was contractual rather than bureaucratic.'[2] We may justly regard the Farmers General as the most highly organized of the groups of accountants.

The Receivers General of Finance formed a much more loose-knit group than the Farmers General. Each of them—and there were normally fifty, more or less, including two for each of twenty generalities in the *pays*

---

[1] Matthews, *The Royal General Farm*, p. 232.   [2] *Ibid.*, p. 203.

d'élection and a small variable number for the *pays d'état*—held his own office which had no legal connection with the others. A very influential accountant summed the matter up in 1783:

The Receivers General make a corps, properly speaking, only through the existence of the common caisse to which they remit the net returns to the Royal Treasury, either in *rescriptions à terme* or in cash. For each Receiver General has his own private *soumission*, his own *etat du Roi*, his personal accounts, and he administers his Generality privately (*privativement*) without any relation to the others, not even between the two *exercices* of the same Generality.[1]

And each Receiver General had his own caisse.

The common caisse, here recognized as the only institution linking the Receivers General together, was created by a Declaration of 10 June 1716. Unlike the general caisse of the Farmers General, which was an integral part of a bureaucratic organization, the *caisse commune des recettes général des finances* was established as an independent fund to hold for the Crown any unspent surplus from the caisses of the individual Receivers General. Thus the *caissier général* of the General Farm, Foacier, received a salary from his employers, the Farmers General; whereas Jean-Claude Geoffroy d'Assy, the *caissier général* of the *Recette générale*, took his salary and bureau expenses from his own caisse according to the decision of the Controller General of Finance, and so did the *premiers commis* of the other bureaux which grew up around the common caisse: the *bureau des soumissions*; the *bureau de comptabilité*; the *bureau de distribution*; and the *bureau des comptes*. These in no way touched the privacy and independence of the individual Receiver General and his caisse.

For each Generality there was one office for the receipts and expenditure of the even-numbered years (*exercices paires*) and another for that of the odd-numbered years (*exercices impaires*) and they had a separate identity and a separate business life. For instance, the Receiver generalship of Montauban for odd-numbered years was created in January 1635 and sold to one Louis Larcher. It passed through the hands of many owners and the last of them, Pierre-Nicolas Mel de Saint Céran, was able to prove clear title to it by showing the receipts for the final accounts his predecessors had submitted to the Chamber of Accounts.[2] During the century and a half of its existence, the office had increased in value from 30,000 livres to 770,000.

[1] Jacques Marquet de Bourgade in a memorandum dated 5 February 1783 (B.N., Coll. Joly de Fleury F 1441).
[2] A.N., F4 2021, *Extrait des registres du Conseil d'état du Roi*. The other holders listed were, Simon Bertholet (1684), François Brunet (1694), Pierre-François Ogier (1700), Pierre Duquesnoy (1739), Jean-Baptiste Bégon (1746).

To the men of the ancien régime the office was as distinct and substantial as a piece of landed property, and other apparently related offices were not even mentioned in the letters of provision and other papers in the hands of the Receivers General.

The difference between the quite unorganized Receivers General and the highly organized Farmers General was to some extent the natural result of a difference in the nature of the taxes they collected. The General Farm collected taxes imposed on the production, sale and movement of goods (*impôts de perception*) of which the yield could not be predicted except within very wide limits. Receipts varied at different times and places according to the vagaries of trade and according to the quality of the collecting organization. Hence, the *perceptions* offered risks and profits which seemed to make them a natural field for the private enterprise of a company of financiers. Furthermore, it was impossible in modern times to collect the *perceptions* efficiently except through a kingdom-wide organization. For all that the *perceptions* remained largely provincial or local, the General Farm, like the trade of the kingdom, owed much of its success to the increasing scale of its operations. It would have been inconceivable to have each Farmer General work a province independently.

The reverse was true of the Receivers General, who collected *impôts de répartition—taille, capitation, vingtième*—quite differently imposed. The Royal Council on Finance decided each year upon the total sum for collection, divided it up among the Generalities, and sub-divided it among the Elections and again among the parishes. As the figures varied little from year to year, there were trends of change rather than sudden alterations. In any event, each Receiver General knew exactly how much he was to collect in his Generality, for the amount was recorded in his biennial *soumission* and virtually assured, except in years of extreme hardship, by the collective responsibility of each parish to pay its allotted portion. With few risks and few profits, the Receiver Generalship lent itself to the creation of a venal office. The Receiver General had therefore come to work alone and to have business relations with his fellows hardly any closer than his relations with other accountants.

Looking at the nature of the taxes he collected, we might have expected the Receiver General to be at the head of a bureaucratic organization—a miniature General Farm, as it were—for the whole of his Generality. Such was not the case. Before 1775 he had a mere legal contract (*traité*) with the Receivers (*Receveurs particuliers des finances*) of each Election in his Generality. By it each Receiver, who had a similar contract with the parish collectors, merely undertook to pay a certain sum out of his caisse to the

Receiver General. In every respect, the Receiver was himself an independent accountant, for he held a venal office and he accounted to one of the Chambers of Accounts. His office was naturally worth much less than that of a Receiver General, but until the changes of the early administrative revolution, there was hardly any other difference between them. Many a Receiver General had risen from the ranks—if we may use so inappropriate a term—of the Receivers by selling the one office and buying the other. Such a change marked a social and financial advance but not an administrative promotion.

On an average the office of Receiver General was worth about five times as much as the office of Receiver. Altogether there were 418 offices of Receiver, 2 for each of the 209 Elections composing the 48 *Généralités*. There was a tendency, however, for these accountants to cumulate two offices, especially the two in the same Election, and in 1775 no less than 101 had done this.[1] The 418 offices were thus held by only 317 accountants; and by 1781 by no more than 276. The value of these offices was not uniform but varied radically, just as the value of the Receiver Generalships did. In 1771 their total value was reckoned at 28,408,462 livres, which was approximately two million livres more than the total value of the offices of Receiver General. Their average value was therefore something over 100,000 livres; whereas 500,000 livres was roughly the average value of the office of Receiver General. A decree during the reactionary period of 1782 recreated two offices in each of the Elections, so that once more a Receiver had either to buy the two or share the work of the Election. As a result the numbers rose once more and at the time of their suppression early in 1791 there were still 322 Receivers.[2]

The value of the offices bore an approximate relation to the amount of revenue which passed through their hands. Indeed, this is not surprising because the income of the office, which was largely in the form of a *taxation* or commission, was the signal factor in the market value of the office. Thus in 1780 the Receivers altogether collected something over 139 millions. They took, it was calculated, about 10% of the value of their *finance*, or some 10,000 livres each. The sum passing through their hands was on the average 350,000 livres, so that their services cost the Crown, in legitimate expenses, less than 3%. In the same year, the Receivers General handled crown revenues to the value of 148 millions (they received about 9 millions directly from sources other than the Receivers). Thus each one managed an

[1] B.N., Coll. Joly de Fleury 1436, fols. 141 ff.
[2] A.N., D vi 1, Amelot, *Mémoire sur l'organisation des bureaux de l'administration de la caisse de l'extraordinaire*, MS.

average of three millions a year. At 10% they received 50,000 each, of which half represented the 5% of their *finance*, about 2% the operating expenses allowed and 3% their own profit or net earnings. This represented a cost to the Crown of 0·166% or one six-hundredth. When Joly de Fleury evaluated the forty-eight offices afresh in 1781 he did so in such a way that they totalled 30 millions. But they ranged in value from the offices of Paris, each worth 1,280,000 livres, down to those for Bourges, at 250,000 livres.[1]

Part of the revenues from the royal domains and forests was collected by a separate system of venal receivers. They had business dealings with the Farmers General, who arranged the collection of the other part of the domain revenues, but they were quite independent. The funds in their charge came from two main sources: rents, fees, dues and fines known as *droits féodaux casuels* or *revenus casuels*; and the wood and other forest products customarily sold during the last three months of the year. There were 481 offices altogether, of which 353 were minor or local: 152 *Receveurs particuliers des domaines et bois*, 152 *Receveurs des amendes dans les maîtrises des eaux et forêts*, and 49 *Gardes généraux et collecteurs* of those fines. The more important *charges* with the large caisses were sixty-four offices of *Receveurs generaux des domaines et bois* and sixty-four offices of *Contrôleur general des domaines et bois*, created so that each of thirty-two Generalities would have a Receiver General and a Controller General for even-numbered years and a similar pair for odd-numbered ones. These offices tended to cumulate to such an extent that in 1774 there were only thirty-six Receivers General for thirty-one Generalities. The offices of Receiver General alone represented an investment of 5,871,810 livres and in the period 1748–67 earned for them an average of 301,591 livres a year or approximately 5% of their investment. Less rich and powerful than the main corps of accountants, the Receivers General for Domains and Forests managed less revenue than their cost seemed to warrant and at the beginning of the reign their days were already numbered. Pursuing studies undertaken by Terray and Turgot, Necker was to abolish their offices in August 1777, and to turn over their duties to an organized Crown company, the General Administration of the Domains.[2]

In addition to the large corps of receivers, there were many individuals

---

[1] Royal Edict of October 1781. The offices were ranked as follows: Paris, Tours, Bordeaux, Rouen, Riom, Orléans, Châlons, Metz and Alsace, Caen, Poitiers, Montauban, Flandres, Alençon, Lyon, Amiens, Limoges, Lorraine, Auch, Franche Comté, Grenoble, Moulins, Soissons, La Rochelle, Bourges.

[2] A.N., F4 1082 contains much information on these accountants; and so does the Edict ordering their suppression, reproduced in Isambert, *Collection des décrets*.

charged with the collection of specific revenues, for when the Crown created a new tax or a new fund it often created an office for a receiver to collect it. Thus, when a special surtax of 6 *deniers* per livre of the *capitation* was ordered to be collected for the rebuilding of a royal palace in Paris, Claude-Gilbert Geoffroy de Montjay bought the office of receiver and collected it.[1] There was also a receiver of the *Capitation* of the Court, Boisneuf; a Receiver General of the *Boëtes de Monnayes de France*, for revenues from minting processes, Du Chauffour and then Bellaud; a Receiver and Payer 'de la Bourse commune des banquiers expédition-naires de Cour de Rome à Paris', Pierre Roustain; and a *régisseur des économats*, Marchal de Sainscy, to collect the revenues from vacant bene-fices and other ecclesiastical properties acquired by the Crown. Prominent among the receivers of special revenues was the *Receveur général du clergé*, Bollioud de Saint Julien and then François-Roche Quinson, who took in the funds of the *don gratuit ordinaire*, voted by the clergy at their quinquennial meetings and amounting to 16 or 18 millions most years. The clergy also paid under protest another 1,300,000 livres in rentes on the Hôtel de Ville.[2]

III

The accountants whose business was to pay out crown revenues were more specialized on the whole than their colleagues on the collecting side. Where-as the caisses of many receivers were used for making payments, most spending caisses did not collect in detail but received crown funds in large sums from comparatively few sources. In some respects paying out was more difficult and exacting work than receiving, for it required elaborate records and a great deal of incidental paperwork to justify and verify each payment. This was partly why nearly every Payer or Treasurer worked with a Controller—sometimes two or three—who kept the registers and receipts and whose business it was to identify and register those to whom payments were made. But the organization or articulation of the spending caisses went no further than that.

The spending caisses were even less organized than the receiving caisses, but we may distinguish six or seven different groups of them. The most coherent was the group of *Trésoriers payeurs des rentes sur l'Hôtel de Ville*.

---

[1] *Arrêts du Conseil* dated 26 July 1776, 30 September 1781 and 20 November 1786; and *Lettres patentes* dated 5 August 1778.

[2] In 1775 the costs and fees of the Receiver General of the clergy amounted to 132,000 livres. The clergy also had their own network of accountants for their own finances, in-cluding *Receveurs des décimes* (tithe collectors) of which there were 128 in 1791 when they were suppressed. (A.N., D VI 1, Amelot, *Mémoire sur l'organisation des bureaux*... MS.)

After many changes, their numbers remained stable at 50 from 1720 to 1758 when 19 new offices were created; then 4 more were added in 1760 and 6 more in 1768, making a total of 79, each with a Controller. An Edict of May 1772 reduced them to 30 Payers each with 2 offices worth a total of 600,000 livres and 30 Controllers, with 2 offices totalling 90,000 livres. Their remuneration included 5% of the *finances*, a *taxation* and *droit d'exercice* amounting to 9,000 livres for the Payers and 2,700 livres for the Controllers, and a further 3,000 livres for the bureau expenses of each Payer.

The offices were, of course, hereditary and quite independent one from another inasmuch as each received the public at his own premises and rendered separate accounts to the Chamber of Accounts. They were divided in the first place by the creation of offices for the payment of the rentes on specific loans. As new rentes were constituted, new offices were set up for *payeurs* who would pay them. Thus, for example, three *payeurs* managed the rentes on the clergy and no others. But even groups such as those three were in no way integrated and arranged no division of labour. Instead, each one managed all the procedures of the paying process but for a few *rentiers* only. The *rentiers* were listed in alphabetical order of the first initial and the Payers divided the list among them, each taking the names beginning with certain letters of the alphabet, and each paying only during certain fixed hours of the week. The system permitted variations in the paying procedures; and in the formalities of identifying and qualifying himself the *rentier* met delays and difficulties no less exasperating than the bureaucratic obstacles of today.[1]

For every Payer there was a Controller who had the responsibility of keeping a register of all the *rentiers*, their names and titles, the nature of their rentes and the amount, the name of whoever actually collected it. They did this, according to their own report, '...in the midst of the tumult and agitation of a crowd of people all pressing, quarrelling over their turns, talking all at once, tormenting either the Payer or the Controller with frivolous and importunate remarks and sometimes by violent and impatient outbursts'.[2] The Controller had responsibility to the *rentiers* to verify their titles and prevent fraudulent applications. A *rentier* who could prove an error against a Controller could collect the sum due from the Controller himself. In addition, the Controller had another duty which was to send a copy of his records annually to the Chamber of Accounts. Their registers

---

[1] M. J. D. Martin, *Etrennes financières* (Paris, 1789), ch. 5; and *Encyclopédie méthodique. Finances* (Paris, 1787), vol. III, pp. 482 ff.

[2] *Mémoire concernant les offices de contrôleur des rentes de l'Hôtel de Ville* (Paris, décembre 1789), p. 6 (B.N., Lf⁸⁰ 85).

were inspected quarterly by the corps of *Payeurs des rentes*. In the words which they themselves were fond of quoting from old legislation, the Controller was 'tierce personne entre le Roi, le payeur et le rentier'.[1]

Each Payer kept his own office quarters open to the public one day a week whenever he wished and he employed from two to five clerks to assist him. The forty Payers in the later 1780s employed a total of about 180 or 200 clerks.

The *Payeurs des rentes* formed a *compagnie* or corps somewhat like the Receivers General of Finances. They had long recognized a *doyen* and *sous-doyen* and elected a syndic to speak for them as a body, but in a general meeting of 3 January 1762 they drew up a document of nine articles creating a committee 'in which business which may concern the service of the King and the public, and the interests of the corps in general, and those of the members in particular, may be brought up and discussed before being put before the entire corps'.[2] This committee included the *doyen*, *sous-doyen*, 4 other members elected for life, and 6 others elected annually, 3 from the Payers functioning that year (*en exercice*); and 3 from those not functioning (*sortis d'exercice*). They were to meet at 4 p.m. every Thursday in the assembly hall of the corps, and to keep records and memoranda as they saw fit. So organized, the corps of Payers of the rentes endeavoured with remarkable success to protect its reputation and standing by keeping watch over its members lest they should go bankrupt or otherwise incur the scandal of an inquiry by the Chamber of Accounts. Considering that they presented the Chamber with more than a hundred folio volumes of accounts each year (which they themselves drew up, unlike other accountants who were obliged to rely on the *procureurs* of the Chamber), they were justly proud of their records.

The Payers attached to the sovereign courts and other bodies, for the purpose of paying the *gages* of their members, were different to all appearances from the Payers of the rentes. In particular, they usually counted as officers of the bodies they served and were so listed in the *Almanach royal*. Yet they all had more or less similar functions and the ministers of the first reform period, beginning with Terray, tended to see them as a group or a type. If we remember that the close grouping of the Payers of the rentes was a professional association, not a functional one, then the group of *Payeurs des gages* does not seem to be very different, for all that they were

---

[1] *Mémoire sur les rentes et sur les offices de payeurs et contrôleur*... (Paris, 1789), p. 12 (B.N., Lf⁸⁰ 85); *Les Quarante Payeurs des rentes, financiers héréditaires*, p. 3 (Lf⁸⁰ 90); and *De l'acquittement de la dette publique*... (Paris, 1792), p. 9 (B.N., Lb³⁹ 5931).

[2] The full text of this *délibération* is appended to the *Mémoire sur les rentes et sur les offices de payeurs et contrôleur*... (Paris, 1789) (B.N., Lf⁸⁰ 85).

6-2

scattered through the pages of the *Almanach royal* rather than named in one list as the Payers of the rentes were.

An absence of definition, however, makes it difficult to establish the precise number of them. The Parlement of Paris had three offices of *Receveurs-payeurs des gages—ancien, alternatif* and *triennal*—and three Controllers to match. The other eleven parlements (the Parlement of Metz dated only from 1775) usually had one or two *payeurs* and an equal number of Controllers.[1] The *Cour des aides* of Paris had three offices of Payer and three of Controller. In principal, there were twelve provincial *Cours des aides* which might have had Payers and Controllers, but nine of them were combined with the *parlements* or *chambres des comptes* of the same provinces, leaving only three independent *Cours des aides* at Bordeaux, Montauban and Clermont. Much the same held true for the twelve Chambers of Accounts, because those in Languedoc, Normandy, Provence and Burgundy were combined with *Cours des aides*, and therefore only eight of them had their own Payers and Controllers.[2] In addition there were from one to three Payers, each with a Controller, for the *Secrétaires du Roi de la Grande Chancellerie*, for the *Officiers du Roi de la Grande Chancellerie*, for the *Officiers du Grande Conseil*, for the *Officiers du Châtelet de Paris*, and for the *Cour des Monnaies de Paris*. Likewise, there were other bodies in the provinces, such as the *Conseil provincial d'Artois*, the *Cour des Monnaies* in Lyon, each with a *Trésorier-payeur des gages*. Taken altogether, there can hardly have been less than fifty *Payeurs des gages*, and as many Controllers, attached to various courts and councils.

The two groups of Payers were distinguishable by their functions, one disbursing rentes and the other *gages*. A third group of accountants, marked by no such definite function, appears in the *Almanach royal* under the general head, *Trésoriers des deniers royaux*. We look in vain for a satisfactory definition of this category but most of those in it managed the funds

---

[1] The letters-of-provision in the A.N., V^1 series usually show only one accountant, even though there might be two or more offices, *ancien, alternatif*, etc. Thus in 1762 Pierre Cassaigne became *Receveur-payeur, ancien, alternatif et triennal* for the officers of the Parlement at Bordeaux (V^1 415). In 1764 Jacques-Philippe Devaux became *Payeur ancien et mytriennal des gages* for the officers of the Chancellery attached to the Parlement of Flanders at Douai (V^1 424) etc. The multiplication of offices under these titles—*ancien, triennal, mi-ancien, alternatif, mitriennal, quatriennal*—was a device ostensibly to divide the work among several accountants, but in reality to sell as many offices as possible. In the reign of Louis XVI, as the end of the system drew near, there was a tendency to consolidate these various offices. For a brief account of this aspect of the system see *Encyclopédie méthodique. Finances* (Paris, 1783–7), 'comptables'.

[2] For the Paris Chamber of Accounts there were three offices of Payer and three of Controller until 1775 when an Edict of July suppressed them and created instead a single office for Bertrand Dufresne (A.N., AD IX 432).

allotted to a particular organization or a special purpose other than the paying of rentes and *gages*. Very different from rentes and *gages*, the pensions and salaries (*traitements*) of clerks and other employees, however, were usually on the table of an organization's expenses along with the rent of bureau premises, the price of heating, paper, candles and other miscellaneous costs. These and the provision for materials, travelling, messengers, fell to the caisse of the Treasurer General of the organization.

More than fifty Treasurers General, as many Controllers General and a great many sub-treasurers or *Trésoriers particuliers* managed the funds for some thirty organizations and purposes which for convenience we may group roughly according to function. The bureaux of the Secretaries of State stand out as being the largest and most expensive. For the Department of War and various associated bureaux in peacetime there were two *Trésoriers généraux de l'ordinaire des guerres, de la gendarmerie et des troupes de la maison du Roi*, two Treasurers General *de l'extraordinaire des guerres*, a Treasurer General *de l'artillerie et du génie*, a Treasurer General *des gratification des troupes*, a Treasurer General *des fortifications*, two Treasurers General and Payers *des invalides*, three Treasurers General *des ligues suisses et grisons*, a Treasurer General *de l'école militaire*, and a large and variable number of Controllers. Funds for the Marine Department were in the hands of two Treasurers General, two Controllers, and a Treasurer General and Controller for the *Invalides de la marine*; and there were two Treasurers General and two Controllers General for the American Colonies. The titles of the fifteen Treasurers General for the Royal Households, everyone matched by a Controller General, would make tedious reading, and the list is much longer if it includes the accountants for the separate households of Mesdames and Messieurs, prominent members of the royal family. No accountant was recorded, on the other hand, for the fourth secretariat of state, for Foreign Affairs, which had its own financial arrangements; and finally, the department of Henri Bertin concerning mines, agriculture and similar matters, made no obvious mark on the system of caisses and accountants during its relatively brief existence (1763–81) for it was only a ministerial grouping of bureaux which otherwise remained unchanged.

A considerable number of paying accountants can only be described as miscellaneous and, indeed, Jacques Necker was to find no better term for the expenditures of their caisses than 'dépenses diverses'. Governments of a later age might have grouped many under titles such as Interior and Public Works: the Treasurers General and fifty-two *Trésoriers particuliers* for the *Ponts et Chaussées*; the two Treasurers General, one for the *Barrage et l'entretènement du pavé de Paris*, and the other for the *Turcies et levées* and the Treasurer General for the Paris Police; the two Treasurers General for the *maréchaussée* (territorial police); the Treasurers General of the *pays d'état* for Burgundy, Languedoc, Brittany and Provence. But the very idea underlying such titles as Interior and Public Works, the idea of a unified state with uniform centralized institutions, was foreign to the ancien régime. A national revolution occurred before the Department of the Interior was created in 1791. Twenty years earlier, when the accountants had not been subjected even to Necker's rough groupings, their names appeared with the names of other accountants, one by one, as free from the bondage of any functional order as the bureaux whose funds they held.

The Receiver General for *revenus casuels* stands out from the rest as one with a title which explains nothing of his functions, and with a caisse too large to be passed off as miscellaneous.[1] No caisse was more characteristic of the ancien régime for it managed the revenues from the sale of venal offices and from the incidental taxes on their inheritance, purchase and retention. These amounted, in 1780 for instance, to over three million livres, most of which was paid out again in the form of salaries and other costs of the many administrative bureaux which the Crown assigned to the *revenus casuels*. In the year 1747, for another instance, the caisse received 4,230,701 livres and paid out all except 185,067 livres.[2] Thus it was a paying caisse, as its inclusion in the list of *Trésoriers des deniers royaux* suggests and, indeed, until April 1664 the title of the office had been Treasurer of the *partie casuelle*, the fund from the sale of offices. Little wonder that even in the eighteenth century this accountant was still sometimes called the Treasurer General of the *partie casuelle*.[3] But for all that, he was also a receiver, collecting revenues at source rather than taking them in annual lump sums from the caisses of the General Farm or the Receivers General, as did most paying caisses. He managed an independent revenue fund of about the same size as those of the Receivers General of Finance.

His business throughout the kingdom, and not merely a single Generality, required a considerable number of employees. Most of the work in the provinces, however, was in the hands of more than a score of Receivers who were just as independent as the *Receveurs particuliers des finances* and the

---

[1] This is not to be confused with the *revenus casuels* of the royal domains.

[2] A.N., F⁴ 1076; and *Encyclopédie méthodique. Finance*, vol. I, p. 209.

[3] An Edict of April 1664 abolished the three existing offices of *Trésorier des parties casuelles* and instead commissioned two *Receveurs des revenus casuels*. But an Edict of February 1689 created two offices under the same title, and another Edict of December 1695 added a third. (B.N., Coll. Joly de Fleury 1443, Moreau de Beaumont, *Mémoire sur le trésor royal et sur les comptes...*) and *Mémoire sur l'administration des finances* (May 1780), fol. 256.

Trésoriers particuliers des ponts et chaussées. They do not figure at all in the provision for his own caisse and bureaux in Paris. These were laid down in an Edict of December 1716 which revised the office, and another of June 1717 which named a certain Bertin to it. The *finance* of the office was then fixed at a million livres, to yield Bertin and his descendants an annual *gage* of 50,000 livres, the usual 5%. His operating budget, like those of most accountants and their bureaux, was complex. For the year 1776, before Necker's reforms had changed the old establishment, he spent 140,600 livres as follows:[1]

Table 1. *Expenses of the Treasurer General for Revenus casuels in 1776*

	livres
Stipend (*gage*) of the office of Treasurer	50,000
To the Treasurer as commission (*taxation*) and expenses (*frais*) .	20,000
To the Treasurer, commission of a *sol pour livre* (5 %) on the product of vacant offices, about	13,000
To the Treasurer, gratuity	9,000
For the preparation of his accounts	10,000
For his clerks	14,700
For his bureau expenses	6,000
For the Treasurer, for an increase of clerks and bureau expenses .	15,500
Gratuities for his clerks	2,400
Total	140,600

The revenue from one of the major taxes on the system of venal offices, the *droit de marc d'or*, did not flow into the caisses of the *partie casuelle* but into the caisses of two special Treasurers instead. The *Trésoriers du marc d'or* were attached to the Chancellery and therefore not listed with the *Trésoriers généraux des deniers royaux* at all. Nevertheless, in many respects their business resembled that of the Receiver General for *revenus casuels*. They collected the *marc d'or* tax from every holder of a royal office, including accountants, but once only, usually at the time the crown issued the royal letters of provision. Copies of these letters in the Chancellery records nearly always have the amount of the *marc d'or* listed at the top right-hand corner immediately beneath the amount of the *finance*, if the crown rather than a previous owner was selling the office, and in any case immediately above the amounts of two supplementary taxes, the *droit de sceau*, about a quarter of the *marc d'or* duty, and an honorarium or fee amounting to about one-sixth of the *marc d'or*. Thus, for example, letters of provisions for Jean-Claude Gurber, *Contrôleur général des rentes*, list a *finance* of 106,000

[1] A.N., 4 AP 190.

livres, a *marc d'or* of 504 livres, a *droit de sceau* of 125 livres and an honorarium of 83 livres, 12 *deniers*.[1] These duties were also levied on letters of nobility, letters of *dispense d'âge* and—after 1770—on a wide range of other official documents, making a total annual receipt of about 1,400,000 livres for each of the two Treasurers.[2] From 1761 they were required to pay the rentes on certain crown loans backed by the Order of the Saint Esprit, rentes amounting in 1778 to over 1,100,000 livres a year.

Their own offices were each worth 500,000 livres at the beginning of the reign and together with the offices of the two Controllers represented a total investment of 1,200,000 livres. According to the Treasurers' own declaration they each received only a *gage* of 5% on the first 200,000 livres and another of 4% on the second, or a total *gage* of 18,000 livres. In addition a *taxation* of $2\frac{1}{2}$% of the funds flowing through their caisses brought in about 17,500 livres a year. But because they had to pay 5% on the full 500,000 livres to their creditors who had advanced the price of their offices, as well as 3,600 livres each for a staff of three clerks and bureaux expenses, their net income was hardly 6,900 livres.[3]

Heading the list of *Trésoriers des deniers royaux* were the two Keepers of the Royal Treasury, whom I have nevertheless reserved until the end in order to emphasize that they were hardly any different from the rest.[4] They had seats on the *Petite direction des finances* and certain other small distinctions. Yet their offices, as revised by an Edict of June 1748, were each worth only 1,200,000 livres—no more than those of the Receivers General for Paris and only slightly more than the Receiver General for *Revenus casuels*—and those offices were the family property of the two Keepers, to be inherited, sold or willed away like the offices of other accountants. Their bureaux were somewhat larger than most and they each received an annual allowance of 60,925 livres, raised to 85,925 livres by Necker, for expenses and the salaries of their clerks. Then, their own emoluments included 1,500 livres *gages du Conseil*; 12,000 livres for the year in which each was *en exercice*, for in the usual manner one managed the work of even-numbered years and the other of odd-numbered years; and the usual *gage* of 5% of their original investment, or 60,000 livres. These and occasional payments for special tasks such as the management of loans and lotteries, permitted them each to employ a score of clerks, *caissiers* and office-boys.

[1] A.N., V¹ 441.
[2] A.N., F⁴ 1936; and *Encyclopédie méthodique. Finance*, vol. III, pp. 66 ff.
[3] A.N., F⁴ 1936.
[4] Much information taken from *Encyclopédie méthodique. Finance*, vol. III, p. 739, 'Trésor royal'; and from B.N., Coll. Joly de Fleury 1443, fol. 224, Moreau de Beaumont, *Mémoire sur le trésor royal et sur les comptes que rendent les gardes du trésor royal*, MS dated June 1781.

Two supplementary office-holders, the *Conservateurs des saisies et oppositions faites au trésor royal*, received and endeavoured to sort out various claims on treasury funds, especially those assigned for payment to people with debts; and their clearance certificates (*certificats de quitus*) were needed along with those of the Chamber of Accounts by office-holders relinquishing their offices and expecting reimbursement. If the Keepers did not have Controllers of the usual type, much the same work was performed for them by the two *Gardes des registres du contrôle général des finances*, and at the beginning of the reign the Keepers were accountable for the funds in their caisses in much the same manner as other accountants, except that their accounts went before the Royal Council on Finance for approval before being sent to the Chamber of Accounts.

Throughout the reign a large part of the Crown's revenues never reached the caisses of the Keepers of the Royal Treasury, but was received and paid out again by other accountants. In the early years of the reign such funds did not even appear in Treasury records and indeed it was not until the Revolution that the Treasury accounts came to show all government funds. The practice of the ancien régime was to arrange for payments to be made by convenient accountants, often locally. As late as 1787 records show the *maréchaussées* (territorial police) of the Ile de France paid 261,588 livres by the Receivers General; a part of 26,706,000 livres interest on foreign and provincial loans paid by the Treasurers of the *pays d'état* and only a part of it by the Keepers of the Royal Treasury; over 159 million livres paid out in rentes by the General Farm; and many other payments by these and other accountants.[1] For what the estimates of the Ministers of Finance were worth, early in the reign they showed (as in Table 2 on page 90) the part of annual revenues actually accounted for by the Treasury.[2]

Whatever the error in these figures, there can be little doubt that the caisses of the Keepers formed no aggregate fund of government revenues. We may see the Keepers of the Royal Treasury, especially at the beginning of the reign, as merely the most important of the accountants, *primus inter pares*, with no general command of government funds and no authority over other accountants.

They held their offices and disposed of them like family property, much as other accountants did, and the families nourished by the offices of Keeper of the Royal Treasury were among the most successful. The Keeper for even-numbered years was, from 1749, Charles-Pierre Savalette de

---

[1] Mathon de la Cour, *Comptes rendus*, pp. 201 ff. Calonne's figures.

[2] The figures for the early years are from Mathon de la Cour, *Comptes rendus, passim*; and for 1788 the figures are from Braesch, *Finances et monnaie révolutionnaires*, deuxième fasc., pp. 71–108.

Table 2. *Revenues accounted for by the Treasury, 1773–88*

Year	Gross ordinary revenue (without loans)	Deductions of sums paid out by other caisses	Net sums sent to the Treasury
1773 (Terray)	348	143	205
1774 (Terray)	362	165	197
1774 (Calonne)	353	156	197
1775 (Terray)	366	156	210
1775 (Turgot)	370	157	213
1776 (Turgot)	378	163	215

For the years just before the revolution, by which time various Ministers had struggled to improve the accounts, the figures showed the Treasury to be accounting for less than before:

1787 (Calonne)	474	236	238
1788 (Brienne)	472	258	214

In addition, the revenues from loans and other 'extraordinary' funds were supposed to flow into the Treasury. For the year 1788 there were expected to be 168 millions from such sources, altering the figures as follows:

1788 (Brienne)	640	258	382

Magnanville, and from 1773 his son, Charles-Pierre-Paul Savalette de Langes was named as his assistant and heir-apparent (*survivant*) in the office. Then, in November 1785 their positions were reversed and the father became assistant and heir-apparent to the son.[1] They were both members of the Paris Parlement, Masters of Requests and Councillors of State; the father served for a while as Intendant of Tours; he was third degree noble and the son, of course, fourth degree noble. With their *robe* connections, the Savalette family were socially perhaps above the holders of the office for odd-numbered years, the families of Micault and Laborde, but these had powerful relations in the world of finance. Joseph Micault d'Harvelay succeeded his famous great-uncle, Jean Pâris de Montmartel, in the office of Keeper of the Royal Treasury in 1755 and held it until January 1785 when he turned the office over to his nephew, François-Louis-Joseph Laborde de Méréville, who had served as his assistant and heir-apparent since 1777.[2] When Laborde de Méréville finally acquired the office in 1785, he took as

[1] A.N., P 2742, Lett. Pat. of 7 Feb. 1782, 14 Feb. 1773; P 2743, Lett. Pat. of 19 Nov. 1785.

[2] A.N., P 2743, Lett. Pat. of 26 January 1785, Letters of *dispense d'age* of the same day to admit Laborde de Méréville, even though he was under the regulation age of twenty-five. A.N., P 2513, Lett. Pat. of 13 Dec. 1776, 29 Nov. 1776 and 22 Sept. 1776.

his assistant and heir-apparent his father, Jean-Joseph de Laborde, who had been court banker for a few years until 1769. Micault and Laborde *père* had become related by marrying sisters, and as these ladies were also the daughters of a rich Belgian court-banker, Nettine, and as a third sister had married Ange-Laurent de Lalive de Jully, *parlementaire*, ambassador, rich art collector and brother of a Farmer General, these Keepers moved in the highest financial circles.[1]

[1] A.N., T 200⁷, a dossier on d'Harvelay's succession in 1786 shows that Jean-Vivant Micault de Courbeton, d'Harvelay's brother, was one of the *régisseurs* of the Powder and Saltpetre Commission. The three Nettine sisters were Anne-Rose-Josèphe, wife of d'Harvelay and then, by a second marriage, of the Controller General, Calonne; Marie-Louise-Josèphe, wife of Lalive de Jully from 1762; and Rosalie-Claire-Josèphe who married Laborde in August 1760. Active in the public events of his time, Laborde de Méréville served in the American War under Rochambeau; in 1789 he was a member of the Comité de Trente who met at Adrien Duport's house to prepare the election of deputies to the Estates General; and he himself became a deputy for the third estate of Etampes and emigrated to London in 1793, where he died in 1802. (Jean Bouchary, *Les Manieurs d'argent*, vol. III, p. 256; Herbert Luethy, *La Banque protestante*, vol. II, p. 680 and, for many of these figures, François Bluche, *L'Origine des magistrats du parlement de Paris, passim.*)

5
PRIVATE ENTERPRISE IN
PUBLIC FINANCE

FRANCE had no central or public bank in the ancien régime. Most countries in western Europe set up such banks in the course of the seventeenth and eighteenth centuries, but the Bank of France was not formed until the year 1800. Turgot's *caisse d'escompte*, founded in 1776, did not perform any of the main functions of a central bank except for a while early in the revolution when Necker gave its bills legal currency and began to rely on it for short-term advances. The revolutionary *caisse de l'extraordinaire* served the same purpose on a somewhat greater scale until the governments of the Directory resumed the habits of the ancien régime in matters of public banking. As for the ancien régime, more has been written to explain why the royal government had no central bank than to describe how it managed without one.[1] A thorough inquiry into the sources of short-term credit during the ancien régime—an obscure and thorny investigation beyond the scope of this book—would reveal the most useful secrets about the régime. An exhaustive study is not necessary, however, to show that in the reign of Louis XVI, by which time the British government could depend entirely on the Bank of England for its advances, the French government had to rely upon its own accountants and taxing agencies for financial credit of a short-term nature.[2] In this aspect of their work, the accountants appear to have been private businessmen engaging in short-term loans for profit.

Considering the general structure of the financial system, we can see at once that two of its features were likely to create a need for continual short-term advances and there is no lack of evidence to support our reasoning. On the one hand a vast network of separate caisses, each holding a deposit of government funds, kept those funds divided in innumerable little pools, so to speak. On the other hand, there being no large central pool, no aggregate

---

[1] Paul Harsin, *Les Doctrines monetaires et financières en France* (Paris, 1928); Paul Harsin, *Caisse d'escompte et banque d'état*; and Marcel Marion, *Histoire financière de la France, depuis 1715* (Paris, 1914), ch. 3; and other financial histories by Gomel, Stourm, etc.

[2] P. G. M. Dickson, *The Financial Revolution.*

fund, the functions of receiving and spending were to a great extent confused. Every caisse both received and spent. Therefore, every caisse was nearly always either overdrawn or else holding an unspent surplus, and over the entire system, as critics pointed out, there was invariably a great deal of money 'stérile et morte pour le service',[1] and at the same time a fluctuating, artificial debt. While some accountants had excess funds at their disposal for weeks and even months, others could only meet their commitments by drawing upon some form of temporary credit. So stated, the system seems to present a problem with an obvious solution: why not, we might ask, create a common fund into which the accountants could all pay their surpluses and from which they could all draw their advances? But we might just as well ask why countries at war did not create a common authority from which they could all get peace and justice. The common fund was eventually created in an administrative revolution stemming from a new vision of efficient public organization and from a social and political revolution which swept away the system of venal offices and other private rights in the public domain. Until then, the ancien régime made many, probably most, of its payments by means of advances of a few weeks or months on which it paid interest.

There was another reason for short-term borrowing that was not inherent in the system but resulted from government policy. As taxes were collected at a slow and variable rate throughout the fiscal year and sometimes even after it had passed, convenience dictated a system of advances that could permit the government to spend money before it had actually been collected and, at best, as soon as its collection had been authorized. In its most obvious form, discounting future revenue was accomplished by tax-farming and, as Professor G. T. Matthews has explained, the Farmers General undertook in every six-year lease to put half of the price of the lease at the disposal of the Crown in regular annual instalments.[2] In addition, the Farmers General made frequent special advances beyond the terms of the leases by means of their own credit notes, which they were prepared to issue in the 1780s at a cost to the Crown of only 4 %.[3] The Domains

[1] This phrase appears, for instance, in the reforming edicts of Necker and Loménie de Brienne (see below, pp. 109, 150 and 205).

[2] G. T. Matthews, *The Royal General Farms in Eighteenth-Century France* (New York, 1958), pp. 13 ff., 217 ff. and ch 8. Dr Matthews explains clearly the role of the General Farm in royal finance, and for this reason I have said little on the subject in the present chapter.

[3] An official summary of short-term advances in 1780 was followed by a note: 'We have not included in this table the interest at 4 % which the King pays to the Farmers General on the daily advances which they make beyond the price of their lease.' (B.N., Coll. Joly de Fleury 1438, fol. 223.)

93

Administration and the *Régie générale*, created during Necker's first ministry, offered the Crown similar services in *anticipations* on the revenues from the domains and the excise taxes. As the Crown fell into deeper and deeper financial difficulties, it turned to the caisses of these agencies, large pools of revenue fed by taxes, and mortgaged them with more and more credit advances. For instance, an *arrêt du Conseil* of 6 January 1788 authorized the *Régie générale* to issue its own notes on behalf of the Crown and during the rest of that month the *caissier* issued 334 credit notes to a total value of a million livres. These were no doubt cashed as they fell due, but on 1 January 1789 there were 1,335 notes in circulation worth over 4 millions.[1]

The revenue from the *taille*, the *capitation* and the *vingtième* was discounted in a slightly different way by requiring the Receivers General at the beginning of each year to send a number of rescriptions to the spending departments, which could use them to make payments or else cash them during the year according to need. Each Receiver General signed his own rescriptions drawn on his clerks in his Generality and as a rule was personally responsible for them. He sent them in the amounts and to the agencies prescribed in the *état du Roi* or the *état de distribution*, which he received from the Royal Council on Finance. Thus, legally he undertook to collect the total annual sum recorded in his *soumission*, and at the same time he engaged himself to advance a part of that sum, in the form of rescriptions, before he had himself received it. But the rescription was not merely a legal agreement; it was a negotiable instrument which derived its value from the personal credit of the Receiver General. The Receiver General might enjoy sound credit with lenders because of the prestige of his office, but at the same time the Crown depended upon his credit to procure its advances. 'The rescriptions and notes of the Farm, in particular,' a lawyer wrote in 1776, 'take the place in this country of the public banks established in other kingdoms.'[2]

On the paying side of the system, there was a similar practice. The Treasurers, Payers and others with responsibility for royal services made necessary payments, whether or not they happened to have royal funds in their caisses, by advancing the money and eventually recovering it with 5% or 6% interest in the form of *remplacements*. Tables of royal cash orders (*ordonnances de comptant*) show frequent and often large sums to many accountants for 'remplacement de sommes payées' or for 'remplacements

[1] A.N., G² 109, Gougenot to Cornu de la Fontaine, 27 April 1789.
[2] Coquereau, *Mémoires concernant l'administration des finances sous le ministère de Monsieur l'abbé Terray*, p. 25.

de ses avances',[1] Almost anyone, it appears, might be called upon to serve his King by advancing funds. In 1786, the postmasters advanced the cost of the royal trips to Cherbourg (203,682 livres), to Compiègne (84,080 livres) and to Fontainebleau (120,789 livres, doubtless for many trips).[2] The Treasurers General were one of the greatest sources of credit on the paying side, however, and their notes became a kind of permanent currency in the ancien régime. According to a reliable report, abbé Terray was considering in 1770 suspending the redemption of all Treasurer's notes but thought better of it on learning that many accountants were using them as cash in making payments for the Crown. The Treasurers General for Marine and Colonies and their agents at Québec issued enormous sums in the form of their notes and bills of exchange, and it is significant of their important role in colonial finance that the government never tried to abolish them even though it tried again and again to do away with the card money issued by the Intendant of New France.[3] The colony was, indeed, almost entirely financed by short-term credit notes of one kind or another, and these ran into hundreds of millions as became apparent in the crisis of 1715–17 after the War of Spanish Succession and in the crisis of 1759–63 after the Seven Years War.

All these advances were for the purpose of making payments assigned to the caisses of Treasurers, Receivers General, tax farmers and others, but for the business of the Royal Treasury there were special arrangements. The two Keepers could not furnish enough short-term credit to meet the obligations of their caisses, and in any case the Ministers and their advisers thought it unwise for the Crown to put such a large operation in the hands of any individual. The experience of having this business managed by a Court Banker, such as Samuel Bernard and Jean Paris de Montmartel, led to the temporary suppression of the Court Banker on 1 January 1767 and a permanent, severe reduction in his work and status in 1778 when the *Premier commis des finances* and the Keepers of the Royal Treasury assumed this part of his duties. Thereafter, the man entrusted with the financial services of the Department of Foreign Affairs was called 'Court Banker', but his work was only a small part of the earlier functions.[4]

---

[1] Two such tables are: (1) *Etat des ordonnances de comptant, année 1779* (Paris, 1790) (B.M. R.623) and (2) *Etats de comptant de l'année et des restes de l'année 1783 avec la table alphabétique des personnes qui y sont employées* (Paris, 1790) (B.M. FR.551).

[2] A.N., F⁴ 1085, *Etats des recettes et des dépenses du trésor royal* (Aug. 1786 to March 1787).

[3] Adam Shortt, ed., *Documents Relating to Canadian Currency, Exchange and Finance During the French Period* (Ottawa, 1925), 2 vols. *passim*; also, J. F. Bosher, 'Government and Private Interests in New France', *Canadian Public Administration* (June 1967), pp. 252 ff.

[4] On the position of Court Banker, see *Encyclopédie méthodique. Finance*, 'Banquier de la cour'. A.N. AB XIX 327: Conférence 2 (1790), Dufresne refers to Joseph Durvey as 'le banquier de la cour, c'est-à-dire l'homme chargé du service des Affaires Etrangères'.

Whoever managed the credit operations for the Treasury—and this is the vital point—the money was advanced by a small and variable group of about a dozen financiers, most of them accountants, who undertook to *faire le service du trésor royal*, according to the expression of the time, and who were described as *les faiseurs de service*. What they did was to discount rescriptions, *assignations* and notes of the General Farm and other agencies, each man furnishing cash every month to the amount he had pledged at the beginning of the year. In November and December the Minister and his assistants prepared a plan of the *service* for the next year by engaging financiers to pledge monthly advances, and four times during the year this plan was reviewed in preparation for the quarterly demands on the Treasury.

During the first ten years of the reign the name appearing most often and for the largest sums in the treasury service plan was that of Nicolas Beaujon (1718–86), Court Banker until 1778 and Receiver General for La Rochelle and then Rouen.[1] His advances to the Treasury, usually the largest single contribution, were as shown in Table 3 for years in which I have found figures:[2]

Table 3. *Nicolas Beaujon's advances to the Treasury*
(in millions of livres)

Year	Total of the Service	Beaujon's contribution
1771	151	36
1772	169	48
1773	208	61
1774	191	46
1780	130	30
1781	135	40
1782	154	30
1783	150	30

Each of the two Keepers, Micault d'Harvelay and Savalette, advanced nearly as much as Beaujon most years. D'Harvelay, indeed, lent more (36 millions) in 1783. These three taken together usually contributed more than half of the total sum. The other lenders included five Treasurers General; five Receivers General;[3] a cashier of the Indies Company, Pierre

[1] André Masson, *Un Mécène Bordelais, Nicolas Beaujon* (Bordeaux, 1937).
[2] Figures compiled from several sources, mainly B.N., Coll. Joly de Fleury 1438, 1441 and others in that series.
[3] The five Treasurers General were: Baudard de Saint James, Mégret de Sérilly, Beaugéard (for Brittany), Randon de la Tour, and Fontaine de Biré. The five Receivers General were: Jean-Jacques de la Fretté (b. 1728), Tourteau de Septeuil, Bollioud de Saint Jullien, Marquet de Montbreton and Duruey.

de Mory; Jacques Necker during his first ministry; and two men grown rich in banking, war finance and other business—*capitalistes* in the language of the day—who were closely associated with government financial policy and sometimes influential. These were Jacques Marquet de Bourgade (1718–84), friend and adviser to the Minister, Joly de Fleury, and Jean-Baptiste Magon de la Balue (1713–94), Court Banker briefly in 1769 and member of an important commission under Loménie de Brienne. Some of these contributed annually to the service, others only occasionally. The plans for three sample years, which I have combined for convenience, were as follows:[1]

Table 4. *Advances to the Treasury* ('*le service*'), *1780–3*
(*in millions of livres*)

Name	1780	1781	1783	Analysis of 1783		
				Notes of Gen. Farm	Rescriptions	Assignations on farms and *régies*
Beaujon	30	40	30	24	6	—
d'Harvelay	23	24·03	36	12	6	18
Savalette	22·5	24	24	—	—	24
Baudard de Saint James	9	4·27	12	—	6	6
de la Fretté	7·5	12	3·6	—	1·8	1·8
Mégret de Sérilly	12·97	8·6	12	—	6	6
Fontaine de Biré	—	—	—	—	—	—
Magon de la Balue	9·6	9·6	12	—	4·8	7·2
Tourteau de Septeuil	4·24	8	8	—	4	4
Marquet de Bourgade	2·88	2·88	—	—	—	—
Bollioud de St Jullien	5·88	—	—	—	—	—
Jacques Necker	2	—	—	—	—	—
Beaugéard	0·6	—	—	—	—	—
Randon de la Tour	—	1·55	1·57	—	1·57	—
Pierre de Mory	—	—	2	—	—	2
Marquet de Montbreton	—	—	9	—	9	—
TOTALS	130·17	134·93	150·17	36	45·17	69

These were reasonably normal or representative years in respect of short-term lending to the Treasury. Of course France was at war until well into 1783, but if we may judge from the total advances quoted for other years, war was not of immediate importance:[2]

[1] These lists are in B.N., Coll. Joly de Fleury 1438, fol. 223, 1435, fol. 237 and 1441, fol. 38. The list for 1781 notes ten million livres in *assignations* not in the table. Fontaine de Biré was listed with Mégret de Sérilly for the advances of 1783.

[2] The most reliable of these figures come from A.N., F⁴ 1078, 1079, 1082 and other *cartons* in this series of accounts and these are for 1771 to 1776. The figure for 1788 is

Table 5. *Advances to the Treasury ('le service'), 1769–88*

Year	Total	Year	Total	Year	Total
1769	154	1775	221	1782	154
1771	151	1776	214	1783	150
1772	169	1777	192	1787	255
1773	208	1780	130	1788	240
1774	191	1781	135		

The notorious crisis of February 1770, when the sources of short-term credit dried up, caused hardly a ripple in this system. Abbé Terray, the Minister at the time, suspended payments on outstanding notes of the General Farm and on rescriptions, amounting to some 200 million livres according to his estimate, and made arrangements to redeem them little by little over the ensuing years.[1] He did this only in order to be able to issue new rescriptions and notes for the service of 1770. Nothing in the information at our disposal suggests that any fundamental change occurred in this process before the revolution.

The credit notes of accountants and financial agencies were traded on the Paris *bourse*, or money market, and other accountants were among the purchasers. An official of the Royal Treasury explained a typical procedure:[2]

[Assuming] I am a Receiver General of Finance and today, the first of the month, I have received from my *Receveur particulier* in the provinces 200,000 livres which I need not pay to the King until the 30th of the month. So I send to the *bourse* and there I have purchased for me, at a discount of 5 % or 6 %, 200,000 livres worth of rescriptions or Treasurer's notes (*billets des trésoriers*). These are authorized by the government and will reach maturity on the 30th of this month or in the first few days of next month. I can therefore give them as cash at the time I make my payment. These profits are so certain, these transfers of funds so public, that they are calculated by the government in favour of the financiers in the agreements (*traités*) which it makes with them.

quoted from Loménie de Brienne by Egret, *La Pré-revolut. française*, p. 312. Those for 1780–3 are from B.N., Coll. Joly de Fleury as in the preceding table. And the rest are from Mathon de la Cour, *Collection des comptes rendus*, pp. 75, 189, 220.

[1] The *billets des fermes* were eventually repaid in part by a lottery system until an arrêt of 2 December 1782 announced that the Farmers General would purchase those remaining in other hands. The rescriptions were repaid at the rate of 3 millions a year, also by lottery, until an arrêt of 26 June 1785 announced that the Receivers General would buy up the remaining 32,500,000 livres. (*Encyclopédie méthodique. Finance*, vol. 1, p. 115 and vol. 3, p. 493.) Also, Mathon de la Cour, *Collection des comptes rendus*, p. 65.

[2] Dufresne de Saint Léon, *Etudes sur le crédit public* (1784) (B.N., Rés. *E593), p. 361. On the Paris *bourse*, George V. Taylor, 'The Paris *bourse* on the Eve of the Revolution, 1781–89', *American Historical Review* (1962), pp. 951–77.

The government has even engaged one of its Treasurers to take the funds collected by the *Receveurs particuliers des Fermes* established in the provinces and in exchange to give them his notes, bearing interest when the payments they undertook to make falls due. And the Farmers General, being bound to pay funds to this same Treasurer, give him these notes as cash.

The rescriptions and other notes of accountants, thus bought and sold, mingled with the shares of private companies and with the notes of private banking firms.

The most expensive abuses of this system of short-term credit were procedures of the Treasurer General called *jeux de caisses*. These abuses depended on the Treasurer's freedom to use the funds in his caisse until they were needed for departmental expenditures. The funds at his disposal came from his own private borrowing and from regular Treasury remittances for departmental expenditures, in the form of rescriptions or, if the money was transferred from a distant source, in the form of bills (*traites*) which did not need to be cashed for a few weeks or at least a few days. He could also increase his resources by delaying his payments. With cash, or paper which could be temporarily converted into cash, the Treasurer advanced funds to the Keepers of the Royal Treasury, who gave him rescriptions cashable for interest in six, eight or twelve months. The legitimate rate of interest was 5·55% per year but the Keepers could find ways of paying up to 8%, and in any event 1% was the usual commission allowed for an accountant handling such negotiations. One well-informed author calculated that the Treasurer General for one of the major spending departments could expect to get credit, in one form or another, amounting to about 15 million livres a year on which he would have to pay 5% interest, but which would earn him an average interest of 7%. Thus, he would earn a net 2% profit, or 300,000 livres. In addition, by multiplying money transfers in the form of short-term bills (*traites*) he could make a net profit of 100,000 livres on twenty-five millions so transferred. One of the larger Treasurers General could, in this way, cost the state a total of 1,150,000 livres of which he would himself get 400,000 livres.[1]

[1] *Eclaircissements sur l'organisation actuelle du trésor public* (Paris, 1790) (B.M. FR 502). This was profit through his *jeux de caisses* over and above his more legitimate earnings which, for the Treasurer of the War Department spending some 84 millions, might come to 850,000 livres in commissions (*taxations*) and 75,000 livres in indemnities or *remises*. If, as the author says, we subtract from this total income of 1,315,000 livres various expenses:

Expenses of office	100,000 livres
Printing, accounting, etc.	70,000
Employees' wages	168,000
Sub-treasurers' wages	177,000
There remains as net earnings	810,000

7-2

As these procedures suggest, *public* credit as we know it was nothing more than the goal of a few reformers such as John Law, Véron de Fort-bonnais, and Jacques Necker; and until the revolution brought the victory of the movement they stimulated, the government depended upon the personal credit of financiers, especially its own accountants. In the view of those who worked with this system, there was an informal partnership of Crown and financiers. Nicolas Beaujon stated the theory of it succinctly in a memorandum to the Minister, l'Averdy:[1]

The nation's credit consists in the credit of the King and of the individuals engaged in banking operations. It is through the harmony of these two types of credit that the requirements of war can be met and things restored after the peace by plans of economy. The King's credit increases that of the bankers and [in turn] gains strength from the extension of the bankers' credit and from the esteem and confidence which they enjoy among the public.

Closely linked with this idea was another just as fundamental to the system: that all accountants and agencies should collect and otherwise manage government funds for profit incentives—*taxations, remises* and so on—rather than for fixed salaries. They should have personal financial interests at stake and be able to grow rich or to fail according to their abilities. The most compelling reason, as Joly de Fleury put it, was that 'the credit of Treasurers who are only clerks and whose salary is fixed becomes nil for the service, so to speak, because the confidence of the public is ruled more by opinion than by reality'.[2] In other words, people were willing to lend money only to rich businessmen, not to salaried civil servants. Calonne made the principle even more explicit in conversation with the wife of a would-be Receiver General for the Generality of Tours: 'a financial office as important as that for Tours cannot be entrusted to a man with no fortune; and henceforth I shall admit to these offices only those whose means will guarantee for the King the management of the sums with which I shall entrust them'.[3]

The business life of an accountant had an extraordinarily active private side, though it was not clearly set apart from his work for the Crown. A variety of loans and investments sometimes made his royal office seem like only one of his business assets. To begin with, most accountants borrowed the capital sum needed for the purchase of the office. Simon-Charles Boutin, for example, in 1780 borrowed half of the *finance* of one million

---

[1] Masson, *Un Mécène Bordelais*, p. 165, dated 1764.
[2] B.N., Coll. Joly de Fleury 1439, fol. 36, point 6.
[3] A.N., T* 594, manuscript journal of Harvoin, p. 27.

livres for his office of Treasurer General of the Marine from four sources.[1] His fellow Treasurer General of that department, Baudard de Saint James, raised 714,000 livres of his purchase-price in loans from nine friends, relations and business colleagues.[2] Jacques Guillot de Montgrand paid 480,000 livres for his Receiver General's office in 1781, 300,000 livres of which he borrowed from Jean-Baptiste Pia, 'ancien maître en pharmagie [sic]' and from Nicolas Rollin, 'bourgeois de Paris'.[3] The last of the Receivers General told the National Convention that they had been in the habit of buying their offices with funds borrowed in most cases 'on bearer-demand notes (*billets au porteur*) which they continually renewed by virtue of their sound credit'.[4] The same was claimed for the *régisseurs* and the tax farmers:[5]

No one is ignorant of the fact that the funds of the majority of *régisseurs*, as of the *intéressées* [in the General and other tax farms] do not belong to them, and that they have borrowed these funds, some on receipts from their caisses or commitments for the term of the *régie*, and promise to renew them if circumstances permit.

When the affairs of the Farmers General were being wound up during the revolution, some four thousand families claimed to be their creditors in one way or another.[6]

The borrowing of accountants and farmers did not cease with the purchase of their offices. Like certain notaries of the time, the accountants attracted people with savings to invest. Sometimes these loans were temporary or short-term holdings. To take a typical case, a resident of a small

---

[1] A.N., P 2520 *quittance* dated 28 December 1780 showing debts to Charles-Philippe Simon de Montboissier Beaufort Cainallard, baron de Montboissier (200,000 livres); to François Méthivier, bourgeois de Paris (119,000 livres); to Louis Véron, bourgeois de Paris (100,000 livres); and Louis-Pierre, comte de Jancours and his wife, Louise-Elisabeth de la Chaste, comtesse de Jancourt (81,000 livres).

[2] A.N., P 2517, *quittance* registered 19 July 1779 showing debts to Marie-Louis Berthelet, veuve de Daniel-Louis Denis de Lausac, conseiller au parlement (20,000 livres); to sieur de Villefroy, representing Catherine-Marguerite Lefebvre, widow of Simon-Charles Cousin, Trésorier de France (Paris) (25,000 livres); Alexandre-François-Jérôme Dargouges, conseiller d'état and his wife, Marguerite-Françoise de Le Fabvre de la Sabre (25,000 livres); to Mlle. Marie-Suzanne-Françoise Dargouges de Fleury (30,000); to Léonard-Philippes Desvieux and Louis François Desvieux, military officers (102,000); to Alexis-Janvier Lalive de la Briche, introducer of ambassadors (100,000); to Lesval, cessionnaire en partie du marquis de la Somme (68,000); to Bourgeoisie de Crethieuville, the same (60,000 livres); and to Joseph-Benoist Blanchard de Bensenvaux, écuyer (284,000 livres). The *quittance* signed 22 January 1779.

[3] A.N., P 2521.

[4] *Pétition des ci-devant receveurs généraux à la convention national* (B.N. Lf[76] 33).

[5] A.N., D VI 6, No. 38, memorandum dated July 1790.

[6] A.N., F[4] 2022, *Réclamations des ci-devant fermiers généraux*.

town in Maine wrote to a Receiver General, Marquet Desgrèves, on 3 December 1788:[1]

I have received a small reimbursement, Monsieur, which I have not yet had occasion to reinvest. In the meantime, I would like to put this sum, which is only eight or ten thousand livres, in safety; and for that I cannot do better than apply to you. Please let me know if you are willing to take this money, on which you may pay me whatever interest you wish, as I would like in that regard to put my conscience in safety as well as my money.

All accountants appear to have been entrusted with sums from many people and to have incurred many debts with tradesmen and others. There were regular procedures for an accountant's creditors to follow if ever he went bankrupt. Forming a legal union to recover their investments, these creditors became a recognized interest group with a legitimate claim on the accountant's assets. One bankrupt accountant hastily made arrangements to satisfy the Crown by renouncing his office, and then in order to avoid his other creditors he persuaded the governor of the Bastille to imprison him.[2] Nowhere in this case, or any others I could find, was there any suggestion that accountants were doing anything illegal in contracting debts to purchase their offices or for other purposes.

If accountants borrowed, they also invested, and in a wide range of enterprises. Gabriel Prévost, a Treasurer General for the *Ponts et Chaussées*, is a good example of an active accountant. In 1778 he had investments of 12,000 livres in a spinning business at Sers, 30,000 livres in a royal cloth-making concern at Bourges, 30,000 in forges at Beaumont and at la Belouze (Nièvre), 4,000 in acid manufacturing, 50,000 in mines in lower Brittany, 50,000 in the military hospital company, 60,000 in the General Insurance Company of Paris and a large but undetermined sum in the official Spanish gunpowder and saltpetre company, the commercial firm of Pedegache and Co. in Lisbon and several shipping concerns.[3] The investments of the Marine Treasurer, Baudard de Saint James, were even larger and spread over an even wider range of enterprises.[4] Marquet Desgrèves invested in a soap factory, and gave substantial support (over 150,000 livres in the first six months of 1786 alone) to a certain Wilfelsheim who managed a new laundry near Saint Denis, la Buanderie de la Briche. These two also planned a national laundry, a *blanchisserie nationale* in Paris for which

[1] A.N., T 165¹⁵, letter from 'Louvigny, viennay au val, près Mamers, au Maine'. The reference to conscience shows scruples about taking interest on his money and so transgressing religious principles.
[2] C. N. Roland, *Receveur particulier for Chartres* (Roland, *Mémoire au Roi*, p. 15).
[3] 'Types de capitalistes parisiens à la fin du XVIIIe siècle', *Centre de recherches sur l'histoire des entreprises*, Bulletin 2, Oct. 1953.
[4] *Loc. cit.*, p. 27; Legoherel, *Les Trésoriers généraux*, p. 348.

coloured drawings in the file show a winter drying room large enough to hold 9,000 pieces of laundry.[1] The Meulan family of Receivers General made heavy investments in America.[2] Millin Duperreux, Receiver General and administrator of the Royal Lottery, owned most of the shares in a paper factory at Essonne.[3] The stock of the Paris Water Company was purchased by Magon de la Balue, Micault d'Harvelay, Mégret de Sérilly and Baudard de Saint James.[4] Probably all the greater accountants engaged in business of many different kinds.

Even the lesser accountants, like the Receivers (*Receveurs particuliers*), often invested in land or engaged in a variety of private and public enterprises. Charles Pillon, for example, owned land in Paris to the value of 184,200 livres.[5] But let us take one example of a Receiver and explore his business life in order to show how active and widespread it might be. The career of Charles-Nicolas Roland will serve to illustrate what a hard-working financier might accomplish. In 1756 he began to work for a Receiver General as a mere *caissier* at the usual salary of 3,000 livres a year and he kept this post even after he purchased the Receivership of Orleans for 150,000 livres, in 1771. Three years later he also became *caissier* and one of the *régisseurs* in charge of the Forest of Grésigne on behalf of its owner, the comte de Maillebois. In 1774, Turgot offered him a salary of 6,000 livres to manage the caisse for receiving the returns from sales of government grain stocks and from the duties on grain exports. Not content with the cumulation of all these posts, in 1778 Roland formed a partnership with two old friends, one an architect and the other like himself 'intéressé dans les affaires du roi,' for the purchase of the Château de Ternes with its sixty *arpents* of land for 170,000 livres which they borrowed under the assumed name of Le Sieur Normand. They also bought two great houses in Paris, the Hôtel de Conti (rue des Poulies) and the Hôtel de Créqui (rue de l'Oratoire) for an unspecified price, all these properties being 'objets de spéculation' to be resold at a profit. Meanwhile, Roland himself owned another house at Sablons worth about 22,000 livres, with the furniture included. He had lent 80,000 livres to an Italian artist, Bocciardi, for the purchase of the office of *Sculpteur des menus plaisirs du Roi*, and another 48,000 livres to a merchant jeweller of his acquaintance. A dying Receiver General of Domains and Forests in Flanders had entrusted Roland with the business of his office, and Roland had carried on the business for the sons until the eldest had succeeded to the office and died, leaving it to the next son who, Roland

[1] A.N., T 165[15].　　　　　　　　　　　　[2] A.N., F[4] 2021.
[3] A.N., T 200[12] where these investments are explained at length.
[4] Bouchary, *Les Manieurs*, vol. I, p. 57.　　　　[5] A.N., F[30] 199 and P 2847.

declared, owed him 30,000 livres. The capital for these ventures came from a variety of sources, notably another financier, Joseph Duruey, who in 1779 held Roland's notes to the value of 180,000 livres; from a numerous group of lesser creditors of whom the most troublesome proved to be an Italian actor, Carlin (or Arlequin), for the sum of 52,500 livres; and from Roland's own profits and the dowry of his second wife. There were many others. All these activities show clearly enough that Roland was a businessman and that his office as Receiver for the Election of Chartres was merely one of his business assets.[1]

The most striking manifestation of private enterprise in the management of public funds was the series of bankruptcies among officials. There had always been such bankruptcies, for they were an intrinsic part of the system and continued until the revolution changed the system. This was because the accountants and all who managed funds were personally responsible for the solvency of their caisses, because they were only accountable to the Chamber of Accounts or the Royal Council and subject to no continuous supervision and because their business for the Crown was hardly any different from their other business affairs and was, in any case, not kept separate. To guard itself against loss, the Crown held the price paid for an office as security, and if necessary the property of the accountant as well. The law also held a wife's property liable in case of her husband's failure. Yet for all this, the position of accountant to the Crown did nothing to protect the individual businessman from the sort of financial failure which might befall anyone engaged in trade and finance. The concern of the government was only with the security of its own funds, not with the maintenance of the accountant's safety and solvency. Just as the *Cour des aides* or the Châtelet might pursue a financier suspected of bankruptcy by his creditors, so the Chamber of Accounts prosecuted every accountant who was unable to meet his financial commitments or who was unaccountably absent for a few days; they put official seals on his papers and property, arrested him if they thought necessary and investigated his business affairs very thoroughly. Indeed, not only absence or failure of an accountant but also his death brought a Chamber inquiry into his affairs. Sometimes a large deficit in a caisse came to light only in the regular posthumous inquiry or in the investigation of a suspicious absence, but however such a deficit was discovered and whether the Chamber held it to be the result of dishonesty or of misfortune, they showed an inflexible rigour in their sentences because they held debt itself to be a crime. When the editors of the *Encyclopédie méthodique. Jurisprudence* drew a distinction between unavoidable

---

[1] Roland, *Mémoire au Roi* (1784), *passim*.

financial failure (*faillite*) and fraudulent bankruptcy (*banqueroute*) they were putting forward a suggestion for reform, not a statement of legal practice. Thus, an accountant might engage in free enterprises in the public domain, but if he failed the courts would compound his misfortune. The system was arranged to punish failure, but not to prevent it.

In 1787 the Chamber of Accounts informed the King that more than fifty accountants or their *caissiers* had gone bankrupt in the previous twenty years.[1] I have found trace of thirty-five bankruptcies between the end of the Seven Years War and the revolution, and a simple analysis of them shows that the incidence of failure was highest among the separate, least organized accountants and lowest in the organized corps.[2] Beginning with the most highly organized, we observe that no Farmers General appear to have failed, at least not with losses to the Crown, and this for the reason that the corps took collective responsibility for the failure of an individual member and tided him over his difficulties in such a way that the Crown suffered no loss.[3] The Chamber of Accounts customarily put seals on the papers and property of a dead Farmer General as for any other accountant, but during the reign of Louis XVI apparently never discovered any large debt to the Crown beneath the seals. The corps of Payers of the rentes proved to be hardly less secure. They appear to have suffered only one failure, that of Joachim-André-Louis Gossey Desplasses in 1779, and they avoided others through the collective responsibility of their corps, 'a corps which has its eyes open on its members, and which forestalls complaints that might be levelled against them'.[4]

When we come to the corps of Receivers General, we find an organization which could prevent some failures but not others. François-Joseph Harvoin fled abroad on 21 January 1787, unhappily convinced that he could not meet his commitments, and the Chamber of Accounts treated the case as a bankruptcy from 23 January when it put seals on his property; but the day before Harvoin took his desperate step, the *Premier commis des finances*, Gojard, reported Harvoin's plight to Calonne, the Minister, and offered a solution which Calonne approved and which they mentioned as the remedy used 'in 1784 in similar circumstances for Monsieur Landry'.[5] This was to

---

[1] *Remontrances de la chambre des comptes*, 11 Feb. 1787 (B.N., Lf²⁷ 33), p. 14.

[2] The principal source is A.N., series P, in which I have scanned most of the volumes of the *Journal*, the *Plumitif* and the *Mémoriaux* of the Chamber of Accounts; but I also searched sequestered papers of several accountants and the papers of Joly de Fleury in the B.N.

[3] Individuals did, of course, get into difficulties and suffer seizure of their goods. An excellent example is Antoine-François Bouret de Valroches who owed 1,560,000 livres in *fonds d'avance* in 1774. (A.N., T 200¹²).   [4] *Mémoire sur les rentes*... (B.N., Lf⁸⁰ 85), p. 18.

[5] A.N., F⁴ 2021, the letter is unsigned but marked 'approuvée' by a minister. For Harvoin's case, see below, p. 183.

have Harvoin turn his registers over to the committee of the Receivers General who would report on his financial situation to the Minister as soon as possible, and in the meantime to arrange for the Keepers of the Treasury or for another Receiver General, Joseph Duruey, to meet Harvoin's commitments and to guarantee his rescriptions. If Harvoin had not fled, these procedures might have saved him from bankruptcy as they had saved Landry earlier, and the case might never have come to the notice of the Chamber of Accounts. In 1780, the Minister and the Committee of the Receivers General seem to have managed to assist Meulan out of the funds in the common caisse in a similar way.[1] Meanwhile, in that same year another troubled Receiver General, Watelet, seems to have considered appealing to the committee of the Receivers General (of which Harvoin was then a member!) for financial help, but decided at last not to do so only because his deficit of over a million livres was partly due to his misuse of royal funds for his own purposes, and this he wished to conceal. Watelet appears to have saved himself from bankruptcy only by cunningly shifting the debt to the account of his clerk and *Receveur particulier*, Roland.[2] Two other Receivers General, however, Thiroux de Montsange and Millin Duperreux, were not saved from bankruptcy in the 1780s, but the first owed a debt to the Crown that was not discovered until his death in 1786 and the second was in a special case by virtue of holding an additional office of Administrator of the Royal Lottery.[3] At least four more Receivers General failed but all in the early years of the revolution when the manifest threat to the system of caisses and accountants made them particularly vulnerable and when economic recession put unusual pressures on them.[4]

[1] Pierre-Louis-Nicolas Meulan and his son, Charles-Jacques-Louis, both Receivers General, were in financial difficulties by 1785 because they had lost a lot of money in the American War. In 1780, a Marine Treasurer, Le Rey de Chaumont, was persuaded by Sartine to assist the Meulans, and so gave them 1,200,000 livres in return for their notes. When Sartine left the Marine Ministry, Necker persuaded de Chaumont to deposit the Meulan notes in the Royal Treasury and on 14 March 1784 Gojard asked the Minister to authorize him to urge the repayment of them. An arrangement was made for the Meulans to pay 558,208 livres in the form of liquidated offices and other assets and the rest in annual payments of 64,179 livres to end in 1794. They seem to have kept up these payments until 1 July 1788, at least (A.N., F⁴ 2021).

[2] Or so Roland convincingly argues. (C. N. Roland, *Mémoire au Roi*, pp. 12 ff.)

[3] Thiroux owed the Crown 1,336,218 livres at his death (A.N., F³⁰ 199 and P 2744); for Millin, A.N., T 200¹² and F³⁰ 199. In 1781 Millin already owed the Crown 364,000 livres in rescriptions (B.N., Joly de Fleury 1435, fols. 162 ff.) and when the bankruptcy was declared in 1786 he was believed by the Chamber of Accounts at Rouen to owe 757,088 livres.

[4] These were Maurice-Alexandre Marquet Desgrèves who fled abroad on 11 May 1789 leaving debts of some 2,408,758 livres and an office worth only 1,010,000 (A.N., P 2846 and F³⁰ 199); Pierre-Nicolas Mel de Saint Céran who also fled, on 16 June 1790, leaving debts to the Crown of 707,134 livres (A.N., P 2847 and F³⁰ 199); Jacques Guillot de Montgrand

It was the unorganized accountants, not formed into corps, who went bankrupt in the greatest numbers: a *Payeur des gages des secrétaires du Roy* (Cadeau); at least three Receivers General of the Domains and Forests between 1763 and their abolition in 1777;[1] at least seven *Receveurs particuliers*;[2] no less than ten Treasurers General;[3] a Receiver of the *communautés réligieuses* (Bourgault Ducoudray); a *Régisseur des économats* (Marchal de Sainscy); a Receiver of the *saisies réelles* (Roulleau); three *Caissiers* for the *régie des droits réunies* (Quinquet), the Postal Farm (Billard), and the Treasurers for Brittany (Le Roux); altogether a total of twenty-seven out of thirty-five failures recorded in the papers of the Chamber of Accounts. Even admitting the possibility of unrecorded failures, allowing for errors on the part of the Chamber, as for instance in the cases of Harvoin and Baudard de Saint James which may have arisen only from suspicion of debt to the Crown and turned into bankruptcy by the Chamber's very investigation, there is nevertheless a remarkable coincidence of financial failure and absence of organization.

Certain cases of bankruptcy show admirably how the financial system confused public funds with private funds, and public functions with private ones. These features of the system appear clearly in the case of François-Pierre Billard, *caissier-général des Postes* from 1756 to 1769.[4] Billard was an ambitious and enterprising businessman who invested in a wide range of financial projects. He helped to form an agricultural company to clear and develop new agricultural land in Berry. He formed another which began to clear and develop an estate at Ormesson which Lefèvre d'Ormesson leased in 1764 for this purpose. The company was planning to build a soap factory, among other ventures, and it was formed for these purposes of four mem-

declared bankrupt in September 1790 with a debt to the Crown of 682,449 livres (A.N., F[30] 199); and Louis Richard de la Bretèche reported bankrupt in 1792, owing 899,824 livres (F[30] 199).

[1] These were Jacques-Benoît de la Croix declared bankrupt in 1763; Michel-Henry Fabus bankrupt in 1765; and Henry-Augustin de Malezieu bankrupt in 1772. (A.N., P 2511, 2843, 2826, etc.)

[2] These were Louis-Alexandre Buisson (1776), Jean-Elie Forien (1787), Nicolas Franquet (1779), René-Louis Goupil (1779), Jean Médard Liger (1777), Claude Pillon (1790), Charles-Nicolas Rolland (1779) and possibly two others called Clouet and Saussaye.

[3] These were Louis-Paul Bourgevin de Norville (Police Treasurer, bankrupt 1769), Jean-Baptiste-René Mouffle de Géorville (Marine—1769), Louis-Etienne Préaudeau de Monchamps (Artillery—1778), Jean-François Caron (*Marc d'or*—1779), Claude-Pierre Radix de Sainte-Foy (*Maison d'Artois*—1781), Gabriel Prévost (*Ponts et Chaussées*—1778), Louis Dupille de Saint-Séverin (*Troupes de la maison du Roi*—1786), Claude Baudard de Saint James (Marine—1787), Antoine-Jean-François Mégret de Sérilly (War—1787), and Antoine Bourboulon (*Maison d'Artois*—1787).

[4] The papers bearing on the case are in A.N., T 2[3-4] and T 2[5-6].

bers including Billard joined together by an act of 15 April 1769, with each member subscribing five shares totalling 40,000 livres. He also invested in a factory at Charité-sur-Loire, in the *régie des droits réunies*, in another land development company to clear and sell land at Captalat in the *landes* region near Bordeaux, another to do the same in Normandy, in a company which he called the Moeres of Flanders and of which he was *syndic*, and in the company which collected the *octrois* of Bordeaux. He was also one of sixty people and a *syndic* in an insurance company. The two enterprises which he expected to be most lucrative were the land-development companies in the Bordelais and in Normandy. In all, he invested a large sum of something over 5½ million livres.

Approximately half of that sum Billard borrowed from private sources. As *caissier-général des Postes* he enjoyed a reputation for soundness and as his affairs grew over the years his credit improved. Most of these loans—about two million livres—were from people who wanted a secure investment for their savings and who simply deposited their money with him personally against a simple receipt. Another 395,000 livres came from people who placed their money in the company to which the postal service was farmed out or from people to whom the company owed money and who therefore held the receipts of the postal company rather than of Billard personally. The other half of the money which he invested he took little by little over the years from his caisse. By the end of 1769, it amounted, according to the administration of the company, to no less than 3,300,000 livres.

In December 1769 Billard got into difficulties through misjudgement and what he afterwards declared to have been imprudence. He could not pay an unforeseen claim on him. Needing help, he went to his employers and explained his circumstances in the expectation that in their common interest the postal farmers would tide him over the difficulty.[1] They were sympathetic at first but soon decided to bring criminal charges against him for using the funds from his caisse. Accordingly, on 16 December he was arrested and imprisoned in the Bastille to await trial at the Châtelet. As usual in such cases, he was immediately declared bankrupt, and his creditors took legal action to recover their investments.[2] Very quickly, before the case had time to spread over too many legal jurisdictions, the Crown ordered the whole affair to be confined to the Châtelet with appeals to the

---

[1] The Postal Farmers whom he dealt with were: Thiroux de Montsange and Jean-Jacques de la Freté.

[2] At the head of the creditors, and representing the rest, were Julien Guillain de Prestre, comte de Seneffe et de Turnhoud and Jacques-Louis Guillaume Bouret de Vezelay, écuyer, Treasurer General of the Artillery, who had a memorandum of thirty-six pages printed to explain their case in 1770.

Parlement of Paris. Claims and counterclaims appeared as his creditors endeavoured to make his debtors pay. All the incidental business was not settled for many years but Billard himself was sentenced on 12 February 1772. His property was confiscated. He was condemned to be publicly exposed for two hours under a notice, *Caissier prévaricateur dans ses fonctions* and then to be banished from France. A devout Catholic, he went to live in Rome. The courts might even have hanged him if a powerful protectress, Madame du Barry, had not intervened in his favour. Yet the historian must find it hard to avoid the conclusion that Billard, for all his misdeeds, had been made a criminal by the financial system in which he had worked.

Had this case occurred at almost any time after the French revolution, there would have been little doubt that Billard had embezzled public funds. In 1772, however, Billard drew up a statement in his own defence which throws quite a different light on the case. It contains, in effect, an indictment of the financial system of the ancien régime, and what we know of the system from other sources lends weight to the statement. He refers to

the fairly general opinion among *caissiers*, and those who by profession are entrusted with some administration of money, that they are entitled to use dead and sterile funds (*les fonds morts et stériles*) when that use is consistent with the service which they owe and when they find in the state of their affairs assured means to replenish their caisses. The very principles of political administration lead to tolerance of this practice which within limits encourages the circulation of money in the Kingdom.[1]

Several more of the arguments on which Billard rested his main defence add to the picture of his business activities and of his attitude to them. He claims that he borrowed the money and did not steal it because he took it openly and replaced it in his caisse with receipts acknowledging that he had taken it. His account books, he says, are all in order. The postal administrators knew of his business ventures and for the previous thirteen years had approved his accounts in which his receipts in the caisse were recorded. During those years his business dealings never once interrupted or prejudiced the services he rendered to the postal company. Therefore he had done everything expected of him. He would have continued to give satisfactory service if the administrators had not taken action against him. There was no question of bankruptcy or failure when he went to see them on 14 December 1769, but (he continues) only a temporary difficulty, and it was the legal action of the postal administrators which precipitated the

---

[1] See his printed, *Requête à nosseigneurs du parlement en la grand'chambre* (1772), 120 pp., p. 17.

failure by destroying the investors' trust in him. In any event, he adds in a brilliant thrust, 'if he had succeeded in his project, he would have enjoyed the consideration which follows prosperity; has he become guilty because he has been unsuccessful?'[1]

As for the question of a criminal abuse of public trust, Billard pointed out that he was not the holder of a public office but merely an employee of the postal farmers. The *caissier des Postes* took no oath and was not approved or recognized as accountable to any court or by any of the laws which applied to Treasurers and other accountants. The funds in his caisse, he held, were not public funds. Therefore he had broken no law and abused no public trust. The whole affair concerned only him and his employers and should be tried as a civil rather than a criminal case.

The case of Billard shows how government funds were not kept separate from private funds and how they could be dissipated in the private enterprises of employees or accountants. The case also shows that the supervision of a *caissier*, and *a fortiori* of an accountant, was distant and uncertain. It follows that the distinction we are accustomed to draw between public and private finances, or between officials and financiers, had little if any meaning in eighteenth-century France. Indeed, we find the term *financier* defined as 'A man who manages the *finances*, that is, royal funds. In general, this name is given to every person known to have interests in the farms, *régies*, enterprises or affairs concerning the King's revenues.'[2] The financier was not an official at all, even though he managed royal funds and this private or semi-private status meant that the Crown could control him only by having recourse to legal process. As the case of Billard shows, the system functioned in such a way that the courts might recover lost Crown funds by liquidating the office and other assets of the unfortunate accountant, but only at great expense and after much litigation. What were these courts, and in particular the Chambers of Accounts, whose duty was to arraign accountants suspected of bankruptcy or dishonesty? What did they think they were doing?

---

[1] *Loc. cit.*, p. 32.
[2] *Encyclopédie méthodique. Finances*, 'financier'. Cf. Necker, *De l'administration*, vol. III, p. 122.

6

THE CHAMBER OF ACCOUNTS

ON THE EVE of the French revolution, the First President of the Paris Chamber of Accounts, Nicolay, wrote in a letter to Jacques Necker, 'if for the last fifteen years the Chamber of Accounts had been left to do its work, and there had been accounting and better accounting, we should not be where we are today'.[1] This was the reproach of a conservative mind opposed to the reforms of the King's ministers and devoted to a sovereign court which his family had presided over for nine generations. The Chambers of Accounts were enemies of reform hardly less than the famous Parlements, but they threw the weight of their opposition into the relatively obscure and technical cause of defending the financial administration. They were bastions of the system of venal accountants and separate caisses.

There were seven Chambers of Accounts after July 1775 when a royal Edict suppressed the Chamber of Blois, and they were no mere courts of audit. In an age when judicial authority had not yet been separated from executive and legislative authority, except in the books of political thinkers, the magistrates of sovereign courts did not confine their work to judging cases sent before them. The justices of the Chambers believed the entire supervision of the Crown's finances to be their primary right and duty. By the eighteenth century they had long lost any direct initiative in making financial policy, but they still enjoyed the right to register all royal acts bearing upon financial matters—the acts they would be expected to enforce in law—and if they did not agree with a measure they could send a deputation to put their remonstrances before the King.[2] The King might take many weeks to reply and when he did so a long formal disagreement could ensue. In these disagreements the Chambers had parliamentary pretensions and saw themselves, like the Parlements, as intermediaries between the ruler and the people, guardians of the established financial order. All the

[1] A. M. de Boislisle, *Chambre des comptes de Paris, pièces justificatives pour servir à l'histoire des premiers présidents (1506–1791)* (1873), p. 742, Nicolay to Necker, 25 November 1788.
[2] They did so notably on 28 April 1776, 16 April 1780, 17 March 1782 and 11 February 1787.

accountants and controllers, except the very minor ones, were subject to one of the Chambers. Even the Controller General of Finance, with a royal commission as an *ordonnateur*, took an oath before the Paris Chamber 'to obey the commandments of the Chamber and generally to do what a good officer is supposed to do in his office', and he undertook to send them the registers of the *Contrôle général* six months after the expiry of each fiscal year.[1] In the royal letters of provision conferring a venal office upon an accountant or controller, one of the Chambers invariably appeared as the instrument of the royal will, formally committed to receive the new officer's accounts in due course and to take any steps necessary to protect or to recover the Crown's funds in his charge. Here was where their real authority lay.

They passed judgement on the accounts of an officer partly for the sake of the office he held. Before an office was sold by the Crown or by one owner to another, the appropriate Chamber certified that the accounts for all of its fiscal years were settled or being dealt with in some way. This certificate was a brief history, often beginning with the very creation of the office and listing the prices at which it had changed hands and the full name of every owner. Accountants came and went but the office had a life of its own and a certain virtue which the Chamber of Accounts endeavoured to preserve. In the view of the Chamber the purchase price of the office was a warranty or surety bond posted by the accountant as a pledge of security. It is hard, indeed, to distinguish between the *cautionnement* which the salaried cashier or other employee paid over to the Crown as a simple surety bond and the *finance* which the venal office-holder paid. The main difference in practice was one of jurisdiction: the *Cour des aides* or perhaps the Royal Council on Finance would have judicial authority to deal with a dispute over a *cautionnement* but not over the *finance* of a venal office. This was a sum which the Chamber of Accounts was free to count to the credit of the accountant on his balance sheet. An accountant with a debt to the Crown was not supposed to recover his *finance* unless it exceeded the amount of the debt. Even if he gave up his office or lost it through a law abolishing it, the Crown did not refund his *finance* until he had submitted satisfactory accounts. Necker, for the many offices he abolished, adopted the policy of repaying one-third of the *finance* when the Chamber had received the accounts, one-third when it had judged them, and the remaining third when it had pronounced them cleared.

An account submitted to the Chamber was essentially two columns of entries, one of receipts (*recettes*) and the other of expenditures (*dépenses*),

---

[1] B.N., MS fr. 11012, fol. 77. Boislisle, *Chambre des comptes*, p. xxxiii.

divided into chapters of principal types.[1] The task of the Chamber was to verify the regularity of each entry and then, by comparing the total receipts with the total expenditures, to conclude whether the accountant was *en retard* (had received more than he had spent) or *en avance* (had spent more than he had received). The Chambers traditionally dealt with accounts in four distinct phases with titles which are roughly self-explanatory: *la présentation*, in January by the accountants and their attorneys; *l'examen*, in detail by an auditor to verify each entry against any receipt and to review the arithmetic; the *rapport*, by the auditor to one of the presidents of the Chamber; and the *jugement*, to pronounce the account acceptable, inadmissible, needing correction or otherwise. For all this the Chamber needed five other sets of papers as well as the account itself: a *bordereau* or summary of the totals of receipts and expenditures for each chapter in the account; the *état du Roi* signed by the Royal Council on Finance, a table of the receipts and expenditures the accountant had been instructed to make; the *état au vrai* or report to the Crown corresponding to the *état du Roi* and reporting on how the instruction had been carried out; the *acquits* or receipts signed by the people to whom he had paid Crown funds; and the previous account. All these papers were used at once in the final stage of the Chamber's examination, the *jugement*, as an official explained:

Five people were appointed for the settlement of the account: one had the *état du Roi*, another the *état au vrai*, the third the previous account, the fourth the new account, and finally the fifth had the receipts. It was in the margin of the account itself and the *bordereau* and next to each entry that the [final decision] was written. It was after having added up all these subsidiary entries that the totals of receipts and expenditures were fixed and the final state [of accounts] established.[2]

This process was evidently an inquiry into the accountant's management of his government account, but nothing more. The records put before the Chamber, even taken all together, did not reflect the state of the accountant's other business activities or the life of his caisse as a whole, and they were not intended to do so. They were essentially similar to the statements of account which a present-day banker sends to his clients; that is, they showed how the accountant had managed the various Crown funds entrusted to him, carrying out all royal instructions for collecting and spending, but they told nothing of whether the accountant was thriving or going bankrupt. Therefore, quite apart from the delays in accounting—necessarily a matter of years in some cases—the Chambers of Accounts were in no

---

[1] Coustant d'Yanville (H.), *Chambre des comptes de Paris, essais historiques et chronologiques, privilèges et attributions nobiliaires et armorial* (Paris, 1866–75), pp. 309 ff.

[2] Turpin, *Mémoire concernant la comptabilité des finances rédigé par l'agent du trésor public* (Paris, 1790), p. 11.

position to know and control the business activities of an accountant, even by putting all his accounts together, but that was not their objective. The Chambers saw themselves, not as the administrative supervisors of the accountants, but rather as judicial courts 'trying' each accountant for his management of Crown funds, acquitting the honest and the accurate, pressing the slow and lazy, correcting the mistaken and condemning the dishonest.

The Chambers watched their flocks of accountants at a certain distance, yet they had the most far-reaching authority to apprehend the suspect and to judge the guilty. They could order an accountant to cease his functions and put another in charge of his books. They could assign penalties for overdue accounts. When an accountant died they could affix seals to his accounts and, when they judged the King's interests sufficiently protected, could lift the seals again for the heir to the office. They could go so far as to sell the goods and liquid assets (*mobilier*) of an accountant to recover money due to the Crown (but not his real estate, which was the business of the *Cours des aides*). For theft or fraudulent misuse of royal funds the Chamber of Paris could join with the Parlement to declare the death penalty. How, we may ask, were the Chambers able to wield these powers to any purpose when their auditing methods told them virtually nothing about the current business activities of an accountant? The financial history of the reign of Louis XVI shows that a Chamber usually took action against an accountant only when a crisis in his affairs attracted its attention. If he died, or was absent for more than a few days, went bankrupt outright, suffered the loss of one of his offices through a reform, or cheated too obviously in his management of the money in his government account, then the Chamber was inclined to suspect him of debt to the Crown. It often brought the full weight of its authority down upon the unfortunate person and conducted a thorough investigation into his affairs which it had hitherto known only vaguely if at all. As Clavière and others were to point out in 1790, this was a system for punishing abuses, not for preventing them.[1]

Whenever the Chamber discovered a debt to the Crown, either in faulty accounts or in the balance sheet drawn up after an investigation, it put the recovery of the debt in the hands of the *Contrôleur général des restes*. This important official held a venal office in the Chamber—there was one in every Chamber—for the express purpose of taking whatever legal action was necessary to recover debts, and during the eighteenth century the Crown also commissioned the one in Paris to perform a similar function for the Royal Council with the title, *Contrôleur général des bons d'état du*

---

[1] See below, p. 301.

Conseil.[1] In Paris the emoluments of the last of them but one, Alexandre-Claude Basly, who took office on 6 September 1761, included a stipend of 3,000 livres, an expense account of 5,000 livres for employees and office costs, and a commission of 5% of whatever he collected. From 1781 he was assisted by Gérard-Maurice Turpin who took his place a few years later.[2] The task of the *Contrôleur général des restes* was made easier by the power of the Crown to put its claims on the estate of a bankrupt accountant before those of other creditors. If there was any money to be had from a financier's assets after a failure, the *Contrôleur général des restes* took it in the King's name, though not without a struggle sometimes with the *Cour des aides* acting on behalf of the accountant's family and creditors.

The pursuit was rigorous. For example, the liquidation of the estate of Jérôme-Robert Millin du Perreux, Receiver General of Finance for Rouen and Administrator of the Royal Lottery, began in October 1783, soon after his financial failure, with ushers and witnesses visiting the château of le Perreux, near Nogent, to seize it provisionally for the Crown and to draw up an inventory of all Millin's assets.[3] In this the Chamber and the *Cour des aides* were both present, the one for the business papers and other moveables and the other for the house and grounds, but at Rouen they happened to form a single court. The family were ordered to change nothing, and sometime later Madame Millin had a sharp exchange with the attorney general of the *Cour des aides* (Lombard) because her children had built a toy theatre on the estate. Meanwhile, the *Cour des comptes, aides et finances* of Rouen discovered a total debt of 757,088 livres and its Controller General of the Remains proceeded to sell Millin's assets: shares in a paper factory at Essonne, forests of timber, houses, lands and so on. Other creditors, such as Millin's associates in the papermaking business and Madame Millin's doctor, had to apply to the *Cour des comptes, aides*, etc. for reimbursement.[4]

The Millin case shows that in its action against an accountant, a Chamber of Accounts did not always have the field to itself. Other courts might intervene. If the courts of more than one province became involved, as in the

---

[1] From 4 May 1761 to 1774, however, the Crown revived an earlier practice of having a separate *Contrôleur des bons d'état du Conseil* who was Pierre-François Boucher. The *Contrôleur général des restes* for Montpellier was Jacques Granier from 1768, and from the same year Jean-Jacques-François Le Fèvre held this office in the *Cour des comptes of Rouen* and Jacques Ducreux the same office in the Chambre des comptes of Dauphiné (A.N., V¹ 441).

[2] A.N., F⁴ 1082; D x 2; and D vi 8, memorandum of Dufresne dated 24 February 1784.

[3] A.N., T 200¹².

[4] Among the associates in the paper concern were Armand Leclerc, Terray's *premier commis des finances* earlier, and his son, a Receiver General.

Millin case when the Paris courts stepped in after a little while because the accountant's business had been mainly in Paris, then the litigation might be very slow and complicated. Very commonly a *Cour des aides* proceeded against a bankrupt accountant as soon as the Chamber of Accounts did, and the two courts continued to work on the case, independently for the most part, until the royal council had assigned the case to the one or the other. Certain functions fell within the purview of only one court by common consent. The examination of the financial accounts was obviously the work of the Chambers and the liquidation of moveable goods including the office itself fell to it also, whereas the confiscation and sale of real estate fell within the jurisdiction of the *Cours des aides*. The creditors including tradesmen, business clients as well as friends who had lent him money, and the heirs in case of death, all filed their claims in the *Cour des aides*.

A case might come to the attention of the *Cour des aides* first, and occasionally a conflict flared up into a serious struggle, as for example in 1779 over the cases of two *Receveurs des tailles*, Charles-Nicolas Roland (Chartres) and René Goupil (Saumur). The Crown at first intervened in favour of the *Cour des aides* by a decision of 5 November, but on 16 April 1780 the Chamber submitted remonstrances to the King who ordered a commission of the *Conseil d'état privé* to investigate. This commission reported on 29 September in favour of the Chamber of Accounts. With that the conflict died down for a time.[1]

There were conflicts with other sovereign courts, too. Throughout the 1760s the Paris Chamber clashed often with the Parlement, as we may see in remonstrances sent to the King on 9 September 1770 to protest against the Parlement's resolution to break seals which the Chamber had affixed on the property of a bankrupt accountant's creditor.[2] The Chamber supposed this man to have taken part in a theft of Crown funds, and they wrote, 'The Parlement is the judge of ordinary theft, but not of thefts of royal funds.' The argument turned, in this and other cases, upon the definition of royal funds and however the argument ended, the conflict appears to have stopped when the Parlement was exiled in Maupéou's *coup d'état* of 1771. Another longstanding rivalry went on throughout most of the eighteenth century with the Treasurers of France, the magistrates in the twenty-four courts called Bureaux of Finance, who had jurisdiction over the royal

[1] A.N., 2741. The Commission, set up on 25 April 1780, consisted of three Councillors of State, Joly de Fleury, Taboureau des Réaux, Dufour de Villeneuve and a Master of Requests, de Menc.

[2] A.N., P 2827, fol. 290, the case of André-Jean-Baptiste Le Roux, commissioned by arrêts of 9 and 30 August 1763 to finish the accounts of the Receiver General of the Estates of Brittany. The creditor was Nezer.

domains.[1] The criminal court, the Châtelet, could also run foul of the Paris Chamber as it did, for instance, in 1788, and so could the *Cour des Monnaies*.[2]

These rivalries were signs of an underlying struggle by the Chambers of Accounts to defend what they regarded as their ancient rights, to extend their field of action and to fortify their social prestige. In this they resembled all the other sovereign courts and, indeed, every corporate group of the ancien régime. In seniority or ancient title, always a major claim to respect in Bourbon France, the Chamber of Paris came second in the hierarchy of sovereign courts, having been established since 1320, whereas the Parlement of Paris had sat since 1303, the *Cour des aides* since the end of the fourteenth century, the *Grand Conseil* since 1497 and the *Cour des Monnaies* since 1552.[3] The Chamber claimed to be one of the heirs of the medieval *curia régis*, like the Parlement, the *Cour des aides* and the *Grand Conseil*, and quite superior to the *Cour des Monnaies*, originally a scion of the Chamber itself and to the Bureaux of Finance created out of the medieval *trésoriers de France* in the sixteenth century. In general during the eighteenth century the men of the Paris Chamber of Accounts ranked, with those of the *Cours des aides* and the *Grand Conseil*, as somewhat lesser than the *parlementaires* but somewhat greater than the men of the *Cour des Monnaies*, the Bureaux of Finance, the *bailliages* and the Elections.[4]

As a social group, the Chambers of Accounts were a considerable part of the *noblesse de robe*. Their fees (*gages*) were listed in the Crown's expenses for 1776 as approximately one-tenth of the total fees of the magistrature as a whole.[5] In this list, the twelve Parlements cost very little more and the

---

[1] Boislisle, *Chambre des comptes*, pp. 1 and 737; Jean-Paul Charmeil, *Les Trésoriers de France à l'époque de la Fronde* (Paris, 1964).

[2] A.N., P 2516, Edict of September 1778, art. 7, increasing the powers of the Chamber at the expense of the *Cour des Monnaies*. Boislisle, *Chambre des comptes*, p. 1.

[3] François Bluche, *Les Magistrats de la Cour des Monnaies de Paris au XVIIIe siècle, 1715–1790*, p. 13.

[4] Bluche, *Les Magistrats du Grand Conseil au XVIIIe siècle, 1690–1791* (Paris, 1966), p. 42.

[5] The total figures were given as follows (A.N., 4 AP 190):

Gages de la Magistrature, 1776

	livres		livres
12 Parlements	1,443,624	Chancellerie	1,490,067
7 Chambres des comptes	1,014,995	Secrétaires du Roi du grand	
4 Cours des aides	328,250	collège	2,105,318
Cour des Monnaies de Paris	118,700	Bureaux des finances	1,837,344
Grand Conseil	165,000	Officiers des elections	594,261
Cour souveraine de Nancy	145,550	Bailliages	330,988
Châtelet de Paris	62,000	Gages attribués à différents	
Conseils souverains d'Artois,		offices	112,053
d'Alsace et de Perpignan	162,000	Officiers municipaux	569,322
		TOTAL	10,479,442

four *Cours des aides* very much less. About 36% of the fees allotted to the Chambers were paid to the magistrates of the Paris Chamber, and this seems to have been roughly proportional to their share of responsibilities in the Kingdom, for their jurisdiction extended over thirteen Generalities (out of thirty-four). There were altogether 284 members of the Paris Chamber —a *premier président*, 12 *présidents*, 78 *maîtres*, 38 *correcteurs*, 82 *auditeurs*, 29 *procureurs*, 30 *huissiers* and a few others—and the venal offices they held represented a total capital of 27,500,000 livres.[1] The value of these offices and the names of the old families which held them, Pasquier, de Machault, Bouvard de Fourquex, le Marié d'Aubigny, betoken a long-standing, respectable group of magistrates. Indeed, the family of the *premier président* Nicolay, had held the office since 1506. Some of their connections were famous rather than respectable: their office of *Receveur des épices* was held by Voltaire's father, François Arouet (1669), who when he died left his two sons and their fortune to the care of the *premier président*, and Voltaire's brother took the office in 1721.

The magistrates of the Chamber of Accounts were a very conservative force. Apart from their strong sense of tradition and their natural inclination to defend the hallowed system of caisses and accounts against reform, the magistrates of the Chamber had a very practical reason for resisting any change that might reduce the number of accountants. They were paid for each account they dealt with and the payments (*épices*) seem to have been large. In 1776 they charged fees amounting to 101,712 livres for the accounts of the Treasury, 360,000 livres for those of the Payers of the rentes, and 499,550 livres for the accounts of the Receivers General. Records for 1783 show that accounts for the General Farm earned them some 120,000 livres. That same year, the total *épices* for all the accounts received in the Chamber came to over 1½ million livres.[2] As we might well expect, the records of the Chamber show that its members opposed attempts to consolidate accounts.

They were conservative even in their most eager and appealing efforts to correct royal acts of despotism and, like the Parlements, they had a way of disguising their own interests as matters of vital importance to the nation. The royal *acquits de comptant* they branded as a fundamental evil in the financial system. These *acquits* were described by the Intendant of the Royal Treasury in 1790 as 'general *ordonnances* which included in composite amounts the sum of various particular *ordonnances* for expenditures

---

[1] Boislisle, *Chambre des comptes*, pp. 1 and lxii.

[2] A.N., 4 AP 190, 'Frais de régie'; Coustant d'Yanville, *Chambre des comptes*, pp. 279 and 288. Accounts in B.N., Coll. Joly de Fleury 1437, fol. 130 show the cost of accounts for the Treasury as 119,055 livres for 1783, of which 101,912 were paid to the Chamber of Accounts.

of all sorts which the King did not wish to expose to the knowledge and examination of the Chamber of Accounts'.[1] The amounts spent by *acquits de comptant* were increasingly large and the discord of the Crown and the Chamber grew with them:[2]

1770	.	.	.	67 million livres
1772	.	.	.	64 million livres
1773	.	.	.	82 million livres
1779	.	.	.	116,176,573
1784	.	.	.	111,784,000
1785	.	.	.	128 million livres

It would be easy to conclude from the Chamber's remonstrances that the magistrates opposed the *acquits de comptant* because they believed these concealed wasteful and illegitimate royal spending. It was, indeed, clear that the Crown used this accounting device for paying higher interest on loans than the 5·55% (denier dix-huit) which the Chambers permitted.[3] Yet the Chamber had two other strong reasons for objecting to the *acquits de comptant*. On the one hand the Crown's use of this device thwarted their ancient prerogatives; and on the other the Crown thereby deprived them of the *épices* which they would normally have collected for their auditing work.

There are other grounds, too, for doubting the sincerity of the Chamber of Accounts in its opposition to *acquits de comptant*. The Chamber had no right to challenge any payment order at all, and in practice restricted its work to verifying the figures, receipts and supporting documents. Therefore, its pretension to a parliamentary role in the kingdom's finances was a sham. Apart from defending its own interests over the *acquits de comptant* and in other matters, it appears to have asked the Crown no questions about spending; had it succeeded in persuading the Crown to abandon these *acquits*, the Chamber would in all probability never have challenged the Crown over the sums spent. After all, the objectives of the Chamber's accounting process were only to maintain the honesty and industry of the accountants, not to review the spending and revenue policies of the Ministers. To use the distinction of the time, it was the *comptabilité* and not the *ordonnancement* which properly fell to the supervision of the Chambers. In any event the delays in accounting amply show that the Chamber was never equipped to review government fiscal policy in a parliamentary way. The very system which the Chamber defended prevented the gathering of information that a parliamentary review would have required.

[1] A.N., D x 2, Dufresne to Camus, 9 March 1790.
[2] *Observations sur la comptabilité* (Paris, 1789) (B.N., Lf²⁷ 36), pp. 11 and 12; B.N. Nouv. acq. fr. 23617; and Marcel Marion, *Dictionnaire des institutions*.
[3] Boislisle, *Chambre des comptes*, p. xxxi.

There is evidence that most accounts reached the Chamber eight or ten years late. The Royal Treasury accounts for the fiscal years 1769 and 1770 were not ready until sometime after 1781, and those for the year 1781 not until 1790.[1] These delays were certainly not due to slackness on the part of the magistrates in the Chamber. The magistrates were lectured in 1778 by one of their senior members who accused many of avoiding service during the greater part of the year because of 'domestic affairs in some cases and the pleasures of youth in others',[2] but the main reasons for delay were inherent in the system which they so energetically defended. An accountant had to keep the books of each fiscal year open until he had made virtually all the receipts and payments set forth in the *état du Roi* for that year, and the Keeper of the Royal Treasury, for example, was making payments in 1777 on no less than fifteen years back to 1763.[3] Also, by an ancient tradition, the Chamber required accounts to be written out in words, not in Arabic numbers, and therefore copyists had to fill many unnecessary volumes.[4] The delays in this process, and the narrow objectives of it, became matters of bitter reproach in the revolution. Until then various ministers in the ancien régime tried to develop a supplementary system of accounting which would serve the Crown's need for information about its own spending processes.

As early as August 1669 Colbert had published an Edict ordering all accountants to report first to the Royal Council on Finance in the form of *états au vrai* before accounting to the Chamber of Accounts. The accounts were to reach the Chamber only with an *état au vrai* duly signed by the Royal Council. The Minister would not have to rely on the Chamber of Accounts for knowledge of the system he was directing. To receive and examine the *états au vrai* Colbert formed in his Department a *Bureau de la vérification des états au vrai* which still functioned, more or less, when Louis XVI came to the throne, but under the supervision of an Intendant of Finance, Lefèvre d'Ormesson, whose family had been in charge of it, as

---

[1] B.N., Coll. Joly de Fleury 1443, 'Mémoire sur le trésor royal et sur les comptes que rendent les gardes du trésor royal', MS by Moreau de Beaumont (1781), fol. 233; and A.N., D x 2, Dufresne to Camus, 16 March 1790.

[2] A.N., P 2740, dated 2 January 1778.

[3] A.N., F⁴ 1082, 'Dépouillement des feuilles du trésor royal'.

[4] Théodore Vernier, *Rapport du comité des finances sur l'organisation de la trésorerie nationale* (1791) (B.M., F.R. 502), p. 29. Parchment was used until a Declaration of 4 October 1772 which ordered the use of paper. The accounts of the past filled four great deposits in Paris which, even after the partial destruction of one of them by fire in 1737, yielded in 1793 over 37,000 pounds of parchment for the revolutionary armed forces and a much greater quantity sold for 443,017 livres. Only 462 volumes were kept, though some of the rest found its way back into archives. (Coustant d'Yanville, *Chambre des comptes*, p. 278.)

well as others, for three generations, since 1720.[1] Except for a brief spell in 1775–6, Lefèvre d'Ormesson kept the direction of this bureau until he became Controller General of Finance in 1783. It is evident from a report he submitted to Joly de Fleury, newly made Minister in 1781, that the bureau for *états au vrai* had long ceased to serve Colbert's original purposes.

Monsieur d'Ormesson will not conceal [he wrote] that his grandfather, his father and he himself have always up to the present signed the *états* [*au vrai*] without examining them, as things of pure formality, except for the little and rarely important litigation to which these *états* gave rise over the refunding of fines on the late submission of accounts...[2]

What prompted these remarks was an attempt by Jacques Necker to revive the accounting process within the Department so that he might have some knowledge and control of the business being done for the Crown by the accountants. To attempt this was to threaten the prerogatives of the Chamber of Accounts and the Chamber became, indeed, one of the conservative forces hostile to Necker's reforming policies.

The Chamber especially disliked Necker's policy of establishing *régies* for royal business that had hitherto been leased to tax farmers and other syndicates of businessmen. The *régie* was a direct management by royal administrative agents (*régisseurs*) who worked on behalf of the Crown, drawing whatever funds they needed for expenses only with royal permission and paying all returns over to the Crown. *Régisseurs* normally worked for salaries rather than for profits, although, when they worked in a mixed system called a *régie intéressée*, they also received a proportion of any profits earned. In eighteenth-century books of reference, the *régie* was defined as the opposite of a farm; men in public life commonly favoured one or the other and debated which was the best. One of the most vital differences, which books then as now did not always make clear, was that farms were accountable to the Chamber of Accounts whereas *régies* were accountable to the Royal Council on Finance, i.e. the Department of Finance. To take the business of tax farmers and put it *en régie* was therefore to rob the Chamber of Accounts of some accounting business, and at the same time to increase the direct jurisdiction of the Finance Department. Necker did this on a massive scale during his first ministry (1777–81) when he created the *Régie générale des aides*, the *Administration générale des domaines* and the

---

[1] B.N., Coll. Joly de Fleury 1448, printed *Notice historique sur l'origine du bureau de la vérification des états-au-vrai*, 4 pp.; and manuscript memorandum of Lefèvre d'Ormesson, 'Etats au vrai de tous les comptables', dated 25 June 1781; and fol. 88, *Arrêt du conseil*, dated 10 August 1777.

[2] *Loc. cit.*

Recette générale. The Chamber of Accounts and many financial interests then understood, better than some modern historians since, what a blow this was to the system of caisses and accountants. In this as in other matters, the Chamber being a veritable bastion of the system was fundamentally opposed to Necker and his policies.

When the Chamber of Accounts talked of reform and of abuses, it meant something quite different from Terray, Turgot, Necker and the reforming officials whose thoughts and plans heralded the changes to occur in the French revolution. When Turgot was received by the Chamber to take his oath of office, the First President said to him in a ceremonial address:

> You will find in the magistrates of this august company enlightenment, zeal and disinterest; their functions associate them with your work. Every time someone has wanted to despoil or to damage their jurisdiction, he has unfortunately given rise to nothing but abuses.[1]

Again and again through the reign, the Chamber referred to any interference with its own accounting process as 'abuses'. Ministerial attempts to have accountants report more often and more fully to the Department of Finance, to save failing accountants from disaster, to sort out major bankruptcies by commissions of the Royal Council, to abolish offices and consolidate the accounts pertaining to them—all these drew forth magisterial complaints and advice to the Ministers and sometimes remonstrances to the King. In the chorus of the *révolte nobiliaire* could be heard voices from the Chambers of Accounts, not the trumpetings of the *parlementaires* or the bass notes of provincial noblemen, but hesitant murmurs of men with a cause already lost. On 4 February 1789 they named a commission to draw up 'a plan of claims concerning the multiple abuses which have been the unfortunate and fertile seed of the decay in the finances and the ruin of the State'.[2] What they saw as abuses appear in retrospect as the beginnings of great reforms.

---

[1] B.N., MS fr. 11012, fol. 71, dated 31 August 1774.
[2] Boislisle, *Chambre des comptes*, p. 743.

PART 2
THE BUREAUCRATIC
REVOLUTION

7
THOUGHTS OF REFORM

THERE WAS little practical and informed writing about the central administration of finance until after the revolutionary events of 1788-9. Then a large number of deputies to the National Assembly and members of the public at large gradually educated themselves in matters of public finance through the inquiries of legislative committees and the compilation of reports by executive officials. Books, pamphlets and printed debates among the politicians and others came gradually to reflect the issues of administrative reform with some clarity and detail; but in the decade before the revolution it was quite otherwise. There was, of course, no lack of public interest in the financial difficulties of the Crown, and these were among the practical matters that drew the attention of many thoughtful Frenchmen, as Daniel Mornet tells us, after the publication of *L'Esprit des lois* (1748) and the early volumes of the *Encyclopédie* (from 1751) and especially after the disasters of the Seven Years War.[1] Yet writers tended to fasten almost entirely on the mere budgetary balance of revenue and expenditure. The Crown's problem, as most of them saw it, and as most historians have tended to see it since, was to find more money and to spend less, although the delicate questions of government expenditure were broached less readily than matters of revenue. Hence, most of the pamphlets and treatises of the time are about the systems of taxation, ingenious tax substitutes or supplements, ways of dealing with the debt, court spending and the like. About the organs of the central administration there was conspicuously little. Even on those subjects which writers did discuss they quickly exhausted their knowledge. 'It is impossible not to deplore the injustice of popular ideas on all these subjects', Mathon de la Cour wrote in 1788 in the preface to his published collection of accounts.[2] Calonne heaped scorn on what pamphleteers at his time were writing about financial questions and it would be difficult to disagree with his conclusion.[3] Many books and tracts appealed to the heart

---

[1] Daniel Mornet, *Les Origines intellectuelles de la révolution française* (Paris, 1933), p. 117.
[2] Mathon de la Cour, *Collection des comptes rendus* (Lausanne, 1788), p. iv.
[3] *Réponse de Monsieur de Calonne à l'écrit que Monsieur Necker a publié en avril 1787*, pp. 129 and 365.

with patriotism, reforming zeal and a sense of injustice; very few showed knowledge or practical sense.

The main reason, no doubt, was that the royal government had always been secretive about its finances and time and again had forbidden public discussion in print of financial questions. No government accounts were published until 1781 when Necker's *Compte rendu au Roi* appeared and it proved to be far from reliable. The last detailed explanation of the financial system was the sixteenth-century work of Jean Hennequin with supplements by the editors of later editions.[1] Certain books of the eighteenth century, notably the writings of John Law, Véron de Fortbonnais, Jean Melon and Moreau de Beaumont, commented with authority on the financial administration but with little information about the accountants and their caisses or the system of short-term credit. The physiocrats and many others drew public attention to economic theory where practical questions of financial administration seldom entered in, and this is another reason for the general ignorance of public finance. Economists of a dogmatic cast of mind, Dr Quesnay, the elder Mirabeau and their disciples wrote interminably about their own doctrine of taxation—a single tax on agricultural production—and encouraged a great many people to confine their thoughts within rather narrow sectarian limits.[2] Yet the ordinary observer of public affairs hardly needed the distractions of physiocracy or the discouragements of the Crown to keep him from studying the institutions of public finance, for these were forbidding technical subjects at best. 'Voltaire used to say', remarked a writer in 1789, 'that the public does not properly understand a slightly complicated arrêt on a financial matter until six months after it is published.'[3] We look far indeed to find writers who displayed precise knowledge of the financial system and its defects.

There were nevertheless a few who published thoughts both critical and pertinent. They were all officials of one kind or another and this goes far to explain their competence in the subject, though not their inclination to discuss it. In a literary or intellectual sense, none of them could hold our attention even for a moment, but they stand out as practical men with systematic thoughts of reform. They are examples of a large group of reformers and critics which cannot be identified either with the *philosophes* and physiocrats, largely ignorant of the financial administration, or with the main body of financiers and officials who understood the system and believed

---

[1] Jean Hennequin, *Le Guidon général des finances* (Paris, 1585); another edition with the notes of Vincent Gelée (1595); and another revised by Sébastien Hardy (1644).

[2] See the works of Georges Weulersse, *Le Mouvement physiocratique en France* (Paris, 1910), 2 vols.

[3] M. J. D. Martin, *Etrennes financières*, première année (Paris, 31 January 1789), p. 243.

in it. Necessarily rather specialized, these critics and reformers most often dealt only with one or two particular aspects of administrative reform. Only those men who criticized the system of caisses and accountants, the credit system, the bureaux of administration and other aspects of the central administration need take our attention in this chapter.

One of the most remarkable was Louis-César-Alexandre Dufresne de Saint Léon (1751–1836) who began a career in the service of one of the Keepers of the Royal Treasury, Savalette de Langes, in 1777 and on 2 October 1786 became a *premier commis* with a salary of 10,000 livres a year and six men under his direction.[1] Meanwhile, he had begun to write on the subject of public credit because, he wrote later, he felt 'bored with hearing credit discussed with that insignificant lightness with which people in Paris talk about everything'.[2] He read widely, he tells us, in the works of Adam Smith, Véron de Fortbonnais, Jacques Necker, Pancton (*Métrologie ou traité des mesures, poids et monnoies*), David Hume, abbé Raynal, Isaac de Pinto, the Encyclopedists and others; and at the same time he had the benefit of his own official experience and that of acquaintances such as Armand Le Clerc, who had been Terray's *Premier commis des finances*.[3] On many matters of public finance Dufresne de Saint Léon speaks with authority. Some of his writings he published in 1784 as a book, *Etudes sur le crédit public*, if printing a single copy for his own use and 'accidentally' allowing the printer to run off a few more copies can be called publication. The manuscript of an unpublished essay fell into Necker's hands, and when Necker returned to the Department of Finance in August 1788 he invited Saint Léon to be *premier commis* of the *Bureau des dépêches* at a salary of 12,000 livres.[4] It was Saint Léon who went to escort Necker back to the capital after the seizure of the Bastille on 14 July 1789. A conservative and royalist in the revolution, like so many of these administrative reformers, Dufresne de Saint Léon eventually emigrated until the first empire when

[1] He was born in Paris on 15 April 1751 and died there on 11 January 1836; married Madeleine-Sophie Vanrobais. At the beginning of 1791, he was appointed to head the *Direction général de la liquidation*. A member of the *Feuillants* and *Société de 1789*, he was arrested and interrogated on 22 November 1792 and on the list of émigrés from 15 prairial year II until 9 Fructidor, and his property, including the Château de Joeurs near Etampes, was not released until 11 Fructidor year III. By an *ordonnance* of 14 October 1818, he was granted a retirement pension of 2,007 francs effective 30 June 1818 for service totalling 31 years, 8 months and 29 days. By the time he died he was a *Conseiller d'état honoraire* and a *Chevalier de la Légion d'Honneur*. (A.N., F^{IA} 565; D XI 2, letter of Delessart to Camus, 23 Dec. 1790; T 1617; *Bulletin des Lois*, 1818; *Almanach royal* (1817), p. 157 and (1818), p. 191.)

[2] Dufresne de Saint Léon, *Etudes sur le crédit public* (Paris, 1784), p. 1.

[3] *Ibid.*, p. 363.

[4] Dufresne de Saint Léon, *Etude de crédit public et des dettes publiques* (Paris, 1824). In a *note préliminaire* he writes of his life and of his previous book on public credit.

127

he returned and took up a financial post as secretary to the *Commission de liquidation des créances anglaises* which he held until his death.

A very different career and other reforming interests are revealed in three books with copious autobiographical notes by Charles-Nicolas Roland. The earliest work, a *Mémoire au Roi Louis XVI en dénonciation d'abus d'autorité* (London, April 1784), is the story of Roland's life as *caissier* to the Receiver General for Orléans, Watelet, for twenty-three years, and *Receveur des tailles* at Chartres concurrently for the last eight of those years, until his career came to a dramatic end in 1779 when he became embroiled in a quarrel with his Receiver General and suffered five years of complicated legal prosecution for bankruptcy. In 1784 he fled to England and then went out to Cape Breton Island for two years as Royal Storekeeper under the English governor. The events of 1789 provoked him to write two books on matters of finance and food supply and soon brought him back to Paris, now sixty years old but passionately interested in seeing the financial administration reformed.

Roland's reforming interests appear to have begun under Turgot and Necker, well before his personal disasters began. In his earliest book he tells how he met Turgot, accepted a minor post under him on 15 October 1774 and then gave him opinions on some financial projects.[1] A few years later, during Necker's first ministry, Roland worked out a plan to abolish the Receivers General of Finance—or so he tells us in 1784—and let Necker know of it in January 1780, not long before the Minister put such a plan into effect. Whether or not Roland was right about this, he believed that Necker had followed his plan, 'an operation which I regarded and still regard as the most essential for the improvement of the State's revenues and for the comfort of the people, especially the poorest class. . .'[2] Roland believed, furthermore, that the Receivers General and the Chamber of Accounts had marked him as their 'future destroyer' and for this reason pursued him with interrogations and imprisonments for the next five years. Considering the detail and the artlessness of Roland's story, and its similarity to others at the time, I am inclined to believe it, but this is not necessary to establish Roland as an expert and serious critic of the financial system. His views and plans are clear enough in the book of 1784.

Another unusually well-informed critic of the financial administration was also an accountant, a provincial Treasurer for the Marine and Colonies posted to La Rochelle. This was Simon-Joseph-Louis Bonvalet des

---

[1] *Mémoire au Roi* (1784), p. 109. This was at a salary of 6,000 livres a year, and by arrangement with Albert.

[2] *Ibid.*, p. 44.

Brosses (1742–1800).[1] In December 1769 he retired from his office and spent much time thereafter working out a scheme for a public bank and trying to interest the government in it. Of his various publications and reforming efforts, those bearing upon financial reform he finally published in 1789, but he then claimed to have been developing them for twenty years.[2] There is no reason to doubt the claim—Mahy de Cormeré and others had done the very same thing—and we may, I think, properly count him among the pre-revolutionary thinkers and planners. Des Brosses spoke to Turgot about his ideas, he tells us, and later sent his work to Calonne's secretary, Acarias de Serionne, who apparently responded by arranging to have him exiled to a distance of more than fifty leagues from Paris. Calonne personally approved of this severe treatment, very probably because des Brosses was a penetrating critic of the system of accountants and caisses which Calonne was sustaining and defending.

Three other knowledgeable critics of the financial system, of whom less is known, were Louis-Henri Duchesne de Voiron, who served as a *premier commis* in the bureaux of Trudaine de Montigny and then as Intendant General of the Household for the comtesse de Provence;[3] Stanislas Mittié, sometime Controller and Travelling Receiver for the Domains Administration in the Generality of Paris;[4] and Jacques-Philibert Rousselot de Surgy, sometime clerk in the Department of Finance and the principal author of the *Encyclopédie méthodique. Partie finance* (1783–7) which reproduced the preambles of Necker's major reforming laws and also long passages from his early books, together with comments of explanation and approval.

[1] Born on 19 March 1742 in La Rochelle and died on 16 June 1800 in Charenton (Seine), Simon-Joseph-Louis Bonvalet des Brosses was the son of Jean-Jacques Bonvallet, Receiver of the *décimes* at La Rochelle, and Marie-Marguerite Gazeau. There was a paternal uncle, Pierre-Alexis-Joseph Bonvalet des Brosses and a maternal cousin, Simon-Marie Billaud, *avocat au parlement*. Among his papers are various manuscript writings including a 'Discours sur le commerce prononcé à Lille le 20 Novembre 1782', and a 'Plan général, caisse de commerce' dated 23 April 1785 and which reproduces part of the book published in 1789, and some autobiographical notes showing that he composed his first study of a *banque royale* in response to an invitation from an influential person called de Rozambourg who, he claims, showed it to d'Aiguillon, de Boines, Terray and Foulon. Later he showed it to Turgot, Necker, a certain Bréard, Fourqueux, Dupont, Villier de Terrage, Abeille. It was shortly after Abeille had advised 'patience, courage and discretion' that Bonvalet was banished from Paris and went to live in Lille (A.N., T 1270–1; and F⁷ 5846; and my article, 'Government and Private Interests in New France', *Canadian Public Administration* (Toronto, June 1967), p. 251).
[2] Bonvalet des Brosses, *Moyens de simplifier la perception et la comptabilité des deniers royaux* (1789) (B.N., Lb39 7248) contains some personal recollections.
[3] A.N., Papers of Lefèvre d'Ormesson, 144 AP 133, dossier 6, memoirs of 29 May 1787 written by Duchesne. Also, *Observations sur un projet d'administration présenté en 1787* (1 November 1791) (B.N., Rp 7613).
[4] Mittié, *Plan de suppression des fermiers généraux, des receveurs generaux des finances...* (Paris, 1789) (A.N., D VI 1).

129

Jacques Necker and another high-ranking figure, Auget de Montyon (1733–1820), deserve to be in a class by themselves because they reflected on the fundamentals of public administration with such perception that we may justly regard them as precursors of French administrative thinkers in the nineteenth century. These two had very different backgrounds and although they were fairly well acquainted they were not friends and Auget de Montyon was one of Necker's harshest critics. If we confine our attention to their main ideas on administration, however, we cannot help but find them remarkably similar. Furthermore they stand out from the others I have mentioned by virtue of their high positions in the administration. Of Necker's career there is little to add to what has long been common knowledge. What must be stressed is that he had brilliant insights into the fundamental shortcomings of the financial administration, insights which are necessarily lost on almost anyone who reads his books out of the proper context. De l'administration des finances de la France (1784) must seem trivial if we interpret the financial problems of the ancien régime, as most historians do, in the terms of Turgot's economic theories or in the terms of Calonne's proposals for tax reform.[1] Where others of his time saw economic and revenue problems, Necker saw problems in public administration. Where many historians see only impending social and political revolution, there is evidence of an administrative revolution in which Necker played a part. When the successive governments of the revolution reformed the royal bureaucracy to serve as the civil service of modern France, they were putting into effect general ideas which few men had written down and none but Necker had expressed both in writing and in practical reforms.

The careers of Necker and Auget de Montyon contrast sharply. Whereas Necker came to Paris as a total stranger, foreigner, commoner and protestant, and twice became Minister of Finance without any other official experience, Auget de Montyon never became Minister but had a long and varied career in the higher ranks of the financial administration.[2] It would be difficult to find a person with stronger connections in the official world of eighteenth-century France than de Montyon. His grandfather had held office in the Bureau of Finance for Paris, his father an office of maître in the Paris Chamber of Accounts. His mother was a member of the Pajot family,

[1] J. F. Bosher, 'Jacques Necker et l'état moderne', Rapport annuelle de la société historique de Canada (1963), pp. 162–75.
[2] This was Antoine-Jean-Baptiste-Robert Auget de Montyon, and there is a very good biography of him by Louis Guimbaud (Paris, 1909). My information comes from it and from the works of François Bluche, and from the Montyon papers, Archives de l'Assistance Publique, Paris.

daughter of a *secrétaire du Roi* and related to Receivers General, magistrates in the Parlement and the Grand Conseil, and Intendants in the provinces. His father's first wife had been the daughter of a Treasurer of *Ponts et Chaussées* and his half-sister married Bouvard de Fourqueux, Intendant of Finance, magistrate in the *Comité contentieux des finances* and Controller General for a few days in May 1787. Auget de Montyon lived with the Bouvard de Fourqueux in their Paris house for more than twenty-five years and during that time their daughters, his nieces, married prominent officials, the elder, Trudaine de Montigny, an Intendant of Finance, and the younger, Maynon d'Invau, a Controller General of Finance. With these connections and a comfortable family fortune, Auget de Montyon had no difficulty in becoming a lawyer in the Châtelet, a Master of Requests, an Intendant in the provinces of Auvergne, Provence and then La Rochelle, a Councillor of State (1776), Chancellor to the comte d'Artois, and a member of the Royal Council on Finance (June 1788). But there was another side of his life which helps to explain his administrative thought.

As a young man Auget de Montyon began to frequent the salon of Madame Dupin, the wife of a cultivated Farmer General, and there he met Mably, Raynal and especially Montesquieu. From this beginning he went on to visit the salons of Madame du Deffand, Mademoiselle de Lespinasse and Madame Necker and so made the acquaintance of many other *philosophes*, including d'Alembert and Helvétius, but his ideas were influenced by Montesquieu more than by any other. Not impressed by either Rousseau or Turgot, whom he wrote about rather scathingly, he remained attached to the *L'Esprit des lois* which shaped his intellectual development with positive ideas of government. These thoughts and his official experience led him to reflect a good deal on what he termed 'the science of administration'. Needless to say, his reflections seem to have no connection with the main body of political thought in eighteenth-century France, but they have something of the spirit of the German cameralists of his own time and of such nineteenth-century Frenchmen as Claude-Joseph Lalouette[1] and the marquis d'Audiffret.[2] Seen in the revolutionary generation he appears politically reactionary and in the Restoration a quaint old-fashioned monarchist. He had been best-known for his philanthropy and for two books, one a rather harsh essay on the Ministers of Finance of the ancien régime and the other a remarkably precocious demographic study published in 1778

[1] Ex-sous-Préfet, member of the legislature, author of *Eléments de l'administration pratique* (Paris, 1812) (B.N., R 6342).
[2] Financial reformer, and author of *Système financier de France* (enlarged second edition (Paris, 1854), 4 vols.).

under an assumed name, Moheau.[1] What brings him to our attention now is the draft of an unpublished manuscript to be found among his papers, apparently written sometime during the reign of Louis XVI before the revolution and entitled, *Des agents de l'administration.*[2]

In this unfinished work Montyon set forth some general ideas about public administration. By this expression he understood more or less what many people understand by it today: government surveillance of public health, the growth and movement of the population, the food supply, trade, agriculture, security, the arts, finance and all matters of common interest. 'The art of administration', he wrote, 'is to combine the general interest with special interests, to make the corps of the state serve the happiness of individuals and to have individuals serve the force and prosperity of the state.' He held the single word, *administration*, in its widest possible sense, to mean the direction or command of other men, and how far his ideas went beyond this platitude may be judged from the section 'De la décision', which reads like a chapter on 'decision-making' in an American textbook of today, or from the section, 'De la langue, du stile [sic], du ton de l'administration', in which he recommends brevity and practical commonsense in lines like: 'I have said to more than one Controller General that a Minister should have a pen only for signing.'[3] He was original, among French writers of his time at least, in his beliefs that administrators should have to pass written examinations and that administration should be not only an art to be practised but also a subject of study with its own peculiar ordering of facts and ideas and its own method. Others were shortly to treat administration as a special subject, Roederer, Barnave, Lalouette, to mention only a few, but they all did so during the revolution or later when the fundamental ideas of the subject had become obvious to all thoughtful observers. Few indeed took up those ideas before the revolution,

---

[1] This work, *Les Recherches et considérations sur la population de la France*, was ascribed to Montyon by Guimbaud and more recently by Edmond Esmonin, 'Montyon, véritable auteur des *Recherches et considérations sur la population*, de Moheau', *Population* (April–June 1958), pp. 269–82. The work of Montyon as an agronomist is the subject of a study in Pierre Léon, ed., *Structures économiques et problèmes sociaux du monde rural dans la France du Sud-Est* (Bibl. de la Fac. des Lettres de Lyon, fasc. XIII) (Paris, 1966).

[2] Archives de l'Assistance Publique de Paris, 3 rue des Minimes, papers of Auget de Montyon, carton 7, a pile of loose papers about an inch thick, and unnumbered. Henceforth referred to as Montyon, *Des agents*.

[3] Or again of formalities in letters, 'In social relations it is perhaps not a bad thing that one man assure another that he feels affection and consideration for him, that he has the honour to be his obedient servant, attached, humble, respectful; all these polite lies, these insignificant exaggerations, are at least the signs of feelings which ought to bind men together. But in the discussion of affairs what does it matter that a man loves or does not love, is or is not a servant? Dans une lettre d'affaires les compliments sont aussi étrangers que dans une lettre de change.'

as Montyon did.[1] 'There has been a lack of progress in the science of administration,' he thought, 'because up to the present this method has not been followed. Some have known only facts, others have had opinions only according to reasoning and abstract ideas. No one has married facts and reasoning, no one has raised facts to principles.' But Montyon believed that progress in the knowledge and practice of public administration was imminent. 'The time for reform of the administration seems to have arrived...' and in another place, 'I believe I can predict a reform and an improvement in the principles of administration.' When he came to the point of suggesting the nature of the expected improvement, Montyon put forward an idea that was probably the most influential of all ideas in the administrative reforms to come:

Every power whose object is not determined, whose limits are not set, and whose abuses are not controlled must become oppressive. Human nature is too vicious or at least too weak to permit men to be put in the hands of other men. For the happiness and safety of the King's subjects, therefore, we must introduce the balance of powers in the administration as in the political constitution... *we must apply to the composition of social power the general rules of mechanics*, introduce forces and counterforces, an action and a resistance, a great impulsion without excessive rapidity, and an ordered movement.

Few men can have stated so deliberately the idea that the central administration ought to be reconstructed according to mechanical principles, but in a cruder form the idea was already widespread.

The general notion of administrative bodies as machines was neither new nor original. Colbert had used the word 'machine' to describe the royal councils;[2] as early as 1704 the Farmers General had used it for the tax farms;[3] and in 1758 Cardinal Bernis had described a prime minister as someone who would alone direct 'all the springs of the machine';[4] in 1769 Jean-Baptiste-Bertrand Durban published a book, *Essais sur les principes des finances*, using the machine in a series of metaphors to describe the financial administration. Very probably this image had supplanted the older image of an organization as a body or organism with head, heart and limbs as a result of the writings of Descartes, Newton and others in the seventeenth century who taught thinking Europeans to envisage the universe as a machine. During the eighteenth century the mechanical image

[1] Roederer, *Œuvres*, vol. VI, pp. 2 and 557; Barnave, *Œuvres* (1843), vol. II, p. 98; Lalouette, *Eléments de l'administration pratique* (Paris, 1872).
[2] Pierre Clément, ed., *Lettres, instructions et mémoires de Colbert* (Paris, 1863), vol. II, p. 55.
[3] J. F. Bosher, *The Single Duty Project* (London, 1964), p. 99.
[4] Marcel Marion, *Histoire financière de la France*, vol. I, p. 188. See, for the growth of the notion of mechanism in general, Jean Erhard, *L'Idée de la nature*.

had grown richer by the spreading of Newton's ideas and of inventions, and by the interest they aroused in the *Encyclopédie* and elsewhere. The concept of the machine became gradually more fertile, capable of stirring the imagination and suggesting fresh possibilities of organization. In the reign of Louis XVI the image developed, perhaps unconsciously, into a source of criticisms and suggestions for administrative reform or (to state the case more cautiously) it influenced critics of the financial system.

To Auget de Montyon the machine obviously suggested continuous and impersonal process. He argues, for instance, that all the heads of bureaux in a government department should be regularly called together to discuss the work of the department. They would form, he writes, 'a kind of special council without form, without title, a repository of principles and errors in finance which might prevent a change of Minister from giving the political machine one of those blows which can arrest its movement or disturb its organization'.[1] To Dufresne de Saint Léon, as to many others, the machine suggested virtues of unity and simplicity, and he would have consolidated the management of the rentes in order to reduce 'the complications of that machine'.[2] Again it is precision and accurate operation which seem to be in Mittié's mind when he refers to 'the multiplicity of the driving springs and the corresponding wheels in that vast machine'.[3] To the twentieth-century mind most, not to say all, of these ideas can be expressed in the word 'efficiency', the main quality of a good machine, and this was the sum total of what Necker and other administrative reformers meant by such terms as 'order', 'uniformity', 'economy', 'regularity' and 'simplicity'. These words abound in Necker's works together with arguments in favour of rational organization and fixed principles of operation which, like Nature's laws, would not admit of privileged exceptions or special favours.[4] Like most administrators of the time, he denounced 'the spirit of system', by which he meant the doctrines of the Physiocrats and any others opposing empirical government with *a priori* systems, but that was an altogether different argument. He brought to bear what he called 'the spirit of order and economy' in criticizing the financial administration.[5] These terms and the ideas they expressed were to find echo again and again during the revolution in lines like the following by the editor of the famous and influential *Moniteur*: 'Thus order puts things and persons in their places;

[1] Montyon, *Des agents*, MS.
[2] Dufresne de Saint Léon, *Etudes sur le crédit public* (1784), p. 88.
[3] Mittié, *Plan de suppression*, p. 2.
[4] Necker, *De l'administration des finances de la France* (1784), vol. II, pp. 428, 431, 443; vol. III, pp. 141, 363.
[5] *Ibid.*, vol. II, p. 395.

everyone has no more work than he can do; all is simplified and there is an economy of men, time and money.'[1]

The machine image tended to change the accepted place of common clerks and secretaries in the scheme of things. They no longer seemed to be mere appendages like domestic servants or harmless scribes. For good or ill, according to the writer's point of view, they were becoming integral parts of 'machines' in which the smallest pieces were essential to the functioning of the whole. Auget de Montyon was prepared to devote a chapter to them because, he said, they are such necessary 'administrative instruments' that good ones can bring success to the weakest administrator and bad ones can bring to nothing the decisions of even the most enlightened, or else so overload him with work that he will lose sight of his true objectives.[2] Whereas de Montyon went on at length to explain and even to praise these 'mechanical beings', another writer of the time, L. S. Mercier, made them a subject of mockery in his journal of intelligent gossip, *Le Tableau de Paris*. Mercier suggested that the inventor, Vaucanson, might invent a mechanical 'commis-scribe...holding his paper straight before him, ruling his registers, dipping his pen in the ink-well, writing and even calculating a little', and the Farmers General might purchase them by the dozen.[3] But in another place Mercier discusses more seriously the power of the common clerks when organized.

Bureaucracy, [he writes] is a word created in our time to designate in a concise and forceful manner the extensive power of mere clerks who in the various bureaux of the ministry are able to implement a great many projects which they forge themselves or quite often find in the dust of the bureaux, or adopt by taste or by whim.[4]

His intention is not to mock them, he goes on to explain, for they all have in their minds some of the precious quality of order which may temper the extravagance of grander men than they. He merely wishes to record the prodigious influence of ministerial bureaux recognized by the common people in creating the new word 'bureaucracy'.

It was only a short step from these reflections to the view that common clerks, properly organized, might very well do their work without the noble magistrates to command them. In administration, bureaucracy offered an alternative to aristocracy. John Law, commoner and foreigner like Necker, had observed many years earlier, during his time as Finance Minister, that so long as his vast organization employed only common clerks it had been

[1] *La Réimpression de l'ancien moniteur*, vol. VI, p. 187.
[2] Montyon, *Des agents*, MS.
[3] Vol. X, pp. 11–14.　　　　[4] *Ibid.*, vol. IX, p. 57.

successful and had functioned with 'order, clarity and simplicity'.[1] As soon as important and influential people had been named to take command, however, the organization had been more and more hampered by 'awkwardness, suspicion, private arrangements and confusion'. In the 1780s others were arguing that magistrates were unnecessary. Mittié believed that directors, *premiers commis, chefs* and *sous-chefs* could perfectly well administer the financial bureaux by themselves with only the Minister to command them.[2] Necker, too, thought salaried clerks with strong ministerial leadership quite capable of doing the work of the accountants and other venal officers, and he reported that he and his former *Premier commis des finances*, Bertrand Dufresne, had once agreed that Dufresne was doing more work than all of the forty-eight Receivers General put together.[3] In Necker's view a financial system composed entirely of salaried clerks would have only one major defect: the 'protection' of clerks by the nobles and the wealthy was so general in France that merit would soon become a minor factor in the selection and promotion of employees. Private interests would continually interfere with public administration as they had always done in the past.

One of the main ideas apparent in much writing on administrative reform is that government or public service ought to be more clearly distinguished from the realm of private affairs. In many people's minds the general welfare deserved to be better guarded against private or local interests. 'When the administration is directed by wise principles', Montyon wrote, 'it will have the strength not to nominate to a vacant post, and it will prove that it does not give posts to persons, but persons to posts.'[4] Pursuing a different line of thought, Bonvalet des Brosses defined a proper system of financial administration as one in which employees should have no other employment but devote all their working hours to the public service. He believed public service and private employment to be incompatible.[5] In another place he argued for a clear and rigorous distinction between public and private funds so that the *deniers royaux* would be treated as government funds from the moment they entered one of the official caisses and would not be used by accountants and cashiers for their own private purposes. To show that the accountants regarded such funds as

---

[1] John Law, *Œuvres complètes*, ed. Paul Harsin (Paris, 1934), 3 vols., vol. III, 'Histoire des finances pendant la Régence', p. 332.

[2] Mittié, *Plan de suppression*.

[3] Necker, *De l'administration* (1784), vol. I, pp. 106 and 139.

[4] Montyon, *Des agents*, MS.

[5] Bonvalet des Brosses, *Moyens de simplifier* (1789), p. 11. Cf. Necker, *De l'administration*, vol. I, p. 105; and also P. J. Malpart, *Plan d'administration des finances* (London, 1787), p. 10.

their own and mingled them with other funds Bonvalet told the story of an experience he had had while working as a Marine Treasurer at La Rochelle.

In the war of 1757, when Beaujon, Goossens and Company suspended their payments and for the service of the Marine we were obliged to substitute our own credit, all our credit notes [*effets*] were accepted and discounted by these same Treasurers and Receivers who had claimed that they had no funds with which to redeem the rescriptions we had tried to use.[1]

There may, in this instance, have been no government funds in their caisses but there was no way to be sure of this. In such a system, the accountants were profit-making businessmen taking full advantage of their offices to exploit a crisis, and they were able to do so because the public funds in their charge had no clear identity. To recommend a clear separation of public funds and private was to believe in a state or common wealth which was something more than the mere sum of private fortunes in the country. Dufresne de Saint Léon made this thought explicit: there is a public wealth destined for use in the general interest and it ought to be clearly marked and protected.[2] He disagreed with the physiocratic idea that the wealth of a country consisted of the net product of its land.

The venality of offices, a form of private interests in the public domaine, was one of the worst evils of the financial system in the eyes of Duchesne,[3] Necker and Mittié.[4] The latter's tract had great force and point because he dealt directly with the main question of whether administrative agencies would function if those in charge of them had not bought their offices or else posted surety bonds and were not working for profit on commissions. Would the salaried civil servant be as responsible as the venal accountant, the *intéressé* to use the term of the time? This question was as vital then as the present-day question of whether medical doctors will work properly as salaried public employees. When Mittié roundly asserted that purchased offices and surety bonds were unnecessary and harmful, can he have suspected that in a year or two others would take up the same cause?[5] Dufresne de Saint Léon and Bonvalet des Brosses also spoke firmly againt *caution-nements* and *fonds d'avance*, but for a different reason. They believed the venal system of caisses and accountants to be a vicious form of borrowing.

[1] Bonvalet des Brosses, *Moyens de simplifier*, p. 89. The reference to Beaujon etc., is to financiers entrusted with naval financing.
[2] Dufresne de Saint Léon, *Etudes* (1784), pp. 19 and 333.
[3] Duchesne, *Observations sur un projet d'administration présenté en 1787* (Paris, 1791), p. 10.   [4] Mittié, *Plan de suppression*.
[5] For example, Etienne Clavière, *Réflexions sur les formes et les principes auxquels une nation libre doit assujetir l'administration des finances* (Paris, 1791), p. 36: 'En un mot qu'est-ce qu'une caution pour un malhonnête homme? Un honnête homme en a-t-il besoin?' See below, p. 233.

The French system of short-term credit, founded on the private caisses of accountants, came in for a variety of criticisms and so did the long-term borrowing in the form of the purchase-price for offices. Necker denounced the prevailing view that accountants and tax farmers were 'indispensable middle-men of public credit; as if that credit did not have its own force and as if it needed the support of a variety of agents who themselves only have the confidence of the public by reason of the offices and connections they are known to hold from the government'.[1] Another argument, put forward by Dufresne de Saint Léon, was that lending to the Crown gave the *financiers* power over the Ministers of Finance: however good their intentions as ministers their hands were tied by their obligations to all these powerful creditors.[2] It would be infinitely better, Bonvalet des Brosses thought, to set up a *caisse nationale* or central bank to do all of the Crown's banking business, to discount all its rescriptions, to make all money transfers and all short-term advances.[3] He had worked out the structure and operation of this institution in great detail and to him it seemed the best alternative to the system of caisses and accountants.

For Bonvalet des Brosses and Roland, themselves former accountants, the faults of the system were inherent in its very nature. Large sums of money, they wrote, pass from caisse to caisse more or less at the disposal of the individual accountant at least for short periods of time; and because of these sums the accountants enjoy sound credit with lenders and can borrow large private sums for long-term investments. Furthermore, accountants are almost certain of never having to make good deficiencies in their accounts, but even sound accounts do not necessarily reveal how an accountant is enriching himself by the cunning use of the funds in his charge.

There is perhaps not a Treasurer, not a Receiver anywhere who fails to receive a sum of money each day [wrote Bonvalet]. But in the system as a whole that sum is ignored or treated with no special consideration. Yet it is by the aid of these same receipts that in a *charge* or office paid 1,500 livres or at most 1000 *écus* a year there are Treasurers and Receivers who acquire ten, twenty, thirty and sometimes up to 100,000 livres in rentes.[4]

The Controllers can seldom follow receipts and expenditures closely enough to prevent abuses, even if they wish to, and therefore no one but the accountant himself knows at any particular moment how much cash is in his caisse or how much ought to be in it. All anyone knows is that he redeems rescrip-

---

[1] Necker, *De l'administration* (1784), vol. I, p. 107 and vol. III, p. 125.
[2] Dufresne de Saint Léon, *Etudes* (1784), p. 70.
[3] Bonvalet des Brosses, *Moyens de simplifier*, bk. II, pp. 11 ff.
[4] *Ibid.*, p. 2.

tions and cashes notes when they fall due—or else goes bankrupt. For debts can grow as well as profits in the secrecy of the individual caisse. Whether it is thriving or declining, the total business life of the caisse is not revealed in the accounts.

No aspect of the system aroused more criticism than the accounting procedures. In a chapter on 'The Abuses of Accounting', Bonvalet des Brosses maintained that nearly all accounts were needlessly in arrears by ten, fifteen, twenty years or more and that there was not a single major accountant who kept his accounts well enough to be able to report on his caisse at the request of the Minister. The reason, he argued, was not that every man was personally dishonest but rather that the system forced him to behave dishonestly. 'It is not within the power of even the most scrupulous accountant to abandon these practices! Consequently it is up to the government to destroy them.' Roland, too, wished to see greater clarity, order and economy in the accounting system and went so far as to propose reducing all the Chambers of Accounts and other financial courts to one national court of accounts—what the Revolution finally accomplished.[1] Duchesne, for his part, wondered rhetorically how such an abusive system had endured for centuries and how foreigners would think of French finances and the vigilance of French courts when they learned that a Treasurer General of the Marine had gone bankrupt in 1787 after submitting no accounts since 1771.[2] By 1787 these late accounts had become a subject of general scandal and the Assembly of Notables voiced complaints about them.[3] This Assembly was conservative on most matters but in this took a parliamentary attitude that government accounts ought to be printed and published.

The argument for publicity in 'public' accounts, and indeed in all aspects of government finance, received a tremendous force from Necker's writing. If many before him had written about the virtues of a free press, none had ever impressed upon such a large public the importance of publicity in the financial system. Not only did he publish accounts in 1781, but he also ridiculed the secrecy in which the Crown had always shrouded its business affairs, and other critics of the administration naturally took up the same line of argument. Dufresne de Saint Léon, critical of Necker for some things, praised him for publishing the *Compte rendu*. 'His enemies', he wrote, 'then accused him of doing a bad turn to the Ministry by putting his successors in a strict obligation to follow his example, under threat of arousing suspicion and exaggerated fears by their reticence. But why would they not follow

---

[1] *Mémoire au Roi*, p. 43; *Le financier patriote* (1789), p. 131.
[2] A.N., d'Ormesson papers, 144 AP 133, dossier 6. He was referring to Baudard de Saint James.
[3] B.N., Nouv. Acq. Fr. 23617, fols. 206–9, 244, 247 and 306.

that example?'[1] The next Minister to do so (unless we count Calonne's reports to the Assembly of Notables) was Loménie de Brienne whose *Compte rendu au Roi*, published on 29 April 1788, fed the growing popular opinion in favour of published accounts. This pressure threatened the entire system of accountants and separate caisses, a system ill-adapted to the process of current accounting and annual auditing necessary for useful public accounts. Calonne pointed out in his opening speech to the Assembly of Notables how difficult he had found it to arrive at the figures he was putting before them.[2] Conservative defender of the system as Calonne was, he did not go on to draw the conclusion that the caisses ought to be consolidated and the accountants reduced in number, but others in the Assembly of Notables did so. They were thereby reviving one of Necker's main reforming principles.

By the time the revolution began there was already a movement in favour of a single caisse, a consolidated or aggregate revenue fund, but it had begun earlier in the more moderate form of complaints about the 'multiplicity of caisses'. Turgot, indeed, had thought of reducing the number of caisses and accountants but his thoughts on this subject remained buried in a letter to a friend.[3] Necker, on the contrary, repeated his ideas in his early popular writings and so gave them to a public more and more interested in reforms of the financial administration. 'Sometimes', he wrote in 1784, 'it is on the pretext of making accounting easier that the numbers of collecting and spending agents are increased...[but this motive] is absolutely frivolous.'[4] Accounts can themselves be divided into clear and distinct parts without any necessity for dividing the funds they deal with into separate caisses under independent accountants. There are far too many caisses and they ought to be consolidated into a very few, and those few made subsidiary to the Royal Treasury and accountable to it. Developing this argument against multiple caisses, Bonvalet des Brosses reckoned every French city to have an assortment of twenty or twenty-five Treasurers and Receivers who kept government funds divided in as many separate caisses. At any particular moment there were surpluses in some caisses and shortages in others, but the Minister could not balance the one against the other because he was necessarily ill-informed about the business life of the caisses. That was, after all, still in

---

[1] Dufresne de Saint Léon, *Etudes* (1784), p. 41.

[2] Speech of 22 February 1787, printed in 16 pp., e.g. in B.N., Joly de Fleury 1038–43, fol. 116. Another strong voice for published accounts was that of Mathon de la Cour in the preface to his *Collection des comptes rendus* (1788).

[3] Turgot, *Œuvres*, ed. Schelle, vol. v, p. 573, Turgot to Dupont de Nemours 17 October 1778.

[4] Necker, *De l'administration*, vol. III, p. 125.

the realm of the accountant's private business. The Crown therefore borrowed money—sometimes its own money—to make up the temporary shortages of some accountants while other accountants were investing their temporary surpluses at a profit. The main purpose of Roland's plan for suppressing the financial offices of Receivers General was to prevent the enormous costs of leaving royal funds in the hands of accountants 'who lend part of these funds to the King at interest'.[1] Roland and Bonvalet des Brosses, who knew the system intimately, believed that there ought to be a single caisse into which all revenues would flow and from which all payments would be drawn, and it could have a subsidiary caisse in each town, thereby putting all the funds of the Crown continuously at the disposal of the government. There were variations on this theme: another pamphleteer, P. J. Malpart, recommended a single caisse for the revenues and eight specialized caisses for making payments, paying being more detailed and exacting work than receiving.[2] But it was the cry for a *caisse unique* which caught the imagination of the revolutionary generation of administrative reformers. At the Assembly of Notables the Archbishop of Aix, Boisgelin de Cucé, drew up a memorandum under the title, *Mémoire sur la suppression des caisses intermédiaires* and almost immediately the various committees (*bureaux*) of the Assembly demanded 'the reduction of all the caisses to a single one'.[3]

Such a reform could not be the work of a moment. Much had already been done to consolidate the caisses by Terray, Turgot and especially Necker, but after 1781 there had been a reaction against their reforms and a revival of many of the caisses which they had abolished. Not until Calonne's fall at the conclusion of the Assembly of Notables did this great reform begin again. Not until 1793 was the work of unifying caisses completed and the Treasury master of an aggregate fund, the heart of the financial system and a truly modern engine of control in the hands of the central government. Although it was achieved in the revolution, this reform was begun early in the reign of Louis XVI and well advanced before it ended. Let us now turn from what was written to what was done.

[1] Roland, *Mémoire au Roi*, p. 58.
[2] *Plan d'administration des finances*, p. 14.
[3] B.N., Nouv. Acq. Fr. 23617, fol. 253 and fol. 391 refer to the memorandum, but I could not find a copy of it, only the synopses in the committee reports.

8

A DECADE OF REFORM
(1771–1781)

IN THE REIGN of Louis XVI the reform of public finance occurred in two phases. The first began in the last years of the previous reign, during the ministry of Abbé Terray, and reached its full development in the first ministry of Jacques Necker. The second began with the fall of Calonne in April 1787 and did not cease until 1794. If we ignore political and social changes for a moment and confine our attention to developments in the institutions of public finance, these two phases appear to be parts of the same process of administrative change. We can see the reforms of the early years—the first phase—as a prelude to the reforms accomplished after 1787. To explain the six-year interval of 'reaction' between the two phases, the subject of the next chapter, it will be necessary to deal with political and social matters, but these may well be omitted from the study of the reforms of Necker and his two predecessors. Their reform measures call for special treatment. This is because their total effect is not immediately obvious and also because the views of them commonly expressed in histories of the period are sometimes misleading.

   Almost anyone with some knowledge of the ancien régime will have formed an idea of the relative merits of the principal ministers and their policies. I venture to think that most people would not hesitate to single out Turgot, the liberal *philosophe*, as the greatest of the three ministers in this period, and perhaps to choose Terray as second in greatness because of his role in the *coup d'état* that Maupéou carried out against the sovereign courts. Necker has sometimes been shown in a better light than Terray, but there can be few books indeed which praise Necker more than Turgot. A glance through the common standard works will show a fairly general agreement that 'Necker was a vain and mediocre *parvenu*—an accountant',[1] who 'renounced great reforms'[2] and devoted himself to 'superficial reforms

---

[1] Pierre Gaxotte, *Histoire des français* (1951), p. 625. Much the same view in Albert Mathiez, *La Révolution française* (1922), vol. I, p. 35.
[2] Ernest Lavisse, *Histoire de France* (1911), vol. IX, p. 77.

of detail',[1] 'half-measures'.[2] To quote a typical judgement, Marcel Marion writes in the standard financial history of France, 'Instead of profiting from [his exceptional popularity] by pursuing with greater chances of success the work of public salvation begun by Turgot, he only ever took half-measures, often very praiseworthy, but quite insufficient, of mediocre importance, done rather to satisfy the vague desire for reform generally felt than to really cure the ills from which the Bourbon monarchy was dying.'[3] More recently Herbert Luethy has brought subtlety and learning to a fresh study of Necker, but his views are much the same.[4] So firmly rooted are these opinions that we even find students of the period working on the premise that Turgot must somehow have been responsible for any statesmanlike measure enacted during Necker's ministry.[5]

Certain other writers have been more discerning or reserved in their judgements of Necker. 'How can we define such a clever man?', asked Olivier-Martin,[6] and Edmond Préclin has expressed a similar hesitation. Perhaps the most salient of the facts which do not accord with the usual view of Necker is the prodigious popularity he enjoyed for a decade after his first reforms. How, we may wonder, could so many people have been so deceived for so long? Why did Necker get the applause which, according to the history books, Turgot deserved? Marion disposed of that popularity[7] by treating it with contempt as a gullible belief in Necker's poses, pretensions and propaganda. Luethy, more ingenious, explained it as a tide of opinion which was turning away from the cynical, worldly society of Louis XV's court and was ready to worship 'the image of the good father and husband' who, unlike most financial ministers of the time, appeared to be honest.[8] Such explanations may account for some of Necker's popularity

[1] Philippe Sagnac, *La Fin de l'ancien régime et la révolution américaine*, 'Peuples et Civilisations' series (1952), p. 362; Marcel Reinhard, *Histoire de France* (1954), vol. I, p. 69.

[2] Henri See, *Histoire économique de la France* (1939), vol. I, p. 170; Marcel Marion, *Histoire financière de la France depuis 1715* (1914), vol. I, pp. 292 ff. And many others, such as Germain Martin, *Histoire de la nation française*, ed. Hanotaux (1927), vol. X, pp. 247, 264; R. R. Palmer, *The Age of the Democratic Revolution* (1959), p. 454; A. B. Cobban, *A History of Modern France* (London, 1957), p. 121; Louis Madelin, *Histoire de la nation française*, ed. Hanotaux (1927), vol. IV, p. 476; Paul Harsin, 'Necker', *Encyclopedia of the Social Sciences* (1934).

[3] Marcel Marion, *Histoire financière*, vol. I, p. 294.

[4] Herbert Luethy, *La Banque protestante en France* (1961), vol. II, pp. 387, 467.

[5] Aline Logette, in a detailed study, *Le Comité contentieux prés le conseil* (Nancy, no date (1966?)), very clearly assumes that somehow Turgot must have been responsible for founding this *comité*, and that Necker could not possibly have been; but her evidence is meagre.

[6] F. Olivier-Martin, *Histoire du droit français des origines à la révolution* (1951), p. 663. Edmond Préclin, *Le XVIIIe siècle* (Clio Series) (1952), pp. 360, 371.

[7] Marion, *Histoire financière*, p. 292.

[8] Luethy, *La Banque protestante*, pp. 408–10.

but certainly not for the admiration of Rousselot de Surgy and his colla-borators in the *Encyclopédie Méthodique*, of Mahy de Cormeré, M. J. D. Martin, Le Brun, duc de Plaisance, Dufresne de Saint Léon, Loménie de Brienne, Robespierre and Marat (in the early years) and so many others of a critical cast of mind. Why did a young clerk in the *Bureau des impositions*, Albert Hennet, regard Necker in 1781 as 'my hero'?[1] Hennet and the rest make two things clear in their writings: they admired Necker for his public spirit or conscience, and they believed his reforms to be very important.

Why have so many historians disagreed with these judgements and been so ready to listen to Necker's critics? There are many reasons, no doubt, but a clue to one of them is to be found in a line Henri Carré wrote in the standard Lavisse, *Histoire de France*: Necker 'renounced the great reforms, but he reorganized the central administration of finance'.[2] Evidently for Carré the reorganization of the central administration of finance is not a 'great reform'. Administrative reform is clearly of minor importance to Sagnac also for he sees Necker's reforms as falling into two categories: first, the 'administrative reforms' by which he means only innovations in pro-vincial administration; and secondly, the 'financial reforms', which to him were nothing more than measures directly intended to increase revenues or reduce expenditures.[3] In Sagnac's thought there is no room for the reform of financial institutions as Necker conceived of it. Even Marcel Marion appears to be only partly aware of the problems Necker was endeavouring to solve, and reserves them for summary discussion in a final chapter so that he can get on with his tale of ministerial struggles to balance a non-existent budget. None of the writers I have cited interprets the financial difficulties of the ancien régime as problems in public administration. None seems to appreciate Necker's concern to increase ministerial knowledge and control of the royal finances, to reduce the influence of accountants and tax farmers, to make the Royal Treasury a central caisse, and to protect royal funds by a vast number of measures which a good businessman would recognize to be essential, the *sine qua non* of management in any enterprise public or private. Of course there is no proof that Necker's reforms if fully imple-mented would have saved the monarchy from the financial disaster which overtook it—but neither is there any proof that the much-vaunted projects of Turgot or those of Calonne would have been any more successful. The revolution took up and developed Necker's policies as much as it did the

---

[1] Albert-Joseph-Ulpien Hennet, *Théorie du crédit* (Paris, 1816), p. 283. Born at Mau-beuge, he became a clerk on 1 April 1779, a *chef* and in 1792 a *premier commis* (A.N., AF II 21^B, pl. 163).

[2] Vol. IX, p. 77.

[3] Sagnac, *La Fin de l'ancien régime* (1952), p. 364.

policies of Turgot and other ministers. For historians to judge them by some theoretical standard is surely futile and misleading. To damn the reform programmes with *argumentum ad hominem* (Necker was pompous, hypocritical, narrow-minded; Terray had an affair with his bastard daughter, etc., etc.) is equally futile. There can be no heroes to the historian. His best course is to follow where the investigation leads him, and the study of reform in the central administration of finance leads inevitably to Necker's first ministry. Terray played some small part in this work, Turgot even less, and Calonne was a major opponent of it.

The cumulative effect of a great series of reforming laws is not always easy to grasp, especially when those laws are intended to accomplish several tasks at once. The order of publication may be dictated by practical circumstance—the accidental order in which committees or experts report, etc.—and so lend an appearance of groping empiricism even to a plan worked out carefully in advance. The clearest objectives or principles may lie behind an apparently haphazard series of laws. In order to see the effect of changes in the financial administration of France enacted in the decade 1771–81 we may usefully separate the regulations into four groups according to whether they concerned the paying *caisses*, the accounting system, the agencies for collecting indirect taxes or the Receivers General. The fundamental objectives were the same for each group but the history of each is slightly different. The paying caisses were very much reduced in number, concentrated in fewer hands and obliged to account to the Keepers of the Royal Treasury; the accounting system was revised on Colbertist principles to give the Minister more knowledge and control; the excise taxes (*aides*) and stamp duties were taken away from the General Farm of Taxes and established as a government agency (*régie*); and the Receivers General, after being made responsible for the accounts of the *Receveurs particuliers*, were reduced from a corps of forty-eight independent accountants to a Crown company (*régie*) of twelve. The first and last-mentioned of these reforms took a great toll of the accountants and roused the dispossessed and their sympathizers to such a fury against Necker that they may well have contributed to his downfall in 1781. But unlike Terray and Turgot, whom they also hated, Necker was shrewd enough to win a long-term political victory over them by publishing the reasons for his reforms in his popular books and so preparing public opinion for the second phase of reform to begin in 1787. A great many of the reading public came to realize that the reforms of the decade ending in 1781 had been for that time a daring and sweeping assault on vested interests accustomed to exploiting public finances for private profit.

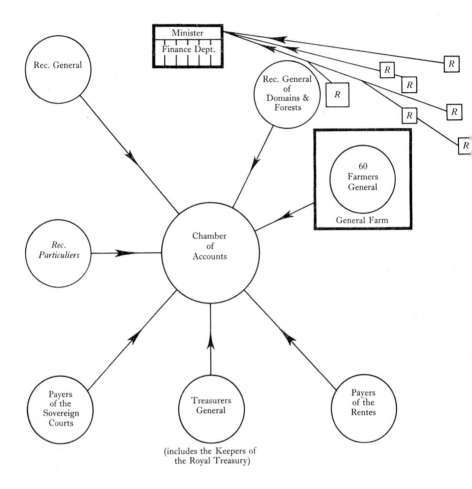

Fig. 1. **The principal corps of venal accountants before 1771.** This shows seven groups of ma[j]
accountants. Of these, the Farmers General and the Payers of the Rentes were comparatively w[e]
organized and unified corps, whereas the Payers of the Sovereign Courts and the Treasurers Gene[r]
were hardly more than loose categories of accountants. The other three, moderately coherent, [?]
somewhere between. The members of all seven groups were accountable to the Chamber of Accoun[ts]
and the royal Finance Department kept watch over them somewhat in the way a client compa[ny]
might keep watch over its bankers. The *régies*, on the other hand, were directly accountable to [the]
Finance Department acting for the Royal Council.

146

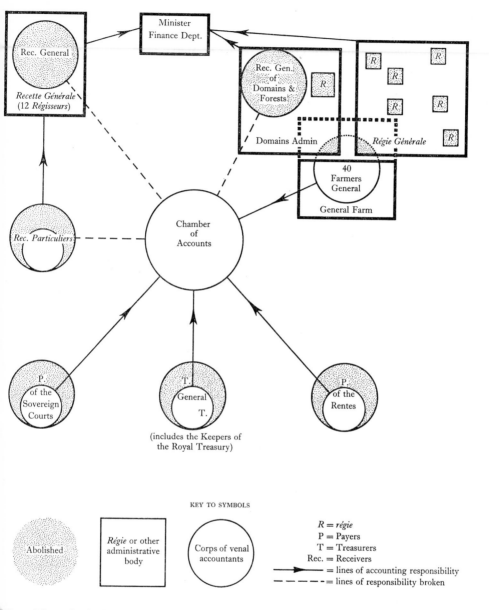

KEY TO SYMBOLS

Abolished

Régie or other
administrative
body

Corps of venal
accountants

R = régie
P = Payers
T = Treasurers
Rec. = Receivers
⟶ = lines of accounting responsibility
– – – – – = lines of responsibility broken

Fig. 2. **The principal corps of venal accountants in 1781.** Here we see the changes made by Terray, Turgot and Necker in the decade 1771–81. Two of the corps of accountants were abolished altogether and the other five were reduced in numbers. Three new *régies* were created to replace the suppressed corps, to take over some of the duties of the General Farm and to incorporate the previous small *régies*. The *Receveurs particuliers* became accountable to the Receivers General. Only four of the original seven corps were left to account to the Chamber of Accounts as before. The Finance Department was integrated by abolishing the Intendants of Finance.

The series of laws concerning the paying caisses prepared the way for the founding of the modern French treasury in March 1788, and a great deal of preparation was certainly needed. The various corps of paying accountants were numerous, incoherent and powerful. The Payers and Controllers for the sovereign courts were the first to be struck down in any great numbers, a task vigorously undertaken by Terray in the wake of Maupéou's destruction of the Parlements, *Cours des aides* and other courts in 1771. Edicts of February, March and October 1772 suppressed the offices of the 'Payeurs des gages des différentes cours' and their Controllers, the Receivers General of Finance to take over their remaining payments. Some of these offices were inevitably revived when Louis XVI restored the Parlements and *Cours des aides* in 1774, but only one for each court whereas there had originally been several. This trend continued under Turgot with the suppression of the *Payeurs des gages* of the Paris criminal court, the Châtelet, and the assignment of their duties to the *Receveurs des impositions*; the reduction of the offices of the *Payeurs des gages* for the Paris Chamber of Accounts from three to one; and the suppression of the three offices of Treasurer General of the *Boëttes de monnaie, payeurs des officiers de la Cour des Monnaies* and their three Controllers, with provision for the Receivers General of Paris to do their work. The preamble of this last edict, published in May 1776, declared that the Crown had drawn up the edict of March 1772 'with a view to reducing the number of accounting officers in the kingdom', and so saying removed any doubt that these scattered laws expressed a common purpose.[1]

With that same purpose in mind, Terray also began to reduce the numbers of Treasurers attached to the major spending departments: the Treasurers General for Marine and Colonies from four to two, and the Treasurers General of the King's Household from two to one.[2] But these changes and Turgot's abolition of one of the two Treasurers for the *Bâtiments du Roi* proved to be only *hors d'œuvres* to Necker's more sweeping reforms. In the households of the King and Queen he suppressed all eighteen offices of Treasurer and Controller in favour of a single *Trésorier payeur général* and then, not to mention the abolition of 406 domestic posts of *Bouche et Commun*, he replaced the ten offices of Intendant and Controller General of the royal

---

[1] A.N., P 2511. All the various laws and regulations, of which this chapter is essentially a study, I have read in four main collections: (1) the records of the Paris Chamber of Accounts, A.N. series 'P'; (2) the Rondonneau Collection in the A.N., A.D. IX 431 etc.; (3) the printed collection in the B.N., F 21201 etc.; (4) *Œuvres complètes de Monsieur Necker publiées par Monsieur le baron de Staël* (Paris, 1820), vol. I, less complete than the others but with its own pieces not found elsewhere.

[2] Edicts of February and November 1771.

furniture, stables and so on with a *Bureau général* to consist of five commissioners appointed by the King and two magistrates from the Chamber of Accounts under the presidency either of the Secretary of State for the Royal Households or the Minister of Finance.[1] Likewise in the recently formed household of the King's younger brother, the comte d'Artois, Necker arranged for the replacement of five Treasurers by a Treasurer General.[2] Meanwhile the offices of no less than twenty-seven Treasurers and Controllers attached to the War and Marine Departments were abolished and in their place one office of *Trésorier payeur général des dépenses* attached to each Department.[3] The result of this process was that the funds for each of the three major spending departments were to be centrally managed in the caisse of a single Treasurer General. As for the work of the suppressed Controllers, it passed from the hands of the venal officers into the bureaux of the Minister's *Premier commis des finances* where we accordingly find three new administrative posts, one for the *contrôle* of each new Treasurer General.[4]

When we come to the lesser spending departments, we find the same process of consolidation taking place. The regional *Trésoriers particuliers* for the *Ponts et Chaussées* had already been suppressed in May 1765, and in 1772 Terray abolished the offices of Intendant, Treasurer and Controller of the *Turcies et Levées* and the office of Receiver General of the *Barrage de Paris*. Necker did away with four Controllers and one Treasurer General, leaving a single office of Treasurer General of *Ponts et Chaussées*. Some fourteen other Treasurers, who managed the funds for such purposes as the Paris Police, the territorial forces of the Paris region (*maréchaussées*), subsidies to the Swiss, the veterinary school, mines and agriculture and government grain purchases, were all abolished in favour of one *Trésorier payeur des dépenses diverses*.[5] *Dépenses diverses!* There was a category to conjure

---

[1] Edicts of July 1779, January and August 1780. The five commissioners received an honorarium of 15,000 livres a year each, increased by 5,000 in December 1780 and again by 5,000 on 18 Dec. 1784. Each deposited a bond of 500,000.

[2] Lettres patentes du comte d'Artois, 15 March 1780. Antoine Bourboulon (b. 1737) had already been appointed by Let. Pat. of 19 Feb. 1780.

[3] Edict of Nov. 1778. For the War Department, this was Antoine-Jean-François Mégret de Sérilly (1746-94); for the Marine Department, Claude Baudard de Saint James (1738-87); for the Royal Households, Marc-Antoine-François-Marie Randon de la Tour (b. 1736).

[4] *Almanach royal* (1781), p. 243, and A.N., AB XIX 327, 18ᵉ Conférence N°3. This was not done without resistance in some paying agencies, as d'Ormesson remarked to Joly de Fleury in a memorandum (B.N. Coll. Joly de Fleury 1448, fols. 55-8).

[5] All this by edicts of May 1765, Jan. and May 1772, Feb. and Oct. 1779; an arrêt of 19 Sept. 1779 destroyed the special caisse to which the Farmers General sent the revenues of the principality of Dombes, and diverted those revenues to the Treasury. The *Trésorier général des dép. div.* was David-Etienne Rouillé de l'Etang (b. 1731).

with. By no means all of the various treasurers had been supplanted by this Treasurer General at the time Necker fell in 1781, as a glance at the *Almanach royal* will show, but there were far fewer of them than before. By thus grouping the reforms of the paying caisses we may, I think, interpret them very differently from Marcel Marion, author of the standard financial history of France. He saw all these and other suppressions of offices as mere economy measures by which the Ministers were trying to save the fees and other costs of office-holders; and seen in this light such measures were, as Marion wrote, 'infinitely praiseworthy, but with no effect in the matter of diminishing revenues until the time when the capital of these offices had been re-paid'.[1] Not much money had been saved. These are, then, some of the footling half-measures with which Marion and others reproach Necker. Such an interpretation might, indeed, be put upon the few suppressions by Terray and Turgot done 'with a view to diminishing the multitude of accounting offices, of caisses and of labour and costs which all these accountings cause',[2] although even this is doubtful. When we come to Necker's work, however, this interpretation can only be sustained by ignoring what Necker said in the preambles to his laws, what he did in addition to suppressing accountants and their caisses and what even his successor wrote on the subject. When Necker reduced the many offices of Marine Treasurer and War Treasurer to two general offices of Treasurer General on salaries 'instead of charges with commissions (*taxations*), he intended to create a whole (*mettre un ensemble*) in the administration of payments and to find an economy in it'.[3] So thought Joly de Fleury in 1782. In laws using the royal 'we' in the customary manner, Necker declared the multiplicity of separate caisses to be vicious because it produced 'dead funds' which lay in caisses unknown to the Crown, because it made the inspection of finances unnecessarily difficult and prevented the Crown from 'supervising as we ought the use of all our funds and directing them as a whole', and because it made the accounting process unnecessarily cumbersome.[4] He described all the paying caisses as emanations of the Royal Treasury and undertook to suppress as many of them as possible with a view to forming a unified central treasury.[5] If the suppressions were partly for the sake of economy, they were mainly for the cause of central control over the financial system.

[1] Marion, *Histoire financière*, vol. 1, 308.
[2] Preamble to edicts of March 1772 and May 1776.
[3] B.N., Coll. Joly de Fleury 1439, fol. 34, dated July 1782.
[4] Lett. Pat. of the comte d'Artois 15 March 1780, and edict of Oct. 1779.
[5] Arrêt du Conseil 18 Oct. 1778. Portant établissement d'un nouvel ordre pour toutes les caisses de dépenses.

Further evidence of an intention to unify the system may be found in the new regulations for paying which accompanied the series of suppressions. Whereas Terray devoted much effort to reducing the Payers of the rentes from seventy-four to thirty—a remarkable feat of economy—but went no further, Necker worked to establish central control over the payment of pensions and fees (*gages*). 'His Majesty has observed', said a *règlement* as early as 22 December 1776, 'that the multitude of caisses and Treasurers involved in his receipts and expenditures has permitted as many different ways of assigning the payment of pensions and annual gratifications. From this has resulted a greater difficulty in assembling them for his perusal and a greater facility in obtaining pensions (*grâces*) by various means.' In other words, as later laws made clear, Necker did not believe mere royal assent to new pensions was control enough, because the King judged each request individually on its merits and never reviewed them all together in one list as he ought to have done; and a comprehensive list of pensions was practically impossible to maintain because too many different agencies were paying pensions. Any budgetary scrutiny and control of pensions was impossible and they had multiplied out of all reason. Necker proposed to draw up a complete table of them, classified by department, and to transfer the payment of them all to the caisse of Savalette, one of the Keepers of the Royal Treasury.[1] The Chambers of Accounts were forbidden to pass sums for pensions in the accounts of any other caisse. The departments were instructed to submit the names of all their pensioners, together with proof of their titles to payment. In future, the title to any *pensions, gratifications annuelles* or other *grâces viagères* was to be granted in the form of a standard patent (*brevet*).[2] The pensioners themselves were inevitably expected to submit to the inquisitorial processes of the bureaux and on 7 January 1779 a four-page printed circular instructed them to send baptismal certificates, original titles to payment, full names and dates of birth to the agencies in which their pensions had been granted. This was supplemented later that year by a further eight pages of instructions, examples and printed forms.[3] All these formalities, so widely advertised, may seem like the tiresome excesses of a modern bureaucracy and no progress—until we realize that they permitted a pensioner to be paid simply by signing a receipt whereas he had hitherto been obliged to solicit a royal payment *ordonnance* every year, an uncertain and tedious process for which there were no printed instructions.

[1] Lett. Pat. 8 Nov. 1778, with effect from 1 Jan. 1779, reaffirmed by edict of July 1779, art. IV and declaration of 8 August 1779.
[2] Decl. 7 Jan. 1779.
[3] A.N., AD IX 456, *Instruction pour tous les pensionnaires du Roi sur les formalités..* and *Instruction sur les formalités à remplir par les pensionnaires...*

As for the budgetary scrutiny and control, only these measures, gradually put into effect over the ensuing years, enabled the Crown in 1785 to appoint a special council to study departmental tables of pensions every year in March with a view to putting a summary pension list before the King.[1] Only these reforms made it possible for the National Assembly to publish in 1789 a multi-volume list of pensions on the Royal Treasury.

Terray, Turgot and Necker, while thus engaged in reforming the system of payments, were taking steps at the same time to improve the accounting procedures. In this work, too, there are grounds for believing that Terray and Turgot were intent upon saving money in the most direct way. Each accountant cost the government something for the accounts he rendered to the Chamber of Accounts and the saving of these *épices* was certainly one of the economies the ministers had in mind when they suppressed forty-four *Payeurs des rentes* and the many *Payeurs des gages*. The simplest economy also appears to have prompted Terray to stop the several hundred *Receveurs des tailles* from accounting to the Chambers of Accounts and order them to account in future to the Receivers General of Finance, a saving of some 104,000 livres in *épices*, he reckoned, even after paying something in compensation to the irate Chambers of Accounts.[2] Any doubt about this is dispelled by the Letters Patent of 1 May 1773 reducing all the *épices* for major accounts, including those of the General Farm which were reduced by half. But was it *only* for a paltry 100,000 livres that Terray went to all the trouble of discovering that the accounts of the *Receveurs des tailles* were redundant, of re-assigning various payments from their caisses to the caisses of the Receivers General and the Receivers of Domains and Forests, and of forcing the Chambers of Accounts to register the regulations?[3] Was it *only* to save a small sum of money that Turgot defended this regulation against the remonstrances of the Paris Chamber and added fuel to the flames by consolidating the three or four offices in each election, bailliage, etc., into a single office of *Receveur des impositions*?[4] When we find signs that Terray and Turgot were interested in having clearer and more up-to-date accounts, we may suspect that their quarrels with the Chamber of Accounts were not entirely over *épices*.

---

[1] Arrêt du conseil d'état du Roi concernant les pensions, 8 May 1785; and Lett. Pat. sur la comptabilité des pensions, 4 Nov. 1785. Both acknowledged Necker's earlier legislation. Necker also rationalized the payments of certain stipends, as for example those of the provincial Governors, Lieutenants, and other military commanders of castles, citadels and fortified towns (Arrêt 1 Oct. 1779; Arrêt 8 Dec. 1779).
[2] Decl. 8 May 1772, Arrêt 1 April 1774; Mathon de la Cour, *Collection de comptes rendus*, p. 82.
[3] After a great deal of fuss, in letters patent of 3 July 1773 (A.N., P 2506).
[4] A.N., P 2739, entry for 16 Jan. 1775; edict of August 1775.

The best evidence of Terray's efforts to improve accounting processes is the decision to have the sixty-four Receivers General of Domains and Forests submit monthly accounts to the Department.[1] The decision was not well received by those accountants and in commenting on one of their protests an employee in the Department wrote:

The observations in question appear to have been made less by an administrator than by an accountant [accountants often argued that they were administrators]. They breath emotion from one end to the other. The truth is occasionally twisted in them, the writer uses subterfuge...and seems to have had no other purpose than to turn to ridicule the establishment of *journaux* registers which are perhaps the only way of knowing the true situation of the accountants at every moment.[2]

He went on to point out that these new accounting methods had already proved their value by, for example, enabling the Department to discover a debt to the Crown of more than 200,000 livres in the accounts of the Receiver General for Flanders for the sale of wood on Crown land in 1772. There is evidence of Turgot's interest in improving accounts also, and if there is any doubt about his intention in this respect and Terray's, there can be none whatever of Necker's.

'It has pained us to see', he had the King say in a *Declaration concerning Accounting and the Royal Treasury* [17 October 1779], 'that the picture of our revenues and expenditures was never anything but the result of research and of scattered knowledge assembled under our eyes by the Minister of Finance. The knowledge most needed for our plans and decisions was therefore entirely dependent upon the intelligence and accuracy of one man.' The registers of the Royal Treasury ought to have details of the entire body of receipts and expenditures but in fact have no record at all of the business done in many other caisses. The registers of the Chamber of Accounts are no help in making up for the deficiencies of the Treasury's accounts 'because only after a great number of years are all the individual accounts rendered and made good (*apurés*), and also because these are divided among all the Chambers of Accounts of our kingdom so that only by an immense labour could the total results be formed; and this work, always too late and confused, would never be useful'. This pointed criticism was a part of the preamble to seven articles instructing all accountants to

---

[1] Arrêt, 1 April 1774, insisting on the submission of *journaux* rather than the briefer *bordereau*. Discussion in detail in A.N., F4 1082.

[2] Drouet de Santerre, 'Réponse aux observations qui ont été faites sur les états de situations des receveurs généraux des domaines et bois au 1 Septembre 1774 rélativement aux exercices 1772, 1773 et 1774', A.N., F4 1082. See also, Decl. 4 Oct. 1772, Decl. 18 Dec. 1774, Decl. 12 Jan. 1775 and Decl. 22 Jan. 1775.

account continuously to the Keepers of the Royal Treasury for all royal funds received and spent. These instructions did not put an end to annual accounts to the Chambers, which were to go on as usual; but henceforth every item in those accounts was supposed to be justified by an accompanying receipt (*quittance*) from a Keeper of the Royal Treasury. The business of each fiscal year was to be recorded separately in the Keepers' books, and accountants were supposed to be careful to report the business of even-numbered years to one Keeper and of odd-numbered years to the other. These new arrangements were 'so that on opening the registers of the Royal Treasury one may see clearly the exact relation between the ordinary revenues and expenditures of each year, and the total of the extraordinary expenditures and resources'. The Treasury would thus keep records of all government funds, even if it did not keep the funds themselves.

In another direction, Necker took steps to establish ministerial control over all the caisses, what he called 'rapports efficaces entr'elles et l'administration des finances'.[1] First, he ordered all accountants to keep their books in perfect order from day to day and to be always ready to report on the state of their caisses at the request of the Department of Finance. To see that they did so and to keep the Department regularly informed, he instructed them to submit certified monthly statements of their receipts, payments and cash-in-hand. He specified that henceforth any use of the government funds paid into a caisse would have to be justified by a royal payment order, with the single exception of the accountants' own fees (*gages*) which could simply be taken from the caisses as usual. The Treasurers of the War and Marine Departments were henceforth to draw their funds as they needed them rather than holding large sums in their caisses until needed. In the royal order publishing these instructions, Necker explained that he wanted the Department to have continuous knowledge of all caisses so that the sums in them could be used in the King's service. Without this knowledge, the Crown had hitherto found it necessary to keep reserve funds on hand ('le capital oisif qu'une sage précaution engage à conserver') and had also been obliged to ship funds to places where, had the Department only known, there were funds lying temporarily idle in some caisse. Necker declared that all the caisses were to be opened to ministerial inspection. He did so on a principle which was little more than a myth—one of those useful eighteenth-century myths, like the social contract—by which he held that all caisses had originally derived from the Royal Treasury. Ministerial inspection of the caisses was only a first step.

[1] Arrêt, 18 Oct. 1778. A.N., Coll. Lefèvre d'Ormesson 144 AP 131, 'Mémoire sur l'arrêt du conseil du 18 Oct. 1778...'

Secondly, to supplement these measures, possibly because they were extremely difficult to enforce, Necker took the further step of reviving one of Colbert's edicts dated August 1669 and ordering all accountants to submit their *états au vrai* to the Royal Council on Finance before rendering their annual accounts to the Chambers.[1] He remarked that in general the collecting accountants had been conforming to this old rule, but the paying accountants had not. The Treasurer General for the War Department he subjected to a special regulation, twenty-six articles long, defining the accounting process necessary for the promptness, clarity and simplicity of accounts.[2] To make good use of the *états au vrai* he tried to revive the bureau that Colbert had set up for their verification in the Department of Finance.[3] The total effect of this and the previous step was to provide the Minister with accounts useful for current administrative purposes. Whereas the Chambers of Accounts were interested mainly in verifying the honesty and accuracy of each individual accountant and therefore wanted annual records for essentially judicial purposes, Necker was trying to provide for a system of more frequent accounts to keep the Minister informed of the current state of government business in all the caisses in all parts of the kingdom. He had in mind the efficiency of the system rather than the behaviour of the accountants.

Necker set out, thirdly, to impose administrative control on short-term advances and the use of paper notes by accountants, *caissiers* and others with custody of royal funds. The best proof of his intentions comes from his successor and opponent, Calonne, who later wrote: 'To reject all intermediary credit and to employ only that of the Royal Treasury—such was the system of Monsieur Necker.'[4] A brief regulation in 1778 forbad both cash loans and credit notes (*billets à terme*) unless authorized by the Department of Finance.[5] Two years later a much more fundamental regulation expressed an attempt at 'nationalizing' credit notes by announcing that in future all those necessary for the royal financial services would be guaranteed by the Crown and not merely by the issuing accountant.[6] To be valid all such notes would have to bear a special seal showing that they had been submitted for the approval of the *Premier commis des finances* acting under

[1] Decl. 3 March 1781; Lett. Pat. 1 March 1781.
[2] Decl. 12 June 1781 very explicit on Necker's purposes in reforming accounts (A.N., P 2421 fols. 1–16).
[3] Arrêt du conseil d'état du Roi qui confirme l'établissement du bureau de la vérification des états au vrai... 10 Aug. 1777 (B.N., Coll. Joly de Fleury 1448, fol. 88).
[4] *Réponse de M. Calonne à l'écrit de M. Necker*, Appendix of 62 pp. 'Réponse au chapitre IV de l'ouvrage que M. Necker a publié', p. 32. Cf. Coppons, *Examen de la théorie et pratique de M. Necker* (1785), p. 82, note, says the same.
[5] Arrêt 18 Oct. 1778, art. 5.　　　　[6] Arrêt 24 Dec. 1780.

the orders of the Minister of Finance 'who will render accounts of them to His Majesty' (art. 2). Finally, just as his term of office was nearing its end, Necker specifically ordered the *caissiers* of the General Tax Farm, who were accustomed to doing a little banking on the side, to issue no more notes in future and he instructed all people then holding these notes to cash them within two months.[1]

It is in the light of such measures as these that we must see the complaints of ministerial tyranny levelled against Necker. To assert government control over public funds in the eighteenth century was indeed to exercise a kind of tyranny over the accountants and caisses through the activities of the Department of Finance. It was a 'tyranny' which we have long taken for granted as being necessary for good government. Was the Department equal to the task? Certainly Necker did his best to make it so. 'Never under the twenty-three Ministers who have succeeded him,' one of the departmental clerks recollected in 1816, 'have I seen the bureaux so small in number, produce so much work, and do it with such care. No part, no detail was neglected. Never at any time have I seen merit, talent and seniority more assured of obtaining the advancement to which they had rights...never was the state better served and at less cost.'[2] Others who worked for Necker expressed similar judgements.[3] Certainly the responsibilities of the Department were increasing as a result of consolidating the paying caisses and developing a system of administrative accounts. But these were only two of the four major tasks of reform which Necker set out to accomplish in the field of public finance.

The other two tasks concerned the caisses on the revenue side of the system. Necker undertook to reform the General Farm of Taxes and the Receivers General of Finance, herculean tasks for any minister and politically risky. It has been usual in history books to explain the first of these reforms entirely by a rather sneering allegation that Necker 'wanted to appear to attack the Farmers General'.[4] Undoubtedly he did. He certainly needed as much support as he could muster to compensate for the enmity of the powerful Farmers General. But we are not entitled to pretend that the only other reason Necker could possibly have had for reforming the General Farm was to effect an immediate saving in costs or an immediate increase in revenue, and to pretend further that because his reform did not result in such a saving there was no practical benefit to the government.

---

[1] Arrêt, 11 April 1781.
[2] A. J. U. Hennet, *Théorie du crédit public* (Paris, 1816), p. 267.
[3] Roland, *Mémoire au Roi*, p. 118.
[4] G. T. Matthews, *The Royal General Farms* (New York, 1958), p. 259, citing other authorities.

As any twentieth-century administrator could see, there was in fact all the benefit of organizing the taxing administration rationally in three logical parts and of 'nationalizing' two of them as Crown companies (*régies*) leaving only one to the profit-making company of Farmers General. These processes of rationalizing and 'nationalizing' had the same self-evident worth in Necker's eyes as in the eyes of Colbert, of the revolutionary National Assembly, of the Convention, the Directory, the First Empire and perhaps of all subsequent régimes. The revolutionary governments hardly thought it necessary to justify the destruction of tax-farming by immediate increases in tax-revenues, for the immediate gains were only incidental. So they were to Necker also, and he explicitly stated that there was little immediate financial gain to be expected.[1] In financial administration, he thought order, efficiency and government control intrinsically worthwhile.

The reorganization of all this taxing machinery was far more complicated than would have been necessary merely to appear to attack the Farmers General. It began in 1777 with a series of re-groupings. One act gathered together various duties hitherto collected by six organizations in which some three hundred people had invested, and put them under a consolidated authority of twenty-five *régisseurs* to be called the *Régie générale*.[2] This authority was to have some of the superficial features of the General Farm, especially in being formed in the name of one man, Dominique Compart, who would sign documents in the name of the twenty-five *régisseurs* who, in their turn, would sign contracts as his legal guarantors. But there was a basic difference from the General Farm: the *régisseurs* were not to buy offices but instead to deposit bonds of guarantee and to be commissioned as salaried servants of the Crown. They were not a profit-making private company working the taxes on contract for the Crown; they were a corps of

[1] *Arrêt de règlement concernant les fermes et les régies du Roi*, 9 Jan. 1780 (B.N., F 21201 (27)).

[2] It was formed of (1) the *Régie des droits réunis* under the name of Fouache and collecting duties on leather, on butchering inspections, on gold and silver, on iron, starch and tallow together yielding over 7 million livres; (2) the *Régie des droits réserves* collecting duties on the inspection of cloth, weights and measures, wood, fish, and certain municipal *octrois* from which the total yield was about 6½ million livres; (3) the *Régie des hypothèques* under the name of Piraudeau collecting duties from the registration of property sales which Terray had wisely initiated to protect purchasers from hidden mortgages—duties yielding over 7½ million; (4) the *Régie des quatre membres de Flandres* under the name Nicolas Remy collecting duties on brandy and others in maritime Flanders and Dunkirk amounting to 771,680 livres (in 1776); (5) the *Régie des greffes* which collected duties on a great variety of legal processes imposed by law courts and other such authorities, e.g. contracts of apprenticeship and marriage, baptisms and legal judgements, totalling some 11 million livres a year; (6) the *Régie des papiers et cartons* for duties on paper reorganized by Terray and totalling some 2½ million (in 1786). Some of these had been included in the Farmers General's leases (A.N., 4 AP 190, accounts of 1776; Marion, *Dict. des inst.*).

salaried civil servants commissioned by the Crown, accountable to it rather than to the Chambers of Accounts, and collecting royal funds directly on behalf of the government.

Another act, an edict of August 1777, suppressed all the offices of Receivers General of Domains and Forests, Controllers and subsidiary venal officers, a decision that swept away a total of 481 offices, and also suppressed the twenty-five offices of the *régie* Jean Berthaux set up by Turgot to consolidate various scattered authorities collecting some of the principal duties on the royal domains.[1] In their place Necker formed a single *régie* of eighteen men with subsidiary employees for the collection of all revenues from the royal domains and forests; it was immediately formed under the name of Jean-Vincent René. Three years later these two new *régies* became the nuclei of large organizations, one for excise duties and the other for domains and forests, which Necker set up beside the General Farm. And it was by transferring parts of the General Farm's taxing empire that he built them up. They were to last until 1791.

The new *Régie général* of 1780, formed under the name Henry Clavel, was a combination of the *aides* from the General Farm and the *régie* Dominique Compart formed in 1777.[2] The *aides*, excise duties imposed on the production and sale of alcoholic beverages and a few lesser products, were collected by an organization of some 3,000 regular employees and as many irregular ones who had formed one of the five main departments of the General Farm.[3] Omitting the Paris *aides*, the so-called *entrées de Paris* not included in the transfer, the *aides* yielded nearly twenty million livres (in 1775) which was less than half of the forty-five millions from the salt monopoly (*gabelles*), just less than the twenty-four millions from the tobacco monopoly (*tabac*), about the same as the revenue from the stamp taxes on legal papers (*droits de contrôle des actes*), but more than the sixteen millions yielded by the customs duties.[4] The *aides* were different from the others, as the stamp taxes also were; they each needed a special organization to collect them whereas the collection of the customs and the salt and tobacco monopolies was integrated to some extent. It was thus easy in practice to detach the *aides* from the General Farm, and by no means disastrous for the Farmers General. One reason Necker gave for detaching the *aides* was that they were very similar to the *droits réunis*, the *droits réservés* and various

---

[1] Edict of Aug. 1777 abolishing 64 Rec. Gen. of Dom. and For.; 64 Controllers; 152 Rec. part. des bois; 152 Rec. des amendes dans les maîtrises des eaux et forêts; 49 Gardes généraux et collecteurs des amendes.

[2] Arrêt, 15 Sept. 1780; Lett. Pat. 5 July 1780.

[3] *Encyclopédie méthodique. Partie finances*, I, p. 29.

[4] Turgot's figures cited in Mathon de la Cour, *Collection de comptes rendus*, pp. 127–8.

other taxes already collected by the *Régie générale*. The *droits de greffes* and *d'hypothèques* which were not similar he transferred to the new Administration of the Domains. A second reason for removing the *aides* from the General Farm was that their yield was very uncertain because it fluctuated with the fortunes of the annual wine crop, unlike all other indirect taxes, and the Farmers General were therefore able to incorporate in their leases a profit proportional to the risk they were taking in agreeing to collect the *aides* at a price fixed in advance. 'The King was needlessly paying a large insurance premium', Necker explained in the reforming act.[1] Henceforth the Crown would bear the risks of bad years because the *Régie générale*, like any *régie*, would collect the *aides* directly for the Crown. A third reason for this new arrangement was that a reform of the *aides* was being planned and the government could more easily make changes in any tax or collection system that was in the form of a *régie* for there was no binding legal contract such as the six-year leases signed with the Farmers General.

For some of the same reasons Necker simultaneously created the *Administration générale des domaines*.[2] This body he formed mainly by transferring three similar but separate branches of the taxing system to the *régie* Jean-Vincent René founded in 1777 to collect the revenues from the royal domains.[3] The three transferred services, all for the collection of stamp duties or taxes of one kind or another on documents, were evidently homogeneous, but it is not easy to see how they might be usefully combined with collection of revenues from the sale of wood and other activities on the royal domains. Necker argued, however, that they were much the same sort of tax from an administrative point of view (as the government had implied many years earlier by calling the principal stamp duties *droits domainiaux*), because the domains' administrators were continually obliged to consult the records of the *Contrôleurs des actes* about changes in property-holdings and other matters, and because the domains' administrators employed the clerks of the *droits domainiaux* to collect various taxes imposed on the royal domains.[4] The taxes were different but the collecting bodies were interdependent. Still, the two parts of this *régie*'s work were separate enough that in each of the thirty-four geographical divisions (*directions*) two Directors were appointed, one for Domains and Forests and the other for *la partie du contrôle et les droits domainiaux*. Thus formed as a *régie*, these branches of

[1] Arrêt de règlement du 9 Jan. 1780 concernant les fermes et les régies du Roi.
[2] *Ibid.*
[3] Arrêt, 4 August 1780 and Lett. Pat. 4 Aug. 1780 (B.N., F 21202, 44 et 45). These were (1) Droits de contrôle des actes; (2) Droits sur les papiers et parchemins timbés; (3) Droits de greffes et droits d'hypothèques (from the *Régie générale*).
[4] Arrêt of 9 Jan. 1780; *Encyclopédie méthodique. Finance*, vol. I, p. 616.

the financial administration were open to changes by the government, and two laws which we need not here examine show that Necker intended to make reforms on the royal domains.[1]

As a result of all these changes there were three major organizations collecting indirect taxes where there had been only the enormous General Farm and a great many separate accountants and minor farms. The General Farm remained the largest of the three, for it continued to collect three of the major taxes, the customs duties and the salt and tobacco monopolies, and a number of minor ones, notably the Paris excise duties, the *entrées de Paris*. Although the Farmers General were reduced from sixty to forty by the reforms, the two bodies of *régisseurs* were to number no more than twenty-five each. The gross revenue collected by the *Régie générale* amounted to less than fifty-two millions in 1787 and the Domains and Forests Administration produced fifty millions, whereas the General Farm yielded 150 millions. In the latest reorganization there was only a modest reduction of senior agents, as Necker pointed out, from 104 (60 Farmers General, 25 *Régisseurs* and 19 Domains administrators) to 90 (40 Farmers General, 25 *Régisseurs* and 25 Domains administrators),[2] but the reorganization of 1777 had already done away with several hundred accountants and investors (*croupiers*).

Reductions of personnel were only secondary benefits, however, from this series of plans designed to give the Crown greater administrative control. The two *régies*, indeed, were expressly freed from accounting to the Chambers of Accounts and were responsible instead to the Royal Council on Finance, i.e. the Minister and his Department.[3] The Minister had the right and power to know the business of *régies* and thereby to direct them more easily. The benefit of this arrangement is evident in a correspondence of the late 1780s—crisis years—between the *Premier commis des finances* and the *caissier* employed by the *Régie générale*, in which we find the *premier commis* being informed almost daily of the financial state of the *Régie*.[4] The *régisseurs* were salaried officials and although they deposited surety bonds they did not hold offices with which they could associate others, as did the Farmers General who together were paying twenty-seven *adjoints* in 1780. Moreover the Crown could discharge a *régisseur* much more easily than a Farmer General. But Necker did not intend to let the Farmers General escape altogether from more rigorous supervision by his Department. In a letter to them, dated 29 September 1780, shortly after signing a new six-

---

[1] Règlement of 7 March 1777; arrêt of 14 Jan. 1781.
[2] Edict of April 1780.
[3] Lettres patentes of 25 Jan. 1779; A.N., P 2517, dated 1 March 1779.
[4] A.N., G² 109, Gougenot to Gojard and Dufresne.

year lease with them (the lease called Nicolas Salzard) he requested monthly statements of their collections from the salt and tobacco monopolies and quarterly statements for the customs duties. He ordered their *comité d'administration* to administer certain important parts of their work, especially the treatment of captured smugglers and other prisoners, and he wanted one Farmer General to be on duty each morning at the Hôtel des Fermes, another at the Hôtel Bretonvilliers, to hear complaints from the public and to do something about them.[1] In these reforms Necker had taken a step towards the revolution in which governments were not going to reduce the numbers of civil servants but were going to do away with tax farming and venality as intolerable forms of private enterprise in the public administration of finances.

In the early reforming era one series of laws reduced and consolidated the paying caisses, a step towards the formation in 1788 of an organized Treasury; another developed the Colbertist system of administrative accounts; a third reformed the General Farm of indirect taxes and 'nationalized' parts of it; and a fourth series of laws consolidated the collection of the direct taxes, the *tailles*, *capitation* and *vingtième*. This last exhibits Necker's purposes even more clearly than the others and perhaps that is why he reserved it until as late as April 1780, when his main reforming law announced it as the last of his reforms. What this edict did, in brief, was to suppress all forty-eight offices of Receiver General of Finance (!), discharge thirty-six of the Receivers General outright and organize a selected group of twelve as a *régie* to be called the *Recette générale*. This was a momentous reform because it affected a corps of accountants who separately collected, each in his own Generality, an average of about three million livres a year, or a total of some 140 millions for the entire corps of twenty-four on duty each year. Nothing even remotely as radical as this had been attempted since John Law had suspended the Receivers General on 12 October 1719.[2]

The striking feature of the reform was the establishment of one general caisse instead of the forty-eight. There had been a central *caisse commune*, with other central bureaux, ever since 1716 but only as a rudimentary intermediary between the Royal Treasury and the caisses of the individual Receivers General. Necker now made it the very heart of the *Recette générale*, by ordering the twelve members of the new organization to choose an official *caissier* 'of whom they would be the guarantors and whom the Grand Chancellery would provide with the commission of *Caissier général de*

---

[1] Necker, *Œuvres*, vol. I, p. 165.
[2] An arrêt of 5 Jan. 1721 and Lettres patentes of 14 Dec. 1722 restored them.

la caisse commune des impositions.[1] Thus in one respect the *caissier général* was intended to serve much the same function as the *adjudicateur* in the General Farm, a salaried puppet or titular head who signed documents in the name of the entire company and in so doing provided a legal link between the company and other parties, particularly the Crown. But in another respect the *Caissier général* was to be much more than this because he was to be in charge of the single central caisse to which the provincial Receivers were henceforth supposed to pay revenues from the direct taxes. The salary of the *caissier général*, set at 20,000 livres, reflected these responsibilities for it was double that of the *adjudicateur* of the General Farm.

As a natural consequence of this reform, and one that Necker deliberately planned, the *Caissier général* was supposed to issue all rescriptions in the name of the company and to sign them and have them countersigned by three of the twelve Receivers General. The instruction on this matter included an example of the new printed form for the rescription, apparently designed or at least approved by Moreau de Beaumont.[2] In this way the private credit of the individual Receiver General was swept away at a stroke. Instead of each Receiver General issuing rescriptions in his own name, the *Recette générale* was to take responsibility for issuing all rescriptions and for redeeming them. No longer would the Receiver General be an independent banker flourishing or failing according to the fortunes of his private business; no longer could he go bankrupt and leave the Crown and other holders of his rescriptions to scramble for whatever cash the courts could recover from his estate. The credit notes of the *Recette générale* would henceforth be as sound as those of the General Farm.

Another consequence was that all the payments hitherto made on behalf of the Crown by the Receivers General, each according to his annual *état du Roi*, would now have to be made by salaried clerks and *caissiers* acting as employees of the new organization. Payment would become literally a bureaucratic process. It is well to remember, however, that each Receiver General had always had his own clerical staff out in his Generality where most of the revenues were actually collected from the Receivers, and he had always made payments by issuing rescriptions drawn much like cheques on those *commis*. The real change in the new arrangements was twofold: the staff in the provinces would now work for the organization rather than for an individual Receiver General, and each payment would be made according to a collective decision. Thus the new rescription read, in part, 'Con-

[1] Edict of April 1780; arrêt of 25 June 1780 (B.N., F 21202 (11)).
[2] Arrêt du conseil qui détermine la forme des rescriptions des recettes générales, 25 June 1780 (B.N., F 21202 (11)).

formément à la délibération de Messieurs les Receveurs généraux de [date] je soussigné, Caissier général des Recettes Générales, prie Monsieur [name] Commis à la Recette Générale des Finances de [place] de payer à mon ordre, des deniers de sa recette...'[1] In its systems of payment and employment this organization would function much like the General Farm and the *Régie générale*.

A very large account for salaries was therefore only to be expected. The cost of the *caisse commune* had risen from 40,000 livres in 1770 to 66,000 in 1778 when Necker had reduced it to 45,000 livres. With the formation of the *Recette générale*, he raised it to 96,000 livres a year, not counting the incidental expenses of heat, light, rent and so on, and when Necker retired from office in May 1781 this figure stood at 99,300 livres.[2] The other central bureaux were correspondingly enlarged and we find that for the year 1781 Necker reckoned the organization would cost a total of 1,302,748 livres of which 300,000 for the salaries of the twelve commissioned *régisseurs*, 315,100 for their employees in Paris and the provinces and 687,648 for office expenses, gratifications to zealous employees, travelling expenses, transporting coin and purchasing new premises.[3] This last item was for the Hôtel de Mesmes which Necker arranged to buy, renovate and rename the Hôtel des Recettes Générales. Of course the benefits from the new system were quite incalculable in terms of immediate loss or gain, but that was how Necker's critics chose to assess the reform. Joly de Fleury and Calonne later made comparisons with the supposed costs of the old system and reproached Necker with saving little or no money by this reorganization. Counting only salaries and other obvious costs they may have been right, especially considering that in the short term, the cost of repaying the price of office to the thirty-six discharged Receivers General had to be set against any gains. But the old system had had hidden costs which, although impossible to calculate accurately, must have been very great. At all events, as Necker's supporters pointed out, there would not have been such a hue and cry at the reform, and such haste to return to the old system after Necker's fall, if many people had not lost a great deal of money, influence or both. The reform could not be properly measured in terms of what it saved in immediate costs.

This reform was never fully implemented because the year which elapsed between the publication of the first reforming edict in April 1780 and Necker's fall in May 1781 was too short a time. The names of the twelve Receivers General chosen to direct the organization were announced on

[1] *Ibid.*   [2] B.N., Coll. Joly de Fleury 1438, fols. 156 ff.
[3] B.N., Coll. Joly de Fleury 1435.

28 May 1780 and the Chambers of Accounts registered their letters of commission on 3 June.[1] They chose their *caissier général*, Jean-Claude Geoffroy d'Assy, in the next few weeks and the Chamber registered his letters of commission on 30 June. Throughout the short life of this organization the Receivers General resisted the change as much as they could, and as the twelve *régisseurs* were chosen for being the senior men in the corps (against Necker's wish) we may assume that they undertook their tasks of reform without much enthusiasm. A certain financier who claimed to have prepared Necker's reform plan described the opposition to it as bitter and vindictive.[2] Ten years later, during the French revolution, Bertrand Dufresne still remembered their damaging opposition and refused to hire Receivers General for a new branch of the National Treasury then being organized to replace the old system. He preferred to hire their clerks instead![3] In 1781 Dufresne and Necker were still struggling with difficult tasks of reorganization in Paris and in the provinces, tasks which had not been accomplished by the time the next Minister, Joly de Fleury, was ready to return to the old system.

What had been accomplished by then? During the decade 1771–81 three Ministers of Finance had taken great strides in the direction of a truly public system of public finance and they had organized various financial agencies of the Crown. The collection and management of the major revenues were now in the hands of four organizations: the General Farm, the *Régie générale*, the Domains Administration and (for a time) the *Recette générale*. Three of these were working as Crown companies, collecting funds directly for the government, and the short-term advances they afforded the government were not a source of great personal profit to them. Profits now went into the caisses of the organizations. The spending caisses, too, had been reduced in number and subjected to a regular, close ministerial scrutiny. The remaining accountants and the new *régies* were obliged to account monthly to the Royal Council (i.e. the Department of Finance) which was beginning to be in a position to know the financial situation of the government a little better. Necker had publicly declared the processes of the Chamber of Accounts to be useless for proper central direction of the financial system and had revived and enlarged Colbert's system of providing

---

[1] Arrêt of 28 May 1780; A.N., P 2518. They were François-Abraham-Marie Mouchard; Claude-Henry Watelet; Jean-Marie Richard; Simon-Charles Boutin; Louis Choart; Jean Batailhe de Francès; Jean-Baptiste-Henri Guillot de Lorme; Paul Fayard des Bourdeilles; Charles-Louis Meulan; François-Joseph Harvoin; Claude Desbrest; Nicolas Beaujon (appointed a few days later than the rest for no obvious reason) (A.N., P 2518, fols. 384–405).

[2] Roland, *Mémoire au Roi*, pp. 8 and 58; also his *Financier patriote*, pp. 16 and 22.

[3] A.N., AB XIX 327, fol. 519, Dufresne to Louis XVI, 14 Jan. 1791.

regular accounts for the Minister of Finance. The *contrôle* of the major spending departments was now partly lodged in the bureaux of the Department of Finance. To cope with much heavier responsibilities the Department had been integrated after 1777 by the abolition of the six venal offices of Intendant of Finance. All this showed a policy of developing a bureaucracy, an organized public administration of finances, as an alternative to the private management of government funds by venal accountants with individual caisses. It is this policy which shows the significance of Necker's efforts to suppress the fees and commissions of accountants such as Bertin, the Receiver General of the *Revenus casuels*, in favour of fixed salaries.[1] This policy, clearest in Necker's work, was very similar to that of the Chancellor Maupeou who, together with Terray, had destroyed the Parlements, *Cours des aides* and other courts and set up new courts of salaried justices: both policies were opposed to the system of venal offices. Both policies wounded powerful vested interests and soon suffered political defeat. The venal judges returned with the revival of the sovereign courts after 1774; many of the venal accountants returned with the restoration of their offices after May 1781. As Hennet remarked of the suppressed Receivers General, 'the personal interest of thirty-six men cried out aloud; the general interest of thirty million men remained silent'.[2] One of Necker's critics wrote, 'He wanted to destroy finance (*la finance*)'.[3] The political result of Necker's reforms was a reaction which brought him down and undid much of his work. His successors, Joly de Fleury, d'Ormesson and Calonne worked to restore and to sustain the old system of venal accountants with independent caisses and to found much of the short-term credit of the Crown on their private credit. The nature of that reaction, the subject of the next chapter, shows by contrast what had been accomplished by 1781.

[1] B.N., F 21201 (58) Arrêt du Conseil of 27 Feb. 1780 fixing Bertin's salary at 25,000 livres. This was reversed during the reaction under Calonne by Lettres patentes of 14 March 1784 (B.N., F 21210 (20)).
[2] A. J. U. Hennet, *Théorie du crédit public*, p. 277.
[3] Arch. de l'Ass. Publique, Paris, Papers of Auget de Montyon, 'Analyse d'un manuscrit datté du mois de juin 1781 sur le ministère de Monsieur Necker', in carton 19.

9

SIX YEARS OF REACTION
(1781–1787)

Necker's successor began his work as Minister of Finance on 21 May 1781 and hardly two months later there were strong rumours of a plan to restore the Receivers General of Finance and intimations that all of Necker's work might be undone. One observer wrote 'If the new Minister of Finance once begins to attack some part of his predecessor's plan, there is no doubt that the whole structure will collapse and that his [Necker's] innovations will suffer the fate of Monsieur Turgot's, not a vestige of which remains.'[1] Although too pessimistic and sweeping, this view soon proved to contain a large measure of truth. In the months that followed the new Minister of Finance, Joly de Fleury, undid all of Necker's work on the Receivers General and Turgot's work on the *Receveurs particuliers*. He and a later Minister, Calonne, created or re-created some offices of Treasurer General and Payer of the rentes, reduced the authority of *premiers commis* in the Department of Finance by appointing more magistrates and also revived the private credit of accountants as a main source of government short-term credit. If they did little to alter the new Domains Administration, the *Régie générale* or the General Farm and if they made no great changes in the new accounting legislation, these ministers nevertheless presided over a movement to restore and strengthen the old system of accountants with independent caisses. None of the reforms which Calonne prepared for the Assembly of Notables were intended to change that system; nearly all were planned for the very different purpose of equalizing tax burdens and simplifying tax collections. When the Assembly balked at these proposals and Calonne fell from office, another era of administrative reform was about to begin.

So stated without details or evidence, the idea of grouping the ministry of Calonne together with the ministries of Joly de Fleury and d'Ormesson as a period of 'reaction' will seem arbitrary and even incredible to many readers. We have become so accustomed to Calonne's interpretation of the financial

---

[1] Bachaumont, *Mémoires secrets*, vol. 17, p. 287, 19 July 1781.

crisis that any other at first sight is bound to seem forced and improbable. Every schoolboy knows that the crisis had to be met by taxing the nobles and otherwise changing the taxes along the lines Calonne proposed. If Calonne failed to persuade the Assembly of Notables to adopt this view, he succeeded in convincing future generations. The shortcomings of his view and the events of 1787 are the subject of the next chapter. In this one I hope to show how the three ministers in office from 1781 to 1787 were essentially in agreement with conservative forces that had resisted the reforms of Terray, Turgot and Necker, and how Joly de Fleury and Calonne tried to revive the old system of financial administration.

The years after Necker's resignation have long been recognized as a period of reaction, but in quite a different sense. Aimé Cherest, for example, described the reaction of the nobility, the bishops and other pillars of the ancien régime against reforms tending towards liberty and equality, and he rightly made much of laws such as the Regulation of 22 May 1781 reserving the ranks of military officer for nobles of the fourth degree.[1] This was a social and political interpretation which explained a good deal but made little sense of the struggles over public finance; it was particularly misleading when it reduced the financial issues to two: economy in royal pensions and other favours to the privileged orders, and the taxing of those orders. In such terms—which are those of most books on the period—the reaction appears to be merely resistance to economy and to taxation. There is no denying that there were conflicts over those issues, but in addition there is evidence of a very different struggle over the reform of the system of caisses and accountants.

Resistance to changes in the system was undoubtedly carried on by the various corps of accountants and their creditors, as Necker, Roland[2] and Hennet declared,[3] but a more vocal resistance developed in the Paris Chamber of Accounts. It is easily overlooked because the Chamber was spared the proscription and exile which the Parlements, the Cours des aides and other sovereign courts suffered at the hands of Maupeou and Terray in 1771. Superficially there is even a semblance of cooperation between those ministers and the Chamber, because they both found the Parlements very trying after the Seven Years War and in the 1760s the remonstrances of the Paris Chamber of Accounts were mostly directed against the Parlements. The unhappy fate of the Parlements, however, and the simultaneous beginning of Terray's assault on the venal Payers brought the Chamber

---

[1] Aimé Cherest, *La Chute de l'ancien régime* (*1787–98*) (Paris, 1884), 2 vols., vol. I, pp. 6 ff.
[2] C. N. Roland, *Mémoire au Roi* (1784), *passim*.
[3] Hennet, *Théorie du crédit public* (1816), p. 217.

veering round to attack these reforms. Throughout the decade of reform the King received the remonstrances of many a delegation from the Chamber on many a Sunday at Versailles.[1]

The remonstrances of those years were eloquent repetitions of a few conservative themes. The Chamber of Accounts tried to impress upon Turgot and upon Louis XVI in the very first year of his reign that in Terray's period of office 'les formes antiques et précieuses y étaient subverties', and the interests of both the King and his subjects had been compromised.[2] The Chamber warned of the confusion and delay which they believed would follow upon any consolidation or combining of accounts. This was to be the most fundamental and permanent of the Chamber's arguments. According to their principles of accounting, clear and accurate records were possible only by keeping separate books for each function or type of transaction and for each fiscal year. Thus the Receivers General of Finance had to keep separate records of the collection and expenditure of the *taille*, the *capitation*, the *vingtième* and every other type of revenue in which they dealt. The Chamber believed that the more types of transaction in a caisse, the more numerous the books for the accountant to keep, the slower the official business would be done, and the greater the possibility of error in both accounting and auditing. When the business of a caisse grew beyond the powers of one accountant, the Chamber believed that another office should be created and another caisse. It was a theory of accounting which justified an endless fragmentation of accounts and a division of funds into a correspondingly large number of caisses under as many accountants. It was one of the main reasons why the Chamber opposed the combining of offices, caisses and accounts. For example, when in November 1778 all the various Treasurers for the Department of War were replaced by a single Treasurer General, the Chamber expressed the fear that the immense detail of all these functions would be 'beyond the powers of a single accountant'.[3] And for similar reasons they sent a deputation to Louis XVI on 17 April 1780 with remonstrances against Necker's edict suppressing the Receivers General. When the King refused to retract or change the edict they registered it with stipulations about the accounting procedures.[4]

The Chamber had another difference with Necker, in particular, over the treatment of failing accountants. The disagreement arose over individual cases but stemmed from fundamentally different views of the financial

---

[1] Specifically on 10 January 1773, 21 February 1773, 2 May 1773, 13 July 1773 (or thereabouts), 2 September 1775 *ca.*, 28 April 1776, 21 November 1778 and 17 April 1780.
[2] A.N., P 2739, session of 30 January 1775.
[3] A.N., P 2740, session of 19 November 1778.
[4] A.N., P 2741, the Remonstrance itself drawn up on 15 April.

system. According to the Chamber's theory (and practice) the health of the system was maintained by rigorously pursuing any accountant who failed or absented himself for more than a few days and, if necessary, by confiscating the man's property in order to recover any losses and expropriating his office in order to sell it to a new accountant. The Chamber was quite pitiless in these pursuits, for like a hangman it was thereby earning its living as well as doing its duty. In at least two major bankruptcies, however, Necker thwarted the Chamber's pursuit, partly because he believed that by organization and inspection the system could be made proof against bankruptcy and partly because he could see little point in prosecuting individuals for misdeeds which were really misfortunes arising from faults in the system. In the case of Gabriel Prévost, a bankrupt Treasurer General for *Ponts et Chaussées*, Necker twice ordered the Chamber to leave him alone, and when Prévost voluntarily turned over his goods to the Crown Necker granted him a pension of 6,130 livres a year to be categorically 'insaisissable', immune to the pursuits of all courts and creditors.[1] The other case was the bankruptcy of Jean-Francois Caron, Treasurer General of the Marc d'Or, which Necker likewise removed altogether from the jurisdiction of the Chamber and turned over to a royal commission.[2] To the Chamber, such interference was a danger to the health of the financial system because it would lead to more abuses as soon as other accountants saw that punishment in these cases had been suspended. The way to end bankruptcy, they maintained, was not by reform of the system but by rigorous prosecution of erring individuals. Accountants ought to be weeded out unless they were prosperous. Joly de Fleury and Calonne, each in his time, shared this conservative opinion and acted upon it.

Throughout the first decade of reform, the Chamber was not only disagreeing with the ministers over the financial system; it was also struggling to maintain its own income and position. To abolish an accountant and his caisse was to deprive the Chamber of the annual auditing fee (*épice*) fixed by statute for each set of accounts. As early as 1772 Terray abolished many accounts, infuriated the Chamber by declaring all the auditing fees to be too high and drastically reducing them. A delegation went off to Versailles with a remonstrance on 10 January 1773 claiming that auditing fees had been a recognized source of income for the Chamber ever since a charter of 1511 and that the rates could not be excessive because they had hardly increased since the schedules drawn up by Sully in 1610. 'Taking an average

---

[1] A.N., P 2519, Letters Patent of 23 September 1780; and Letters Patent of 14 August 1780. He turned over his property by contract on 2 February 1780.

[2] A.N., P 2517 fol. 291, arrêt of 25 April 1779 and Letters Patent of 8 September 1779.

year in the twenty years up to and including 1769, these emoluments are less considerable than they were during two of the last years in the ministry of Cardinal Fleury.'[1] The Chamber thought its total income not disproportionate to the earnings of the Parlement. The Crown responded favorably to this complaint. Terray would not withdraw his reforms, but consented to raise the auditing fee for each account of the Payers of the rentes from 8,000 livres to 12,000 and to draw up a new schedule of fees for the accounts of the Receivers General, ranging from 28,000 livres for the Paris accounts down to 7,000 for the accounts from each of eleven lesser Generalities.[2] The Chamber still felt injured but had to put up with its losses and voted compensation to those of its members who had sacrificed the most.

By one of his reforms Terray seemed to threaten the Chamber's very position and power as well as its fees. This was a decision of 1772, which Turgot and Necker later defended, to have all the Receivers (*Receveurs particuliers*, at that time called *Receveurs des tailles*) account to the Receivers General instead of to the Chambers. In the Minister's eyes this measure eliminated a wasteful duplication of audit because the Receivers General accounted to the Chamber for the money received from their Receivers. There seemed no need to account twice for the same funds merely because there were two steps in the collecting process. To the Chamber of Accounts, however, there was much more at stake than the auditing fees. As a result of the change each Receiver General became legally responsible, 'civilement garant', for the official business of the Receivers in his Generality and that shift of responsibility opened the way for challenge of the Chamber's jurisdiction over the Receivers. To begin with, the *Cours des aides* had a right to deal with legal business arising out of contracts like those between Receivers General and Receivers. Then, to complicate matters still further, Turgot's reform of August 1775 encouraged the Receivers to cumulate offices as collectors of municipal *octrois* and other taxes not always subject to the Chamber's authority. If one of these accountants failed or was suspected of fraud, the ensuing legal pursuit could never be confined to one part of his business but was invariably total, with the result that various courts might claim to deal with the case and the Chamber had to engage in long struggles to defend its jurisdiction.

In 1779 two Receivers became the object of such struggles: Charles-Nicolas Roland in the Election of Chartres and René-Louis Goupil de

---

[1] A.N., P 2829, session of 29 December 1772.
[2] These were Soissons, Amiens, Châlons-sur-Marne, Bourges, Moulins, Lyon, Limoges, La Rochelle, Auch, Caen and Alençon, as listed in A.N., P 2506, fol. 76, Letters Patent of 1 May 1773. In 1784 Roland believed that the Chamber had lost a great deal in fees by the reforms of Terray, Turgot and especially Necker. (*Mémoire au Roi* (1784), p. 58.)

Bouillé in the Election of Saumur, both accused of disorder and dishonesty. To the consternation of the Paris Chamber, the Royal Council was at first prevailed upon to reserve these cases for the justices of the Elections, with appeals to go to the *Cour des aides*.[1] Undeterred, the Chamber went about its usual business of pursuit and for some time both courts proceeded to deal with the two unhappy accountants as they saw fit and each petitioned the Crown against the other. The conflict became most acute when the Chamber ordered Roland imprisoned in the 'geôle du petit Châtelet', only to find that the *Cour des aides* had already shut him up in the Conciergerie!

On 6 May 1780 the Chamber heard a letter from the Keeper of the Seals announcing the appointment of a Council commission to hear from both courts and to settle the matter of jurisdiction.[2] Joly de Fleury, future Minister of Finance, was one of the three commissioners.[3] They reported largely in the Chamber's favour and, armed with a decision of the Royal Council (dated 29 September 1780) the Chamber triumphantly proceeded with the cases of Roland and Goupil.[4] This triumph was not complete, however, nor the Council's judgement final. After Necker's fall, when a reactionary edict of January 1782 had restored two offices of Receiver to each Generality, the Crown put them entirely under the jurisdiction of the Election courts with appeal to the *Cour des aides*. Eloquent remonstrances had no effect on this decision, but neither did the decision put an end to the Chamber's efforts.[5] A few years later the magistrates took part in the *révolte nobiliaire* with a sense of grievance and of self-righteousness hardened in many years of struggling over issues like those raised by Terray, Turgot and Necker.

The life of the Chamber of Accounts shows it as a conservative force opposed to any reform of the financial system. Roland, the unhappy victim of the struggles between different courts, believed the Chamber to be working together with the Receivers General to resist all changes.[6] Certainly these magistrates and accountants shared a conservative interest in maintaining the system against such plans as those of Necker and Roland. Yet it does not follow from this that the Chamber was working in league with Joly de Fleury or groups of accountants in any conspiratorial party of reaction. After all the magistrates were painfully aware that Joly de Fleury,

---

[1] A.N., P 2519, 2520, 2741 *passim*, 2742.
[2] Letter dated 25 April, A.N., P 2741, session of 6 May 1780.
[3] Along with Taboureau des Réaux, and Dufour de Villeneuve (Councillors of State) and de Menc (Master of Requests).
[4] A.N., P 2741, session of 15 November 1780.
[5] A.N., P 2742, sessions of 25 May 1782, 25 February 1782 and 13 May 1782; Remonstrances of 17 March and 12 May 1782.
[6] Roland, *Mémoire au Roi* (1784), *passim*.

like Necker, did not have the title of Controller General and was never formally received into the Chamber. It could quarrel with him, as it did over the question of jurisdiction over the Receivers. Not until Calonne's appointment in November 1783 did the Chamber feel that the finances were in safe hands. Yet Joly de Fleury and d'Ormesson were fellow-travellers of the Chambers just as much as Calonne.

Necker's immediate successor, Jean-François Joly de Fleury, seigneur de la Valette (1718–1802) was a nobleman and Councillor of State from a large family of Parlement magistrates. He had himself served in the Parlement of Paris and also as Intendant of the Generality of Dijon (1741). Eighteenth-century writers were seldom kind to him in the little potted summaries of character they composed for the amusement of their readers. Whether or not they were sound, the Minister himself provided the best clue to his financial policy in the choice of his collaborators. Unlike Terray, Turgot and Necker, none of whom had chosen accountants or other financiers to assist them, Joly de Fleury immediately called on a financier who had made a fortune supplying the army in the War of Austrian Succession and the Seven Years War and who had strong family connections among the major corps of accountants.[1] This was Jacques Marquet de Bourgade (1718–84).[2] An elder brother, Louis Marquet de Mont Saint Père, had been Receiver General for many years and had married the daughter of the famous court banker, Paris-Duverney; one of their sons had been a Receiver General since 1773, and one of their daughters had married Calonne, the future Minister of Finance, in 1769. A younger brother of Marquet de Bourgade, Jean-Daniel Marquet de Montbreton, had also been a Receiver General for many years and had married the daughter of a Farmer General, Dumas. There is plenty of evidence that Marquet de Bourgade was devoted to the advancement of these relations, and to the system in which he and his family had done so well.

When Necker had abolished the offices of Receiver General, Marquet de Bourgade's two brothers and nephew had all lost their places; the nephew's office had actually been owned and paid for by Marquet de Bourgade himself.[3] None of these was among the twelve *régisseurs* chosen to direct the new *Recette générale*, and there was small comfort in the appointment of

---

[1] It is to be kept in mind that Necker's connections were in the field of banking and therefore with a different group, not closely allied with accountants.

[2] Information on the Marquet family is largely from François Bluche in his various works, from the series 'P' in the Archives Nationales (papers of the Chambers of Accounts) and from the registers A.N., T 165¹⁻², T 165⁵ and T. 165¹⁵, the papers of Marquet Desgrèves.

[3] A.N., F⁴ 2021: he was reimbursed 869,900 livres for it by an order of 14 December 1781.

the nephew, Maurice-Alexandre Marquet Desgrèves, as one of eight assistants to the original group of twelve. However, Marquet de Bourgade made full use of the opportunities afforded by Joly de Fleury's favour in 1781 to advance the family. An official remarked of Marquet de Montbreton on 28 September: 'brother of Monsieur de Bourgade who had very much at heart to obtain a better Receivership for him, probably that for Rouen, by the good offices of the Minister',[1] and on 12 December he was duly appointed to one of the newly re-created offices of Receiver General for Rouen. At the same time the nephew, Marquet Desgrèves, was appointed to the Receivership for Bordeaux which he had held before Necker's suppressions.[2] The powerful family benefactor, Marquet de Bourgade, appears to have received a salary of 40,000 livres a year during his period of office and to have been made one of the eight *régisseurs* of the postal service on 3 August 1783, less than a year before his death.[3]

All this and more was in consequence of Joly de Fleury's trust in Marquet de Bourgade. Whatever the origin of their friendship (and it may have been in childhood, as they were the same age) these two were very close and from the beginning of the ministry Joly de Fleury was addressing the other as 'mon amy' in familiar little notes on financial questions and signing off with phrases like 'vous avez toute mon amitié'.[4] As for de Bourgade's precise role in the government, the editor of Bachaumont's *Mémoires secrets* knew as early as 8 June 1781 that he was to be

a director of the Royal Treasury, much like Monsieur Necker in the time of Monsieur Taboureau, with the difference that Monsieur de Bourgade will be totally under the orders of the new Minister of Finance and will work only with him [not with the King]. It is believed that Monsieur de Fleury's purpose is to entrust this collaborator with the continuation of the financial operations undertaken by the Director General [i.e. Necker].[5]

Correspondence in the Joly de Fleury papers at the Bibliothèque nationale shows that Marquet de Bourgade did indeed have charge of this part of the Minister's task and may therefore be held largely responsible for undoing Necker's financial reforms. He and the Minister consulted others, particularly a Receiver General, François-Joseph Harvoin, and a *premier commis*, Dailly, but it seems plain that all decisions were taken by the Minister and

[1] B.N., Coll. Joly de Fleury 1435, fol. 161.
[2] Desgrèves was mentioned in Bourgade's will for one-eighth of the property as was also a niece, Jacqueline-Henriette (daughter of Louis) who had married François-Nicolas de la Guillaumye, Intendant of Corsica. Desgrèves was to go bankrupt in 1789.
[3] B.M., FR 551, Etats de comptant, 1783; and Eugène Vaillé, *Histoire des postes françaises*, vol. 6, part 1, p. 115.
[4] B.N., Coll. Joly de Fleury 1434, *passim*.
[5] Vol. 17 (1782), 8 June 1781, p. 218.

his friend. Marquet de Bourgarde remained in this position until Calonne took office early in November 1783 and he died five months later on 12 April.

In choosing Marquet de Bourgade, Joly de Fleury was appointing a financier with strong personal interests in the system of accountants and caisses to take charge of work which had been in the hands of *premiers commis* for more than ten years. Three *Premiers commis des finances* had been chosen, one after another, by the three Ministers: Armand Le Clerc by Terray, Jean de Vaine by Turgot and Bertrand Dufresne by Necker. Each had worked closely with his Minister and had fallen from office with him, and yet unlike Marquet de Bourgade each had served as a regular departmental official listed in the *Almanach royal* at the head of several bureaux. It had been the policy of the three reforming Ministers to have their collaborators in the task of reforming public finances properly appointed as officials of the Department of Finance; and by not so appointing Marquet de Bourgade, the new Minister undermined the power of the Department. He and Marquet de Bourgade put their heads together and selected a colourless clerk, Achille-Joseph Gojard, to succeed Necker's capable and energetic Dufresne in the post of *Premier commis des finances*.[1] Totally dependent on de Bourgade, Gojard did his work in a routine manner as he was expected to do without a thought of reforms like those his three predecessors had collaborated in, and in the meantime de Bourgade went ahead with his reactionary plans for reviving the system of caisses and accountants. Whereas the reforming Ministers and their *premiers commis* had stood for public authority in government finance, Joly de Fleury and Marquet de Bourgade stood for government finance by private enterprise.

One of their fundamental reactionary ideas was that accountants working for private profit would be more energetic, efficient and economical than salaried administrators. Marquet de Bourgade observed to Joly de Fleury that the twelve administrators of Necker's *Recette générale* had paid too much for the transport of money but that this was not surprising 'in view of the fact that these Receivers General had no personal interest in the matter'.[2] For the same reason they decided to do away with the fixed salaries Necker had arranged to pay these Receivers General and other accountants such as Bertin, the Receiver General of the *Revenus casuels*, to restore the old system of commissions (*taxations*) reimbursements (*remises*),

[1] J. F. Bosher, 'The *premiers commis des finances* in the Reign of Louis XVI', *French Historical Studies*, vol. III, no. 4 (1964), p. 490.
[2] B.N., Coll. Joly de Fleury 1438, fol. 10, 7 April 1782.

and other such variable emoluments.[1] In recommending the destruction of Necker's new *Recette générale* to Louis XVI, Joly de Fleury argued that each fiscal year and each Generality required special attention and so the direct taxes of the entire kingdom could not be properly collected 'by a company of which the members being guided by no personal interest are less zealous in their work and often show a diversity of efforts detrimental to the service'.[2] Such was the prevailing view of the matter in the ancien régime when nearly all public services were done for private profit and the notion of salaried public servants was out of favour.

Another idea, probably the most important in the minds of de Fleury and de Bourgade, was that the short-term credit of the government necessarily depended on the personal credit of the accountants. They reckoned that for the year 1782 some 400 millions in credit would have to be found, some of it in long-term loans but perhaps 135 millions in *anticipations* on the revenue of 1783 and as much as possible of the rest in the form of rescriptions.[3] Joly de Fleury reported rather pompously to the King:

I cast my gaze on the *Recettes générales* and was troubled to see that the rescriptions which were of such great help under the administrations of Monsieur Orry, of Monsieur de Machault and in the last war were not at all in my hands. I tried uselessly to revive confidence in those bills; I could not succeed in doing so. Those who do the service, that is, make advances [to the Crown] of one or several millions a month, receive rescriptions but are obliged to offer their own notes on the market. Rescriptions are of little use because people regard them as *assignations* on the Royal Treasury . . . This stagnation can only be attributed to the public opinion which did not approve of the suppression of the Receivers General. This opinion is not without foundations: the twelve administrators who were substituted for the forty-eight Receivers General sign these rescriptions, it is true, but they are not the guarantors of them. The people who lend their money want to have a rich guarantor behind the rescriptions.[4]

He concluded by urging that the Receivers General be reinstated. 'Il est toujours facheux de changer; mais la nécessité du crédit commande...'

[1] B.N., Coll. Joly de Fleury 1435, fol. 184, letter of 24 Sept. 1781. B.N., F 21210 (20), lettres patentes du Roi portant rétablissement des droits de quittance au receveur général des revenus casuels (14 March 1784).

[2] B.N., Coll. Joly de Fleury 1435, fols. 56 ff., 'Copie du rapport fait au Roy', 7 Oct. 1781. They put forward similar arguments for the paying accountants: 'Treasurers by commission on mere salaries cannot be guarantors of their clerks and as they have no personal interest in supervising the work of their clerks, Your Majesty is continually exposed to considerable losses and frauds' (B.N., Coll. Joly de Fleury 1439, fols. 36 ff. 'Travail sur la création des trésoriers généraux de la guerre et de la marine.' July 1782).

[3] B.N., Coll. Joly de Fleury 1434, fols. 174 ff.

[4] B.N., Coll. Joly de Fleury 1435, fol. 56. Later in 1782 we find Joly de Fleury assuring the King that rescriptions are beginning to go on to the market again and will do so on an ever-increasing scale.

As a practical result of these ideas the Minister and his adviser tried to find the richest possible men with the soundest possible credit to fill new and other vacant offices. This was their guiding principle in selecting accountants. For this reason Joly de Fleury declared himself opposed to choosing men according to their influence and patronage, just as Necker had been, but for completely different reasons. Necker had argued that the government ought to choose men for their ability, loyalty and honesty and should base its credit 'not on the signatures of persons it has chosen as intermediaries but on the public establishment (la chose publique) in general'.[1] Joly de Fleury argued that the short-term credit of the government necessarily depended on the choice of accountants with good personal credit and we find him taking wealth into account in his various assessments of candidates for Receiverships: 'Landry *fils*, good subject, intelligent and rich; Bouilhac *fils*, one of the suppressed Farmers General, made himself useful by his work in the Farm, rich and strongly recommended by Madame Adelaide etc.'[2] In the final selection Joly de Fleury and Marquet de Bourgade gave some weight to other factors, but their declared intention was to choose the wealthiest men. As I shall show, Calonne in his time had exactly the same idea.

There was yet a third principle in the minds of these reactionary ministers: only a large number of independent accountants with separate caisses were capable of drawing up correct accounts. Joly de Fleury and Marquet de Bourgade agreed that Necker's twelve-man *Recette générale* could not possibly prepare the accounts hitherto kept by forty-eight independent accountants. The Minister made this point to Louis XVI as a good reason for restoring two Receivers General to each Generality. 'It will be easier to prevent confusion', he said. 'Each one will have a year free to finish his business and to prepare his accounts.'[3] A few months later, in July 1782, he used the same argument to justify the appointment of a second Treasurer General for each of the Departments of War and Marine. In this case, the Secretary of State for the Marine, the marquis de Ségur, objected that a second Treasurer would double the work of correspondence in his Department and cause an extra burden in supervising two sets of accounts. 'I find it very agreeable', he wrote, 'to have to do with only one person and to find in one place all the materials which I need to pursue His Majesty's service.'[4] But Joly de Fleury merely repeated his own arguments in reply and the Minister for the Marine gave way. Had someone with Necker's

[1] J. Necker, *De l'administration*, vol. III, p. 128.
[2] B.N., Coll. Joly de Fleury 1437 fol. 283; 1435, fols. 162 ff.
[3] B.N., Coll. Joly de Fleury 1434, no. 34, fol. 31, 5 Sept. 1781; and 1435, fols. 56 ff.
[4] B.N., Coll. Joly de Fleury 1439, fol. 45.

view of the matter pointed out that anyone or any organization could perfectly well hire accounting clerks to keep any number of account books, as private firms did, Joly de Fleury would have replied that such clerks were not acceptable to the Chamber of Accounts and could therefore have no legal status or responsibility. It would not have been easy to confound him. The system of caisses and accountants, like many institutions of the ancien régime, was internally consistent and the conservative mind, by remaining within the system, could always find arguments for its defence.

Lefèvre d'Ormesson became Minister of Finance on 29 March 1783, when Joly de Fleury was dismissed, and held the post until the following November.[1] Member of a numerous, powerful and well-known family of *parlementaires*, he followed more or less in Joly de Fleury's footsteps for a few months and then, having thought of reforming the General Farm, immediately fell victim to a political onslaught of financial interests which drove him out of office. He had a reputation for laborious and rather pedantic attention to the legal aspects of public questions (next door to stupidity in the minds of eighteenth-century memorialists) and was for the most part a conservative defender of the financial system. This is perhaps not surprising when we consider the long family tradition going back to the sixteenth century and his own career as a Master of Requests and Intendant of Finance which began at the age of nineteen. As a result of this early start and of painstaking investigation in the company of a boyhood friend, his father's secretary, Pierre-Hubert Anson, he knew a great deal about the system and believed in it. He believed in venal offices, the superiority of magistrates and other nobles and the inherent inferiority of clerks and other commoners. His friend Anson, who became a clerk in the *Bureau des impositions* and later played a role in the National Assembly, once accused him of arrogance and wrote, 'I had suspected and now I see more than ever that equality is the basis of true friendship...'[2] The friendship lasted long enough for d'Ormesson during his brief period as Minister to find Anson a Receiver General's office. During his ministry d'Ormesson also assisted the planners of a customs reform project, as Calonne was to do after him, and it was partly in trying to release customs duties from the shackles of the lease to the General Farm that he got into the trouble which led to his resignation. But there is no evidence that he ever tried to change the system of caisses and accountants.

His affiliations and preferences suggest the contrary. Like Turgot and many others from old official families, he had despised and detested Necker

[1] This was Henri-François de Paule III Le Fèvre d'Ormesson (1751–1807).
[2] Anson to d'Ormesson, 31 March 1773 (A.N., 144 AP 129 dossier I, no. 5).

from the moment Necker had been appointed, and he soon had personal reasons for these feelings because he was one of the venal Intendants of Finance whom Necker discharged in June 1777. By his own admission he refused to assist Necker or to accept anything from him.[1] He welcomed the appointment of Joly de Fleury in 1781 with enthusiasm, tried to assist him in every possible way, wrote him many a memoir, and was a party to the restoration of the Receivers General.[2] He retained the services of Marquet de Bourgade. Without further research into his brief period of office we may safely assert that he had more in common with Joly de Fleury and Calonne than with the reformers of the earlier period. But his ministry contributed nothing positive to the reaction, and it was Calonne who developed the work begun by Joly de Fleury.

The active and complicated ministry of Calonne, during the three and one-half years from November 1783 to April 1787, has been interpreted in various ways, but the most convincing explanation of it is the one Herbert Luethy developed in his study of international finance, *La Banque protestante en France de la révocation de l'édit de Nantes à la révolution*.[3] In that book, Calonne appears as a member of a particular group of ancien-régime financiers, one of the social pillars of the régime which included families like the Marquet into which he married in 1769, thereby making Marquet de Bourgade ('mon oncle', as Calonne called him)[4] and Marquet de Montbreton his uncles by marriage and Marquet Desgrèves his brother-in-law; and the family of Micault d'Harvelay, whose widow he was to marry in 1788, thus relating himself to several more of the most powerful financial dynasties.[5] As Minister, Calonne behaved like the *chef d'orchestre* of these ramifying families and conducted a programme of conservative revival, 'the last great effort to restore the society of the ancien régime in its glory and in its splendour'.[6] His policies expressed that society's 'reaction of

---

[1] B.N., Coll. Joly de Fleury 1448, memoir by d'Ormesson of 25 June 1781, fols. 55–8.

[2] *Loc. cit.*; Coll. Joly de Fleury 1443, 'Mémoire sur le département des impositions', by d'Ormesson dated June 1781, fol. 60; and A.N., 144 AP 132, dossiers 1 and 2.

[3] (Paris, 1963), pp. 696–8.

[4] J. M. Augéard, *Mémoires secrets* (Paris, 1886), p. 116.

[5] Calonne first married Anne-Josephine, daughter of Louis Marquet de Mont Saint Père and Louis-Michèle Paris-Duverney, on 12 April 1769. His second wife, Anne-Rose-Josèphe de Nettine, had first married a Keeper of the Royal Treasury, Micault d'Harvelay, in January 1762. After his death Calonne married her at Bath, England, on 2 June 1788. Thus, Laborde de Méréville, who was d'Harvelay's nephew, became a relation of Calonne. Furthermore, this second wife's sister, Rosalie-Claire-Josèphe, had already married Laborde de Méréville's father, Jean-Joseph de Laborde, Court Banker, in August 1760; and another sister had married Lalive de Jully, introducer of ambassadors at Court, rich art collector and brother of a Farmer General. This sister was Marie-Louis-Josèphe (married July 1762). (See H. Luethy, *La Banque protestante*, vol. II, p. 658.)

[6] *Ibid.*, p. 697.

self-defence' against the tendencies of ministers like Terray, Turgot and Necker.

Turning from the field of social history, which Luethy opens before us, to the financial institutions, we must be struck by the determined opposition of Calonne to administrative reforms like those undertaken by Necker before him and by Loménie de Brienne and the National Assembly after him. During the years of his ministry (1783–7), Calonne behaved like a determined conservative in the vital matters of financial administration. He attacked Necker's reforms at great length in print, thoroughly approved of Joly de Fleury's restoration of the Receivers General, created many new venal offices himself, and believed that the public finances were best managed by the private enterprise of accountants and tax farmers.[1] After a long hostile review of Necker's work and much of Turgot's, Calonne concluded,

It is thus—and I could cite many other examples—that these operations allegedly for economy and these badly conceived suppressions, which are always presented as productive of great benefits for Your Majesty's finances, often leave behind them only the infuriating effects of useless innovation, of private fortunes overturned without any increase in the state's revenues, of reimbursement charges on the Royal Treasury, and, what is still worse, of public confidence damaged by changes which must inevitably shake it.[2]

To the book in which he thus attacked the administrative reformers, Calonne appended a careful anonymous defence of the financial system against its critics.[3] In response to the project of one would-be reformer, Bonvalet des Brosses, a former accountant whose criticisms of the system were expert and pointed, Calonne had the man banished from Paris without appeal. When Dufresne de Saint Léon printed his excellent critical study, *Etudes sur le crédit public* (1784), which Necker admired, and a copy fell into Calonne's hands, he ordered Dufresne to stop publication.[4] Yet Durban, who praised the financiers and the tax farms, was Calonne's choice to head the *Bureau des projets* in the Department of Finance. There was no place in Calonne's plans for changes in the system of caisses and accountants, and the famous reforms which he put before the Assembly of Notables in 1787 avoided any such changes. In his reform plans Calonne drew the attention of the Assembly—and of generations of historians later—to the deficiencies in the *tailles*,

[1] *Réponse de Monsieur Calonne à l'écrit de Monsieur Necker* (London, 1788), p. 264.
[2] *Ibid.*, p. 284.
[3] 'Réponse au chapitre IV de l'ouvrage que Monsieur Necker à publié...remise à Monsieur de Calonne par M. de...au mois de février 1783', 41 pp.
[4] Bonvalet des Brosses, *Moyens de simplifier la perception et la comptabilité* (1789), pp. 89, 110; Dufresne de Saint Léon, *Etudes du crédit public et des dettes publiques* (Paris, 1824), 'note préliminaire'.

the *aides*, the *gabelles*, the customs duties and such-like, all of which he planned to reform or replace by other taxes. Admirable though Calonne's programme was, it provided for alterations mainly in the form and management of the taxes, and left to his enemies the rationalizing and 'nationalizing' of the administrative system at its centre.

Calonne's view of the system was in many ways like that of the Chamber of Accounts. It was doubtless a sign of his respect for the Chamber that when he went before it on 13 November 1783 to be sworn in, he did so with a new and extraordinary pomp, accompanied by a retinue of Councillors of State, Masters of Requests, Intendants of Finance, Farmers General and others. The *Premier président* made him an unusually flattering speech of welcome, even suggesting that he gave off 'sparks of genius', and in his reply Calonne made an unmistakable allusion to Necker's 'empirical and violent remedies of which not even the memory should be recalled'.[1] As Calonne then suggested, he shared the beliefs of the Chamber, of Joly de Fleury and of other conservatives that the system required no reforms but only careful attention to the appointment of accountants and whenever necessary their legal prosecution. He believed that accountants ought to be rich, first and foremost, because their credit was the foundation of the Crown's credit. It was on those principles that he turned the misfortune of an elderly Receiver General, Harvoin, into a general disaster for the whole family. The son had for years held the strongest possible assurances of succeeding his father in the office, but Calonne took someone else instead because, as he said to the son's wife, 'a financial office of the importance of that of Tours cannot be entrusted to a man with no fortune; and henceforth I shall admit to these offices only people whose means will guarantee, with all security for the King, the management of the sums I shall entrust to them'.[2] He went on to explain that only rigorous disciplinary action against the accountants would overcome financial failures. Calonne's was a conservative voice, a voice of reaction against administrative reform. He was anxious to make the system work, not to change it.

The bare facts of the reaction carried out by Calonne and his two predecessors are quickly told. Joly de Fleury restored the forty-eight offices of Receiver General of Finance, two for each Generality, by an edict of October 1781, and by another of March 1784 Calonne added two more for Paris to replace the administrative Director of Paris Impositions and his

---

[1] Bachaumont, *Mémoires secrets* (1 Dec. 1783), vol. 24, pp. 66–7; B.N., MS fr. 11012, fol. 68; Boislisle, *Chambre des comptes de Paris*, p. 723.

[2] A.N., T* 594, *Journal de tous les évènements relatifs à la malheureuse affaire de Monsieur Harvoin, père, receveur général des finances de Tours*, MS fol. 27. For more on the Harvoin case, see below, chapter 10.

bureaux. Having destroyed Necker's organized agency for collecting the *taille* and other direct taxes, Joly de Fleury had also to make the rescriptions once more the instruments of the individual Receivers General. This he did by an arrêt of 16 October 1781 which allowed each Receiver General to issue and to honour his own rescriptions with only the endorsement of the general *caissier*, Geoffrey d'Assy. In the same month d'Assy was ordered to distribute the accounts, kept centrally since 1 January, so that each Receiver General could account retroactively to the beginning of the year and thus expunge the brief Neckerian reform from the record.[1]

In the winter of 1781–2 Joly de Fleury and Marquet de Bourgade turned their attention to the lesser but more numerous offices of *Receveur particulier*. There had been two for each of 209 Elections until Turgot had ordered the union of the two gradually as they fell vacant by the death of incumbents. By December 1781 the situation of the 418 original offices was this: 132 of these accountants each held one office, 101 had held two offices even before the Edict of August 1775, and 42 held two offices as a result of that Edict. Thus 276 men held the original 418 offices and in the course of time they would eventually have been reduced to 209. But Joly de Fleury reversed the process by an Edict of January 1782 which re-created the 418 offices.

Certain vestiges of coherence remained. The *Receveurs particuliers* were still accountable to the Receivers General rather than to the Chamber of Accounts, and the corps of Receivers General was provided with a stronger central committee to act in its name on certain matters much like the committee of the Payers of the rentes. Joly de Fleury, de Bourgade and d'Ormesson decided in February 1783 that this would be a committee of eight and would meet twice a week, on Monday and Thursday at 11 a.m., to discuss matters raised by any Receiver General or by Ministers of the Crown. Its first members were Batailhe de Francès (first *doyen* or chairman), Harvoin, Beaujon, de Vaines, Desbrets, Baron, de Lorme and Chanorier and five of their signatures were required on any document the committee issued. Yet this body had very little authority, as Bourgade explained: 'the manner of governing a farm or a *régie*, where all is known, must not be confused with the collection of taxes which have no relation from one province to another and for which each Receiver General is accountable only to himself and directly to the King'.[2] This was a far cry from Necker's highly organized *Recette générale*.

---

[1] Letters Patent of 7 Oct. 1781.
[2] B.N., Coll. Joly de Fleury 1441, fol. 99. Also, the edict of October 1781, article IX concerns this committee.

On the paying side of the system Joly de Fleury created a second office of Treasurer General for the War Department and another for the Marine Department. These were major offices and they each sold for the enormous sum of 1,600,000 livres to experienced accountants, Fontaine de Biré (War) and Baudard de Saint James (Marine).[1] Then, in May 1784 Calonne restored the office of Treasurer for *offrandes et aumônes, dévotions et bonnes œuvres du Roi* for a certain Jacques-Joseph Lenoir who was to receive and spend funds from the Treasury, as before Necker's time, under the direction of the King's Grand Almoner. In September 1784 Calonne re-created twenty offices of Payers of the rentes to sell for 300,000 livres each and as many of Controller at 80,000 livres each, and raised the total corps of Payers of the rentes to forty, almost as many as Terray had found in 1769. By a Declaration of 19 March 1786 Calonne created sixty offices of *Agent de change* to sell for 100,000 each.

This was no wholesale restoration of the situation as it had been in 1769 and there were even certain minor suppressions.[2] Yet the trend was clearly reactionary, and it was arrested only by the events of 1787 which led to Calonne's downfall and the beginning of a new era of reform. Looking back over the entire span of the reign, we cannot help but see the six years from the fall of Necker to that of Calonne standing out unmistakably as a period in which the transformation of the system of caisses and accountants stopped and the ministers made efforts to revive the system. Those reactionary efforts failed in the course of 1787.

[1] Edicts of June 1782. The new accountants were Marie-Sébastien-Charles-François Fontaine de Biré, Letters of Provision of 8 June 1782; and Claude Baudard de Saint James, informed of his appointment by Joly de Fleury in a note of 13 June 1782 (Coll. Joly de Fleury 1439, fol. 42).

[2] An edict of April 1782 suppressed all the provincial military Controllers from 1 January 1782 and another of July 1785 suppressed the six offices of *Receveur particulier des impositions de Paris*.

10

THE FINANCIAL CRISIS OF 1787

THE FINANCIAL difficulties facing the Crown in 1787 have always appeared to be merely the old budgetary problem of trying to meet heavy obligations with too little revenue. This, indeed, was the view Calonne took of it. When he put the problem before the famous Assembly of Notables on 2 March, he gave the public their first official knowledge of the annual deficit—over 100 million livres, while the revenue amounted to only 475 millions and the total borrowing since 1776 had reached 1,250 millions—and he proposed to increase government revenue by a new 'subvention territoriale' or tax in kind on agricultural produce.[1] This measure, together with auxiliary reforms of the *gabelle*, the customs duties, the *corvée* and other parts of the tax system, became the subject of a serious quarrel between Calonne and the privileged orders represented in the Assembly. The conflict ended with Calonne's discharge on 8 April. Because this political crisis revolved around Calonne's proposals for tax reform, historians have tended to see the financial crisis of the time, in terms of those proposals, as a matter of insufficient revenue and inappropriate taxes. This view, however, is a reflection of Calonne's belief that the system of financial administration was satisfactory, and many of Calonne's contemporaries did not share that belief. During the first six months of 1787 a series of spectacular financial failures among the accountants drew attention to the faults in the system of caisses and accountants. To examine these failures and their causes and results, is to throw a different light upon the financial crisis of 1787.

The first case began on 20 January 1787 when one of the senior Receivers General of Finance, François-Joseph Harvoin, abandoned his caisse and fled to Antwerp where he took refuge in a monastery. He had been an adviser and assistant to Joly de Fleury; and he was presently serving as treasurer to the princesses Victoire and Adelaide, and also as director of the bureaux which drew up the *états du Roi* for the Receivers-General of Finance. On the day he fled, but before his disappearance was yet known, a letter to the Controller-General (almost certainly from Gojard, the *Premier commis des finances*) announced:

[1] Jean Egret, *La Pré-révolution française, 1787–88* (Paris, 1962), p. 5.

183

Harvoin finds himself unable to honour his rescriptions which will fall due on the twenty-second of this month. He is lacking three hundred and some odd thousand livres. It appears certain that he will be short of at least as much again for the months of February, March and April. This situation is all the more disturbing in that it is impossible to allow protest over rescriptions because the result would be to discredit these bills in a way most damaging to the service. It is therefore absolutely necessary to provide for their payment by having them redeemed either by the Royal Treasury or else by Monsieur Duruey who could then be reimbursed.[1]

No sooner had Calonne approved this course of action than he learned of Harvoin's disappearance.

Harvoin's chief *caissier*, Jacques Monet, had immediately informed authorities in the *Cour des aides* and the Chamber of Accounts who had put seals on Harvoin's property that very day and soon afterwards commissioned Monet to carry on with Harvoin's *exercices*. The Crown, arbitrating between the two rival courts, allowed the Chamber of Accounts to pursue the case, and the Chamber immediately began criminal proceedings against Harvoin. Only gradually over a period of months did it emerge that he had neither made off with public funds nor engaged in dishonest practices nor even gone bankrupt in any simple sense of the term. He had broken the law only by abandoning his caisse, and this because he had been frightened that he would not be able to raise the several hundred thousand livres which he needed to honour his rescriptions for the service of his Generality until receipts began to come in. The failure ultimately appeared as merely a failure of nerve, hardly surprising in a man seventy-two years of age and partly paralysed as the result of a stroke some years earlier. His son described the stroke as 'une attaque d'apoplexie qui a affaibli les organes de sa tête'.[2]

The case was a complex one. It is possible that the *caissier*, Monet, who had long managed most of the old man's business, had plotted or done something to cause his flight, as the son later came to suspect. It is probable (as de Montholon, a magistrate in the Chamber of Accounts, said) that Harvoin was rigorously prosecuted because he had made many enemies through a life-long interest in various reform projects.[3] It appears almost

[1] A.N., F⁴ 2021, letter dated 20 January 1787.
[2] A.N., T* 594, *Journal de tous les évènements relatifs à la malheureuse affaire de Monsieur Harvoin père, receveur général des finances de Tours*, 312 fols. in MS containing 604 entries; followed by 96 fols. containing copies of 198 documents bearing on the case; and including a number of loose memoranda. The present quotation is from a memorandum dated 23 January 1787. This source will hereafter be abbreviated as 'Harvoin, *Journal*'.
[3] Harvoin, *Journal*, fol. 46, entry of 11 March 1787. Montholon spoke of 'projets sur le régiment des gardes, sur les communautés, sur toutes les cours de magistrature, sur les finances etc., enfin il a eu tort avec tout le monde'.

certain that he owed the Crown little or nothing when the value of his abandoned office and other confiscated assets were weighed in the balance.[1] This did not appear, however, until later. The publicity of the case in that spring of 1787 made considerable impression on opinion. As in all cases of accountants investigated by the Chamber of Accounts, Harvoin was immediately rendered bankrupt by the effects of the investigation itself, whatever the state of his affairs before. His creditors united to recover their investments and two of them, Carrelet de Loisy and Brousse, the one a magistrate in the parlement of Dijon and the other a lawyer attached to the parlement of Paris, went off to Antwerp and there succeeded in obtaining a court order for the seizure of the jewels and money which Harvoin had taken with him.[2] Meanwhile his son and son's wife made the rounds of Paris in a vain endeavour to keep the Receiver-generalship in the family. Malesherbes, Gojard and many others received them sympathetically but Calonne soon gave the office to another accountant and explained to Madame Harvoin, 'Your husband has nothing, and financial offices are not made to create nor to restore the fortunes of individuals...The conduct of his father renders your husband unworthy to succeed him in the office...'[3] The effect of all this activity was to advertise the affair even more widely.

Almost simultaneously another long and mysterious case began over the failure of one of the two Treasurers General for the Marine, Claude Baudard, baron de Saint James.[4] Son of a Marine Treasurer before him, rich in an ostentatious way, with a large house and bagatelle in Neuilly, three houses in Paris and a reputation for unquenchable ambition, he had built up an extraordinarily wide range of business enterprises. Mines, manufacturing, the famous Le Creusot founderies, the shipping ventures of his friend Beaumarchais, the Paris Water Company, the Northern Commercial Company, supplies of wood and equipment to the Navy, the *Caisse d'escompte* created in 1776, and other banking interests: all these had absorbed millions of livres, borrowed and invested by Baudard de Saint James. Many of these concerns he also managed or directed. His office of Treasurer General was therefore only part of an immense business empire and Calonne naturally relied on him to advance money to the Marine Department. In the course of 1786, however, Baudard de Saint James found himself pressed on all sides for more money and at the same time less and less able to meet

---

[1] Harvoin, *Journal*, a memorandum from Saint Aubin to Harvoin *fils* dated 2 March 1788, reckoning a surplus of 4,278 livres in Harvoin's dealings with the Crown.

[2] A.N., P 2847 and P 2744.

[3] Harvoin, *Journal*, fol. 28.

[4] A.N., P 2847 and P 2744; Legohérel, *Les Trésoriers généraux...*, p. 348.

his commitments by recovering investments. Times were hard for the Crown too. When Calonne decided to raise 70 millions by ordering the administrators of the *Caisse d'escompte* to increase their capital fund, Saint James, one of those administrators, reached the end of his resources. That was in January 1787 and on 2 February Saint James voluntarily turned his accounts over to the Crown, confident that an investigation would show them to be in proper order, and interned himself in the Bastille to protect himself against courts and creditors while awaiting the result. The very same day the Royal Council named a commission to investigate and appointed a temporary manager to carry on the business of his office.[1] Baudard de Saint James had many enemies and the case was further complicated by suspicions that he had played a part in the scandalous affair of the diamond necklace.[2] Six months later, on 3 July, he died leaving a wife and young children, but the case went on for some years. He was suspected of dishonest practices which had resulted in a debt to the Crown of fifteen thousand livres, another of 1,814,000 livres to the Invalides de la Marine, and some 13 millions in debts to private individuals. Although the investigation eventually showed his management of his Receiver-generalship to have been quite honest and sound, such a conclusion to such a notorious scandal was out of the question in 1787 and 1788.[3] Furthermore, his bankruptcy had ramifications expensive to the Crown and it shook the government's credit system to its very foundations. The case of Baudard de Saint James made a profound impression and was recalled years afterwards as a black mark on the financial system of the ancien régime.[4]

The third failure of the year occurred on 17 February when the Crown ordered seals put upon the possessions of Louis-René-Marchal de Sainscy, the *régisseur des économats* or, as he was sometimes called, the *économe du clergé de France*.[5] The duties of this office were to collect the revenues from

---

[1] A.N., P 2744. Louis-Charles-Thomas Bizouard was appointed by letter of commission dated 6 February 1787. The Royal Commission was composed of two Councillors of State, Le Noir and Perrin de Cypierre; the Lieutenant General of Police, de Crosne; three Masters of Requests, Charpentier de Boisgibault, Albert and de la Porte. Albert was asked to lift the seals formerly affixed by the royal commissioners at the request of the *Contrôleur des bons d'état du conseil*, Gérard-Maurice Turpin.

[2] *L'affaire du collier* in 1784–6 developed over a diamond necklace which the Cardinal de Rohan purchased for the Queen at the suggestion of the Comtesse de la Motte, and which disappeared. Obscure and complicated, the affair threw suspicion on many people.

[3] 'Types de capitalistes parisiens à la fin du XVIIIe siècle: le problème des investissements', *Centre de recherches sur l'histoire des entreprises*, bulletin no. 2 (Oct. 1953), pp. 25–31; Luethy, *La Banque protestante*, pp. 437 and 689.

[4] Rougier de la Bergerie (Jean-Baptiste), *Opinion*... (Paris, 9 April 1792), p. 18; Adam-Philippe, comte de Custine, speech to the National Assembly on 20 Nov. 1789 (Arch. parl. vol. x, p. 147).

[5] J. Borie, *Rapport*... (B.N., Le^{33} 3G (13)).

vacant church benefices and from confiscated ecclesiastical property such as that of the Jesuit Order. The post had been in the family for a long time and Louis-René had inherited it from his father, Louis-Pierre-Sébastien, on 2 April 1782. At that time the accounts showed a deficit of 1,460,573 livres, but Calonne made arrangements for the gradual repayment of these arrears. By the time of his declared failure Louis-René himself had run up a deficit of more than two millions, according to his successor, and most of this had not been recovered by 1792 when the *régie des économats* was abolished.[1] Meanwhile, at the suggestion of the Director-General of the économats, the Crown had named an *avocat au parlement* to assume the responsibilities of the office and to complete the Marchal de Sainscy accounts.[2]

On 5 March 1787, less than three weeks after the case of Marchal de Sainscy had begun, officials of the Chamber of Accounts put seals on the house of yet another major accountant, the Treasurer of the comte d'Artois, Antoine Bourboulon. His predecessor, Radix de Sainte Foy, had also failed only six years before and the Chamber of Accounts was therefore doubly concerned at Bourboulon's failure. According to Montholon, magistrate in the Chamber, Bourboulon had embezzled at least 100,000 livres.[3] On 11 March the Chamber made an inventory of his belongings and respon-sibilities, including eleven servants and six horses; on 22 March the comte d'Artois appointed Philippe Silvestre to continue the *exercices* of the office;[4] a week later the Chamber decreed Bourboulon's arrest, too late because he had already fled to England. On 21 May the Chamber ordered the sale of his property, including the office itself which was worth 300,000 livres. The office was soon sold to a *premier commis* in the Finance Department, Drouet de Santerre, who managed the affairs of the comte d'Artois until 1818 and whose son carried on until the prince was crowned Charles X in 1824. Among Drouet de Santerre's papers, a memorandum on the Bourboulon affair shows an original debt of more than a million livres reduced to 256,000 after the sale of all assets, and standing at 155,000 livres in records of the *Cour des comptes* dated 3 June and 1 July 1814.[5]

Yet another major failure, that of Antoine-Jean-François Mégret de

---

[1] B.N., F 21313 (59), *arrêt du conseil*, 13 May 1787; A.N. F⁴ 2680, an exchange of correspondence between Marchal de Sainscy and Calonne shows that the father left the office with a deficit of 1,460,573 livres.
[2] Isidore-Simon Brière de Mondetour, named by *arrêt du conseil*, 13 May 1787 (B.N., F 21313 (59)).
[3] Harvoin, *Journal*, fol. 59.
[4] A.N., P 2744.
[5] A.N., P 2844. Luethy, *La Banque protestante*, p. 693. The papers of Barthélemy-Pierre Drouet de Santerre and his son Anselme-Barthélemy are in the library of Cornell University. Memorandum dated 28 January 1815.

Sérilly, occurred on 1 June, and this was as serious a matter as the failure of Baudard de Saint James because Mégret de Sérilly was one of only two Treasurers General for the War Department. Furthermore he was deeply involved in some of the same enterprises and appears to have been financially shaken by Baudard's failure. Son of a distinguished Intendant, Antoine Mégret d'Etigny; nephew of another Intendant bearing his own name, and also of a Treasurer-Extraordinary for War, Thomas de Pange, Mégret de Sérilly had been appointed by Necker in 1778. On 4 June 1787 commissioners of the Chamber of Accounts visited his house and found that his books showed a deficit of 5,410,179 livres and his caisse held effects to the value of only 344,802 livres, so that he appeared to be in debt to the Crown by over five millions.[1] His chief clerk, Guesdon, was commissioned to settle his affairs; twenty-one of his other employees, and his *premier commis*, Berlinger, were all discharged; his office was suppressed; and his caisse with all outstanding obligations passed to the other Treasurer General for War, Marie-Sébastien-Charles Fontaine de Biré, who henceforth managed both offices.[2] Letters-patent of 9 July 1787 laid down rules for the sale of Mégret de Sérilly's property, including the château de Theil near Sens, and the division of the proceeds among his creditors and the Crown.[3] His wife, Marie-Louise Thomas de Domangeville, succeeded in temporarily stopping the sale of his jewels, wine, laces, furniture and other valuables, set for 7 January 1788, but the Chamber of Accounts soon set aside her objections and resolved on 14 March 1788 to proceed with the sale. The claims arising out of this bankruptcy had by no means all been met by the end of 1790.[4] Mégret de Sérilly himself survived, however, until 10 May 1794 when he was executed as a counter-revolutionary.[5]

Mégret de Sérilly was the fifth major accountant to fail during the first half of that fateful year of 1787. All these failures in so short a period constituted in themselves something of a crisis, for they stood out as the worst series of bankruptcies for many a year. News of them reached even across the Atlantic to Nova Scotia where Roland, who had escaped in 1784 after his own bankruptcy, heard with great interest of 'the quantity of bankruptcies of financiers, receivers and payers of all kinds'.[6] Looking ahead I could find no trace of any more failures until two years later when a Receiver

---

[1] A.N., P 2517, Letters of provision dated 24 March 1779; A.N., P. 2744 entry for 8 June 1787.
[2] B.N., F 21313 (74), Letters Patent dated 18 June 1787; B.N., 23631 (46); B.N., 21313 (81), edict of June 1787; A.N., P 2844.
[3] B.N., F 21313 (93).
[4] A.N., P 2845; A.N., AB XIX 327, report of 30 September 1790.
[5] Chevallier, *Journal de l'Assemblée des Notables*, p. 67.
[6] Roland, *Le Financier patriote*, p. 11.

General, Marquet des Grèves, went bankrupt in May 1789; and looking backward I find evidence of only two failures in 1786, both of them older debts which merely came to light in 1786 (one of them posthumously), no failures at all in 1785, and only one each year in 1784, 1783, 1782, and 1781.[1] The only other year during the reign of Louis XVI in which so many accountants failed was 1779, when there is evidence of five somewhat lesser cases: two *Receveurs particuliers* (much smaller fry), a Payer of the rentes, a *Trésorier du marc d'or*, and the *Receveur des communautés réligieuses*.[2] There can be little doubt that the series of five major failures early in 1787 was the worst in the quarter century preceding the revolution.

As we might well suspect, this crisis was not a mere coincidence of failures because there is evidence of great strain on other accountants, many of whom nearly failed also. On 5 April, the bishop of Toulouse, Loménie de Brienne, wrote in his journal, 'They are obliged to support Messieurs de la Balue, Le Normand and de Savalette who are doing the *service* and are not sufficient for it'.[3] On 12 April the bishop of Aix, Boisgelin de Cucé, wrote:

The *service* is being carried on only by means of sums dispatched from the Royal Treasury. The public is withdrawing its funds, and everyone wants to be paid. Monsieur de Sérilly can no longer sustain himself alone. The sieur Duruey is in difficulties. There is not a moment to lose... Bankruptcy is being caused by the public itself which does not give its money when the minister is without credit.[4]

On 29 April 1787 the Paris correspondent of the *Gazette de Leyde*, 'always perfectly informed on these matters'[5] declared that royal bills (*effets*) were suffering more each day from a gradual decline in value, which was affecting other kinds of public securities. The rescriptions and *assignations* were not being renewed. On the following day Vidaud de la Tour, an official attached to the Assembly of Notables, reported a conversation with a clerk of the Finance Department who predicted that if steps were not taken to revive public credit the service would have to be suspended and government payments would cease.[6] It was under the pressure of such hard conditions, such a severe shortage of credit, that the five major failures occurred.

The predicament of the government has its place in a general financial

---

[1] These were, in the order listed, Dupille de Saint Séverin (Treasurer for the War Department), Thiroux de Montsange (Receiver General), Marie-Louis-César Roulleau (*Commissaire, receveur et contrôleur aux saisies-réelles*); Jacques-Paul Cadeau (Payer of the Company of *Secrétaires du Roi*), Millin Duperreux (Receiver General), and Radix de Sainte Foy (Treasurer to the comte d'Artois).

[2] These were, in the order listed, Roland, Goupil, Gossey Desplaces, Caron and Bourgault Ducoudray.

[3] Chevallier, *Journal de l'Assemblée des Notables*, p. 53.

[4] *Ibid.*, pp. 66 and 69.

[5] Egret, *La Pré-révolution*, p. 52.   [6] *Ibid.*

crisis on which Herbert Luethy and Jean Bouchary have thrown much light.[1] Throughout the ancien régime a great number of financiers and bankers, French and foreign, had always engaged in speculation with securities, public and private, long-term and short-term; in the reign of Louis XVI this business had become more volatile with speculators buying and selling on the Paris *bourse*, combining and competing to realize profits in everything from insurance and real-estate to international exchange operations. Government finance was a part of all this, in no way protected and, indeed, hardly distinguishable. Much has been written to suggest that rampant financial speculation, with all its profits and its failures, was most often the work of foreigners like John Law, Jacques Necker and various Swiss and Belgian immigrants, all battening upon the ancien régime and somehow corrupting it. This cherished myth will not bear examination. Any serious study of the financial system will show it to have been fundamentally and characteristically dependent on the private enterprise of its agents, however respectable, Catholic and French they might be.[2] The crisis of these years was not primarily the work of foreigners: for example, in 1786 Calonne encouraged a syndicate of speculators to keep up the price of Indies Company shares with the aid of Treasury funds. These activities were publicly denounced by the comte de Mirabeau in a pamphlet so forceful and eloquent that Calonne had Mirabeau arrested on 18 March 1787.[3] This noisy affair not only compromised Calonne in the view of the Assembly of Notables, then in session, but also contributed a good deal to the instability of the financial world at that time. The repercussions of this affair and of the five great bankruptcies of royal accountants were at the centre of what Luethy has called the 'convulsions of 1786–7'. The shares in the Compagnie des Eaux, the Indies Company, the insurance companies and securities in general were all declining in value. Many financiers were on the verge of failure. There was no total crash like that of John Law's *système* in 1720, but instead a severe general crisis which shook public confidence in the financial system.

This financial crisis was in turn a result—or at any rate a part—of the general economic depression which C. E. Labrousse has described. Winegrowers' revenues, so fundamental to the general prosperity of the countryside, diminished steeply after 1783 so that, for instance, the Receivers of the *taille* in the election of Reims, the largest wine-producing region of Champagne, declared their collections to have reached 'a state of crisis and of

[1] Luethy, *La Banque protestante*, pp. 686 ff.; Bouchary, *Les Manieurs, passim.*
[2] This is shown in Luethy, *La Banque protestante*. See also Chevallier, *Journal de l'Assemblée des Notables*, p. 126.
[3] Mirabeau, *Dénonciation de l'agiotage.*

impotence', the worst in thirty years. From 1785 to 1787 there was a general clamour throughout Champagne, Languedoc, Guyenne and many other regions.[1] Again and again in different contexts and with varying evidence, Labrousse asserts that 'for both prices and profits, the lowest point in the decline was reached in 1786'.[2] By that year there was far less money about than usual and investments declined. The textile and other industries were already in difficulties. 'Le zéro de 1786' was naturally reflected in a growing resistance to taxation, a 'réaction fiscale' which could only threaten the credit of accountants because they depended squarely upon the expectation of tax revenues. Who would risk purchasing rescriptions and *assignations* which might never be redeemed? Our twentieth-century concept of the cyclical recession is invaluable for interpreting the economic conditions of that time, but the men of the 1780s, whatever the deficiencies of their economic theory, were perfectly capable of responding to conditions in accordance with their own immediate interests. The failure of five major accountants shows that conditions in 1787 were hard indeed.

The Chamber of Accounts believed—or behaved as though it believed— that the fate of the accountants was in every case due to their own faults. As early as 11 February 1787 it wrote in a remonstrance to the King, refer- ring to the case of Baudard de Saint James, 'The scandal of this new bank- ruptcy leads us naturally, Sire, to seek the causes which multiply them to infinity. There are several causes: *le luxe, l'avidité et surtout l'impunité.*'[3] The Chamber went on to complain that in less than twenty years fifty accountants had gone bankrupt with losses to the Crown totalling 40 million livres, but none of them had been punished. In the case of Harvoin the Chamber immediately ascribed his flight to bankruptcy, apparently owing in turn to misuse of royal funds. Again, de Montholon of the Chamber expressed the opinion that four bankrupt accountants had all failed because they had embezzled large sums of money.[4] Acting upon its belief of guilt, the Chamber prosecuted the cases which fell to it with all the rigour at its command.

The bankrupt accountants may have been dishonest and greedy, as the Chamber thought, but their failures can hardly have been results of their dishonesty. Given the nature of the financial system, the Chamber was surely mistaken in assuming that honesty should meet with success and dishonesty with failure. It seems more likely that disaster was a consequence of not finding credit with which to honour rescriptions and meet other

---

[1] Labrousse, *La Crise de l'économie*, p. 473.
[2] *Ibid.*, pp. 578 ff.
[3] *Remontrance de la chambre des comptes*, 11 Feb. 1787, 16 pp. (B.N., Lf²⁷ 33), p. 13.
[4] A.N., P 2744, entry for 24 Jan. 1787; Harvoin, *Journal*, fol. 59.

obligations. Certainly the old man, Harvoin, fled because he could see no way of raising the money to redeem his rescriptions until the tax revenue began to come in. In a similar predicament Baudard de Saint James deliberately turned his books over to the Controller General. The records of these cases even suggest that Harvoin and Baudard de Saint James may have been innocent of any great irregularity in their management of royal funds. However that may be, bankruptcy in such a system was not an ethical issue but an economic and institutional one. As we have seen, an investigation by the Chamber would itself bring on a bankruptcy by destroying confidence in the accountant's credit; and his credit would also suffer in hard times when money was scarce.

Calonne also, like the Chamber of Accounts, took a conservative view of the financial crisis. He appears to have seen no reason to change the system of caisses and accountants, and his policies were intended rather to support and improve it. With all his personal interests and family connections in the world of finance, he was naturally well aware of its difficulties, and beginning in 1786 he made efforts to sustain the money market with Crown funds.[1] It was in this endeavour that he began working through the group of speculators whom Mirabeau exposed. Not that Calonne saw the difficulties as a cyclical crisis to be tided over; but he believed that the government would benefit from a general confidence and prosperity which he hoped to stimulate by every means at his disposal. And the funds of the Treasury were at his disposal. True to the ideas of Jacques Marquet de Bourgade, Nicolas Beaujon, Joly de Fleury and all those who had directed financial policy since the fall of Necker in 1781, Calonne believed the credit of the government and that of private financiers to be interdependent and mutually sustaining. There was nothing irregular in what Calonne did to manage the fate of government finances at the *bourse*, nothing the least bit inconsistent with a system of administration in which private and public finances were inextricably bound up together. Calonne saw no essential difference between public funds and private, and he was ready to commit either to maintaining confidence and prosperity.

Accordingly, to some extent he was prepared to underwrite the credit of failing accountants. When Harvoin first got into difficulties, on 20 January, Calonne approved the payment of his rescriptions by the court banker, Joseph Duruey, or else by one of the Keepers of the Royal Treasury. On that occasion, Gojard pointed out that in 1784 the Receiver General, Etienne-Nicolas Landry, had been supported in a similar manner.[2] This

[1] Luethy, *La Banque protestante*, p. 691.
[2] A.N., F4 2021, Gojard (?) to Calonne, 20 Jan, 1787.

was a common practice and it infuriated the Chamber of Accounts. It was precisely against such assistance that the Chamber was protesting when it wrote to the Crown on 6 February 1787,

It is tempting to believe that by an incredible coincidence, the greater the fraud in cases of bankruptcy the greater the measure of royal protection and favour... In a word, Sire, these unfaithful accountants who have pillaged Your Majesty's coffers, instead of being punished...have almost all obtained either salaries or pensions.[1]

The Chamber and the *Cour des aides* were all the more willing to prosecute the bankrupt accountants because Calonne seemed to connive in what the courts believed to be the results of dishonesty. On 24 January, after preliminary investigation, the Chamber already believed Harvoin guilty of 'misappropriation of royal funds' and ordered his arrest. However, on close inspection there turns out to have been little fundamental difference between the attitude of the courts and that of Calonne. Once the fat was in the fire, the courts in hot pursuit of an accountant, and the bankruptcy therefore inevitable, Calonne was no longer concerned to sustain the unfortunate man. Punishment seemed to Calonne perfectly in order. To Madame Harvoin he said, 'all the accountants allow themselves the greatest disorders; the indulgence which has tolerated these disorders has multiplied them to a revolting degree; rigour alone can make each one attend to his duty'.[2] The only difference between Calonne and the courts was that they looked immediately for dishonesty in every case of failure whereas Calonne was prepared to believe that some were due to weakness. Both were founded upon a conservative belief in the system of caisses and accountants. Neither wished to change the system, and nowhere was there a hint of such a change in the reforming proposals that Calonne put before the Assembly of Notables.

Nevertheless the complaints of the Chamber of Accounts, published on 11 February 1787, can hardly have passed unnoticed in the Assembly of Notables which opened its first session only eleven days later, because the Assembly was perfectly well aware of faults in the accounting system, of criticisms levelled at accountants and of many bankruptcies. Mirabeau's pamphlet, too, made a sensation during their meeting. While Calonne remained silent on these matters, the Assembly became interested in them and took up the cause of administrative reform. Much of what was said in the Assembly on these subjects was merely vague opinion, such as members

[1] *Remontrance de la chambre*, p. 14.
[2] Harvoin, *Journal*, fol. 26.

of the Assembly passed upon most of the matters they debated. There were expressions of surprise that the latest accounts from the Keepers of the Royal Treasury to the Chamber of Accounts were of 1772 and 1773, indignation at this and other evidence of long delays in the accounting process, sharp criticisms of the Crown's use of *acquits de comptant* which had risen from 64 million livres in 1772 to 128 million in 1785,[1] attacks on the accountants for using public funds in their personal ventures and going bankrupt, and arguments in favour of reducing the numbers of officials wherever possible. The *bureau* of the duc d'Orléans counted seventeen departments in the Ministry of Finance, eleven of them (it said) created since 1783, and increasing numbers of commissioners, Farmers General, and other high officials, many of whom might well have been laid off. All this was only general criticism, but on 3 May there began a series of recommendations directed specifically at the system of caisses and accountants.

It was the archbishop of Aix, Boisgelin de Cucé, who first brought the faults of the system to the attention of the Assembly. The clerical group in the Assembly—seven bishops and seven archbishops—were the most outspoken and determined opponents of Calonne; and Boisgelin together with Loménie de Brienne, archbishop of Toulouse, even went so far as to send a memorandum to the Queen predicting bankruptcy if the Controller General was not soon discharged.[2] That foreboding piece, written on 12 April, was not merely political propaganda nor even a judgement on the state of the deficit. It represented a different policy of financial reform which Boisgelin had already put before the Assembly in a memorandum of 2 or 3 April entitled, *Mémoire sur la suppression des caisses intermédiaires*.[3] In this memorandum Boisgelin launched a full and frank attack on the system of caisses and accounts. This attack had momentous consequences.

All the *bureaux* of the Assembly of Notables passed approving comments on this memorandum and some were enthusiastic. One wrote:

The *Bureau*, after hearing a memoir on the suppression of intermediary caisses, considered that no better moment could be found to suppress a crowd of receivers, treasurers, clerks and employees, when complaints of speculation originate in the multiplicity of intermediary caisses, and when enormous bankruptcies make all these disorders felt.[4]

[1] B.N., MS Nouv. acq. fr. 23617, fol. 244.
[2] Chevallier, *Journal de l'Assemblée des Notables*, p. 66.
[3] I could find no copy of this memorandum, notwithstanding the references to it in Chevallier, *Journal*; but there are many detailed references to its contents in B.N., MS. Nouv. acq. fr. 23617, fols. 253 ff.
[4] B.N., MS Nouv. acq. fr. 23617, fol. 284.

Another recommended 'the reunion of all the royal caisses, which would first of all remove from the hands of the accountants funds sufficient to facilitate the suppression of their offices and the reimbursement of the greater part of their *finances*'.[1] A third *bureau*, after reading Boisgelin, wanted 'the reduction of all the caisses to a single one'.[2] One bureau saw in the memorandum 'a precious principle' worthy of the government's attention: the simplification of the administration of receipts and expenditure.[3] And yet another criticized the accountants for using public funds in their own business ventures and thereby entailing public losses when they went bankrupt.[4] Not all of these bureaux were arguing in favour of a strong central administration of finances, and one of them even suggested turning the collection of taxes over to the provincial assemblies,[5] but all were critical of the system of caisses and accountants. All could see advantages in consolidation.

Here was a reform that was not a part of Calonne's programme. Calonne had avoided any measure of change directed at the central administration of finances, for he had no desire to restrict the initiative and independence of the accountants. Believing in the system, he had tried to direct the attention of the Assembly of Notables towards taxes and purely fiscal problems and had even evaded the issue of administrative reform in his pamphlet debate with his opponent, Necker, who was committed to a consolidation of the caisses system begun ten years earlier during his first ministry. The issue was raised in the Assembly nevertheless, and it appealed to the notables undoubtedly because the suppression of caisses was a direct remedy for the alarming series of bankruptcies among accountants in that spring of 1787, undoubtedly because the Chamber of Accounts was complaining loudly about the accounting practices of the accountants, and almost certainly because an attack upon the system of caisses and accountants was necessarily an attack on Calonne. Here was a proposal for reform which directed attention towards financiers and officials and away from the privileged landowning classes. 'What do the parlements ask?' Brissot de Warville wrote in August 1787. 'A regular financial administration which will prevent the past disorders forever.'[6] In the terms of the social interpretation of the French revolution, as primarily a struggle between the bourgeoisie and the feudal nobility, this was a conservative reform; that is, it was intended to strengthen the existing social and political arrangements rather than to change them. Yet at the same time its effect would be to strengthen and

---

[1] *Ibid.*, fol. 271. [2] *Ibid.*, fol. 251.
[3] B.N., Coll. Joly de Fleury, MS 1041, fol. 210, dated 4 May 1787.
[4] B.N., MS Nouv. acq. fr. 23617, fol. 251, dated 2 May 1787.
[5] *Ibid.*, fol. 284. [6] Brissot de Warville, *Point de banqueroute* (1787), p. 19.

rationalize the machinery of central government. In terms of administrative history, the suppression of the *caisses intermédiaires* which Boisgelin proposed was another step in a revolution that was to distinguish public power from private wealth and to equip the state with a modern financial bureaucracy.

Lest these reflections should seem to exaggerate the significance of one modest manuscript put before the Assembly of Notables and forgotten by historians, a brief scrutiny of events during the following years—and the subject of the next chapter—will show that Boisgelin's proposals were implemented even before those of Calonne. After Calonne had been discharged on 8 May, a friend and colleague of Boisgelin, Loménie de Brienne, succeeded him as Minister of Finance and immediately set out to reform the system of caisses and accountants. After suppressing a number of the principal caisses in the autumn of 1787, the following March he combined those of the remaining Treasurers General and of the Keepers of the Royal Treasury in one organization which he called the Royal Treasury. This was the true founding of the Public Treasury, for it was the first time it had been an organization and not merely the caisses of independent Keepers and other accountants. The reform of the central administration of finances thus began immediately after the crisis of 1787 and after Calonne's fall, whereas Calonne's fiscal reforms had to wait until after the social and political revolution of 1789 had cleared the way for them.

II

THE FOUNDING OF THE
MODERN TREASURY

IN THE SYSTEM which Calonne hoped to preserve, the Royal Treasury did not exist as an organization but only as two venal Keepers, one for odd-numbered years and the other for even-numbered years, each with his own separate caisse and his own employees. Though these Keepers were considerable accountants and their caisses large, hundreds of other caisses held substantial deposits of royal funds which never found their way into the Treasury caisses or even into the Treasury accounts. Hundreds of accountants in the royal service managed government funds according to the wishes of the Finance Minister but not under his inspection or control; and in the absence of an aggregate central caisse, the Finance Minister was obliged to do the Crown's business by drawing on a multitude of separate caisses like so many bank accounts. The accountants managed Crown funds in trust, as it were, almost like private businessmen obliged only to draw up annual financial statements and accounts.

Like any other accountants the Keepers of the Royal Treasury could have gone bankrupt and, indeed, the one on duty in 1787 during the meeting of the Assembly of Notables was on the verge of doing so. For this and other reasons Calonne's successor, Loménie de Brienne, planned and carried out a fundamental reorganization of the paying caisses, including those of the two Keepers, and so created the modern French treasury. This great reform was hardly noticed at the time. For one thing, it occurred during the great stress and excitement of the *révolte nobiliaire* when the sovereign courts were challenging the authority of the Crown, and for another, the reform was disguised as a measure of economy. It was partly intended to save money, but not only in the direct way of reducing expenses. The legislation, cast in Neckerian terms, shows the main intention to have been the establishing of treasury control over government funds and the eventual subordination of all other caisses to the Treasury. This revolutionary step soon proved successful. Over the years that followed, the new Treasury never ceased to grow at the expense of other financial agencies, swallowing up caisses and accountants until it became the commanding centre of the entire system.

197

The founding of this organization in March 1788 was clearly a matter of profound importance in the history of the financial administration. All the evidence I have been able to muster—indicative but hardly conclusive—points to Loménie de Brienne himself as the founder of the Treasury. He put the legislation before the King and from time to time in the ensuing years was mentioned as the author of it. One high official who was in a position to know, as he became second-in-command of the Treasury in August 1788, went out of his way in later reminiscences to insist that Brienne had been the founder.[1] If this is true, it is inconsistent with the most common estimates of Brienne's character and achievements in memoirs and histories, for they usually dismiss him as a shallow intriguer with no understanding of finance. These need not detain us long, however, as Jean Egret has already rehabilitated Brienne and shown his reform projects to have been serious and intelligent.[2]

The reform of the Treasury seems to have been a logical part of Brienne's policy for meeting the immediate needs of the government in 1788. He was obliged to budget for no less than 240 million livres in short-term advances for that year, and even if he could draw upon fresh private resources from financiers and bankers in the time-honoured manner, the Treasury would have to be rendered as sound as possible, proof against bankruptcies of the kind which had overtaken so many accountants in 1787, if such a vast sum in *anticipations* and rescriptions was to be floated on the market.[3] Furthermore, the founding of the Treasury as a public organization, the 'nationalizing' of it, so to speak, accorded well with another emergency measure that Brienne prepared the following August, when it became apparent that the state of the money market was such that bankers and financiers would not take the *anticipations* and rescriptions: he decided that the Treasury would make payments in paper notes backed by royal decree! This decision was embodied in the infamous arrêt of 16 August 1788, too often loosely interpreted as a declaration of bankruptcy. Only to believers in the traditional system of depending upon the private credit of accountants and tax farmers, admittedly the majority of observers in 1788, did this seem like bankruptcy. To Brienne this seemed like a natural step. As he afterwards wrote, the government would thereby have been able 'to provide for its own expendi-

---

[1] François-Pierre Cornus de la Fontaine, *Lettres à l'auteur de l'écrit anonyme intitulé: De la comptabilité des dépenses publiques...* (Paris, 1822), p. 11.

[2] The usual disparaging view of Brienne may be found in, for instance, Baron de Besenval, *Mémoires* (Paris, 1821), pp. 244–6; Aimé Cherest, *La Chute de l'ancien régime* (1787–1789) (Paris, 1884), p. 211; J. Egret, *La Pré-révolution française* (Paris, 1962), *passim*.

[3] Loménie de Brienne, quoted at length in Jean-Louis Soulavie, *Mémoires historiques et politiques du règne de Louis XVI* (Paris, 1801), vol. VI, pp. 238–9.

tures without depending on the bankers'.[1] Having nationalized the Treasury, Brienne was thus trying to nationalize the currency. There was a tremendous outcry at the time and Brienne was forced to resign, but less than three years later the National Assembly deliberately adopted the same expedient. As Brienne then pointed out, his own plan of August 1788 'was perhaps not so absurd as people would have us believe'. But however sound it had been financially, the measure had been politically defeated by various forces of opposition, not least by the coalition of interests which had earlier sustained Calonne.[2] Brienne resigned on 25 August after helping to arrange for Necker to succeed him.

Brienne's work of suppressing and consolidating financial offices, culminating in the union of caisses to form the Royal Treasury, was a revival of the work suspended when Necker fell in 1781. Not since Necker's first ministry had such blows been struck at the system of caisses and accountants. There was more than a close resemblance, however, between these two ministries. We find signs that Necker and Loménie de Brienne approved of each other's reforms and that Brienne may therefore have learned from Necker. When Louis XVI appointed Brienne chief of the Royal Council on Finance on 1 May 1787 it was with the intention of also appointing a Controller General of Finance to work under the Council's orders. Technically speaking, therefore, we must remember that Brienne had replaced Vergennes, who had died in February, rather than Calonne who had been discharged in April. The post of Controller General remained vacant. At the time of his own appointment, Brienne recommended the appointment of Necker in the strongest terms, and seems to have greatly admired Necker.[3] The King refused and Brienne eventually selected a manageable junior, Laurent de Villedeuil and in September 1788 replaced him with a quiet lawyer, Claude-Guillaume Lambert, whom Necker had favoured in his first ministry and was to recall for a second term as Controller General in 1789. It was in Lambert's time that all the major reforms were done and although he played second fiddle to Brienne he was named as the *rapporteur* to the Council in much of the legislation founding the new treasury. When Necker returned to office after Brienne's fall in August

[1] *Ibid.*, p. 245. Furthermore, the notes of the *Caisse d'escompte*, already used by the Treasury, were to be voted up to 170 million by decrees of the National Assembly as early as 19 and 21 Dec. 1789.

[2] *Ibid.*, 'A la tête de ces ennemis était Monsieur Le Comte d'Artois, pressé par Calonne et ses partisans, par les Polignac, par les Vaudreuil et toute cette classe de favoris qui regardait le Trésor public comme une source intarissable où il leur était permis de puiser.'

[3] P. Chevallier, *Journal de l'Assemblée des Notables de 1787* (Paris, 1960), p. 123; André Morellet, *Lettres à Lord Shelburne, passim*; Soulavie, *Mémoires*, pp. 237–54.

1788, he wrote that he had long meditated combining the paying caisses and thoroughly approved of what Brienne had done to form the Treasury.[1]

To name Loménie de Brienne as the founder of the modern Treasury is not to pretend that he did it all alone or even that this reform figured very prominently among his activities in those agitated months. He was the director of a broad programme of reforming activity in which many others assisted, and first among them his secretariat. The first secretary was a young man from Auxerre, Pierre Soufflot de Mérey (1760–1837).[2] If we may judge from his writings many years later, Soufflot de Mérey was one of the reforming officials of that time who formed a milieu of their own which is not easy to assess. He was conservative in the sense that he defended many old institutions, had little respect for the physiocrats or for Turgot and detested 'that spirit of system which condemns with intolerance all which does not bear the stamp of novelty, all which is not in harmony with what la néologie calls liberal ideas, philosophic ideas'.[3] At the same time, like so many other officials, he worked vigorously at reforms which, though they seemed to shrink into insignificance during those stormy years, remained among the enduring work of the revolution. Nothing in the introduction to the Compte rendu au Roi of April 1788, which he is supposed to have written, leads us to think that he was any the less conservative while serving as premier secrétaire to Brienne. Nevertheless his views were in no sense inconsistent with administrative reforms stemming from a desire for order, efficiency and firm public authority over public funds. Loménie de

---

[1] Eclaircissements sur l'organisation actuelle du trésor public... (Paris, 9 Nov. 1790), p. 11 n. This pamphlet commands confidence by its precise and ample information and the intelligence of its reasoning.

[2] Often mentioned but nowhere properly identified, Soufflot de Mérey was born at Auxerre (Yonne) in 1760 and served as a councillor in the bailliage of Auxerre before joining Brienne's staff, and in 1790–1 he was 'procureur syndic de l'administration du district d'Auxerre' and travelled several times to Paris as a delegate until his exclusion on 22 Fructidor Year III. In the meantime, he had been arrested and imprisoned on 20 Floréal Year II and was not cleared of charges until 8 Vendémiaire Year III. He became an active member of the Banque Territorial formed by acts of 1 Fructidor Year VII and 1 Brumaire Year VIII and published a pamphlet on it. He married Jeanne-Amélie Garnier Deschênes and, a second time, Anastasie-Louise Bosset. After the revolution he appears to have lived on revenues of property in Paris which included no. 25 rue des Sentier (in 1805), the 'petit hôtel de Nivernais' and from 1813–19 the 'grand hôtel de Nivernais', 10 rue de Tournon (until he lost it in a legal battle with the Ministry of War), another large house in the rue de Clichy and a house in which he was living in 1817, 6 rue de Seine. He died on 28 November 1837, aged seventy-seven, in another house which he owned at 8 rue du Doyenné. Two nephews signed his death certificate: Pierre-Jules Soufflot, administrateur des messageries royales, chevalier de la Légion d'Honneur, and Paul-Emile Soufflot de Magny, ancien procureur du Roi. (Archives de la Seine, DQ¹⁰ 126, dossier 3189; DQ¹⁰ 1597; DQ 335 dossier 12645; and his acte de décès.)

[3] Soufflot de Mérey, Considérations sur le rétablissement des jurandes et maîtrises (Paris, An XIII, 1805), pp. 45–58.

Brienne employed him from the summer of 1787, if not earlier, until August 1788, at an annual salary of 12,000 livres and a considerable expense account.[1] In addition Soufflot de Mérey employed the large number of eight clerks and two office-boys at salaries totalling 16,000 livres.[2] Every Minister of Finance, every Controller General, had a private secretary. No other chief of the Royal Council, certainly neither Maurepas nor Vergennes before him, had employed so many secretaries in addition to those of the Controller General, and they are something of a testimony to his ministerial activity.

Brienne also appointed an advisory committee (*comité consultatif*) for the discussion of plans concerning the improvement of the finances and the order of service of the Royal Treasury. It was to meet weekly at Brienne's house mainly to discuss 'matters connected with the handling and distribution of the funds of the Royal Treasury'.[3] If the formal appointment of this committee is to be taken as a guide to its activity, it could hardly have had enough time to prepare the entire reform project because the members were named by an *arrêt du conseil* of 15 March 1788 and the treasury reform act, in all its detail, together with a supplementary regulation, was published at the end of that month. It is therefore possible that Loménie de Brienne provided for the advisory committee as part of his plan at the same time that he drew up the founding legislation. The Regulation of 30 March shows in several of its provisions that the advisory committee was to be responsible for implementing the reform and this was possibly the committee's entire purpose.[4] They may have had nothing to do with the original planning.

On the other hand, it seems more probable that Brienne had been consulting this committee—or certain members of it—for some time before their formal appointment on 15 March. In the first place, the Minister certainly needed expert advice in order to draw up these reforms. Secondly, although the members of the advisory committee do not seem at first sight to be the sort of people he might have called on to assist in the project from the beginning, a more careful investigation of them shows that they might very well have been willing and able to reform the Treasury.

Two of the four members we might have expected to find serving

---

[1] See payments to him in A.N., D X 3 (1788), F⁴ 1087 *passim* and F⁴* 71.

[2] These were Chabanetz (2,400 livres), de Verville (2,400), Chavallerie (1,800), Feres de Saint Hilaire (1,800), Mailly (1,500), Barthélemy (1,500), Perrotet (1,800), Malius (1,200) and two office-boys at 800 livres each.

[3] *Arrêt du conseil*, 15 March 1788 (B.M., 27 d 15 (74)).

[4] *Règlement général du Roi pour la manutention du trésor royal*, 30 March 1788, cited in Isambert, *Recueil des anciennes lois*, vol. 28, p. 521; original in B.M., R. 623.

ex-officio on the advisory committee. Claude-Guillaume Lambert (1726–93) had been working under Brienne as Controller General since September 1787, and fundamental laws such as the arrêt of 15 March 1788 named him as the formal *rapporteur* to the Royal Council. Nothing in his career suggests that he might have been opposed to the treasury reforms, especially as he seems to have been something of a Neckerite. His association with Brienne probably owed something to their service together as members of the same committee in the Assembly of Notables. With him on Brienne's advisory committee was another who served *ex-officio*, Achille-Joseph Gojard, the *Premier commis de finances* who supervised the treasury work in the Department of Finance. Gojard was certainly not a Neckerite, having been chosen by Bourgade and Fleury in 1781 to replace Necker's *Premier commis des finances*, and Necker was to discharge him the moment this became possible in August 1788. But all the signs are that Gojard was a neutral civil servant. He had certainly not been an adviser to any of the ministers he had served since 1781 and in his time the post of *Premier commis des finances* had become one of routine administration, unconnected with the policies of any particular minister. Brienne thought him a politically uncommitted official.[1] His work with treasury matters obviously qualified him to be a member of the advisory committee.

The reasons for the choice of the other two members are far from clear but we may form a hypothesis about them from certain scraps of information. Both of them, Jean-Baptiste Magon de la Balue (1713–94) and Simon-Emmanuel-Jullien Le Normant (1740–?), were financiers with fortunes based upon banking rather than venal offices and with strong connections of family and friendship in banking circles. Magon de la Balue, member of a ramifying family of financiers active in Brittany and Paris, had been banker to many noble houses, including the house of Artois, and to the royal court for a short time in 1769.[2] In the years 1767–9, he had played a part in the attempt to form a government bank, the abortive *caisse d'escompte* formed to discount rescriptions, assignations and other such bills, thus providing short-term credit to the Crown. That first *caisse d'escompte* had had certain features in common with the new Treasury of 1788: they were both government organizations intended to take over some of the functions hitherto provided by groups of separate accountants acting as free business agents.

---

[1] Soulavie, *Mémoires*, vol. VI, p. 238; Bosher, 'The Premier Commis des Finances', *French Historical Studies* (Fall 1964), p. 491.

[2] E. Daudet, 'La conspiration Magon, récit des temps révolutionnaires', *Revue des Deux Mondes* (1911), pp. 356–90 and 624–55; H. Luthy, *La Banque protestante*, vol. II, pp. 391 and 732; A.N., T 957¹ *Testament* dated 6 July 1783; Cornell University Library, Papers of Drouet de Santerre, H 42, showing that Magon de la Balue died on 1 Thermidor, Year II aged eighty-one' etc.

They were both based on the idea that an organization backed by government fiat would afford greater security. Was it only a coincidence that Magon de la Balue helped to organize both of them? Was it nothing but coincidence that Bertrand Dufresne was a *caissier* in the first *caisse d'escompte* and in August 1788 became Intendant of the new treasury organization; that Magon de la Balue purchased the premises for his own bank, 22 Place Vendôme, from Dufresne; that another *caissier* of the *caisse d'escompte*, Bénigne Dollé, was one of Magon de la Balue's closest friends and named executor in his will? Were these links between the two organizations of no significance? Or was Magon de la Balue in some measure a believer in that kind of organization? At the very least we may assume that he did not feel inclined to defend the system of accountants against reform.

The fourth member of the advisory committee, Le Normant, was Receiver General of Finance for Tours, in which office he had succeeded the unfortunate Harvoin, and before that he had been Receiver General for La Rochelle since 1781. Yet before buying these offices he had already made a fortune in business and banking and, as Joly de Fleury remarked in 1781, had come 'to establish himself in Paris for the quiet enjoyment of his fortune, which is considerable'.[1] It seems certain that he, like Magon de la Balue, did not depend on his venal office for his income and his functions as accountant were secondary. Having none of the usual close family connections with other accountants, and having had much business and banking experience, he was very possibly not opposed to an organization like the new Treasury. Is it fanciful to imagine that men like him and Magon de la Balue would look favourably on innovations such as double-entry bookkeeping which article 13 of the new regulations ordered for the books of the principal caisse in the new Treasury? Certainly the advisory committee undertook to enforce such regulations; and they may even have planned them in the first place. In order to assume that they prepared the reform project we have to assume that they worked several months without official identity because they were not publicly appointed until 15 March 1788. This may well have been the case, but I could find no evidence one way or the other.

Whether or not the advisory committee was new, the founding of the Treasury in the Spring of 1788 was not a sudden or unexpected measure. There was a series of smaller reforms leading up to it from the crisis of 1787 in which Loménie de Brienne took control of financial affairs. These were

[1] B.N., Coll. Joly de Fleury 1435, fol. 170. Closely connected with the Le Couteulx family of bankers, Le Normant became Secrétaire du Roi in place of Antoine Le Couteulx on 1 August 1777 (A.N., V² 49–50).

reforms which consolidated certain caisses in the hands of accountants who in March 1788 became the administrators of the new Royal Treasury. The first were laws dealing with the immediate crisis, such as the edict of June 1787 which for reasons of economy suppressed Mégret de Sérilly's office of Treasurer General for War and assigned the business of the caisse to the other Treasurer General, Fontaine de Biré.[1] In November an edict suppressed three major caisses, and the offices of the accountants who managed them, with effect from 1 January 1788: the *Revenus casuels*, the *Marc d'or* and the *Amortissements*.[2] The receipts of the first two were turned over to the Domains Administration; the payment of rentes formerly by the Treasurer of the *Marc d'or* was assigned to the Payers of the rentes at the Hôtel de Ville; and the work of the Treasurer of the *Caisse des amortissements* devolved upon Savalette de Langes, one of the Keepers of the Royal Treasury and a future administrator of the new Treasury. These suppressions were accompanied by an order that the functions of the suppressed Treasurers were to cease totally on 31 December 1787 and they were to pay all the funds in their caisses over to the Royal Treasury within the following ten days.

Meanwhile, on 13 October, an arrêt provided for a stricter and more orderly payment of pensions and served as a sequel to Necker's measures on pensions and an introduction to more detailed regulations such as one of 24 June 1788 laying down new terms for the payment of naval pensions. Like all pensions, those of the Marine had been assigned to the Treasury in 1779, but the Minister for Marine had retained an annual 400,000 livres 'for secret expenses' until Loménie de Brienne suppressed this allowance with effect from 1 July 1788. On that date, pensions on the naval secret fund, to the amount of 110,130 livres a year, were transferred to the Treasury.[3] Coming after all these measures, the organizing of the Treasury appeared as merely another step in the same direction and one that was mentioned in advance by Pierre Soufflot de Mérey in the *Compte rendu au Roi* which Brienne put before the King early in 1788.[4]

The reform of the Treasury, like the reforms just cited, was ambiguous.

[1] B.M., 27 d 12. Fontaine de Biré, Treasurer General since 1782, had been summed up by Joly de Fleury: 'de Biré travaille depuis plus de 30 ans dans cette partie [war finances]; ancien Trésorier provincial à Lille et Trésorier de l'armée pendant la dernière guerre [Seven Years War]; réunissant à une grande expérience la meilleure conduite, la fortune, le crédit, et le vœu général de tous les gens du métier et autres qui ont eu à faire à luy.' (Coll. Joly de Fleury 1439, fols. 38–9.)

[2] Isambert, *Recueil des anciennes lois*, vol. 28, pp. 442–9; and also B.M., 27 d 12 (4).

[3] Isambert, *Recueil des anciennes lois*, vol. 28 and B.M., 27 d 12 (37). *Etat nominatif des pensions, traitements conservés...* (B.N., Lf^{81} 3), p. 276.

[4] pp. 150 and 177.

On the one hand, it could be viewed purely as a saving of money on administrative costs by a reduction of the number of employees and procedures. Soufflot de Mérey seemed to take this view when he referred to 'the profits to come, especially to those which will result from a well-organized Royal Treasury and a well-ordered accountancy'.[1] In this light, the laws suppressing accountants and their caisses appear much the same as the edict of January 1788 which formally suppressed 173 offices in the Queen's Household with a total *finance* capital of 1,206,600 livres.[2] Undoubtedly Brienne intended the treasury reform to be an economy measure in the most direct sense of saving money on salaries and other expenses, and yet this was clearly only a gain of secondary importance in his mind. The 'economy' expected from a rational control of public spending by a powerful central treasury was far more than a mere saving of operating costs. Any doubts about this are dispelled in the founding edict.

Its preamble explains some of the faults of the financial system briefly and clearly: the evils of separate caisses, especially the needless complexity of the paying procedures, the absurdity of having funds in some caisses 'dead and lost for the service' while others are overdrawn. 'Finally', it states near the end,

it has happened that some treasurers of these different caisses, not always separating their own affairs from those entrusted to them, the disorder overtaking their fortunes has rebounded upon our Royal Treasury, either through the advances made to them or by the confusion of the bills and the difficulty of distinguishing those which had a connection with our service, or again by the debts which it has often been impossible to recover in their entirety in spite of the precautions taken by the law.[3]

In short, the edict made perfectly clear that the founding of the treasury was a measure of simplification and consolidation whereby the Crown intended not only to save money but also to exercise stricter control over public revenues. Calonne and the other ministers of the reaction against Necker's measures had followed the Chamber of Accounts in trying to control the accountants who managed public funds rather than the funds themselves. Brienne, like Necker before him, was endeavouring to increase ministerial control of public funds by means of reorganization.

The raw materials for the new Treasury were eight major caisses, of which three disappeared altogether and all ceased to function independently.

[1] *Compte rendu au Roi* (1788), p. 150.
[2] B.M., 27 d 12 (7).
[3] *Edit du Roi, portant suppression de tous les offices de gardes du trésor royal*, etc. (March 1788), 8 pp. (B.M., 27 d 12 (10)).

These were the caisses of the two Keepers of the Royal Treasury and of the Treasurers for War, Marine, the Royal Households, royal buildings, roads and bridges and miscellaneous expenditures (*dépenses diverses*). Beginning on 1 July 1788 the Royal Treasury was to assume their functions with five interdependent caisses: one each for War, Marine and Colonies, Pensions and all expenditures arising from government debt, miscellaneous expenditures (including the royal households, the royal buildings and the roads and bridges) and a general caisse to maintain central control of all receipts and disbursements. Only seven, not eight, accountants were affected by the reform because Necker had earlier joined the roads and bridges service to the miscellaneous expenditures. Two of the seven, David-Etienne Rouillé de l'Etang (*Dépenses diverses*) and Antoine-Jean-Baptiste Du Tartre (*Bâtiments du Roi*) were, in the text of the law at least, removed and given duties outside the Treasury.[1] The other five were made Administrators of the Treasury. The most striking feature of the reform was not the economy it effected, which was certainly small, but the articulated structure of the new organization.

This was visible in a number of ways. The five accountants, their venal offices abolished, were now to be called *administrateurs* and to have fixed salaries of 50,000 livres a year. Their *finance* capital was to be converted into a surety bond, fixed at 1,200,000 livres each, on which the Crown would pay 5% just as it did to *caissiers* and other non-venal employees in financial services. No longer separate venal office-holders, they were to be collectively responsible for most aspects of treasury work. All salaries of their employees, hitherto a matter for the individual accountant to decide himself, were to be at the charge of the Crown, and the Controller General of Finance was ordered to prepare an annual budgetary table of all employees. These salaries had formerly appeared nowhere in the government accounts except as lump sums which the accountants could distribute as they wished, but henceforth they would appear among public expenditure accounts, or such was the intention. For this purpose the administrators were ordered to compile general accounts of all treasury business, that is of all funds passing through each caisse, and to present them to the Royal Council on Finance in April of each year in the form of *états au vrai*. When the Council had approved these tables, the administrators were then to render their accounts to the Chambers of Accounts, each for the caisse in his charge.

At least two observers of the time who recorded these changes were

---

[1] Dutartre was somehow able to ignore the laws of 1788 and to continue as *Trésorier des bâtiments du Roi* (Martin, *Etrennes financières*, vol. i, ch. 3, supported by Delafont-Braman, *Rapport sur la comptabilité du sieur Randon de la Tour*, B.N., Le 3³³ (G) (11)).

perfectly aware of their nature. The author of a manuscript *Nouvelle à la main* noted in his entry of 5 April 1788 that the Treasury with its five administrators would be under a *directoire* to include two Councillors of State, d'Ormesson and Villedeuil, and two general inspectors, Magon de la Balue and Le Normant.[1] He reported further that it was expected to move on 1 July 1788 into the Hôtel of the Indies Company where it would be protected by a contingent of French and Swiss guards. He concluded from his information that quite apart from the economy which would result from the new régime, there was 'the very precious advantage of knowing day by day the true state of the finances and of abridging the accounting process by having accounts gathered at one point and all payments made in a single caisse'. In his entry of 15 April he recorded having heard expectations that the new Treasury would extend its organization into the provinces where it might share operations with the Provincial Assemblies, 'the intention of the government being that public funds remain as little as possible in the hands of accountants'. A few months later, after the Treasury had begun its work, a book published on 31 January 1789 described its organization in some detail and with many similar comments on the control over public funds which it afforded the government.[2]

Let us examine the new Royal Treasury. It consisted of five departments, each with a caisse and each with an administrator at its head. The first department, headed by Laborde de Méréville, one of the former Keepers, was that of the General Caisse. This was intended to be the central caisse through which all the funds of the Treasury would pass and be accounted for. Indeed, article 4 of the Regulation of 30 March 1788 explained its pre-eminence over the others in unmistakable terms: '...in view of the impossibility of having all expenditures paid out by one and the same caisse, the General Caisse will have four auxiliary caisses for the service of the four other departments. It will pay the required funds into them and accounts of these payments will be rendered to it every evening'.[3] The second department was administered by Savalette de Langes, the second former Keeper, and its function was to pay all pensions, interest and reimbursement of royal assets stemming from loans, sinking funds, the shares of the Indies Company and all such matters. It did not, of course, pay the *rentes* which the forty Payers at the City Hall were to go on managing until 1793. The third department, for War, remained under the administration of Fontaine de Biré who had managed all military funds since the failure of Mégret de

---

[1] B.N. Rés., LC² 2225, MS, entry for 5 April 1788.
[2] M. J. D. Martin, *Etrennes financières* (B.N., Le²⁵ 137), ch. 3. Isambert, *Collection des décrets*, vol. 28, p. 521.

Sérilly. And similarly, Simon-Charles Boutin, who had alone managed Marine expenditures since the failure of Baudard de Saint James, continued to deal with Marine finances in the fourth department. The fifth department was put in the hands of the former Treasurer for the Royal Household, Marc-Antoine-François-Marie Randon de la Tour. Its function was to make the payments for the royal households, for all the purposes which Necker had originally gathered together under the general head, *Dépenses diverses*, and for others since added to that category. In 1792, the accounts committee of the Legislative Assembly held him responsible for nine separate accounts which he was supposed to have kept from 1 July 1788 in his department of the Treasury and which give an idea of the diversity of the matters in his hands. He made payments to or for the administration of (1) police, commerce, transport, mines, food supplies (*subsistances*) and stud farms; (2) the postal system and *messageries*; (3) the royal *loteries*; (4) the Paris guard and the *maréchaussée* of the Ile de France; (5) the *turcies et levées* or building and maintenance of dykes along the Loire and some of its tributaries; (6) royal buildings; (7) Paris streets; (8) the roads and bridges service; and (9) the rentes on the corporation of trades and crafts (*arts et métiers*). The accounts for the *Ponts et Chaussées* were particularly complicated because expenditures were made through twenty-seven sub-treasurers, one at Dunkirk and one for each of twenty-six Generalities. There was another such network of fifteen provincial Payers of the rentes secured on the Paris corporation of crafts and trades. Little by little, the Treasury was to grow from these beginnings into one of the largest and most powerful agencies of the central government.

Already, by the primary arrangements which went into effect on 1 July 1788, the Treasury increased its control over the funds of the major spending departments. These departments, particularly those for War and Marine, had hitherto taken the funds provided in the *états du Roi* for spending, and departmental Treasurers had kept such funds in their caisses for weeks or even months. Henceforth the Treasury was to hold these funds until it received payment-orders from a Secretary of State or other *ordonnateur*. In consultation with the spending departments the Treasury made up weekly estimates of anticipated expenditures, and on these estimates the general caisse of the Treasury paid weekly sums to the auxiliary caisses. These caisses in turn paid the money out little by little on signed orders from the departments. This change in procedures was effected by transferring the main caisses of the spending departments to the Treasury.

What this change saved the Crown in profits formerly taken by the Treasurers is impossible to count exactly, but it must have been considerable because the Treasurers had been allowed to hold funds in their caisses or to invest them in various ways until needed for departmental expenditures. One well-informed writer estimated that the War Department Treasurers had earned profits of up to fifteen or eighteen thousand livres a year by investing the funds of their departments.[1] These profits were now wiped out. The new Treasury effected another saving by managing its own transfers of funds from one place to another instead of allowing the Treasurers to use the delays permitted for transfers as an excuse for holding funds long enough to make profitable use of them.

The formation of an organized Treasury was not an isolated reform but closely connected with a simultaneous endeavour to bend accounts to the purposes of central financial planning. In the minds of the reformers the Treasury and the accounting system were inseparable, twin objects of the same reforming enterprise, for if the Treasury could be adapted to controlling government expenditure then there would have to be a plan of expenditure, i.e. a budget. The preparation of an annual budget was an English parliamentary institution which French governments were gradually and belatedly to adopt. The very first attempt at a French budget, as Frédéric Braesch has shown, was the *Compte rendu au Roi au mois de Mars 1788*, 'l'aperçu des recettes et dépenses de l'année 1788', which Loménie de Brienne and Soufflot de Mérey prepared at about the same time as the founding of the Treasury and eventually published on 27 April 1788.[2] Just as in the preparation of the new Treasury, Brienne called upon four expert advisers to assist in drawing up the budget and these, named on 16 February 1788, were chosen from the four principal corps of collectors: a Farmer General (Alexandre-Victor de Saint Amand), a Receiver General (Louis-Jacques Baron), a *Régisseur général* (Didelot) and a Domains Administrator (Salverte).[3] According to Brienne's plan, the new Treasury was to implement the new budget beginning on 1 July 1788. On the same day, the central caisse of the Treasury was to begin keeping its books according to the prescribed double-entry system so that a running balance would always be available to the Minister and so that the final accounts, the *compte effectif*, for the fiscal year ending 1 July 1789 could be published. The treasury administrators were henceforth responsible, according to the edict of March 1788 (article VIII) for preparing annual accounts in the form of an *état au vrai*, the counterpart of the budget, and submitting them to the Royal Council each year in April. For the Treasury's *état au vrai* the

---

[1] *Eclaircissements sur l'organisation actuelle du trésor public* (Paris, 1790).
[2] F. Braesch, *Finances et monnaie révolutionnaires* (Paris, 1936), fasc. ii.
[3] *Arrêt du conseil d'état du Roi par lequel Sa Majesté nomme une commission pour l'examen* (16 February 1788), 3 pp. (B.M., 1480 bb 18 (6)).

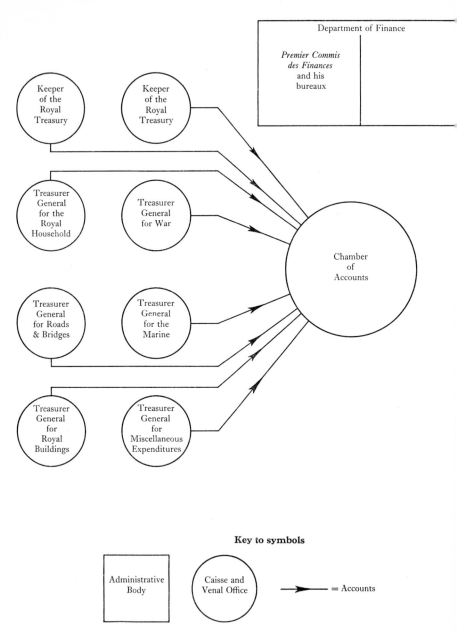

Key to symbols

Administrative Body   Caisse and Venal Office   ➤ — = Accounts

Fig. 3. **Some of the principal spending caisses in 1787 before the Royal Treasury wa organized.**

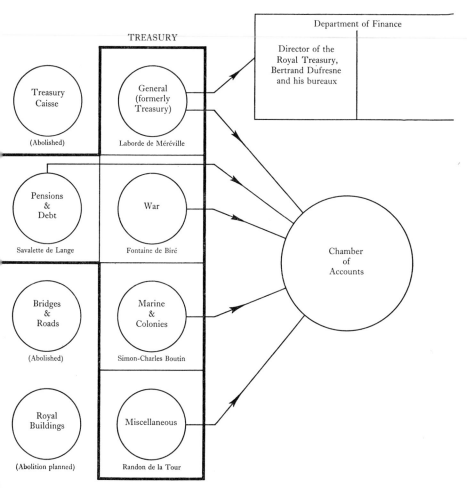

TREASURY

Treasury
Caisse

(Abolished)

General
(formerly
Treasury)

Laborde de Méréville

Pensions
&
Debt

Savalette de Lange

War

Fontaine de Biré

Bridges
&
Roads

(Abolished)

Marine
&
Colonies

Simon-Charles Boutin

Royal
Buildings

(Abolition planned)

Miscellaneous

Randon de la Tour

Department of Finance

Director of the
Royal Treasury,
Bertrand Dufresne
and his bureaux

Chamber
of
Accounts

g. 4. **Organizing the Royal Treasury in 1788.** Fig. 3 shows the eight major caisses which were to
affected by the creation of an organized Treasury in 1788. In 1787, they remain still separate and
dependent, sending accounts individually to the Chamber of Accounts and only *états au vrai* to the
epartment of Finance. Fig. 4 shows how Loménie de Brienne founded the Royal Treasury as an
ganization by incorporating five of the major Treasurers into a single agency. At the same time,
abolished the offices of the three other principal Treasurers and transferred their duties to the new
reasury. In this way, the independent caisses became part of an organization for the first time, and
e venal Treasurers became salaried administrators. At the same time, each of these Treasurers
tained his caisse until the reorganization of 1791 which created a single caisse or consolidated
venue fund.

Meanwhile, an *Intendant du trésor royal* had been appointed to the Finance Department and from
ptember 1790 he was entitled *Directeur*. He administered the bureaux formerly under the *Premier
mmis des finances*. In the autumn of 1790 the *Directeur* and his bureaux were transferred from the
sintegrating Finance Department and became part of the Treasury. The Chamber of Accounts
on disappeared and the Treasury became the centre of the financial system. Before 1795, it had
adually absorbed the remaining separate caisses one by one.

Council would prepare (or have prepared) the published accounts for that fiscal year and also the budget for the next year.

These rearrangements implied a revolution in the financial system. In respect of its accounts, the Treasury had become a corporate entity, almost as it were an accountant, collectively responsible to the Royal Council. Instead of issuing several budgetary *états du Roi*, to each of the Keepers of the Treasury and other separate paying accountants and receiving from each of them an *état au vrai*, the Council would now issue one budget (*aperçu*) to the Royal Treasury and receive in return one *état au vrai*. By ordering the publication of annual accounts, Brienne was involving public scrutiny as a control device and quite deliberately, or so it appears from the preamble to the *Compte rendu* in which Soufflot de Mérey wrote, 'there is no abuse that order and publicity will not succeed in destroying'.[1] An orderly treasury and a set of public accounts were together intended to be an engine of financial management, but they could only be truly effective if they accounted for all public funds. So long as there were still accountants with independent caisses receiving and spending funds which did not pass through the Treasury, the budgetary control of the government would be imperfect.

To make the Treasury truly central to the system, controlling the flow of public funds like a great commanding valve, was the final goal of these reforms, and it was not to be reached until 1793–4 and then only temporarily. Not until the nineteenth century were French governments to achieve that measure of control over public funds. Yet Brienne took a great step forward and his documents of 1788 were already pointing the way. The edict of March 1788 declared, 'our finances have long suffered the innumerable inconveniences from the multitude of the caisses in which our revenues are paid successively in order to meet the expenses for which they are destined'. And the *compte rendu* threw these imperfections of the system into relief, and showed that the General Farm and other caisses were making payments amounting to nearly half of the revenues of the state, payments which had never been properly accounted for and which would be better made by the Treasury. The editors argued that the General Farm, for instance, ought to deduct nothing but its own operating expenses from the funds it collected on behalf of the Crown.[2] Brienne, like Necker before him, was planting seeds of reform which governments of the revolution would harvest in later years.

These reforms were among the minor subjects on which the royal government and its critics disagreed in the period of the *révolte nobiliaire*.

[1] p. vii.   [2] p. 9.

To the Chamber of Accounts the reforms were already something of a revolution and when they received the edict of March 1788 they appointed a commission to study it.[1] On 28 April 1788 the Chamber decided to register the edict with many misgivings and two pages of stipulations. They believed it a mistake for the Crown to pay the salaries and other operating costs of the Treasury because, they said, Necker had tried to do this with the Treasurers for War and Marine in 1778–81 and the system had proved a failure and was replaced in 1782 with the old system of payments to venal office-holders responsible for their own expenses. The Chamber had doubts about the proposed accounting system. Brienne had instructed the treasury administrators to submit accounts to the Chamber, each for the caisse of his division in the usual way, but he intended the accounting system primarily to inform the Minister and the Royal Council of treasury business. To maintain their threatened position in the financial system the Chamber proposed to name commissioners to inspect the general caisse of the Treasury every month without charge to the crown, and it rested this stipulation on ancient laws.[2] Meanwhile the Keeper of the Seals, Lamoignon, had been preparing his *coup d'état* against the sovereign courts, and the Chamber of Accounts was suspended only a few days after registering the edict of March 1788.[3]

When the Chamber was recalled with the other sovereign courts in September, triumphant in the knowledge that the Estates-General were to meet in May 1789, Loménie de Brienne had fallen, and Jacques Necker had taken his place. But the Treasury was still much as Brienne had cast it. If we may judge from appointments Necker had made to the section of the Department of Finance dealing with treasury business, he thought very highly of the new Treasury. In August he had discharged the *Premier commis des finances*, Gojard, and appointed in his place François-Pierre Cornus de la Fontaine who was to become one of the Treasury commissioners in 1791,[4] and above him Necker had at the same time appointed the

---

[1] A.N., P 2744, entry dated 22 April 1788.
[2] Such as an Ordonnance of 7 Jan. 1407 and Lettres patentes of 7 Feb. 1531.
[3] There is a gap in the *Journal* of the Chamber from the entry of 7 May to that of 24 September (A.N., P 2845).
[4] Born at Montmorency (Seine-et-Oise); married Marie Trudon in 1779 and they had a son, Alexandre-Henri-Simon (d. 1841) and a daughter Anne-Madeleine (d. 1833). He entered the service of one of the Keepers of the Royal Treasury on 18 April 1767 and rose, after long service, including thirty-two months as *Premier commis des finances*, to be a Treasury Commissioner on 5 May 1791; went back into the ranks of the Treasury some-time in the course of the revolution and retired on a pension (2,507 fr. 29 c.) on 25 April 1797 after 30 years and 7 days of service in the Treasury. He became *caissier* of the Bank of France under the Consulat and Chevalier de la Légion d'Honneur; died on 31 October 1818 in Paris. He must be distinguished from another treasury employee who may have

former *Premier commis de finances*, Bertrand Dufresne, with the new title of Intendant of the Royal Treasury and a large salary of 60,000 livres a year. Thus, in some sixteen months after Calonne's fall, the bureaux for treasury affairs in the Department of Finance had grown enormously and the Royal Treasury had become a bureaucratic organization.

The Royal Treasury was to thrive over the next few years. As other financial institutions crumbled under successive waves of revolution—the General Control, the Receivers General of Finance, the General Farm, the *Régie générale*, the National Lottery, etc.—the Treasury inherited many of their bureaux which performed useful services. Each new revolutionary government found the Treasury an invaluable instrument and sought to improve it. Under a changing title—*Trésor royal*, *Trésor public* and finally *Trésorerie nationale*—it waxed ever larger and more powerful. But in spite of its growth it remained basically much the same. The Constituent Assembly added to it and in the spring of 1791 reorganized it without changing either the main body of its personnel or the foundations laid down by Loménie de Brienne. Five years later, Barbé-Marbois sent a report on the Treasury to the Directory from which we learn that there were then twenty-four bureaux with a total of 1,246 employees costing 2,836,233 livres a year. In his covering letter he wrote:

It was five years ago that the National Treasury was set in motion, in conformity with the organization which it was then given and which still exists. This great establishment is presently an integral part of the constitutional edifice and it has necessary, important and continuous relations with all parts of the government. It is, so to speak, the heart of this immense body.[1]

Still later, another Finance Minister described the Treasury of the Consulate and Empire as a restoration of the 1788 organization.[2] All this lay in the future and after many struggles. In 1788 the new bureaucratic Treasury was already the subject of deep conflicts, and to these we must now turn.

been a relation: François-Benoît Cornut de la Fontaine de Coincy, born at Saint Denis (Seine) in October 1745, died on 23 May 1831 in Paris. (*Actes de Décès*, Archives de la Seine; and Daubermesnil, *Corps législatif...* 6 Floréal Year V (B.N., 4° L^{43} 925).)

[1] Barbé-Marbois, letter dated 9 August 1796 in A.N., AF III 130, dossier 611.
[2] Gaudin (duc de Gaëte), *Mémoires, souvenirs etc.*, vol. II, p. 448.

12

STRUGGLES FOR CONTROL OF
THE TREASURY 1787–1793

I

THE ORGANIZATION of the Treasury in the spring of 1788 strained the already uneasy relations of the Royal Council on Finance and the Chamber of Accounts. These two authorities had long been engaged in an obscure struggle, dormant for some periods during which they cooperated in a common endeavour to get the best out of the system of caisses and accountants. Their struggle was always overshadowed by the much more obvious conflict of Crown and Parlements, but yet it grew during the crisis of 1787 and ripened in the following year. The revolutionary National Assembly intervened at a time when the Crown was imposing reforms on the financial system in spite of the Chamber's conservative resistance. The principal reform, the organizing of the Treasury, marked neither the beginning of the struggle nor its end.[1]

In the series of financial failures during 1787, the Royal Council reserved much of the investigation for itself and its own commissions and otherwise encroached upon the jurisdiction of the Chamber. The failure of a *régisseur* was the legitimate concern of the Council, to which all *régisseurs* were responsible, and the Chamber therefore had no complaint to make about the Crown's management of the investigation into the bankruptcy of the *économe du clergé de France*, Marchal de Sainscy. But in the crisis of 1787 the alarm and impatience of the Council impelled it to interfere in the affairs of the Treasurers from the military departments. By an arrêt of 2 February 1787 the Council appointed a commission of six to manage the claims and investigations arising out of the failure of Baudard de Saint James.[2] The cash and effects from his caisse and any other assets were to be sequestered by one of the Keepers of the Royal Treasury, Savalette de Langes. The Chambers, alarmed at this interference, sent representatives to

---

[1] See above, p. 167.
[2] Two Councillors of State, Le Noir and Perrin de Cypierre; the Lt.-Gen. of Police, de Crosne; and three Masters of Requests, Albert, Charpentier de Boisgibault and de la Porte. (A.N., P 2744, entry for 3 Feb. 1787 and Lett. Pat. of 28 Aug. 1787.)

Versailles on 11 February to tell the King that 'the existence of a commission of the Council performing the functions of the Chamber of Accounts in the heart of the capital, affixing seals on the property of Baudard de Saint James...presents too many disadvantages, Sire, to let it pass in silence'.[1] In the same remonstrance the Chamber complained of interference by the Keeper of the Seals and the Controller General of Finance who in the King's name had over-ruled a resolution of the Chamber against an unruly Receiver. The Chamber got little satisfaction in these cases. Then, only a few months later, the Royal Council intervened again, this time by ordering the Chamber to hurry its investigation of the bankruptcy of Mégret de Sérilly, the War Treasurer, and by laying down rules for handling the affair.[2] Such incidents continued to occur after Necker's return to the Department of Finance in August 1788. The Treasurer of the *Caisse des arrérages* died in August, and without waiting for the Chamber of Accounts to begin its inquiry into that disappointing and troublesome caisse Necker appointed a Crown commission to take over the whole affair. There were several angry exchanges on the subject over the next few months and at the end of January 1789 the Chamber held a long discussion of the *Caisses des arrérages* and *amortissements* which, according to one speaker, had suffered abuses 'that have been the unhappy and prolific germ of the dilapidation of finances and the ruin of the state'.[3]

The Chamber professed to see a dangerous indulgence for erring accountants in the Crown's interference and even hinted at collusion. 'In a word, Sire,' they said on 11 February 1787, after reviewing the failures of recent years, 'these unfaithful accountants who have pilfered the coffers of Your Majesty, instead of being punished for their prevarications, instead of serving as a warning through a salutary punishment, have nearly all obtained either salaries or pension.'[4] During the previous year the Crown had protected a certain accountant, Dupille de Saint Séverin, against the Chamber's efforts to imprison him for fraud. The Chamber found further evidence for their suspicions in measures like the Letters Patent of 12 January 1788 ordering the Chamber to suspend the sale of goods confiscated from Mégret de Sérilly, apparently at the request of his wife. A commission

---

[1] *Remontrances de la chambre des comptes* (11 Feb. 1787), 16 pp. (B.N., Lf²⁷ 33).

[2] B.N., F 21313 (74 and 93) Lett. Pat. of 18 June 1787 and 9 July 1787. The case of the *Receveur particulier* concerned Jean-Baptiste-Paul-Antoine Clouet.

[3] The *Trésorier de la caisse des arrérages* was Claude Darras and the Crown Commission was headed by Vidaud de la Tour. Arrêt of 18 Aug. 1788. The Chamber registered letters of commission of 4 Oct. 1788 for Jean-Baptiste-Nicolas Cauchin de la Tour to continue Darras's accounts. The Chamber assembled to discuss the matter on 30 Jan. 1789. (A.N., P 2846 and P 2744; Boislisle, *Chambre des comptes*, p. 742.)

[4] *Remontrances* (B.N., Lf²⁷ 33), p. 15.

of the Chamber drew up a report in 1789 which blamed the Royal Council for insisting on the priority of the *états au vrai* over the accounts due to the Chamber, holding up the accounting process in this way and so shielding accountants from the discipline of the Chamber.[1]

The Chamber's view of financial problems on the eve of the French revolution was profoundly conservative. They believed that there was nothing wrong with the system which could not be righted by finding the men responsible for the trouble and punishing them. A patriotic speech about the debt turned into a tirade against unnamed officials responsible for it, presumably the Ministers of Finance.[2] Whenever an accountant failed in any respect, the Chamber seized on him with almost savage triumph and presumed him guilty even before the investigation. Again and again they blamed the lateness and confusion of accounts, the Crown's use of *acquits de comptant*, the secrecy of financial policy, and the interference in the Chamber's processes; but they never recommended any change in the financial system and they resisted the changes which Ministers of the Crown made. Their attitude was expressed by the *premier président* on 9 September 1787 on the occasion of Claude Lambert's reception as Controller General: France is passing through an historic moment, he said 'a moment of regeneration and of crisis when the art must be to repair everything and to destroy nothing'.[3] Reforms like the organization of the Treasury appeared to the Chamber to be profoundly mistaken.

The organization of the Treasury was a ministerial blow at the system which the Chamber of Accounts believed in. Loménie de Brienne does not appear to have consulted the Chamber about it, though he and Lambert consulted several accountants and other officials. Then, the Treasury was organized for the most part during the period from May to September 1788 when the Chamber was suspended with the other sovereign courts.[4] The arrangements for the Treasury's accounts, such as the provision for a system of double-entry book-keeping and for regular financial reports, were all intended to improve the Royal Council's control and thus indirectly to prevent the Chamber from interfering in day-to-day administration. The Chamber would be relegated to the position of a court of financial accounts —the position, as it turned out, of the future Cour des Comptes. When Necker returned to power, in August 1788, he reinforced these arrange-

---

[1] A.N., P 2843, P 2845, and *Observations sur la comptabilité et sur la juridiction de la chambre des comptes* (B.N., Lf²⁷ 36), p. 1.
[2] A.N., P 2744, *Plumitif de la Chambre*, entry for 17 Aug. 1787.
[3] Boislisle, *Chambre des comptes*, p. 736.
[4] The records of the Chamber show a hiatus from 7 May to 24 Sept. 1788 (A.N., P 2845).

ments by making changes in the Finance Department the better to exercise control over the Treasury.

Since before the reign of Louis XVI the powerful *Premier commis des finances* had supervised the principal caisses and accountants, including the Keepers of the Royal Treasury, on behalf of the Controller General of Finance. Bertrand Dufresne had held this post during Necker's first ministry, 1771–81, and on Necker's fall had been almost immediately replaced by the innocuous Gojard, who had served quietly throughout the period of reaction when the influence of accountants had dominated the financial administration. Upon returning to the Department of Finance in August 1788 Necker called upon Dufresne once more to head the same bureaus. This time, however, he gave Dufresne a new title, Intendant of the Royal Treasury, and appointed a new *Premier commis des finances*, Pierre-François Cornus de la Fontaine, as Dufresne's second-in-command. We may judge the importance which Necker attached to these appointments by the sharp increase in salaries over the annual 24,000 livres which Gojard had received. Cornus de la Fontaine was paid 30,000 livres a year and Dufresne, from his appointment on 25 August 1788, received no less than 60,000 livres. Necker was not one to set up sinecures, and he evidently intended to equip the Department to match the new Treasury and to supervise it. He was establishing ministerial power over the Treasury.[1]

Throughout Necker's second and third periods of office, that is from August 1788 to September 1790, the Intendancy of the Treasury constituted the largest and most expensive section of the Department of Finance. With forty-eight employees organized in seven bureaux under *chefs* who were for the most part paid as much as the *premiers commis* in other sections of the Department, the Intendancy of the Treasury cost nearly 200,000 livres in 1788, and approximately 270,000 livres a year in 1789 and 1790.[2] It was Dufresne and his bureaux who compiled the most complete and reliable accounts for 1789 and 1790, accounts which Necker put before the National Assembly. When the Chamber of Accounts resolved on 10 September 1789 to send the Assembly a memorandum 'on the causes of the depredation of the finances' and six weeks later ordered the publication of that memorandum, it was celebrating and recording its own decline in the face of the Crown's vigorous efforts at reform of the financial system.[3] In the next stage the Crown was going to suffer defeat in its turn.

[1] For details and references see my article, 'The Premiers Commis des Finances in the Reign of Louis XVI', *French Historical Studies*, vol. III (1964), p. 475.
[2] A.N., D x 3.
[3] A.N., P 2846.

II

The changes in the central administration of finance during the period of the National Constituent Assembly—some twenty-seven months from June 1789 to October 1791—are difficult to interpret because the Assembly carried on two different though related kinds of work. On the one hand, debates and resolutions concerning the projected constitution led many deputies to study financial institutions closely in order to improve upon the system that had brought low the Bourbon monarchy. On the other hand, before the constitutional debates were resolved, circumstances forced the Assembly to take a number of steps which necessarily affected the outcome of the debates. Thus the ancient systems of taxation were swept away prematurely in response to popular pressure; thus a pressing need of funds drove the Assembly quite early to despoil the Church; thus the Assembly (and even more its successors, the Législative and the Convention) endeavoured to put its own financial record in a favourable light by sketching in the background an ever-blackening picture of the ancien régime. And thus the Assembly seized and transformed the Treasury, well before discussing its constitutional position and future. To appreciate the Assembly's work in respect of the Treasury, we have to look first at what it did—or rather at what its committees did—and only then can we go on to examine the debates to any purpose.

During 1790 the Assembly engaged in an informal political struggle with the Crown for control of the central financial administration, and in the course of the struggle the Department of Finance was dismantled and eventually discarded, leaving the Crown or executive with virtually no hand in the direction of the state's finances. The Assembly took one of the earliest steps on 17 July 1790 when it assumed the power of authorizing payments, not merely of voting funds. The Crown lost the power of *la liquidation et l'ordonnancement* so that the ministerial tables of fund-distribution no longer served to authorize payments. Not many weeks later, two bureaux in the Department especially concerned with this aspect of payment, the *Bureau de la distribution des fonds* and the *Bureau de l'expédition des ordonnances*, were transferred to the Treasury and thereby removed from the executive Department of Finance.[1] This was only a prelude to a larger transfer, however, and its significance becomes clear when we realize that in the autumn of 1790 the Assembly's Committee on Finance assumed full control of the Treasury.

[1] A.N., F⁴ 1032², Jurieu in a letter of 24 Dec. 1791 refers to the transfer as taking place six months before the 'organization of the Treasury' in the spring of 1791.

These revolutionary events took place in an obscurity which has tended to hide their significance, but evidence of them is not lacking. The first development is succinctly worded in an official document:

Today, 17 September 1790, the King being at Saint Cloud, the sieur Necker, *premier ministre* of finances, having begged His Majesty to accept his resignation; and His Majesty wishing to provide for the administration of the Public Treasury, with which the sieur Necker was especially charged, His Majesty has believed it best to confer it on the sieur DuFresne whose services, experience, zeal and talents are perfectly known and who has hitherto managed (*gérait*) that important part of the administration under the sieur Necker's orders. To this effect, His Majesty has named and names the sieur DuFresne to exercise the Direction of the Public Treasury under his immediate orders with the title of Director General of the Public Treasury.[1]

This letter, which confirmed a *brevet* of appointment dated 9 September, shows only that upon Necker's resignation his duties were divided between Claude Lambert, the Controller General, and Bertrand Dufresne, the Intendant of the Treasury, whose title was changed to Director. Such a division was not unprecedented, and we find (in the same *carton* of the archives, indeed) an earlier *brevet* naming Necker himself Director General of the Royal Treasury on 22 October 1776 when the Controller General was the insignificant Taboureau des Réaux. In the intervening years, however, the Treasury had changed. Whereas there had been only two Keepers, accountants with their caisses and bureaux, now there was a large unified organization under five administrators whose individual powers as venal accountants were waning. Dufresne had been supervising the Treasury from a distance since 29 August 1788 in his capacity as Necker's Intendant of the Treasury with bureaux which were part of the Department of Finance. But in September 1790 he and his bureaux were transferred from the Department to the Treasury. In this fundamental reorganization Dufresne's bureaux became part of the Treasury and he came to direct the whole. This was a most important change.

The evidence for it begins with a decree voted on 11 September 1790, the same day that the Assembly ordered the over-zealous community of Arcy-sur-Aube to release Necker and allow him to continue his journey out of the country. On a motion of a member of the Finance Committee the Assembly decreed that 'from 1 October next, the Intendance of the Public Treasury and its bureaux will be united in the building occupied by the Public Treasury, and the house occupied at present by the Intendance of the

[1] A.N., D vi 1. A brief correspondence about Dufresne's appointment.

Public Treasury will be turned over to the bureaux of the General Administration of Finance'.[1] The decree evidently provides only for a physical removal, but on 9 November 1790 an anonymous authority, perfectly well-informed on many matters, wrote: 'Since the retirement of M. Necker, the Public Treasury has been administered by a Director General', and went on to explain that the administrators of the Treasury were working under the Director's orders.[2] If any further evidence is needed, we have an official table, published about the same time, showing all the bureaux of the Department of Finance, and it significantly omitted Dufresne, Cornus de la Fontaine and all the bureaux of the former Intendance of the Treasury. This table was followed less than a year later by another showing the bureaux in the Treasury as they were before the reorganization of 1 July 1791, and it records not only the Director General himself and his *Premier commis des finances*, but also various bureaux from their Intendance scattered through the list.[3] Had these bureaux been listed all together in a group it might have been possible to interpret their union with the Treasury as existing only on paper, but they were unmistakably integrated in the organization. These indications find support in a second development of September 1790, the virtual seizure of the Treasury by the Finance Committee of the National Assembly.

This committee had been dealing with Necker through a special subcommittee ever since a public announcement of 1 September 1789 that it would do so, and partly to shift the burden of this consultation Necker invited the Assembly in March 1790 to allow some of its members to serve on a proposed *Bureau de trésorerie*.[4] This invitation refused, Necker's resignation in September posed the problem of consultation for the Assembly, which needed continuous financial information, and also for the Treasury which was in such a penurious state that it could no longer make its scheduled payments.[5] Clearly, the committee would have to deal with the new Director General of the Treasury, but for all his new title and royal commission Dufresne was only a salaried employee, not a minister of the Crown, and irrespective of his position and ability he enjoyed none of Necker's prestige. 'This is the moment', said a Deputy in the Assembly on

---

[1] *Procès-verbaux de l'assemblée nationale* (11 Sept. 1790), p. 5.
[2] *Eclaircissements sur l'organisation actuelle du trésor public* (9 Nov. 1790), p. 2.
[3] *Bureaux de l'administration générale* (Paris, 1790), 15 pp. (B.N., Lf⁹⁹ 6); and *Etat des bureaux de la trésorerie nationale* (Paris, 1791), 27 pp. (B.N., Ff¹⁵⁷ 11).
[4] Bernardin, *Roland et le ministère de l'intérieur*, p. 150; *Archives parlementaires*, vol. 12, pp. 150 and 354.
[5] As Dufresne wrote to the Finance Committee on 6 Sept. 1790. (*Moniteur*, réimpr., vol. 5, p. 580).

4 September 1790, 'to charge the Committees on Finance and Constitution to take in hand the direction of finances.'[1]

And they did. The comte de Montlosier writes in his *Mémoires*, 'It had spread through Paris...that...since the retirement of Monsieur Necker our Committee on Finance had seized the Public Treasury. As in general our committees seized everything, this rumour was possibly not without foundation.'[2] Dufresne had his first conference with the Finance Committee on 23 September 1790 and thereafter met them weekly until 7 June 1791, a total of thirty-two meetings. Only twelve specially appointed members of the committee attended—the 'comité de douze'—and they referred some matters to meetings of the whole. But if they were careful not to abuse their mandate, they were evidently in command of the Treasury. Dufresne has left a manuscript register of their minutes, a very full record in which it is clear that the committee continually asked Dufresne for information and advice but took decisions themselves or else by introducing decrees in the Assembly.[3] 'You know, Monsieur,' Dufresne wrote to Bailly, the mayor of Paris, on 3 February 1791, 'in the delicate position in which I am, I neither can nor should take anything upon myself.'[4] The widest possible range of financial affairs, including fundamental reforms of the Treasury itself and other agencies, were discussed and decided in these meetings. Here, indeed, was the centre of the financial administration from Autumn 1790 until the following summer.

This period of uneasy cooperation between a legislative committee and a royal executive agent came to an end in summer 1791 when Dufresne lost his post. One of the reasons for his dismissal was that he criticized the growing deficit and debt resulting from the radical reforms of the National Assembly. Sharing the beliefs of Necker and other royal officials, Dufresne saw the revolution as a regeneration of royal finances, Crown and parliament collaborating to defeat the selfish private interests which at every social level obstructed the order, efficiency and authority of government. In letters and memoranda which he sent to Louis XVI in November and December 1791, Dufresne showed how the Assembly had increased the deficit and had only made the debt worse by an unbusinesslike use of paper *assignats*. His figures were probably accurate—no one was better equipped than he to calculate debt and deficit—and he was indifferent to the revolutionary efforts that had led to such heavy expenditure, impervious to the

[1] Gaultier de Biauzat immediately after Necker's letter of resignation was read (Arch. Parl., vol. XVIII, p. 559).
[2] (Paris, 1830), 3 vols., vol. 2, p. 210,
    A.N., AB XIX 327. Cf. Braesch, *Les Exercices budgétaires 1790 & 1791*, p. 7.
[4] B.N., MS fr. 11696, Dufresne to Bailly, 3 Feb. 1791.

spirit of those dramatic years and deaf to abstract principles like popular sovereignty and the rights of man. He believed not in revolution but in improvement. For him an efficient Public Treasury and a competent government were goals in themselves, and he feared that the revolutionary forces were sacrificing them to wild ideals. He expressed bewilderment (and passionate loyalty) in a letter to Louis XVI written on Christmas Day 1791, in which he summed up the financial situation and concluded: 'this is the deplorable state to which new systems have brought the finances of the most beautiful kingdom in the world, which might so easily have also been made the happiest'.[1] The revolution was entering the republican-democratic phase in which Dufresne, like Louis XVI, would have no place, and the Treasury would be no longer an end in itself but a revolutionary instrument.

Long before then, while the National Assembly was taking legislative command of the Treasury it was also dismantling the Department of Finance and so destroying whatever power the King and his ministers still had over the public finances. Taking over the Treasury was a step in this process, and Dufresne unwittingly assisted in the destruction of the Finance Department by engaging in a personal rivalry with the Minister, Lambert. 'These two kings of finance,' an observant official remarked on 17 October 1790, 'one wants no master and the other no equal; and their disunity, manifested by their lower officials, is in some ways even becoming scandalous.'[2] Lambert, like all the royal ministers in general, came under a furious attack during the later months of 1790 in the National Assembly, in the Jacobin Club and in large sections of public opinion. Forty-four of the forty-eight Paris *sections* were reported to have adopted a resolution of the *section* of Mauconseil calling for the dismissal of all the ministers.[3] On 4 December 1790, Louis XVI appointed Valdec de Lessart to replace Lambert as Controller General of Finance and de Lessart wrote to the Assembly calling himself Minister of Finance, but it was already an empty title.[4] A few of his bureaux were transferred, like those of Dufresne, to the Treasury and the rest were divided between two new Departments, for *Contributions publiques* and *Intérieur*, duly set up by a decree of 27 April 1791. De Lessart became Minister of Interior, and the new Minister of Public Contributions turned out to be Tarbé, the chief *premier commis* of the former *Bureaux des impositions*. According to the Assembly's intention, neither of these had any control over spending or budgetary policy, which was coming to be made in the Treasury so far as it fell to any administrative

[1] A.N., C 224, dossiers 160, 165 and 166.
[2] Claude-Charles Coster, *Journal manuscrit*, vol. i, entry for 17 Oct. 1790.
[3] *Ibid.*, entries for 22 Oct., 23 Oct., and 8 Nov. 1790.
[4] *Procès-verbaux de l'Ass. nat.*, vol. 17, session of 4 Dec. 1790.

agency. Few voices were raised in favour of creating a Department of Finance to replace that of the ancien régime. Meanwhile, another part of the old financial system, the Chamber of Accounts, was marked for suppression on 2 September 1790 and actually done away with a year later by decrees of 17 and 29 September 1791. These old antagonists had both lost control over the financial system.

III

While the Treasury was the object of political struggles it was also a subject of legislative debate. The Estates General first met in May 1789 mainly to discuss the Crown's financial difficulties, but on 11 July 1789 the revolutionary National Assembly decided to put off all basic decisions about the financial system until the foundations of a constitution had been laid down. Accordingly, when the fundamentals of finance eventually came up for debate, they were treated in terms of the constitutional principles of separate powers. Should financial administration properly belong to the legislature or to the executive? Should the Treasury be subject to executive or legislative control? These issues appeared again and again in different guises throughout 1790 and had not been decided by the time the Constituent Assembly had finished the constitution, which was its main work, and formally disbanded on 27 September 1791. The constitution of 1791 was ominously silent on these questions. In the meantime the constitutional debates had resulted in temporary practical compromises.

The constitutional issues first appeared in a proposal which Jacques Necker, as Minister of Finance, put before the Constituent Assembly on 6 and 12 March 1790.[1] Having had great difficulty in answering questions from the Assembly, referring to the Assembly's growing need for accounts of revenue and expenditure and other information, pointing out the burden these demands laid on the Ministry of Finance, hinting at his own ill health and probable resignation, Necker proposed a *Bureau de trésorerie* (a Treasury Commission), to assume responsibility under the King's authority, for determining daily expenditures (*ordonnancement*), deciding upon methods of payment, watching over all receipts and expenditure, and supervising all the work of the Treasury. The crux of the plan was that the King would choose the commissioners from among the deputies in the Assembly. Necker knew that such a mingling of the executive and the legislature would run contrary to the principle of the separation of powers but he argued that the Assembly should make an exception for financial administration. It was a clever proposal that would have involved the

[1] *Arch. Parl.*, vol. XII, pp. 150 and 354.

224

Assembly in collaborating with the Department of Finance to solve the problems of the moment and might have forestalled the development of the Assembly's committees on finance and taxation with their antagonism to the Department. Many members of the Assembly got the impression that this proposal might put the Treasury within the power of the Crown and this impression was amply reinforced by a letter of support for the proposal which the Assembly received from Louis XVI on 25 March 1790. There was nothing obviously sinister in this, for the Treasury had always been legally at the King's command, like all parts of the administration, and the Finance Committee was divided on the issue. Its chairman, Montesquiou-Fezensac, believed in a compromise like that of Necker, arguing that in the administration of public finance there ought to be a close cooperation of the executive and the legislature. He thought finance different from the other parts of the government and not suited to being rigidly assigned to either the Crown or the legislature. A majority of the Committee were opposed to Necker's plan, however, and the Assembly, too, rejected it on 26 March. They mistrusted royal and ministerial power and disapproved of any confusion of the executive and legislative parts of the government.

For almost six months thereafter there was no further discussion of this issue in the Assembly. The deputies carried on with their vast programme of legislation and left the planning of the Treasury to the Finance Committee which was not idle but came to no conclusion until prompted by a resolution in the Assembly. On 4 September 1790 the deputies heard Necker's letter of resignation and immediately afterwards adopted a resolution by Gaultier de Biauzat that the two Committees on Finance and on Constitution should prepare a decree 'for the organization and direction of the Public Treasury'.[1] In the following weeks, while Louis XVI appointed Dufresne to the post of Director General of the Treasury, the Assembly grew more and more uneasy about the future of the Treasury and on 21 October applauded a deputy who asserted that 'this deposit [the Treasury] ought to be entrusted to reliable hands, and the present ministers are not worthy of it'.[2] Gaultier de Biauzat stood up immediately to ask that the three committees on Finance, Constitution and Taxation be asked to report the very next day because there was not a moment to lose. It was decided to hear them three days later, but because of disagreements within the committees, and among them, nearly two months elapsed before the first of their reports was read on 11 December. Not until the following March, 1791, a whole year after Necker had put forward his proposal, did the Assembly take any decision on the constitutional position of the Treasury.

---

[1] *Arch. Parl.*, vol. xviii, p. 559.   [2] *Arch. Parl.*, vol. xix, p. 740.

Long before then the Finance Committee had in fact assumed control. What disagreements in the Assembly caused this delay?

A majority of the Finance Committee were more interested in making the Treasury an efficient executive agency than in determining its constitutional position. All the reports from this committee show a concern for the practical details of organization and functioning. This was mainly because their most experienced members were men of the ancien régime who were waging the same old struggle as before for a rational system of public finance: Le Brun, former secretary to Chancellor Maupéou and with strong memories of Terray; Anson and Dailly, both *premiers commis* in the Department of Finance during Necker's first ministry; Boisgelin de Cucé, the archbishop of Aix, so active in the clamour for a single caisse during the Assembly of Notables; Lecouteulx de Canteleu, banker and friend of Magon de la Balue; and others.[1] Their task as they saw it was to improve the administrative machinery of public finance and they resented having to deal with what their spokesman, Lebrun, described as 'metaphysical questions'.[2] At first they assumed that the Treasury would be part of the executive bureaucracy, subject to the close supervision of the legislature but administered by an official chosen and appointed by the King. When arguments were brought forward in favour of making the Treasury an agency of the legislature, and not part of the executive branch at all, the Finance Committee raised several strong objections. One was that such an arrangement would be contrary to the principle of the separation of powers. The legislature ought not to take responsibility for the execution of the laws it made because then it would be in no position to hold the executive responsible; and the whole point in separating the powers of government was to allow the nation, through its representative assembly, to supervise the executive at work. If the new constitution provided for the legislature to take executive command of the Treasury and to appoint the administrators of it, then national criticism of the Treasury's actions would fall on the legislature and the constitution when it ought to fall on the executive.

Another and more characteristic line of argument was practical: financial administration would not work well as a whole if parts of it depended upon the legislature and other parts on the Crown, and such an arrangement would be inefficient. There must be a unified command. 'It was the insubordination and independence of the secondary caisses which in the previous reign and in recent times gave rise to the great sores of [illegiti-

---

[1] Others who publicly shared their point of view were Dupont de Nemours, Briois-Beaumetz, de Jessé and d'André.
[2] *Arch. Parl.*, vol. XXIII, p. 736.

mate] finance, the wild dissipation of the Treasurers and the scandal of the nation.'[1] An even more practical argument, which drew applause from the Assembly, was that except for the deputies from Paris and those who had lived in Paris a great deal, 'there will not be four people in the Assembly qualified to decide who are the persons most capable of being [Treasury] administrators'.[2] It was immediately after this outburst on 9 March 1791, by d'André, deputy for the nobility of Aix, that the Assembly decided to have the Treasury administrators chosen by the King. On this crucial point the Finance Committee and its supporters had their way, at least for a few months. The legislature was merely to supervise the Treasury, as the Finance Committee had been doing since September 1790.

Using the time-honoured categories especially invented for the political groups in that parliament without parties, we may describe the Finance Committee and its supporters, some of them called *monarchiens* or *impartiaux*, as belonging to the Right and the Right Centre. They were opposed chiefly by men of the Left and Left Centre including most of the Taxation Committee (Dupont de Nemours was an exception), a few sympathetic observers outside the Assembly such as Condorcet and Clavière, and republican democrats like Pétion de Villeneuve and Robespierre.[3] These had a common suspicion of the King and his ministers and a fear of royalist counter-revolution which made them want to keep the Treasury well away from the Crown.

The Taxation Committee argued that public finance was a distinct constitutional power that ought to be kept separate from both the executive and the legislative powers. To arrive at this conclusion the Committee identified eleven financial functions of government, first the voting of public expenditures, secondly the voting of taxes to pay those expenditures, and so on to the seventh, which was the Treasury's function of holding and distributing public funds, and to the eleventh, which was the final accounting process. These functions the Committee held to be one integrated process of government that ought not to be divided even though some of the eleven functions might be interpreted as legislative, others as executive and others again as judicial. There ought to be a supreme directory of financial administration.[4] This ingenious train of argument did not win much

---

[1] (Lebrun), *Arch. Parl.*, vol. XXI, p. 374 (11 Dec. 1790).
[2] (d'André), *Arch. Parl.*, vol. XXIII, p. 748.
[3] Condorcet, *Sur la constitution du pouvoir chargé d'administrer le trésor national* (1790); Clavière, *Lettre à M. Beaumetz sur l'organisation du trésor public* (1790).
[4] Dupont de Nemours called it 'a political monster' and de Jessé said it was 'unknown to all the politicians ancient and modern from Zoroaster to the author of the *Contrat Social*, and it will upset, or at least complicate uselessly the machine of government' (*Arch. Parl.*, vol. XXXIII, p. 744).

15-2

support in the Assembly, but the Taxation Committee made a much greater impression with an argument that the legislature must be allowed to make appointments to this separate financial part of the government:

> ...if all the high-ranking posts in these *régies* are at the nomination of the government and under its inspection, the government [the Crown] will evidently have at its disposal a very numerous and redoubtable army. It will also have the crowd of people who aspire to belong to that army; for one holds men much more by the hopes one flatters them with than by the goods one assures them of; and with 30,000 jobs to give, the government will be able to capture 100,000 individuals.[1]

The English government has access to the Treasury both directly and by having posts to offer, the Committee warned, and it has been able to corrupt the legislature and the electors. If the French government were in a similar position it would do the same or worse. 'Put the army and the finances in its hands', Robespierre warned on 9 March 1791, 'and you will have adopted the most infallible means of constitutionally restoring despotism.'[2] Fear of corruption thus roused by the Taxation Committee and others did not dissuade the Assembly from approving royal nomination of the treasury administrators—that would come later—but it did bring them to contradict the Finance Committee on the related question of whether there should be one administrator or several.

The Finance Committee, according to its report to the Assembly read by Lebrun, proposed to organize the Treasury under one administrator, in a position much like that of Dufresne since Necker's resignation. The main argument was that a single administrator would be able to command the Treasury much more efficiently than a group. 'That unity of direction,' Lebrun said, 'that unity of power has not been proposed by your committee, it is nature who has done it, it is reason which demands it...'[3] All action is individual, and in any executive organization there must be a mainspring or *primum movens* to keep all the subordinate agents active. The Committee had in mind the principle by which a ship was best commanded by a single captain, an army by a single general, and they doubted the executive capacity of a group.

To this argument the Taxation Committee raised the objection that a single administrator chosen by the King would in practice be nothing less than a minister with something of the hateful powers of a Controller

---

[1] *Rapport concernant les lois constitutionelles des finances*, drawn up on 10 December 1790 and read on 20 Dec. by Roederer. Others who had signed it were Dauchy, La Rochefoucauld, Defermon, d'Allarde and Jary. (*Arch. Parl.*, vol. xxi, p. 583.)

[2] *Arch. Parl.*, vol. xxiii, p. 746. Others, too, repeated this warning.

[3] *Arch. Parl.*, vol. xxiv, p. 8 (10 March 1791). Two other members at least, Tuaut de la Bouverie and Tronchet, agreed.

General of Finance. Even some members of the Finance Committee bridled at the thought. 'I do not know what it is to administer the Public Treasury,' said Briois-Beaumetz, 'and what I very much want is that it should not be administered. I knew well what it was to administer the Treasury in the time when it used to live by loans, by anticipations, by drafts of funds, by false payments, by promises to pay and so much other financial juggling by which the nation was oppressed'.[1] The Assembly eventually adopted the proposals of another member of the Finance Committee, Montesquiou-Fezensac, who also believed that the Treasury did not need to be administered as an executive department because it should be nothing more than an immense counting house and safety deposit for holding public funds between the two actions of collecting and spending. At his suggestion the Assembly adopted a decree on 10 March 1791 to the effect that the Treasury would not be subject to any ministry or executive department, but would be governed instead by a committee of six, named by the King, to meet not less than three times a week and take all decisions in common, four of the six members being a quorum. A legislative committee was to supervise the Treasury.[2]

In these arrangements the Finance Committee and its right-of-centre supporters had succeeded in preserving the important power of royal nomination. This did not mean, however, that the opposing groups were permanently defeated or that their arguments in favour of legislative control were weak. On the contrary, they and their arguments belonged to the early stages of the republican movement. They were inclined to interpret the position of the Treasury in a republican way, as did Roederer in a speech of 27 November 1791:

The Treasury is not royal, it is national. The administrators of it are therefore essentially keepers of the national funds. They are, it is true, named by the King, but not because they keep the King's money, not because they represent royal power, but because it has seemed to you that in the choice of men for these national functions there could be no better elector than the King.[3]

The republicans were only a small minority in the Constituent Assembly, but their numbers increased in the Legislative Assembly, elected in Autumn 1791, as fears and resentments of the new régime accumulated. One of those fears was that the Crown might use its financial powers in the cause of counter-revolution. The Treasury itself remained, indeed, a permanent centre of royalist opinion, but on 10 August 1792 the republican and demo-

[1] *Arch. Parl.*, vol. xxiv, p. 10 (10 March 1791).
[2] *Ibid.* p. 14 (10 March 1791).
[3] A.N., Roederer papers, 29 AP 82.

229

cratic forces overturned the régime, suspended the King's authority and the constitution of 1791 and held elections for a new assembly, the National Convention. This body decided that the legislature should command the Treasury and so stated in the constitution it drew up in February 1793, the so-called Girondin Constitution which provided for three elected Treasury Commissioners. Shortly afterwards the Jacobin Constitution of 24 June 1793 restored the nomination of the commissioners to the executive, subject to strict legislative supervision, but these short-lived documents were never properly implemented and the constitution of 22 August 1795 gave the legislative assemblies of the Directory period complete control of the Treasury.

Throughout the revolutionary years from 1790 to 1800, republican principles consistently required the nation's representatives to guard the Treasury against the dangers of executive authority. An executive minister, as Condorcet reasoned in 1790, might fall victim to a coalition of financial interests such as had influenced ministers in the ancien régime, perverting the public revenues to private ends. If the legislature controlled the Treasury through a permanent national commission, then such a sinister coalition of financiers would be obliged as a first step to direct its efforts to the much more obvious and unconstitutional objective of replacing the commission with an executive minister, 'that is, of introducing corruption into the public administration'.[1] Legislative command over the Treasury to defend the general interest against private interests: this was one of the republican constitutional principles.[2] It was threatened by financiers, such as those who formed the Bank of France in 1800, and by royalist opinion like that of Cornu de la Fontaine in his *Idées sur l'administration des finances* (1800). For ten years the royalists and the financiers were kept at bay. Not until the Bonapartist *coup d'état* and the constitution of 13 December 1799 was the Treasury turned over to the executive, a Minister of the Treasury appointed and the republican financial system corrupted for imperial ends.

[1] Condorcet, *Réflexions sur la constitution du pouvoir* (1790), p. 21.
[2] L. Duguit, H. Monnier, R. Bonnard, *Les Constitutions*, 7th ed. (Paris, 1952), *passim*.

13

TOWARDS A SINGLE CAISSE

THE ROYAL TREASURY flourished and expanded in the French revolution because every government of those busy years used it as an instrument of financial reform. With its help the Constituent Assembly (June 1789 to September 1791), the Legislative Assembly (September 1791 to August 1792) and the various régimes of the Convention (September 1792 to October 1795), including the Committee of Public Safety, all carried on the great tasks of rationalizing and 'nationalizing' the institutions of government finance. They were difficult tasks and the reform process was destined to go on into the nineteenth century. But when the Directory period began in Autumn 1795 the financial administration of the republic had already been largely cut free of the nettles and thickets of the ancien régime, those special interests and private enterprises that had maintained financial disorder at public expense. By 1795 the Treasury was at the centre of the system and commanding it. A single caisse received all revenues in one form or another, issued the funds for all expenditures, and so controlled the funds of the central government like a large valve.

While the independent caisses, the venal accountants, the tax farms and the Chambers of Accounts were disappearing in the revolution, the Treasury was gaining by every turn of events. It became not only a tool in the hands of the reformers but also their greatest beneficiary. In the numbers of its employees, the Treasury grew from 264 in 1789 to 490 by 1793, 1,026 by 1795 and 1,246 by April 1796. The cost of these employees rose accordingly from 781,300 livres in 1789 to 1,290,100 livres in 1793 and 2,836,233 livres in 1796.[1] These increases were not autonomous; the Treasury did not grow fat by a Parkinsonian process of making work for itself. It was built up by successive governments which continually reorganized it and watched its structure very closely. All the signs are that the employees worked harder and to more purpose than under the ancien régime, while their salaries were certainly much reduced, especially in the upper ranks. The growth of the Treasury is all the more remarkable because it took place

---

[1] A.N., C 260 dossier 552; AF III 130, letter from the Commissioners dated 7 April 1796; F 30 106, July 1796; B.N., Lf[157] 11, 1791; A.N., D x 3.

during lean years. Through this revolutionary activity the republic developed a financial administration with a power Louis XIV can hardly have dreamed of.

The most fundamental steps in this financial revolution were those leading to the destruction of the venal accounting offices and most agencies with independent caisses, especially the General Farm of Taxes. Little by little the entire system was subordinated to the Treasury so that public funds could be clearly identified and protected from private exploitation. Under the ancien régime, Terray, Necker and Loménie de Brienne had already laid the foundation for this work and pointed the way. But even in March 1788 when the Treasury was founded as a public organization, it stood as little more than a grouping of major paying caisses in the midst of a jungle of receivers, treasurers and payers who had purchased their offices, and of farms, *régies* and sovereign courts with various kinds of power over public funds. The events of 1789 had little or no immediate effect on these arrangements, but the changes of later years were, of course, the work of the National Assembly, composed mainly of officials, professional and business men wielding the authority of the sovereign nation.

In 1789 there was a strong feeling among them in favour of setting aside the reforms of financial institutions until the main terms of the kingdom's constitution had been worked out. 'The whole system of finances must, indeed, stem from the Constitution', the Finance Committee reported on 16 November.[1] Although circumstances obliged them to take many decisions even in their early sessions, they were able to avoid most of the complex work of reconstruction until Necker resigned in September 1790. Whatever differences arose to strain their relations with Necker, many of them trusted and respected him as a sort of financial caretaker during the first critical year beginning in summer 1789. In the eyes of Marat and Hébert at least, the Assembly was following Necker's leadership.[2] The social and political issues were in the forefront during the early months, but the financial crisis kept reappearing on the floor of the Assembly. Beneath the dramatic struggle of the Third Estate against noble and clerical pri-

---

[1] *Arch. Parl.*, vol. x, p. 70.

[2] Marat, *L'Amie du peuple*, nos. LI, LV, LXXV and others of November and December 1789; Hébert, *Le Père Duchesne*. To appreciate this view of Necker, it is necessary to consider how much more favourably the Assembly thought of him than of all other royal ministers. The emotion which swept the Assembly and the Hôtel de Ville at Necker's dismissal on 13 July was equalled only by the general delight at his recall three days later, an enthusiasm which contrasts strangely with their mournful and apprehensive silence on hearing 'the disastrous news' about the fall of the Bastille. (*Arch. Parl.*, vol. VIII, pp. 228, 233 and 239.) Even though his popularity waned during 1790, he remained in charge of financial administration, a rather sanctimonious figure bound to fall victim to the challenge of the Assembly as it slowly educated itself in matters of financial administration.

vilege, there was a different though related struggle to impose the authority of the Assembly upon private rights in public finance.[1] The 'rights' of venal accountants to exploit government funds for profit were privileges of the aristocracy. In the financial system privilege was marked by independence and disorganization, and we should not be surprised to find that the financial revolution was a triumph of bureaucratic structures. Suddenly, for the first time in French history, government bureaux and other agencies began to be charted, their anatomy exposed in detail so that the legislators could see the name, salary and functions of every official and his place in the bureaucratic hierarchy. Drawing organization charts was part of bureaucratic planning and controlling, but it was also part of the new accounting process, taking stock to see what the public was getting for its money. As reorganization went forward, there was more and more need for treasury control and less and less room for independent accountants and caisses. On 19 October 1790 Dufresne, the Treasury Director, told the Finance Committee of the National Assembly that there should be no more *anticipations* of any kind, nor any payments by any independent caisse. 'All funds will be received and all will be paid directly at the Public Treasury.'[2]

The first major accountants to be disbanded were the Receivers General of Finance and the *Receveurs particuliers*, suppressed by a decree of 14 November 1790 with effect from 1 January 1791. This was not an inevitable consequence of abolishing the taxes they collected, the *taille, capitation* and *vingtième*, for these were replaced by other taxes on land and other property which the old receivers might well have been employed to collect. But the revolution led to a change of men and system as well as a change of taxes. Large numbers of *cahiers de doléances*, sent to the Estates-General with the elected representatives in May 1789, called for the suppression of the Receivers General and *Receveurs particuliers*, venal offices, and middlemen profiting by tax collecting. Frenchmen detested these nearly as much as the taxes themselves. The National Assembly intended to replace them with more subordinate and dependent officials for whom tax collection would be a paid public function rather than a profitable private business. The same decree that suppressed the old receivers also established new ones, the *Receveurs de districts*, one for each of the 543 newly drawn Districts of France. They were supposed to be elected for six years by a majority vote in the Administrative Council of the District, and their caisses and accounts

[1] By a decree of 28 November 1789, the Assembly ordered its Finance Committee to discover all abuses in this part of the administration and to report on them.
[2] A.N., AB xix 327, 5th Conference.

233

were to be inspected twice a month by two members of the District Directory. Responsible thus to local governments, the District Receivers were subordinated in other ways to the Treasury, bound especially to keep it informed of every collection, expenditure or other transaction by an elaborate system of receipts and books.[1] In consequence the Treasury needed additional staff.

The new Treasury bureaux of General Correspondence with the District Receivers, were planned by Bertrand Dufresne, the Treasury Director, and approved by the National Assembly on the advice of its Finance Committee. Dufresne planned for a total of sixty-nine employees including four Directors, eight Chiefs and eight *premiers commis*, at a total cost of 220,000 livres for salaries and the usual incidental expenses for wood, candles, registers, paper, ink and pens.[2] This and all other changes between September 1790 and July 1791 were the result of the close collaboration of Dufresne and the Finance Committee. According to the new constitutional arrangements, the legislature approved the establishment of additional civil service posts, especially the costs, and the appointments to these posts needed executive or royal approval. Dufresne therefore wrote to Louis XVI on 14 January 1791 asking (and receiving) approval for a list of sixty-nine employees. He wrote,

it is essential to engage only experienced, intelligent and hard-working candidates. In consequence, I beg Your Majesty to allow me to choose the best of those in the various bureaux of the *Recette générale* and the Receivers General. The Receivers General complain at not being called to these posts themselves. It is certain that they were one of the corps of finance which distinguished itself most honourably by its zeal and good services. But the [financial] difficulties which a great number of them are now revealing and the way in which the majority of them have managed their places, make me fear that they are less suitable than their clerks for the subordinate and onerous type of work required for the new collection of general receipts. Besides, the example of what happened in 1781 gives me some uneasiness.[3]

Dufresne had learned a lesson in 1781 when the Receivers General he and Necker chose for their reorganized *Recette générale* had opposed the reform and helped to destroy it. But their clerks were acceptable, and among those appointed to the new Treasury bureaux were many from that hinterland of bureaux between the Receivers General who paid them and the Department of Finance which listed them among its divisions.[4]

[1] Decree of 14 November 1790, sanctioned 24 November.
[2] Authorized, pending general reorganization, by decree of 27 December 1790, sanctioned 2 January 1791.
[3] Dufresne to Louis XVI, 14 January 1791 (A.N., AB XIX 327, fol. 519).
[4] Among the senior employees in Dufresne's list we recognize Villiers, Vauguyon des Essarts, Beckvelt, Lefèvre and D'Houbert.

The most notable addition to the Treasury, not marked on Dufresne's list because made a little later, was Gaudin's bureau of *Impositions de province*. Gaudin writes in his memoirs: 'The administration of Finance, properly speaking, having been transferred by the Constituent Assembly to the National Treasury which it had just instituted, I passed with all my colleagues [nineteen men] from my former department, which was dissolved, to this new establishment...the receipts and the accounting of the receivers formed my particular division....'[1] He had the difficult task of instructing and guiding the new District Receivers through the new Bureau of General Correspondence. All these transfers resulting from the suppression of the Receivers General swelled the Treasury with new bureaux costing 245,550 livres in salaries for 1791 and about 190,000 livres in 1792 and in 1793.[2]

The National Assembly suppressed the General Farm and the *Régie générale* by a law of 27 March 1791, but this had little effect on the Treasury because for some years no new taxes on commodities were enacted to replace the defunct *aides, gabelles, tabac, droits de marque, droits réservés* or *octrois*.[3] The yield of these taxes had fallen off drastically by popular resistance even before their formal suppression; the Farmers General and Receivers General had already received orders to make no further payments after 1 January 1791; remaining stocks of salt and tobacco were turned over to the District Directories for sale; and in November 1791 the long task of winding up the affairs of these companies began. Only three considerable parts of them survived: the administration of the customs duties on the national frontiers, the duties of *contrôle* and *insinuation* on legal documents which became the modern registration duties, and the *marque d'or et d'argent* duties. The first two were put under government commissions (*régie*) and the third was eventually assigned for collection by the Mint administration. Meanwhile, the third great collecting agency, the Domains Administration, had been reduced to a nucleus with a budget of a mere 60,000 livres, and it soon became part of the new Ministry of the Interior.[4]

---

[1] Gaudin, *Mémoires, souvenirs, opinions et écrits du duc de Gaete* (Paris, 1826), vol. I, pp. 9 and 12.

[2] B.N., Lf[157] 11, a list showing the new bureaux for fifty-nine employees and 139,680 livres a year after 1 July 1791, but this is deceptive because the caisse and its employees had been moved into another part of the Treasury, the *caisses de recette*. Also, A.N., F[30] 106 and *Arch. Parl.*, vol. LXIX, p. 665 (29 July 1793).

[3] The *aides* suppressed with effect from 1 May 1791; the *droits de marque* from 1 April 1790; the *gabelle* from 14 March 1790, the *tabac* 30 March 1791 and the lease Mager cancelled on that day. G. T. Matthews, *The Royal General Farms*, p. 278; Clavière, *Mémoire sur la liquidation de la ferme générale et de la régie générale* (Paris, 31 December 1792).

[4] Decree of 16 August 1790, sanct. 19 Sept.; Edith Bernardin, *Roland et le ministère de l'intérieur, 1792–3* (Paris, 1964), *passim*.

The receiving caisses of the Treasury were prepared to manage what little revenue these and other small agencies might gather, and by summer 1793 the Treasury commissioners claimed to be receiving no less than eighteen different kinds of revenue.[1]

The venal paying accountants with their independent caisses had begun to disappear in 1787, not to mention Necker's earlier work of suppression, and the very founding of the Treasury in March 1788 had consolidated several major paying caisses. Twelve Treasurers were listed as suppressed in the *Almanach Royal* of 1791, but fifteen others still survived under the head, *Trésoreries diverses*.[2] These survivors were small fry except for the five Treasurers for the former *pays d'état*, Brittany, Burgundy, Languedoc, Provence and Artois, who were largely receivers from the Crown's point of view, and all were in any case eventually eliminated by the general condemnation of venal offices and the suppression of the agencies they were supposed to pay and of the provincial estates. The Treasury inherited the responsibility for all such regular small payments which the ancien régime had assigned—or would have assigned—to independent venal Treasurers, and accordingly the Treasury's division for miscellaneous expenditures grew from twenty-five employees with salaries totalling 72,900 in 1788 to more than twice that size by 1 July 1791. Two years later, even after the removal of the caisse and other reorganizations in this division, it still employed thirty-six men with salaries amounting to 101,400 livres.

Two other major categories of venal payers, the Treasurers in the provinces and the Payers of the rentes, were not affected by these arrangements because their businesses were too large to be included among the miscellaneous payments. In many parts of the country, especially in seaports and certain frontier towns where there were military and naval costs to be paid, small venal Treasurers did the business of the spending departments. In 1788 there were sixty-three for the War Department, about half of them called *trésoriers principaux* and drawing annual salaries of anything from 1,500 livres to 12,000 livres and the other half called *trésoriers particuliers* paid on a scale ranging from 600 livres to 9,000 livres.[3] The Marine Department kept Treasurers in seven French ports and five colonies with

---

[1] *Compte rendu à la convention par les commissaires de la trésorerie nationale* (B.N., Lf¹⁵⁸ 19, p. 2). The District Receivers were receiving forty kinds by the end of 1794.

[2] p. 269. These were one each for Charges assignés sur les fermes, Régiments des Gardes Suisses, Hôtel royal des invalides, Invalides de la marine, Ecoles royales militaires, Ordre du Saint Esprit, Ordres de Saint Louis et du mérite militaire, Œconomats, Sceau, and Monnaies; and four for Pays ci-devant d'états.

[3] A.N., D x 3, 'Traitements des employés dans les différents bureaux', MS. The ten best-paid *Trésoriers principaux* lived at Lille (12,000), Aix-en-Provence (11,000), Metz (11,000), Strasbourg (11,000), Valenciennes (10,500), Rennes (9,500), Besançon (7,000),

salaries ranging from 15,000 livres for the one in Brest to 3,300 livres for those in Le Havre and Dunkirk.[1] In the early years of the revolution, before the system had been changed, there were reported to be a total of thirty-three such Treasurers for the Marine Department and the *Ponts et Chaussées* combined, and we may therefore assume that the *Ponts et Chaussées* employed twenty-one of them.[2] Altogether there were ninety-seven provincial Treasurers, according to the Treasury Commissioners, and during the winter months of 1790–1 Dufresne and the Finance Committee seem to have intended to replace these partly by the elected District Receivers and partly by the appointment of paying clerks in the spending departments.[3] The District Receivers did undertake the payments for the *Ponts et Chaussées*, the Department of Justice, and the salaries of the clergy, recently added to the public pay-roll, but no law explicitly required the provincial Treasurers of the War and Marine Departments to turn over their duties.

They quietly continued in office until the Constituent Assembly suddenly passed a law on 24 September 1791, right at the end of its term, instructing the Treasury Commissioners to appoint a *Payeur général* for each of the eighty-seven territorial departments and two or three in departments where concentrations of troops or ships required them. Their salaries were to range from 1,800 livres to 10,000 livres and to form a total expense of no more than 300,000 livres. They were, of course, not to purchase their posts but were to put up security bonds or real estate as security. This decree, proposed by Lecouteulx de Canteleu, a banker and deputy for the Third Estate of Rouen, passed almost without discussion because the Assembly was impatient to be finished. To some observers the law looked like an attempt to put the paying process in the hands of the executive, especially when a royal proclamation of 18 December 1791 charged these new officials with all the payments hitherto made by the District Receivers as well as the provincial Treasurers.[4] Protests that this was a reactionary

Grenoble (6,500), Montpellier (6,000) and Amiens (5,400). The ten best-paid *Trésoriers particuliers* lived at Bastia (9,000), Nancy (6,400), Cherbourg (5,400), Colmar (4,500), Dunkirk (3,000), Givet (2,700), Bayonne (2,500), Calais et Boulay (2,400), Verdun (2,400), Landau (2,400), Arras (2,400).

[1] The others were in Toulon (14,000), Rochefort (12,000), Lorient (6,000), and Bordeaux (5,500); and in the colonies of Saint Domingue (12,000), Isles de France et de Bourbon (8,000), Martinique (5,000), Guadeloupe (4,000) and Cayenne (4,000).

[2] *Mémoire sur les principes et les avantages de l'établissement des payeurs généraux* (1792) (8° Le33 3 H (8)), p. 13.

[3] Lebrun, *Report* of 11 December 1790, *Arch. Parl.*, vol. XXI, p. 376.

[4] Rougier-Labergerie, *Opinion et projet de décret sur les payeurs généraux* (9 April 1792) (B.N., L33 3z (7)); and Laffon de Ladébat, *Rapport du comité de l'ordinaire des finances...* (10 Feb. 1792) (B.N., 8° L33 H (6)).

step, especially because the Treasury Commissioners admitted having chosen most of the Payers-General from among the old provincial Treasurers, met with the argument that to combine the operations of receiving and paying in the same hands or to create special payers for the War and Marine Departments would be even more reactionary. The war which began in April 1792 seemed to redouble the need for Payers-General. In spite of criticism, they were still in place at the end of 1794, when the Commissioners praised their devotion, zeal and talents in a report to the Convention, and in July 1796 their numbers had increased to about a hundred.[1] That was still their numbers in 1798, and with their employees and bureau expenses they then cost 1,018,000 livres. In the meantime the paying section of the Treasury had grown a little with the increasing difficulty of supervising wartime expenditures, but complicated reorganizations make it risky to estimate by how much. Certainly the revolution in this part of the public spending system did not swell the Treasury as much as the abolition of the *Payeurs des rentes*.

For reasons which are rather obscure, the Payers of the rentes were by a considerable margin the last corps of accountants to fall victim to the French revolution. Their suppression was not even enacted until August 1793 and their functions did not altogether come to an end for another year and a half. Though they had suffered few bankruptcies and were probably the best of the accounting corps, they were not above criticism or reform. Terray had severely reduced their numbers, the Constituent Assembly ordered their scattered bureaux to be gathered into the former Hôtel de la Recette générale (or Hôtel de Mesmes) for the sake of administrative supervision and public convenience, and in 1790 a majority of the Finance Committee headed by Briois de Beaumetz, proposed that they should be done away with and the rentes paid by a new bureau of twenty-two employees in the Treasury.[2] There was considerable public opinion in favour of such a reform. Lebrun led a minority of the Committee, however, in a defence of the Payers of the rentes, who also defended themselves in a number of pamphlets, and eventually the legislation of 1790 and 1791 left the forty Payers and a larger number of Controllers still at work.[3] Only those few employed in paying rentes on the clergy, the Paris domains, the General Farm, the *Pays d'état* and the Indies Company were suppressed and the rest suffered only a reduction of their fees to 12,000 livres. Their fees and bureau

---

[1] *Deuxième compte rendu par les commissaires*, 20 December 1794 (B.N., Lf^{158} 20), p. 20; A.N., F^{30} 106; Dufresne, *Rapport*, B.N., Le^{43} 1333.

[2] Beaumetz, *Projet sur l'organisation du trésor public* (21 July 1790); *Arch. Parl.*, vol. XVII, p. 240; and *Arch. Parl.*, vol. XXI, pp. 371 and 387.

[3] Some of the pamphlets are in B.N., Lf^{80} 85, Lf^{80} 83, Lf^{80} 86 and Lb^{39} 5931.

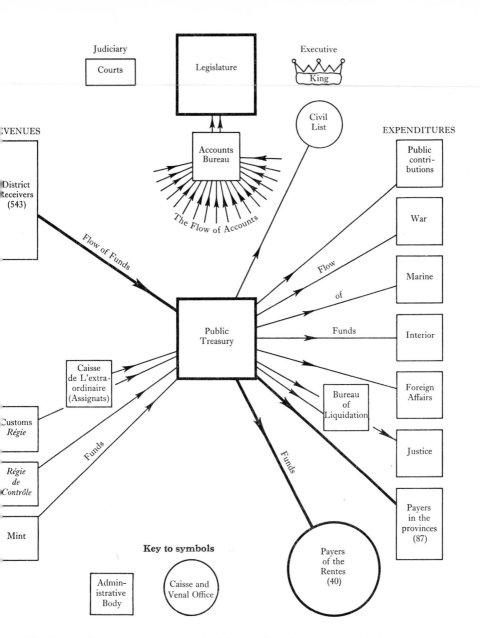

Judiciary

Courts

Legislature

Executive

King

REVENUES

EXPENDITURES

Civil List

Accounts Bureau

Public contributions

District Receivers (543)

War

The Flow of Accounts

Flow of Funds

Marine

Flow

of

Funds

Interior

Public Treasury

Caisse de L'extra-ordinaire (Assignats)

Bureau of Liquidation

Foreign Affairs

Customs Régie

Funds

Justice

Régie de Contrôle

Funds

Payers in the provinces (87)

Mint

Key to symbols

Payers of the Rentes (40)

Admin-istrative Body

Caisse and Venal Office

5. **The financial system in 1791 organized by the Constituent Assembly.** In this diagram, the Treasury stands out at last, by the end of 1791, in the centre of the financial system and in command of it. Acting on the orders of the legislature and executive, the Treasury received all public revenues and paid out all government expenditures. It did not receive the accounts, however, and was itself accountable, like all financial agencies, to the new bureau of accounts. Of the old corps of accountants, only the Payers of the Rentes remained; but in 1793–4, the Committee of Public Safety suppressed them and transferred their duties to the Treasury.

expenses, which had cost a total of 1,292,000 livres, now came to no more than 480,000 livres. Beyond these reforms it might well have been politically dangerous to interfere with the system of paying the rentes during these early years because so many revolutionaries were *rentiers*, and so complicated were the rentes of the ancien régime that no moderate or centre government would risk losing the experience of the old corps of Payers.

Pierre-Joseph Cambon, the financial man in the Committee of Public Safety, was the first statesman successfully to propose 'to republicanize the debt', as he put it. In a long report to the Convention of 15 August 1793, he described the cumbersome methods of payment and the variety of titles, so baffling that 'to recognize and classify them is a science', and put forward a copious reform project.[1] The purpose of the 229 articles approved on 24 August was to create *Le grand livre de la dette publique*, a set of registers on which every rente of more than 50 livres a year would be inscribed and to arrange for a unified system of payment in the Treasury. The process of converting the entire debt in this way was expected to be very long, but the Payers and Controllers were to stop their work altogether before the end of 1794. On 13 April 1794 the Convention heard assurances from Cambon that the Treasury was now capable of paying the rentes and adopted his proposal to abolish the Payers with effect from 20 April. Various political and administrative delays held up the final dissolution of the corps, however, and they were not legally extinguished until 23 April 1796.[2] But long before then the reform added enormously to the Treasury's staff and budget.

Until 1793 only a very small part of the business of paying the public debt fell to the Treasury. The organization of March 1788 committed one of the five divisions, under Savalette de Langes, to deal with pensions and the debt but it was mainly concerned with pensions. In 1790 the *Bureaux des rentes*, still under Gurber, passed from the disintegrating Finance Department to the Treasury but it had only a few clerks and a mere 16,400 livres budget. In 1791 (the Treasury Commissioners of 1796 wrote in retrospect) only four men and 18,000 livres were devoted to matters directly concerning the public debt.[3] The Treasury was therefore much affected by Cambon's act of 24 August 1793 (article 124) which provided 400,000 livres 'for expenses necessary to establish the Grand Livre of the debt and to draw up the first table of payments'. By the time the Payers of the rentes had turned their work over to the Treasury, the five bureaux of the public debt division employed 223 clerks, or more than one-fifth of the

---

[1] *Arch. Parl.*, vol. LXXII, pp. 196, 197, and 706.
[2] Decree of 4 Floréal, An IV in B.M., F26*.   [3] A.N., F30 106.

total.[1] The number was still the same and the proportion only slightly less in July 1796, after further additions to the Treasury and much reorganization. By then, the Grand Livre for the consolidated debt was practically finished and it ran to 316 volumes containing the names of 113,000 *rentiers*. A further 90 volumes had already been filled with the names of about 30,000 holders of life-annuities (*rentes viagères*) but these were only about one-third of what the Treasury anticipated for that category of *rentier*. This work and the payment of the rentes twice a year cost 716,240 livres in 1796, but the Treasury Commissioners planned to reduce this when the Grand Livre had been finished and, in any event, they reckoned that the old corps of Payers and Controllers had cost more than one and one-half million annually in their last years.[2] By July 1796 the Treasury had been managing the national debt for many months and the last of the old corps of venal accountants, the Payers of the rentes, were winding up their affairs.

The dissolution of the venal accounting corps during the early years of the French revolution seems in certain respects to be a development of the suppressions Terray and Necker carried out years earlier. Ignoring the republican-democratic era for a moment, we may discern a continuity in the *liquidation* processes of the twenty years from 1772 to 1792. The Constituent and Legislative Assemblies which governed during the monarchical phase of the revolution, managed the suppression of offices in an impersonal and business-like way, with a respect for property and procedures inherited from the past. They appointed committees of Farmers General and *Régisseurs* to wind up the business of their companies and instructed accountants to draw up their accounts and then to apply for reimbursement of the purchase-price of office. There was not much difference between the elimination of a Payer of the rentes in 1772, a Treasurer of the *Vennerie, Fauconnerie et Toiles de Chasse* in 1778, a Receiver General of the Partie Casuelle in 1787, a Keeper of the Royal Treasury in 1788 and a Receiver General of Finance in 1791. The process was long and slow in every case partly because the governments of the entire period were willing to make equitable settlements in the interests of the accountants as well as of the state. During the winter of 1790–1 we find Dufresne, the Treasury Director, and the Finance Committee of the National Assembly going to considerable lengths to assist accountants in winding up their affairs, and even debating whether the clerks of Receivers General could be said to have been employed 'in the service of the nation'.[3] Only flagrant dishonesty, such as

---

[1] A.N., C 356. [2] A.N., F[30] 106.
[3] A.N., AB xix 327, 10th, 24th and 30th Conferences.

the twenty-seven receivers of the Royal Lottery were guilty of, aroused Dufresne to work indignantly for a prosecution in criminal courts.[1] As for the judging of final accounts, in 1791 this duty passed from the defunct Chamber of Accounts to a temporary Bureau de Comptabilité but there was little or no change in what was expected of accountants. The recovery of money due to the government was the duty of Basly, *Contrôleur général des restes*, and then of his assistant and successor, Turpin, right up to 10 August 1792. True, Turpin had in the meantime lost the venal offices of *Contrôleur des restes* and *Contrôleur des bons d'état* and had joined the staff of the Treasury as its Agent, but the continuity of his work is visible in his reports which show him still working to recover money from various accountants, for instance, the estate of Thiroux de Montsange, a Receiver General who died in 1786, while also trying to make the living Receivers General redeem their rescriptions outstanding at the time their offices were abolished in the revolution.[2] Confiscating the house of Joubert, the Treasurer for the Estates of Languedoc, during the early revolution was no different from confiscating the house of Mégret de Sérilly, the War Treasurer, during the late ancien régime. If the volume of suppressions was greater in 1790 than in 1780, the process had not changed very much from the *liquidation* that was as old as the venal system itself. All this was in sharp contrast to what followed the republican-democratic revolution of 10 August 1792.

The republican years of virtue and terror transformed the business of winding up accountants' affairs into a crusade and then a purge. Among the causes of this change were a popular hatred of financiers, a fear of counter-revolution and a need for money to wage the war that had broken out in April 1792; but a full explanation would undoubtedly lead us deep into political and social history beyond the scope of this volume. On 12 February 1792 the legislature asked the Bureau of Accounting to give its views 'on accelerating and improving the submission of accounts in order to find in the recovery of the arrears the resources which the State has the right to expect from them', and it reported on 3 July urging the Assembly to press the accountants.[3] The first practical step was a decree of the legislature voted on 19 July 1792 to hurry the work of prosecuting accountants and verifying their debts to the nation. Within twenty-four hours of receiving the decree, the District Directories were each to name a commissioner and an attorney who should immediately visit the homes of Receivers General,

[1] B.N., MS fr. 11696. Dufresne to Bailly, 21 Sept. 1790 and 30 Dec. 1790.
[2] From 15 August 1790, Turpin was the Treasury's agent, and he and his clerks drew salaries totalling 14,300 livres until 1 July 1791 and then 16,400 livres (A.N., F[30] 199).
[3] Delafont-Braman, *Rapport fait à l'assemblée* (B.N., Le[33], 3 G (10)); Nicolas-Thérèse Carant, *Rapport sur les comptabilités* (B.N., L[33], 3 G (7)).

Receveurs particuliers and their employees to seize their records. Another decree, proposed on 11 August and approved on 17 October 1792, ordered the work of prosecution transferred from the *Agence* of the Treasury to the Directories of the territorial departments, and Turpin duly turned over all his files on accountants to the *procureur général syndic* of the Paris department. Legal actions of the Treasury Commissioners against accountants (*contraintes*) were likewise transferred and accountants soon found themselves being prosecuted by 'national agents', such as François-Mathieu Alein, section de la Montagne. There was no intention of reducing or undermining the Treasury, and indeed decrees on 17 and 19 September added heavily to its duties, staff and budget for the management of military spending. But it was plain that the governments of the republic thought the usual business and legal methods of the Treasury and other agencies were slow and ineffectual. Turpin showed in his reports how difficult he found the recovery of money from most of the receivers and treasurers, and he singled out only a handful of them for praise, including Le Normand and nearly all the former *premiers commis* who had acquired accounting offices: De Vaines, Dufresne, Anson, Gojard, and Hamelin.[1]

The republican authorities resorted to peremptory orders, confiscations, arrests and executions in what they believed to be the national interest. As early as 11 August 1792 they ordered Bertin, the former Receiver of the *revenus casuels*, to pay 400,000 livres to the Treasury. On 10 December Isaac Melin, former Treasurer for the noble orders of Saint Michael and the Holy Spirit, received an order to pay the Treasury 272,247 livres within three days. A few days later the Assembly heard a report that 'the majority of Receivers have not yet observed the law. Several have become bankrupt, others are trying to avoid making good the deficiencies in their accounts on one pretext or another. All are still holding funds which it is most important to have brought into the public treasury'.[2] The Receivers General were immediately ordered to turn over to the Treasury all remaining funds in their caisses, but that was only a beginning. The bankrupt were Mel de Saint Céran (June 1790); Guillot de Montgrand (September 1790); Richard de la Brèteche (sometime before 1792); and Marquet des Grèves (May 1789). Against the plea of the Receivers General that they had been unable to collect from the· *Receveurs particuliers*, the government ruled that twenty-five of them must redeem a total of 555 rescriptions issued in 1788 and 1789 to the value of over 11½ million livres. Including this and

[1] Report of 19 Oct. 1792, A.N., F³⁰ 199.
[2] Pierre-Mathurin Gillet, *Convention Nationale, Rapport* (21 Dec. 1792) (B.N., Le³⁸ 2610), p. 2.

other debts, forty Receivers General owed the Crown more than 16½ millions, according to the accounts examined up to that time, and there were many more accounts not yet examined and many not even submitted.[1] For the accountants who did not emigrate, the years 1793 and 1794 were a nightmare of arrests, interrogations, confiscations, imprisonments and executions. Gaudin tells how he personally intervened to save them from being executed as a group on 8 May 1794 along with the Farmers General.[2] As it was, in that spring, Mégret de Sérilly, Treasurer for War, Jean-Joseph Laborde, Court Banker, Magon de la Balue and many others perished under the guillotine. After this violent interlude the prosecutions continued in a slower but more business-like way much as before. On 22 July 1795 the Convention gave Fontaine de Biré (Treasurer for War) another year in which to submit his accounts; on 25 August, Savalette de Langes (Keeper of the Royal Treasury) and Drouet de Santerre (Treasurer of the House of Artois) received orders to turn in their accounts within nine months; and so the *liquidation* went on through the Directory period.

If the methods of the republic differed in some respects from those of the monarchy, the two régimes were tending towards the same bureaucratic end in financial administration. This bureaucratic tendency was one of the main features of the revolution in public finance, a far more momentous and revolutionary event than the violence of the early republic, because more enduring. Every régime vied half-consciously with its predecessors to create more efficient organizations for executive purposes. It was to such agencies that the corps of accountants gave up their power and functions, and it was such agencies which saw that they did so. As I have tried to show, the Treasury was the greatest of these, at the very centre of the new financial bureaucracy, and for this very reason the Constituent Assembly tried to shield it from the corruption of the past by creating two separate financial services to wind up the business of the ancien régime: the *Direction générale de la liquidation* and the *Caisse de l'extraordinaire*. The Assembly intended these to be temporary organizations for settling all the affairs of the past or the *finances extraordinaires*, as they called them in a new use of that much-abused term, and to keep them separate from the *ordinaire* or regular financing of the present and future which was the proper business of the Treasury. There was also a political reason for this division in that the *Constituante* hoped to demonstrate to the nation the value of its work by contrasting the orderly, economical public administration of its own making with the confused, wasteful and corrupt legacies of the ancien régime.

The National Convention took a different view, for a number of reasons.

[1] A.N., F30 199.   [2] Gaudin, *Mémoires, etc.,* vol. I, p. 17.

Founded in a revolution against the Constitution of 1791, the Convention never felt obliged to respect the arrangements of the Legislative and the Constituent Assemblies; and also, growing efforts to defend the republic against invasion and counter-revolution quite overshadowed the former concern to distinguish between the liquidation of the past and the financing of the present. More important, that distinction became impossible because the Treasury was obliged to use more and more *assignats* for day-to-day spending. The Finance Committee of the Convention saw no reason for keeping the *Caisse de l'extraordinaire* separate from the Treasury and they hoped for an economy in abolishing it. Furthermore, as the Committee reported on 31 December 1792,

We must return to the principle that the multiplication of caisses is a real obstacle to the establishment of that uniformity which is the principal basis of a good administration. The execution [of financial policy] will never be certain and the inspection of it will never be easy until there exists only one and the same caisse for the consolidation of all the revenues of the Republic and for the payment of all its expenditures.[1]

Outside the Convention, support was not lacking. Consequently, by a decree of 4 January 1793 parts of the *Caisse de l'extraordinaire* were transferred to the Domains Administration and to the Director General of the Assignat Fabrication, and the caisse with its auxiliary bureaux, some thirty men with salaries totalling 64,800 livres, went to the Treasury. This soon entailed an expansion of the secretaries and domestic staff and the Treasury also took over buildings of the *Caisse de l'extraordinaire*.[2]

As well as the funds allotted for winding up the affairs of the ancien régime, the Treasury also came to manage certain parts of the *liquidation* business. There had always been liquidation services, such as the bureau set up by an edict of 1764 to assist in winding up the affairs of the suppressed Jesuit order. Before the separate *Bureau de la liquidation* was formed in 1790, a small bureau with the same name was transferred from the declining Finance Department to the Treasury. Then another bureau was established in the Treasury for the liquidation of venal offices abolished before 1789, and it collaborated with the Agent of the Treasury appointed to do the work of the suppressed *Contrôleur général des restes* of the Chambers of Accounts.[3]

---

[1] Cambon, *Rapport, Arch. Parl.*, vol. LVI (31 Dec. 1792), p. 80.

[2] *Arch. Parl.*, vol. LVI, pp. 191–6; B.M., 924a 90; A.N., F³⁰ 106, ch. 2. Antoine Burté, a former official urged the formation of 'une caisse unique, chargée de l'universalité des recettes et de l'universalité des paiemens' (*Pour la convention nationale*... (Paris, 1792), B.N., Lf¹⁹¹ 3).

[3] Guyton Morveau, *Rapport sur l'établissement d'un bureau*... (Paris, 26 Nov. 1791) (Le³³ 3z).

For a time the Treasury had a bureau for winding up the Indies Company, and two commissioners appointed by a proclamation of 17 December 1790 to deal with the liquidation of the rentes secured on the clergy and on religious orders. When a decree of 8 March 1791 awarded an unemployment allowance of 50 livres a month to all government employees who lost their places as a result of reform, including those of the General Farm and other such bodies, it was the Treasury which paid it.[1] Even after the independent *Bureau de la liquidation* had been established, the Treasury's control over funds implied an obligation to continue doing liquidation work of one sort or another.

A dramatic example of the way in which the Treasury absorbed other caisses, even those founded in the revolution, may be seen in the brief story of the Civil List. Before the revolution the royal households, including the apanages of the princes, had spent sums only less than those allotted to the military departments, and the Treasurer General of the Royal Households, Randon de la Tour, had been attached to the Treasury in March 1788 as one of the five administrators. The following year the Constituent Assembly began to plan the constitution which was to confine the King and the royal family to the role of executive in a government of divided powers. Various committees of the Assembly concerted to draft a decree establishing a *Liste civile* based in name and inspiration upon the British Civil List but, unlike it, intended to provide only for the expenses of the royal family. At the Assembly's invitation Louis XVI wrote on 2 June 1790 to request a fixed annual sum of twenty-five million livres and separate provision for the maintenance of his parks, domains, forests and 'maisons de plaisance'. He also asked the Assembly to pay the arrears of the Civil List and to reimburse the holders of suppressed offices. The Assembly adopted all these proposals by acclamation in a decree of 26 May 1791. Meanwhile the office of the treasury administration for the Maison du Roi, that of Randon de la Tour, had been suppressed with effect from 1 July 1790.[2]

The sum decreed was to be paid in twelve monthly instalments to 'the person whom the King shall choose for this purpose', who turned out to be Jean-Baptiste Tourtault de Septeuil, a former Receiver General of Finance and a *valet de la chambre du Roi*.[3] His fortune obviously bound up with that of the monarchy, so fatally compromised after the infamous flight of the royal family to Varennes on 21 June 1791, the new Treasurer of the Civil List survived only a few months. The revolutionary decree which Vergniaud put forward on 10 August 1792 proposed a National Convention in its

---

[1] A.N., F⁴ 1040, notes on the case of Chabanetti.
[2] By decree of 12 Nov. 1790.   [3] *L'Ancien Moniteur*, vol. 8, p. 499.

first article, suspended the King's executive functions in the second, and in the sixth and seventh articles suspended the Civil List and ordered the records of its Treasurer to be audited and scrutinized by the National Assembly.[1] Tourtault de Septeuil fled that very same day; seals had already been put on his papers as a result of a decree on 17 July 1792. A commission of the Assembly studied the Treasurer's papers and reported that Louis XVI had abused the Civil List by spending money for counter-revolutionary purposes. All payment to employees of the 'ci-devant Roi' on the Civil List stopped on 31 December 1792 and all property on the List was confiscated.[2] As in nearly all such cases, the people named in the List were promised reimbursement for their losses. A director for the *liquidation* of the List, Hocquart, was appointed. His bureaux did not long escape the tendency of those years to consolidate, for Hocquart was denounced to the Committee of General Security and executed on 13 Thermidor, Year III; and on 19 Thermidor, the liquidation of the Civil List became part of the public debt already lodged in the Treasury.[3]

The Treasury was the principal heir of the accountants and of the financial agencies destroyed in the French revolution, and it expanded as their duties devolved upon it. Certain large divisions of the revolutionary Treasury cannot, however, be explained in this way, for they grew up as a result of revolutionary efforts to develop a system of accounting control. Necker had published the principle that the Treasury ought to be at the centre of the financial system and had done a good deal to equip it to account for all government revenues and expenditures through frequent reports and receipts from all the Receivers and Payers. The system was bound to fail so long as it suffered from the resistance and antagonism of accountants and tax farmers, Secretaries of State and Chambers of Accounts. But the District Receivers who began their work in January 1791 and the Departmental Payers appointed the following September were strictly subordinate to the Treasury; the tax farms had been dissolved in the meantime; the ministers of the new executive departments of government could no longer spend anything but what the legislature voted and the Treasury paid; and the Paris Chamber of Accounts met for the last time on 19 September 1791.[4] With all these obstacles removed, the Treasury was legally

---

[1] *Moniteur*, vol. XIII, p. 380.
[2] The Commission reported on 16 September 1792; the suspension decree came on 27 November 1792 (*Moniteur*, vol. XIV, pp. 17 and 583).
[3] *Moniteur*, vol. XXV, p. 431.
[4] Its suppression, voted in principle on 2 Sept. 1790, was pronounced by decree of 4 July 1791, published on 25 August, and decreed again on 17 Sept. 1791 (Boislisle, *Chambre des comptes* (1873), p. cxxx).

the accounting centre of the system and faced only practical difficulties in exercising its great powers. The only other agency with power in the accounting process was a new Accounting Bureau. This bureau was formed to assist the legislature in performing the one major accounting operation which the Treasury was not qualified to do; that is, to sit as a sovereign authority and pronounce judgement on the final accounts of responsible public agencies. The Chambers of Accounts, sovereign courts, had done this in the ancien régime, but the Treasury was not a court or sovereign body of any kind, whatever else it was, and could not be empowered either to settle disputes over accounts or to approve its own records and those of other agencies in the name of the sovereign nation. Therefore, after some debate, the Constituent Assembly decided to keep this authority and function in the legislature, the highest court of the nation, and so founded a bureau of fifteen commissioners to receive and prepare all financial accounts for the legislature's examination and approval.[1] In accordance with the new constitutional arrangements, the King named the commissioners and he got the new bureau off to a bad start in the eyes of public-spirited observers by appointing a brother-in-law of the Justice Minister; a former War Treasurer and brother of a deputy to the Legislative Assembly; a brother-in-law of the Minister of Public Contributions; a relation of the Minister of the Interior; a former Treasurer of the *Vennerie du Roi* whose office had been abolished in 1778; a former director of the Breton tax commission, the *régie des devoirs*, recommended by the deputy to the Assembly, Le Chapelier; at least two men with wives influential at court; and other such men, few of whom knew anything about auditing accounts.[2] Such was only the ancient royal practice, but times had changed and two middle-ranking officials with much experience in public finance were quick to point out the shortcomings of such men and methods. They correctly predicted that it would prove to be necessary to set up an independent body of experts with authority to take legal action to speed up accounts or to prosecute as a result of unsatisfactory ones.[3] The publicity of accounts was necessary but not enough, they argued; and the same independent judicial authority ought to both audit and approve. The system did indeed turn out to be cumbersome because the commissioners were afraid of making mistakes the legislature might discover and because the legislature merely 'aired' accounts and was hardly equipped to pronounce judgement on them.

---

[1] Decree of 17 Sept. 1791.

[2] Antoine Burté, *Observations sur la nomination des commissaires de la comptabilité* (B.N., Lb⁴⁰ 2248).

[3] Burté, *Pour l'assemblée nat., observations rapides...* (B.N., Lf¹⁶⁰ 38); Gérard-Maurice Turpin, *Mémoire concernant la comptabilité...* (1790) (B.M., R 479).

In 1795 the legislature abandoned its authority to judge accounts to the Commissioners of Accounts and only then did the public accounts come to be officially approved in significant numbers. The *Cour des comptes* founded on 16 September 1807 added nothing essential to the accounting authority of the republic.[1]

To put the stamp of official approval on the final accounts of agencies responsible to the nation was an act of sovereignty, necessary and difficult, but still by no means as demanding as the tasks of the Treasury. At their most active and expensive stage, in 1795 and 1796, the Accounts Commissioners employed just over two hundred men and spent less than 800,000 livres, whereas in the same period the major accounting bureaux in the Treasury employed about 500 men and cost about 1,500,000 livres.[2] These figures for the Treasury are only for those bureaux which were formally and entirely engaged in accounting, and many of its other bureaux had accounts sections which, in July 1793, for example, employed a total of 56 men at a cost of 121,300 livres. This category of scattered accounting clerks was the oldest of three to be found in the Treasury by 1795. In the original organization of 1788 we find no central accounts bureau at all but at least thirty-six accounting clerks divided in at least five separate little bureaux as adjuncts to the main functional divisions. Bertrand Dufresne and Necker set up the first central accounting section in response to the clamour of the Constituent Assembly for frequent balance sheets or statements of the Treasury's financial position. Reliable balance sheets were one of the things which reformers and revolutionaries had in mind when working for a powerful central treasury and struggling against the private control of public funds. Adopting a system of double-entry book-keeping such as the naval accounts bureau of the Treasury was already using, the central accounting section began to work out the situation of the Treasury from day to day and 'as though it had to do with one and the same person'.[3]

Since 1791 (the Treasury Commissioners reported in 1796), it has so expanded that it presents in summary and in detail the incoming and outgoing funds not only of the Treasury, but of all the receiving and spending caisses of the Republic. This has increased the number of registers which it keeps up to date to 120 volumes incorporating fifteen or twenty thousand accounts or parts of accounts;

---

[1] Victor Marcé, *La Comptabilité* (Paris, 1893); see laws of 16 Feb., 22 Aug. and 9 Dec. 1795.

[2] These and figures following are from A.N., D x 2, 'Etat de l'organisation et des dépenses du ministère des finances'; Dufresne, Report of An VI (B.N., Le⁴³ 1333); F³⁰ 106; A.N., C 356; *Arch. Parl.*, vol. LXIX, p. 665; A.N., D x 3; *Etat des bureaux de la trésorerie nationale* (1791) (B.N., Lf¹⁵⁷ 11), p. 15; Theodore Vernier, *Rapport* (1791), p. 48.

[3] Vernier, *Rapport* (1791), p. 48.

and with the aid of these registers, there is no information which cannot be obtained. It is a machine unique in its conception and in its parts, considering the precision and exactitude of the results it obtains.[1]

Whatever its virtues, this bureau employed only 16 men in 1791, 31 in 1793 and 48 in 1796. To see why the Treasury employed hundreds of other accounting clerks in addition to these, we must turn to a third category, by far the largest of them, engaged in 1794 mainly to account for vast spending outside Paris during the revolutionary war.

The French declaration of war on 20 April 1792 entailed an urgent need for money in many parts of France and its colonies. Eighteenth-century warfare required a flexible system of financing which made accounting control extremely difficult and the War and Marine Departments had always been the most independent and wasteful spenders of public funds. Much of the effort to control expenditure during the fifteen years from Necker to Cambon was directed against military spending, and on 26 March 1792 the Legislative Assembly was unsympathetic to an urgent appeal on behalf of the War Ministry for greater independence of the Treasury. When the war began to go badly, however, military needs could hardly be sacrificed to the principle of central public control, whatever the cost, and the Treasury Commissioners took it on themselves to pay out more and more funds without even waiting for the decrees of the legislature. The War Department and other authorities were permitted to meet emergencies with funds in the caisses of the District Receivers and Departmental Payers. The Commissioners and the wartime Minister of Finance, Cambon, soon lost track of war expenditures and in 1793 Cambon said to a member of the Convention, 'You will be doing pretty well if you can pierce the shadows that surround the War Ministry. I have been trying to find my way around in them for more than a year and I still cannot see anything very clearly.'[2] The Treasury Commissioners complained to the Convention about the War Department, 'whose financial service has been surrounded by obstacles'.[3] Only with the victories of 1794 could the Convention and the Treasury take steps to clear up the confusion.

They faced a difficult problem which called for a special solution. The prospect of auditing accounts of expenditure from about 900 different sources, which had spent altogether something over sixty billion livres, made them reflect that in the best of conditions the ancien régime had needed at least ten years to clear away the accounts of a much smaller war.

---

[1] A.N., F[30] 106.
[2] *Ancien moniteur*, vol. 19, p. 153 (7 Jan. 1794).
[3] *Compte rendu* (1793) (B.N. Lf[158] 19), p. 11.

In addition, the accounts from the provinces and the colonies had been in arrears when the war began and by 1794 those for the Marine Department were eighteen years in arrears.[1] The District Receivers, inexperienced and hampered by the revolutionary tumult, had rendered few if any accounts since they had begun working on 1 January 1791. The Finance Committee of the Convention thought twenty years—until 1814!—might be needed to deal with all this work in the normal fashion, and to speed it up they hit upon a plan for compressing the three fiscal years of 1791, 1792 and 1793 into one fiscal period. This plan was devised to avoid the usual delays and complexities in distinguishing the business of each separate year. The Convention adopted the plan and declared the period from 1 January 1791 to 22 September 1794, the first day of the Year III, to be 'le premier exercice républicain'.[2] For that period, every receiver and payer and anyone who had paid out public funds was to send accounts and receipts to the Treasury, and by the end of 1794, the commissioners had taken on more than 300 additional clerks to cope with this work. By July 1796 this *section de la caisse des acquits* was employing no less than 428 clerks out of a total of 1,244, and their salaries used 1,275,400 livres out of a total Treasury budget of 3,656,500 livres.[3] This was about as large as the Treasury ever grew before the nineteenth century and, indeed, well before Napoleon's time it had shrunk to less than half that size, its emergency work done. In 1798 the Treasury was expected by the legislature to employ only 582 employees in Paris at a cost of 1,703,000 livres.

The reforms of the Directory period do not fall within the scope of this study because they came after the ancient financial system had already given way to a new one in which the Treasury was in command, the true centre of the national finances. In any case, the constitution of the Year III protected the Treasury against executive interference and the Directory had no control over it.[4] In 1796 the executive Minister of Finance himself urged the legislature to protect it with constant vigilance.[5] At no stage, even during the Terror, had any government dared to risk interfering with its vital functions, and the worst had been some minor purges of its employees, leaving it still, in the words of Jacques Godechot, 'a nest of counter-revolutionaries'.[6] But that is to use the language of the social revolution. In

[1] *Deuxième compte rendu* (20 Dec. 1794), p. 32.
[2] Decrees of 19 April 1794, 5 September 1794, and 16 February 1795.
[3] A.N., F³⁰ 106 describes all this work in great detail. B. Dufresne, *Rapport* (Le⁴³ 1333), for A.N., vi.
[4] Jacques Godechot, *Les Institutions de la France sous la révolution*, pp. 403, 431 and 432.
[5] Barbé-Marbois, *Rapport sur la situation de la trésorerie*, 8 Thermidor An 4 (A.N., AF III 130, dossier 611) the covering letter is dated 22 Thermidor.
[6] *Op. cit.*, p. 432.

the realm of public administration and public finance, there had been no event more revolutionary than the growth of the Treasury and of its control at the expense of the old private caisses and venal accountants. The Treasury proved to be a great organ of revolution. As an administrative machine it seldom failed to impress the legislators who examined it. Theodore Vernier reported to the Constituent Assembly on behalf of a committee:

Your commissioners will not deny that they were astonished at the extent of that vast administration; but in examining and analysing details, their astonishment declined by degrees. What had seemed complicated to them became simple; what they had at first judged to be superfluous ceased to appear so.[1]

That was written before the reforms of 1791, just as Bertrand Dufresne was preparing to turn the Treasury over to the six newly appointed commissioners. It was already a very different organization from the one Dufresne had directed in Necker's first ministry ten years earlier. And although it was to grow larger and more powerful, it was already basically the same as he was to find it in December 1799 when he took command of it for the third time. The revolution in financial administration occurred before the period of the Directory, and although Napoleon built little or nothing on these foundations the governments of the restoration period carried on the work of the revolution.[2]

---

[1] Vernier, *Rapport du comité des finances...sur l'organisation de la trésorerie nationale* (23 June 1791), p. 11 (B.M., F.R. 502). The Committee included Antoine de la Métherie, Philippe-Antoine Merlin, and Théodore Vernier.

[2] Audiffret, *Système financier de la France*, 2ᵉ ed. (Paris, 1854), 5 vols.

14

NATIONALIZING THE DEBT

THE MOST urgent piece of public business in the early years of the French revolution was the debt. The short-term and other irregular and unfunded debts were particularly pressing because the government needed more and more credit in the economic crisis of 1787–90 and then during the war that began in April 1792. During its term of office, the National Constituent Assembly broke with the practices of the royal government by assuming responsibility for all government debts, by taking steps to pay them systematically and, most of all, by doing away with private enterprise in public borrowing. Here was a truly revolutionary change. With financiers and bankers ready to serve the revolutionary government in the old ways, the National Assembly deliberately rejected their proposals. The Assembly was taking an anti-capitalist stand in the national interest and with premeditation. Of course, the legislative decisions were the results of political struggles and debates in which the partisans of private enterprise, such as Dupont de Nemours, Laborde de Méréville, and a great many businessmen suffered defeat. 'We shall have destroyed forever', said Baron de Pinteville de Cernon, a noble deputy from Châlons-sur-Marne, 'the speculations and all other kinds of influence of the capitalists on the public fortune.'[1] Following the course set by the Constituent Assembly, the Legislative and the Convention maintained public management of government borrowing and all the business connected with it, to them one of the most sacred of French institutions. Thus for a time at least did the French revolution whip the financiers out of the temple of the national debt. By what steps did this remarkable revolution come about?

When Necker and Calonne brought the indebtedness of the Crown to the forefront of public attention by their writings and their quarrel, they demonstrated for all to see that even the ministers of finance did not know the full extent of the debt. Calonne's revelations to the Assembly of Notables in February 1787 did nothing to allay curiosity. Thereafter the clamour for public accounts grew louder in the sovereign courts, in pamphlets and journals, in general conversation and in the *cahiers de doléances* which every

[1] *Arch. Parl.*, vol. x, p. 285.

electoral district dispatched to the Estates General with its representatives. The Crown had always made a mystery of its financial processes. Hampered by their own ignorance, the deputies at first hardly knew what questions to ask. 'The fact is that nothing is less familiar to the Assembly than the maze of finance', Mirabeau wrote to his constituents in December 1789. 'The Assembly still has neither the principles, nor the knowledge of the facts nor the theories necessary to judge well what will best suit the nation in this important matter.'[1] But they were learning quickly. Very soon after the revolution of the Third Estate in June 1789 they had appointed a Finance Committee and its sixty-five members had chosen twelve of their number to meet the Minister of Finance, Necker, for regular discussions. This sub-committee (*Comité de Douze*) became a link between the executive bureaux of finance and the National Assembly. Many observers both inside the Assembly and outside it worked out independent opinions on financial questions, but the main sources of information about the debt were the Finance Committee and Necker, followed after his retirement in September 1790 by Bertrand Dufresne, the Treasury Director. Long before the Assembly disbanded in September 1791, it had formed a reasonably clear and detailed view of the debt.

From the beginning of its work the National Assembly was particularly curious to know the short-term irregular and unfunded debts rather than the rentes. The Assembly was no doubt devoted to the interests of the *rentiers*, but that part of the debt was fairly well defined, the annual total of the rentes not inaccurately estimated at 158 million livres in the *Compte rendu* of March 1788, and in a report of the Finance Committee in April 1790 at nearly 168 millions.[2] This annual payment, suspended by the infamous arrêt of 16 August 1788 which had led to Brienne's downfall, posed no problem to the revolutionaries except the practical difficulty of resuming payments. Referred to as the *dette constituée*, it was sacred even to the more radical and hard-pressed Convention which merely reorganized it and arranged for the National Treasury to pay it. Known and respected in the National Assembly, the rentes attracted much less attention than the more obscure and dubious *assignations*, rescriptions and other short-term advances, the pensions and investments in venal offices. These parts of the debt were only slowly brought to light and, once known, described collectively as the *dette criarde* or, more seriously, the *dette exigible*, and marked for urgent repayment. In the eyes of the Assembly, they were evil remains of

---

[1] Mirabeau, *Courrier de Provence*, no. LXXV, p. 17.
[2] Frédéric Braesch, *Finances et monnaies révolutionnaires* (Nancy), fascicule II, p. 142; *Arch. Parl.*, vol. XVIII, p. 353.

the ancien régime and major obstacles to the regular payment of the rentes. This distinction between the short-term, irregular debt, and the long-term or *dette constituée* was fundamental and important.

The rescriptions and *assignations* anticipating future revenue seemed to the Finance Committee to be 'the most expensive and disastrous of loans'.[1] From year to year the royal government had pushed this burden ahead of it like a gathering snowball until forced to suspend redemption of it, as in 1771 and again on 16 August 1788. On the latter occasion, *assignations* on the domains and forests were suspended to the sum of 50,800,000 livres. This afforded only temporary respite. When the Estates-General met on 5 May 1789, Necker told them that 172 millions had been spent in advance on the revenues of the remaining eight months of that year, and the revenues of 1790 were already mortgaged in the amount of 90 millions.[2] Ten months later, on 6 March 1790, Necker reckoned the outstanding *anticipations* on the revenue of 1790 at 141 millions and by the time the National Assembly had published this figure, two months later, the books of the Treasury showed another 40 millions spent in advance of revenues expected in 1791.[3] These figures showed how much revenue the government had consumed in advance, but differently presented as a proportion of total government spending the *anticipations* used in the twelve months ending on 30 April 1790 came to a total of more than 220 millions, or more than one-third of the Treasury's total receipts and expenditures. Even if we subtract 127 millions worth of old *anticipations* redeemed during that year, we still have some 93 millions or a proportion of one-fifth or one-sixth of the total budget.[4] These notoriously expensive advances had come from the Receivers General, the Farmers General and other accountants and farmers.

The National Assembly attacked the *anticipations* at the very root when it decided in principle, in August 1789, to abolish venal offices. If, as the Finance Committee said, the *anticipations* 'rendered the government vassal

---

[1] Read by Montesquiou, 12 March 1790, *Arch. Parl.*, vol. XXXII, p. 141.

[2] *Arch. Parl.*, vol. VIII, p. 12; A.N., AB XIX 327, 'Anticipations sur les revenues de l'état tirées sur 1789, 1790 et 1791' shows that these 262 million livres in *anticipations* had been furnished by the following agents and agencies:

Receivers General	119 millions
Farmers General (including notes) . . .	114 millions
Régisseurs généraux	16 millions
Fermes des postes	11 millions
Ferme de sceaux et de poissy	274,000
Domaines et bois	2 millions

[3] *Adresse de l'assemblée nationale aux Français sur l'émission des assignats* (30 April 1790); and also A.N., AB XIX 327, 'Anticipations sur les revenues de l'état au 1 May 1790'.

[4] Braesch, *Finances et monnaies*, fasc. II, p. 29.

(*tributaire*) of the capitalists',[1] then the decision to remove the capitalists from office was also a blow at the rescriptions and *assignations* they had signed. At the same time, that decision added the price of the venal offices to the debt. There was no question of refusing to repay them because to fail to repay would be to attack the accountants' property, as well as their position in the credit system, and the Assembly could not afford to alienate people unnecessarily by attacking their property without good reason. The Finance Committee reckoned, in a report of 18 November 1789, that these and other *dettes criardes* calling for urgent repayment amounted to over 707 millions as follows:[2]

Anticipations, including suspended *assignations* . . .	225,300,000
Surety bonds of Farmers General, *Régisseurs*, etc. . . .	201,799,400
Price of the offices of Receiver General and other accountants .	119,178,835
Arrears in payment of the rentes	81,000,000
Arrears in payments of the executive departments . . .	80,000,000
Total	707,278,235

That small list was only a beginning, as the Committee realized. The venal offices of the magistrature represented an investment of 450 millions, the offices of the royal households another 52 millions and the military offices over 35 millions. The abolition of 'feudalism' on the famous night of 4 August had entailed the repayment of more than 100 millions to the owners of the feudal tithe; and by confiscating the Church's property the Assembly had found itself with a clerical debt of nearly 150 millions secured on the property. In August 1790 all these and other pressing obligations formed a total *dette exigible* which the Finance Committee reckoned at a capital sum of nearly two billion livres. The annual interest on this sum they put at nearly 89 millions, or more than half the annual total of the rentes (167,737,819 livres).[3] But in 1790 the total regular receipts of the Treasury amounted to only 207 millions and in 1791 to no more than 249 millions.[4] These low figures could not, of course, have been known in advance, but even the most optimistic observer could have seen no way of even servicing the debt, not to mention retiring any of it, out of ordinary revenues.

Meanwhile, during the months in which the Assembly was thus coming to terms with these matters, the royal government which had contracted such confused and apparently endless obligations was continuing to incur more and more of them. On 7 and 27 August 1789 Necker prevailed on the

---

[1] *Arch. Parl.*, vol. x, p. 90 (18 Nov. 1789).
[2] *Ibid.* p. 91.
[3] *Arch. Parl.*, vol. xviii, p. 343 (27 Aug. 1790).
[4] Braesch, *Finances et monnaies*, fasc. I, p. 14 tables.

Assembly to give its blessing to two new loans totalling 80 million livres and these were duly opened to public subscription. The company of Paris notaries lent him 7 millions and the administrators of the Royal Lottery another 3,600,000 livres. On 14 November, however, he told the Assembly that he would need short-term advances of 90 millions to make all the payments due in 1789 and another 80 millions for the same purpose in 1790, making a deficit of 170 millions during the first eighteen months of the National Assembly's life.[1] Three months later the Minister was obliged to report a deficit of 41 millions for the first two months of 1790 alone, because of falling tax revenues, heavy government purchases of grain and other difficulties in that troubled year. He talked of a total deficit of 294 millions.[2] Well before then, on 14 November 1789, he had proposed to meet this crisis by making a national bank, somewhat like the Bank of England, out of an institution he had already turned to for advances of cash in the crisis of August 1788, the *Caisse d'escompte*.

This was a bankers' bank founded by royal charter on 24 March 1776 as a limited company (*société par actions en commandite*) with a capital of 15 millions in 5,000 shares of 3,000 livres each, later raised to 100 millions total. The shareholders met twice a year to examine the balance sheets, fix dividends and elect the board of directors. Forbidden by its charter to trade in goods or shipping, the *Caisse d'escompte* had as its main function to discount bills of exchange and other negotiable paper at the rate of 4%, to issue notes and in a small way to deal in gold and silver, activities intended by the founders to stimulate French trade but destined instead to serve financial speculation and government short-term loans. The *Caisse d'escompte* had already made a disguised loan to the Crown in 1787 when Calonne had succeeded in having 70 million livres from its capital fund deposited in the Royal Treasury. By an arrêt of 18 August 1788 Brienne had prepared to use the notes of the caisse by giving them forced circulation in law. They had been circulating freely for many years in ever-increasing amounts: 20·5 millions in 1781, 44·7 millions in 1783 and 99·2 millions in 1786.[3] On 4 September 1788, Necker prevailed on this caisse to lend the Crown 15 million livres, and on 16 October the same sum again. Similar loans in 1789 came to a total of 100 millions and in 1790 to no less than 300 millions.[4] In addition, a banker in Brest, Gaudelet, advanced the Marine Department nearly 8 millions in 1790 and over 6 millions in the first six months of 1791.

[1] *Arch. Parl.*, vol. X, p. 57.
[2] Speech of 6 March 1790, *Arch. Parl.*, vol. XXXII, p. 46.
[3] H. Luethy, *La Banque protestante*, vol. II, p. 718; R. Bigo, *La Caisse d'escompte*, *passim.*
[4] Braesch, *Finances et monnaies*, fasc. II, p. 43.

257

Thus bankers came to the aid of the Crown and added to the advances of the accountants and tax farmers. With such assistance Necker was able to tide the Crown over until the National Assembly should provide other funds.

Necker hinted at the necessity of a state bank as early as 27 August 1789, so stirring up a certain amount of controversy, but it was on 14 November 1789 that he first put before the National Assembly a plan for transforming the *Caisse d'escompte* into a national bank.[1] He candidly admitted this plan to be against his principles—an admission not lost on the Assembly—and recommended it only as an expedient solution for the problems of the moment. The government urgently needed 90 millions to meet obligations of 1789 and at least another 80 millions for those of 1790. But taxes were yielding less and less in the revolutionary crisis, the balance of payments with England was unfavourable, much-needed wealth was fleeing the country and gold and silver coin was becoming desperately scarce for the people as well as the Crown. The *Caisse d'escompte*, so useful since the crisis of August 1788, would soon stop advancing its notes unless the Crown could find a way of repaying its past loans now falling due.

Necker therefore proposed to grant it the privileges of a national bank for ten, twenty or thirty years and to reform it so that it could immediately issue another 240 millions in notes for the government's use. The notes would be guaranteed by the National Assembly and the King and bear an official stamp with the words, 'Garantie nationale'. To provide a material support the Crown would give the new bank rescriptions and *assignations* on future revenue to the amount of 170 millions and continue to hold the 70 million livres in capital funds which the *Caisse d'escompte* had deposited in 1787. The total capital fund would be raised from 100 to 150 millions by selling 12,500 new shares. The board of directors would be increased from thirteen to twenty-four members, and a commission of the legislature watch over its operations.

In its functions and arrangements, this projected bank was basically similar to previous banks created in moments of difficulty, except that it drew on bankers as well as accountants. For example, in November 1709 the Controller General, Nicolas Desmaretz, had formed a *régie* of twelve Receivers General who undertook to manage a caisse which would issue notes against deposits of tax revenues and other funds. Known as the *Caisse Legendre*, it attracted depositors and served the Crown with bank notes until it fell into discredit in April 1715.[2] Half a century later, after the Seven

---

[1] *Arch. Parl.*, vol. x, pp. 56–65.
[2] A. Seligmann, *La Première Tentative*, pp. 109 ff.

Years War, the Controller General, L'Averdy, established a first *caisse d'escompte* to discount rescriptions and *assignations*, so substituting its impersonal credit for that of the court bankers and individual accountants or *faiseurs de service*.[1] There was no question of replacing one group of lenders by another: the fifteen directors whom the King named to the caisse were drawn from among the major corps of accountants and included also the court banker, Jean-Joseph de Laborde. They were the same men who had been lending to the Crown before the new organization was formed —and who would do so again after it had been suppressed in April 1769. This first *Caisse d'escompte*, premature though it proved to be, was a highly significant attempt to organize the private financiers and accountants as a central discount bank or crown company. There were to be 60,000 capital shares of 1,000 livres each bearing 4% interest, and after the first ten years of business a sum of 1,500,000 livres was to be distributed among the shareholders by a lottery. The government subscribed for 20 millions and de Laborde for another 7 millions, but the shares of the new company did not sell at all well and whether for this or other reasons it lasted scarcely more than two years.

Both of these earlier projects were known to the public at the time Necker proposed his national bank on 14 November 1789, and there was nothing unexpected about his proposal. Plans for public banks had often appeared in pamphlets.[2] Six months earlier, on 5 May 1789, Mirabeau had detected signs in Necker's speech to the Estates General that the minister intended to promote the *Caisse d'escompte*, and Mirabeau was already denouncing to his constituents 'that joint stock company of which the fraudulent failure [i.e., forced circulation of its notes] is hated in Paris and feared in Europe'.[3] Many other voices were ready to spring to the attack or the defence of Necker's plans for the *Caisse d'escompte*, and in November and December 1789 this debate in the National Assembly attracted an attentive crowd of deputies and spectators.[4] Ultimately two decrees of 19 and 21 December 1789 set aside Necker's project and confined the *Caisse d'escompte* to the

---

[1] Established by arrêt of 1 Jan. 1767 and suppressed by another of 21 March 1769. (Luethy, *La Banque protestante*, p. 391; *Encyclopédie méthodique. Finances*, vol. I, p. 157.) The two *caissiers* were Bénigne Dollé and Bertrand Dufresne.

[2] For example, Custine prepared one, and Charles-Claude-Ange Monneron published one on 1 Aug. 1789 (Bouchary, *Les Manieurs d'argent*, vol. III, p. 183).

[3] The memorandum in which Nicolas Desmaretz described the *Caisse Legendre* was published in 1789 by someone who thought it appropriate to the moment (B.N., Lf[76] 97 D). Several influential people had been in Laborde's caisse: Bertrand Dufresne had been one of the *caissiers* and among the directors were Magon de la Balue and Savalette de Magnanville.

[4] *Courrier de Provence*, LXIX (18–21 November 1789) and LXXV (4–5 December).

more temporary and limited role of continuing to lend its notes to the government until 1 July 1790. Later decisions confirmed this defeat and in 1793 the Convention went so far as to suppress the *Caisse d'escompte*. What was at stake in this struggle and why did the Assembly reject the proposal for a national bank?

Many of the established families of financiers who held the accounting offices were opposed to Necker and to the *Caisse d'escompte* as representing banking interests. For many years, but especially since Necker's first ministry (1776–81), Swiss protestant bankers, and even others of Belgian or French Catholic origin, had been a growing threat to the corps of Catholic financiers accustomed to dominating the field of government credit. The families of cosmopolitan outsiders—Julien, Perregaux, Haller, Tourton, Vandemyver, Pache, Cottin, Rilliet and others—had connections in many countries and engaged freely in speculation and foreign trade.[1] Necker showed what a foreign, protestant banker could do by winning the highest financial post in France, by drawing upon Swiss resources to finance the Crown, and by disestablishing large numbers of accountants, who therefore cordially hated him. That hatred found expression in the earlier pamphlets of the revolutionary Mirabeau, such as his *Dénonciation de l'agiotage au Roi* (1787) which struck only at bankers, not at royal accountants. The rivalry of bankers and official financiers was by no means always a simple opposition of two clearly-drawn sides, for bankers like Simon-Emmanuel-Julien Le Normand and Jean-Louis Julien became Receivers General; and also Necker had enemies, such as Etienne Clavière and Isaac Panchaud, among the bankers. Yet as early as 1778, Necker made the *Caisse d'escompte* a bastion of banking interests and even though financiers infiltrated into its board of directors after his fall in 1781, the institution remained suspect to many people. When in November 1789 he proposed to make a national bank of it, the National Assembly had already committed itself to extinguishing the venal offices of the accountants and the posts of Farmers General. The bankers seemed to be on the verge of a great victory. Laborde de Méréville, Administrator (formerly Keeper) of the Royal Treasury and deputy for Etampes, stood up in the National Assembly and read a counter-proposal for a bank in which he and his kind would predominate, a bank not unlike the accountant's *Caisse d'escompte* his father had planned in 1767. For all this opposition, it would be going much too far to attribute the defeat of Necker's scheme to the hostile accountants. The old struggle of bankers and official financiers was already overshadowed in importance by

[1] H. Luethy had developed this interesting thesis in *La Banque protestante*, pp. 446 and 774, etc.

other antagonisms. In particular, the National Assembly and much public opinion outside it detested both financiers and bankers for their profit-seeking activities in government finance. The short-term and irregular *dette exigible* which the Assembly was so anxious to do away with was largely owing to financiers and bankers. We should therefore not be surprised to find that a majority in the Assembly also wanted to dispense with the services of financiers and bankers altogether in order to prevent them from lending the government any more money. In an effort to care for the interests of the *rentiers*, which they took to be the national interest itself, the Assembly regarded the investments of bankers and financiers as altogether reprehensible and, indeed, the very root of the Crown's financial difficulties. It regarded the *Caisse d'escompte* with great misgivings. This attitude no doubt reflected the presence of a great many *rentiers* in the Assembly in contrast to the small number of bankers and even fewer official financiers—no more than half a dozen.[1]

But there was another feature of the Assembly's composition which affected the issue even more: it was a national body and an overwhelming majority of the deputies came from the provinces. The Parisians in it might well have adopted Necker's plan in response to his personal prestige, still very great, and the knowledge and persuasiveness of speakers like Dupont de Nemours, Lecouteulx de Canteleu, Duclos-Dufresnoy, Antoine Lavoisier and the delegation from the *Caisse d'escompte* which addressed the Assembly on 20 November 1789. Few Paris deputies appear to have opposed the project; the *Caisse d'escompte* was, after all, a Parisian institution. Its notes had forced circulation only in Paris, but had the plan succeeded they would have been forced on the reluctant provincial cities also. 'One of the oratorical devices that is most successful', Mirabeau wrote to his constituents in Provence, 'is to show the interest of the provinces in opposition with that of Paris. . .'[2] Mirabeau did so, and his oratory went far to move the Assembly against the *Caisse d'escompte*.

Whatever special interests Mirabeau was able to rouse, or shared himself, the arguments he advanced in print and on the floor of the Assembly made a strong general appeal to the national feelings of the time.

Is it quite certain that a great nation can neither collect its revenues nor establish a wise economy in their use, nor keep its credit, nor pay its debts honourably, without putting all its means, its whole fortune, its entire resources, in the hands of a speculating company which affords it the means for consuming its revenues

[1] Armand Brette, *Les Constituants* (Paris, 1897), 310 pp.
[2] *Courrier de Provence*, LXVIII (18 and 19 November 1789), p. 10.

in advance and renders the same services that a prodigal son expects only of money-lenders?[1]

The shareholders, Paris capitalists, he continued, have been profiting by the national distress and are now seeking to extend their power over the whole country. The public have no need of share-holding administrators but only of wardens of the public interest. At the service of whoever pays them, banks should be confined to the sphere of private trade and industry and kept well away from government. The *Caisse d'escompte* used to serve the absolute monarchy and would be working for despotism now if despotism had triumphed. Is Necker under its sway (Mirabeau went on) that he has proposed, against his principles, to guarantee the credit of this bank so that it will deign to lend us its notes at interest? 'I have proved invincibly that the *Caisse d'escompte*, transformed into a national bank, can only lend us our own credit...Let us dare to feel that at last our nation can aspire, in the use of its credit, to do without useless intermediaries.' Necker's plan will only encourage the 'marches and countermarches of the army of speculators'.[2] With such arguments and with ten years' practice in observing and denouncing capitalists, as he called them, Mirabeau emerged as a prince of the national interest.

He was by no means alone. Among many writers and speakers, four other noblemen distinguished themselves on the floor of the Assembly and in the press by their cogency, knowledge and conviction in opposing the *Caisse d'escompte*: Comte de Custine (Metz), Baron de Pinteville de Cernon (Châlons-sur-Marne), Baron d'Allarde (Saint-Pierre-le-Moutier) and Marquis de Gouy d'Arsy (Saint Domingue). These four, Mirabeau and some deputies of the Third Estate such as Regnaud de Saint-Jean d'Angely, Lavenue (Bazas), and Bouchotte (Bar-sur-Seine) were the main opponents of Necker's project in the Assembly, and the most striking feature of their speeches is a general hatred of financiers and bankers for making profits in public finance.

I have never been able to understand (Custine wrote) the necessity in France... of having a court banker and several fiscal agents to make payments (*faire le service*) and to provide funds in the various departments whose manifold needs... could only be satisfied on very onerous terms, which rapidly raised the fortunes of the fiscal agents to the highest degree of opulence...bloodsuckers on the body politic and with fortunes made by the sweat and blood of the people.[3]

---

[1] *Courrier de Provence*, LXXV (4–5 December 1789), p. 20.
[2] *Arch. Parl.*, vol. IX, pp. 17–23; 705–11; vol. X, pp. 131–5; *Dénonciation de l'agiotage* (1787).
[3] *Arch. Parl.*, vol. X, p. 152 (20 Nov. 1789). C. N. Roland regarded the capitalists as the opponents of patriots (*Recueil d'idées patriotiques* (1789), p. 127).

A royal attorney from a financial court in Burgundy, Bouchotte, expressed a common thought:

People have cried out a great deal, and rightly, against all kinds of aristocrats, but I hope we shall soon attack the plutocracy (*plutonarchie*); it is the worst of all the aristocracies, with no sense of *noblesse* if I may use that term. No grandeur of soul will ever move those whose wealth alone brings them into the government.[1]

Cernon told the Assembly that they had a reliable 'thermomètre' for judging whatever plan they wished to adopt: if capitalists, financiers and speculators found the plan good this would be a sure sign that it was very bad indeed.[2] When the Assembly elected a special ten-man committee to study the proposals of Necker and Laborde, all the members believed that the Assembly would never consent to either. Little wonder that during a shareholders' meeting of the *Caisse d'escompte* Lecouteulx de Canteleu complained that the Assembly regarded anyone who defended the caisse as a banker, financier, shareholder or speculator.[3] Little wonder, too, that on 19 and 21 December 1789 the Assembly rejected the *Caisse d'escompte*, deliberately turning its back on the oft-cited example of the Bank of England and on all plans for a bank of shareholders.

Parliamentary speeches expressing all the violence and indignation of a Marat or an Hébert against financiers might well be dismissed as mere political rhetoric were it not for the practical steps which the National Assembly took to remove all private enterprise from the system of public credit. As it turned out, the Assembly put into effect a revolutionary theory of public credit clearly expressed as early as 1789 by the noble opponents of the *Caisse d'escompte*. The essential idea was that the government need not depend upon the credit of profit-making bankers and financiers but could perfectly well borrow on its own national credit. Hitherto the Crown had required a private or personal guarantee for a credit note of any kind, re-scriptions, *assignation*, etc., so that some individual could always be held responsible, and the purpose of converting the *Caisse d'escompte* into a national bank was to have the shareholders guarantee the bank notes. A truly national government, ran the argument, needs no such private guarantee for its notes. 'If the title of *Nationale* does not carry the guarantee of the nation,' Mirabeau said, 'what will it signify?'[4] The credit system of the nation needs no intermediary agents and indeed, said the Marquis de

---

[1] *Arch. Parl.*, vol. x, p. 277 note (27 Nov. 1789).
[2] *Ibid.* p. 287 (2 Nov. 1789).
[3] Mirabeau, *Courrier de Provence*, LXVIII (18 and 19 Nov. 1789), p. 31.
[4] *Arch. Parl.*, vol. IX, p. 21 (16 Sept. 1789).

Montesquiou, 'all the intermediary agents can only damage the simplicity of that great machine'.[1]

That idea of an intermediary credit (said Lebrun, the very conservative future duc de Plaisance in June 1790), so seductive at a time of distress and of illusion, can no longer stand against the principles and especially the enlightenment of a people for whom administration no longer has any secrets, nor credit any prestige. We need no longer tie the public fortune to all the risks of private fortunes.[2]

The profits of financiers and bankers on loans to the Crown seemed unnecessary and immoral. The system of surety bonds (*cautionnements*), too, seemed intolerable because like the sale of offices it was a form of government borrowing through officials, and the Assembly began to require that the bonds posted by treasurers and others handling government funds should be pledges of real estate instead of bonds. The classic Bourbon theory of public credit by private enterprise was pilloried again and again in the National Assembly, which slowly worked out the theory and practice of a truly national system in which it issued its own notes, the famous *assignats*.

This revolutionary theory stands out all the more clearly against the reactionary arguments expressed by men like Dupont de Nemours, Laborde de Méréville and Calonne. After attributing the entire revolution, no less, to the *Caisse d'escompte*, Dupont de Nemours recommended what he called 'the law of competition' (la loi de la concurrence) by which the government should choose as a public bank the company making the best offer. 'The union of their two credits [the government and the *Caisse d'escompte*] like any other union,' he continued, 'will be a means of force and felicity. It will resemble that of two trees which separated would be too weak to resist the wind but which can support themselves pressed one against the other, their branches and roots interwined.'[3] No government should try to issue its own notes and so to provide for its own short-term credit. Much the same views were held by the famous counter-revolutionary, Calonne, during his term of office as Controller General and in after years. While in England in 1796 he was asked for his opinion of a British financial scheme which entailed issuing paper notes, and whether the government should do this itself or leave it to a private company. Calonne replied:

[1] *Arch. Parl.*, vol. x, p. 62 note (18 Dec. 1789). Condorcet, too, was opposed to the Treasury dealing with any private bank (*Sur la Constitution du pouvoir chargé d'administrer le trésor national*, p. 14.)
[2] *Arch. Parl.*, vol. xvi, p. 175.
[3] *Arch. Parl.*, vol. x, p. 143 (20 Nov. 1789).

The [British] government would find no advantage in doing this operation itself. It would not be appropriate for the government to gain by any benefit the scheme produces, because that would be to profit on the discounting of its own notes. *It is natural that it should leave this profit to those who provide a convenience for the public while bearing all the expenses...*

On the other hand, if the government put into circulation any paper that might be described as paper money, it would thereby expose itself to the imputation of imitating the abominable régime of the French in their fabrication of *assignats* and *mandats*. The dignity of the government requires it to avoid even a suspicion of the least resemblance to that *manœuvre banqueroutière*.[1]

By 1796, it is true, the national paper *assignats* had long been depreciated and discredited, but this was because they had served to finance a war and to pay for the day-to-day business of government in a time of revolution. As early as October 1790 the Treasury had begun to receive *assignats* from a government agency instead of notes from the *Caisse d'escompte*: over 124 million in 1790, and in 1791 nearly 610 million.[2] Had the government been able to reserve them entirely for repaying the *dette exigible*, they would probably have depreciated far less, if at all. In any event, the *assignats* were originally conceived of as part of a revolutionary system for nationalizing the debt and so avoiding 'the snares of private interest', in Mirabeau's phrase. 'Let us fear capital, which has long had a habit of seeking opportunities for fortune in the needs of the State.'[3] Mirabeau, marked by one observer as the leader of the 'friends of the assignats', spoke a good deal on this subject and his splendid eloquence found echoes on all sides and support in the Paris *sections*.[4] 'So long as our credit exists only by the gold of the capitalists,' said a town mayor, deputy for Villers-Cotteret, 'we shall see no money.'[5] The towns as well as the capitalists incurred the censure of the Assembly which refused 'to borrow from the municipalities a credit which they cannot have without the Assembly'.[6] With such ideas in mind, the National Assembly worked out a system for repaying all the debts of the Crown to financiers, bankers and other holders of irregular and short-term investments in royal finance.

At the centre of the system was an agency established to issue paper *assignats* against deposits of funds from a new levy, the *contribution patriotique*, and from the sale of royal domains and church property. The greatest

---

[1] Public Record Office, London, P.C. 1/123, no. 79, Calonne, *Prospectus d'une entreprise utile à l'état et au public*. (Italics mine.)
[2] Braesch, *Finances et monnaies*, fasc. I, p. 14 tables.
[3] *Arch. Parl.*, vol. IX, p. 22 (16 Sept. 1789).
[4] Claude-Charles Coster, *Journal manuscrit*, vol. I (1790), entry of 17 Sept. 1790.
[5] Pierre-François Aubry du Bochet (16 March 1790), *Arch. Parl.*, vol. XXXII, p. 204.
[6] Jacques Defermon (17 March 1790), *Arch. Parl.*, vol. XXXII, p. 207.

of these resources by far was church property and the decision to confiscate it a momentous step. The story of how the Assembly came to do this has often been told. To recount it briefly, the famous resolution on the night of 4 August 1789 to abolish 'feudalism' struck at the tithe (art. 5) and so raised a larger question of church property; Buzot, Dupont de Nemours and other deputies soon proposed the expropriation of the whole of it. There was nothing very novel or original in the proposal, for certain publicists had argued in its favour even before the reign of Louis XVI, and little thought was required, after all, to draw an argument for general confiscation from the notorious example set by the Crown in expropriating Huguenot, Jansenist and Jesuit property. Practical arguments found their place, however, in a more abstract debate over the nature of private property on which two theories developed in the eighteenth century. One to be found in the writings of the Physiocrats and certain American writers held that property, existing in a state of nature and being one of the natural rights of the individual, was therefore beyond the legislative power of government to confiscate or otherwise control. The other maintained that property was inherent in the civil order rather than in nature and that governments therefore had a right to dispose of private property according to the requirements of the general welfare. Such eminent thinkers as Grotius, Pufendorf, Jurieu, Montesquieu, Voltaire, Mably and Rousseau had all espoused this theory in one way or another.[1] It did not necessarily lead to the confiscation of clerical property, for the Church's defenders in the National Assembly, such as Camus and Custine, argued that the Church was making the best possible social use of its wealth by providing for the poor, the needy and the sick. They feared that if sold it would only profit the capitalists, and would be lost to the poor.[2] All the same, during the Autumn of 1789 the principle of social utility served Barnave in his journal, Le Point du jour, Mirabeau in his Le Courrier de Provence, and the majority of deputies in the Assembly to justify nationalizing Church property for the purpose of paying off the irregular part of the national debt. Put to a vote in the Assembly on 2 November, this crucial step was supported by 568 deputies and opposed by only 336, with 40 absent or abstaining.[3]

Approved in law as early as 2 November 1789, the confiscation had still to be carried out and the value of the property somehow applied to the debt.

[1] Jean Signorel, Etude historique sur la législation révolutionnaire rélative aux biens des émigrés (Paris, 1915), p. 154; Charles Bournisien, 'La vente des biens nationaux', Rev. hist., vol. 99 (1908), p. 245.

[2] Custine, Arch. Parl., vol. XXXII, pp. 428–9.

[3] Jean Belin, La Logique d'une idée-force, l'idée d'utilité sociale et la révolution française (1789–92) (Paris, 1939), pp. 231 ff.; Mirabeau, Courrier de Provence, LX, p. 24.

Who would administer these vast holdings in town and country scattered across the kingdom and including, as we now think, some 6% or 10% of all the arable land? To what use would the nation put the property, and if it decided to sell, how would the sale be managed and by whom? The Assembly moved gradually and groped cautiously for answers to these questions, but its policies turned out to be decidedly anti-capitalist. Unlike the monarchy, which had never known any other way of doing business than through profit-seeking intermediaries, the Assembly kept all the major operations of this enormous enterprise firmly in the hands of public agencies. Wherever agencies were lacking, the Assembly created new ones.

Although evidently affected by decisions about the ultimate fate of the property, the immediate management of it was a different question and a separate task. Buildings and estates had to be cared for, the leases, repairs and other business carried on so that the property would not lose value. All this might have been left to the clergy, as some deputies proposed, or turned over to municipal governments. A quarter of a century earlier, the Crown had put the management of the confiscated Jesuit property in the care of Marchal de Sainscy, the venal *économe du clergé*, and his affairs had got into such disorder that he had gone bankrupt in 1787. The revolutionary assembly made no such mistake. Instead, the Assembly first entrusted it to the new departments and districts but then, finding the work not uniformly or carefully done, transferred it to the *Régie de l'enregistrement*, which was the old Domains Administration reorganized.[1] Under twelve administrators in Paris, it had a director of national property in each department with inspectors, *vérificateurs*, clerks and store-keepers and in the National Assembly the Minister of Public Contributions was responsible for it until 10 July 1793.

The Assembly decided in stages to sell the nationalized property of Church and Crown—the royal estates were very early taken over—as the pressure of the debt and a determination to put the state in order affected the legislators. On 18 November 1789 the Finance Committee proposed to sell property to the value of 400 million livres and the Assembly so decreed on 19 December. This was only a fraction of the whole; the Committee thought the remainder worth about two billion livres.[2] Already, however, the practical details of the sale called for legislative decision, and after a great deal of hesitation the Assembly accepted an offer from the Paris municipality to purchase twenty-seven monastic establishments estimated

---

[1] Decrees of 9–20 March and 19 Aug.–12 Sept. 1791. The *Régie de l'enregistrement* was created by art. 15 of the decree of 5–19 Dec. 1790, and organized by decree of 16, 18–27 May 1791. Commission de recherche, *Recueil des textes législatifs et administratifs concernant les biens nationaux* (Paris, 1926), 2 vols., introduction.

[2] *Arch. Parl.*, vol. XVIII, p. 354 (27 Aug. 1790).

to be worth 200 million livres, in order to re-sell them at a profit to the city of one-sixteenth or about twelve millions.[1] At the same time the Assembly resolved to sell another 200 millions worth of property to any other municipalities making offers. A new legislative committee of twelve, the *Comité de l'aliénation* immediately took over the supervision of all this business on behalf of the Assembly, but the essential feature of the arrangement was the intermediary service of city governments. For a time it seemed as though the revolutionary government, like the monarchy of old, was intending to let the middlemen take over this part of its financial business. As we might expect in that nationalistic Assembly, there was strong opposition to this arrangement.

The Assembly rejected one part of the Paris proposal immediately and almost without hesitation. This was a plan for the city to contract a loan equal to one-third of the property's value and to pay the state with fifteen *obligations*, one each year for fifteen years, the government to divide these *obligations* into coupons in denominations small enough to circulate as money. The Assembly rejected these *effets municipaux* on the grounds that the central government needed no intermediary, municipal or otherwise, to make such a loan and to issue such paper notes.[2] Even the decision to sell to municipalities applied only to the first 400 million livres worth of property. When the main holdings of national property went on sale a few months later, the municipalities were no longer in an intermediary position.

Again and again the Assembly witnessed a struggle between the old private and local interests on the one hand, and on the other hand the revolutionary defenders of the national interest. When in August 1790 the Finance Committee wanted guidance in drawing up plans to apply the remaining two billions worth of property to the debt, Mirabeau persuasively argued in favour of an operation which would admit of no other intermediary between the nation and its creditors than the same kind of paper already in circulation, the *assignats* guaranteed by national funds and by the nation. Business syndicates, large landowners, and local oligarchies should be rigorously excluded from every phase of selling property and retiring the debt.

Let us stop regarding capital funds [of land], he said, as if they formed the entire kingdom; and the capitalists who inhabit them as if they formed the bulk of the nation. In the liquidation of the national debt let us prefer the methods most appropriate to the advantage of the greatest number; for it is, after all, the great

[1] Decree of 17 March 1790. Bailly first made the offer on 7 March 1790.
[2] Charles Bournisien, 'La Vente des biens nationaux', *Rev. Hist.*, vol. 99 (1908), p. 253.

number [of citizens] who bear the debt, and it is from the common stock that the debt will be paid.[1]

Gouy d'Arsy, abbé Brousse and Chabroud rose to support Mirabeau in pleading for the method of public agencies, and for the national paper currency. During the next few months the *assignats* found defenders in Cernon, Roederer, Pétion de Villeneuve, La Rochefoucauld and Aiguillon.[2] Even an opponent of the *assignats*, de Toustain de Virey, shared the common attitude to the despised capitalists. Much of the debt was owed to them, of course, but another deputy, Hell, referring disparagingly to the Farmers General as capitalists, warned that much of the money in their hands was lent by honest little people. Many of the opponents of *assignats* were not so much in favour of private enterprise as opposed to a proliferation of paper. But on 29 September 1790 the Assembly decided by a vote of 508 to 423 to reimburse the entire *dette exigible* with *assignats* bearing no interest and issued to the value of 1,200 millions.[3]

A few days later, the Assembly named nine additional members to the *Comité de l'aliénation* it had founded on 22 March 1790, and this committee, now twenty-one strong, quickly became a many-headed executive body, dividing up the work between the members by assigning a geographical region to each.[4] By continually demanding information from authorities in the provinces and issuing instructions to them, each committee member administered the property sales of his region much like a minister of the Crown. The committee also acted by drawing up new legislation on the matter for the Assembly to decree and, if necessary, to enforce. If the administration of sales in the Côte-d'Or department by Camus is any indication, the committee energetically pursued two national policies: first, to get as much money as possible for the central government in order to restore public credit. 'You know, Messieurs,' Camus wrote to the Directoire, 'it is on this great operation that the restoration of public credit essentially depends.'[5] Secondly, they favoured the sale of property in small lots in order to give as many people as possible a stake in the revolution. Rural property, in particular, went on the market on terms intended to encourage small buyers: 12% of the sale price was due within two weeks

---

[1] Mirabeau, *Arch. Parl.*, vol. XVIII, pp. 359, and 361 (27 Aug. 1790). Mahy de Cormeré, an official of the old Finance Department, warned in 1790 against concentrating the sales of state property, 'in the narrow circle of a small number of capitalists' (*Recherches et considération sur l'impôt*, p. 30).

[2] S. E. Harris, *The Assignats*, p. 13.

[3] *Ibid.* p. 31.

[4] Commission de recherche, *Recueil des textes législatifs et administratifs concernant les biens nationaux* (Paris, 1926), vol. I, p. vii.

[5] R. Delaby, *Le Rôle du comité de l'aliénation* (Dijon, 1928), pp. 9, 16 and 45.

of purchase and the remaining 88% in twelve equal annual instalments with 5% due each year on outstanding capital. These terms showed a certain anti-capitalist endeavour to assist peasants in competing with business groups in the district auctions of land and houses.

The *Comité de l'aliénation* found its executive duties much too onerous and after its first year of work, on 30 September 1791, turned over the entire management of property sales to a government agency that had hitherto handled only the money from the sales and the credit operations based on them. This was the *Caisse de l'extraordinaire*, established in principle by a decree of 19 and 21 December 1789 and organized during the year following.[1] It was no less than a treasury for the revolutionary processes of abolishing venal offices, repaying all other parts of the unfunded debt, and otherwise winding up the business and institutions of the ancien régime, thereby carrying the burden of these enormous extraordinary finances during the critical years in which the Royal Treasury was being nationalized and developed as the centre of the new regular or ordinary finances. While the Public Treasury was coming to grips with the financing of the present and the future, the financing of the rejected past devolved upon the *Caisse de l'extraordinaire* until it was abolished on 4 January 1793. The funds for its huge expenditures came principally from the sale of royal and clerical property and from the paper *assignats* issued against the property's value. Thus it appears to have been a public agency doing the work of a bank and, indeed, it was the Assembly's ingenious substitute for the national bank which Necker, Laborde de Méréville, Dupont de Nemours and others had wanted to organize as a joint stock company.

The *Caisse de l'extraordinaire* had two parts, an administration and a caisse. The former part was organized by its first and only Director, Amelot de Chaillou, who had served as Intendant of Burgundy for the previous six years and now, the intendancies gone, accepted this appointment by a commission dated 25 April 1790.[2] His bureaux, which soon employed 165 directors, clerks and office-boys, did not actually handle the money but supervised the centralizing of the *contribution patriotique*, the funds still due from the accountants of the ancien régime, and the returns from property sales, including the *assignats* issued in expectation of sales. It also issued payment orders (*mandats* and *ordonnances*), kept general accounts for the business of the caisse, and compiled inventories of the nationalized pro-

[1] Decrees of 6 December 1790, ratified 15 Dec.; and 30 Dec. ratified 9 Jan. 1791.

[2] Antoine-Léon-Anne Amelot, marquis de Chaillou, 1760–1824. son of the Master of Requests with the same name who in 1776 became the Secretary of State for the Royal Households.

perty.[1] The money itself, whether paper or specie, was in the care of the other division of the *Caisse de l'extraordinaire*, the treasury or caisse proper. Here was the repository of the *assignats*, receiving the new ones from the printers and paying them out on orders from the administration, receiving the spent ones and burning them as the property they stood for was sold. Caring for such large sums of money was a task for an experienced banker and Le Couteulx de Canteleu, deputy for the third estate of Rouen, took this post of Treasurer General on 20 January 1790. When the Assembly expressed hostility to this cumulation of executive and legislative functions, Le Couteulx de Canteleu gave up the post to his elder brother, Jean-Jacques Le Couteulx du Molay who began work on 17 April.[2] Not until the following December did he have the bureaux of this division properly organized and then there were 72 employees in them. After some reorganization in the next six months to meet criticisms by Camus and others in the Assembly, the *Caisse de l'extraordinaire* proved to be ready to take full charge of selling national property and did so on 30 September 1791. Legislative supervision of this business went on until 1825, and in all the administrative changes of later years, the sale of national property remained a public service, never becoming a private enterprise as it certainly would have done under the ancien régime.

The same may be said of the separate though related business of examining all claims on the government, arranging for the *Caisse de l'extraordinaire* to pay them, and so winding up the debts of the ancien régime. The agency charged with these difficult duties, the *Direction général de la liquidation*, was hardly new in conception because the 'liquidation' of a suppressed office or agency, a procedure as old as the venal system itself, had always been done by the royal government. The work of the revolutionary assemblies differed only in that they undertook to wind up virtually the entire system of venal offices, judicial, military and financial, and also to pay various forms of compensation to certain people who suffered in the process of revolution and reform. As an example of the latter, we may mention one indemnity bill providing for 33,718 livres to compensate fifty-two government employees whose houses or other property had been damaged in popular disturbances from 12 July 1789 to May 1792.[3] Put on a legal footing late in 1790, the *Direction général de la liquidation* had a budget of 500,000 livres a year from 1 April 1791, a figure which had grown to 768,000

---

[1] A.N., D VII 1, Amelot, 'Mémoire sur l'organisation des bureaux de l'administration de la caisse de l'extraordinaire', MS; and Camus, *Rapport fait par Monsieur Camus au nom des commissaires de l'extraordinaire...* (1791), p. 3 (B.M., R 623).

[2] A.N., V¹ 539, two *Provisions d'Office* dated 20 Jan. 1790 and 7 March 1790.

[3] Jord-Panvilliers, *Rapport et projet de décret* (23 May 1792) (B.M., F 183).

livres two years later, when 313 clerks were employed.[1] Louis XVI, who wielded the executive power in the brief period of constitutional monarchy, chose one of Necker's men as Director, Dufresne de Saint Léon, who had served from 1777 as *liquidateur* and then as *premier commis* in the service of one of the Keepers of the Royal Treasury. He had continued to serve in the reorganized Treasury of 1788 until Necker had appointed him *Premier commis des dépêches*. It was on 23 December 1790, more than three months after Necker's resignation, that Dufresne de Saint Léon was appointed Director General of the Liquidation and, on the recommendation of the Finance Committee moved into that Committee's own quarters which became known as the *Hôtel de la liquidation*.[2]

On 23 November 1792 he was succeeded by Louis-Valentin Denormandie, formerly a National Accounting Commissioner, who held the post until well into the First Empire. Their reports show how bureaucratic was the business of winding up the ancien régime—which would itself have conducted such an operation through the judicial processes of sovereign courts or royal commissions and the services of venal accountants. With the National Assembly, a court of the sovereign people, ready to decide every issue and to judge every case by decree, an agency like the *Direction générale de la liquidation* had only to proceed by gathering information into a system of dossiers, putting the decrees into effect and applying for new decisions whenever necessary. The Assembly named two Liquidation Committees to follow the business of this agency and to act as liaison.[3]

Dufresne de Saint Léon, Denormandie and their bureaux played a part in disposing of confiscated real estate as well as confiscated offices, but by far the greatest part of their work consisted of verifying and approving claims on the government. They distinguished several kinds of payments among those they had to arrange for: first, the arrears of the executive departments, that is, the claims of departmental employees for salaries, of tradesmen for settlements of accounts, and of others for compensation. Practically all government salaries were in arrears by at least a year and the revolutionary settlement was that Intendants and their bureaux would be paid up to

---

[1] Cambon, *Rapport sur la dette publique* (15 Aug. 1793) (B.M., FR 562, no. 7), p. 130; also, *Etat des citoyens employés dans les bureaux de la direction générale de la liquidation* (25 May 1793), B.N., Lf^{157} 10.

[2] Delessart to Camus, 23 Dec. 1790; Dufresne de Saint Léon to Camus, 4 Feb. 1791 (D XI 2); A.N., AB XIX 327, decision of 29 Dec. 1790. In this office St Léon served for two years and then in Nov. 1792 was arrested and imprisoned on suspicion of counter-revolutionary work. He had been a member of the Feuillants and the Société de 1789. He was cleared of the charges in Feb. 1793 but not reinstated.

[3] Comité de la liquidation created 22 Jan. 1790; Comité de liquidation created 7 Nov. 1790 and composed of delegates from other committees.

1 July 1790 and most other services up to the end of 1790, some later. Secondly, there was the liquidation of judicial, military and financial offices, including some 8,000 municipal offices created in 1771, 14,000 notaries, 392 *Receveurs particuliers*, 50 Receivers General, 5 Treasury Administrators, perhaps 50 Treasurers General and eventually 30 Payers of the rentes. Lower in the scale came a miscellaneous body of offices such as wig-makers, the guild offices (*maîtrises et jurandes*) and the *agents et courtiers de change*. Thirdly, the financial companies had to be liquidated, mainly the General Farm of Taxes and the *Régie générale* legally suppressed on 27 March 1791 and the Domains Administration converted into the *Régie de l'enregistrement*, not only the 40 Farmers General and 40 *Régisseurs* and Administrators but also some 20,000 employees to be compensated for not finding work in the new civil service.[1] Fourthly, there were the debts of the clergy who, as an estate or corporation with excellent credit in the ancien régime, had borrowed heavily, in part for the purpose of lending to the Crown. Fifthly, the royal pensions were in arrears and although many were abolished as being quite unjustified, others were owing to employees, particularly to some 35,000 retired employees of the General Farm, *Régie générale* and Domains administration. Finally, the liquidation service had to settle all claims on the feudal domains of both Church and Crown, including the *économats* or royal management of vacant benefices. All these required immense sums of money and by the end of 1791 the Director General of Liquidation had already recognized claims totalling nearly one billion livres.

The ancien régime could never have paid such large sums, caught up as it was in a system of borrowing from its own accountants and other intermediaries, and few royal ministers had even contemplated the reform of this old credit system. In the French revolution the system's destruction was possible only by the use of the national *assignats*, and these were a necessary instrument in the administrative revolution. Any of the alternative methods put forward would have perpetuated the old private-enterprise system. This was why the *assignats*, at first intended to bear 5 % interest and to serve modestly as notes for the purchase of real estate (*billets d'achat*), became legal tender by a decree of 17 April 1790. As Montesquiou said, speaking for the Finance Committee, the question was not whether to issue paper notes instead of coin; 'notes already exist, and in great number'.[2] The question was to devise a system of government currency notes that would permit the destruction of the *anticipations*, notes of the *Caisse d'escompte*, of

---

[1] Dufresne de Saint Léon, *Mémoire sur la liquidation* (9 Dec. 1791), *Arch. Parl.*, vol. xxxv, p. 681 and B.M., FR 562; and Etienne Clavière, *Mémoire sur la liquidation de la ferme générale et de la régie générale* (Paris, 31 Dec. 1792) (B.N., LE 3⁸ 80).
[2] *Arch. Parl.*, vol. xxxii, p. 146 (12 March 1790).

the General Farm, of the *Régie générale* and other such private paper. Therefore, the decree of 17 April giving currency to the *assignats* (art. 3) also ordered bearers of notes from the *Caisse d'escompte* to change them before 15 June 1790 (art. 12) and announced that the Crown would not renew *anticipations* when they fell due but would repay the bearers with *assignats* instead (art. 15). While waiting for *assignats* to be printed, the *Caisse de l'extraordinaire* was empowered by this act to endorse notes of the *Caisse d'escompte*. The act also reduced the interest on *assignats* to 3%, even this disappeared on 8 October 1790, and from 18 November, *assignats* were legally simple bearer notes, 'au porteur' and no longer 'à ordre'.[1]

The notes of private financiers and banks circulated according to the confidence or the need of those who accepted them; the forces that caused them to circulate were greed of gain, gambling instincts, simple trust or convenience. *Assignats* appealed to few if any of these and the patriotism to which the National Assembly appealed did not sustain the *assignats* for more than a few months. When they were first issued, the King announced them in a proclamation of 19 April 1790 and invited his subjects 'to favour the credit and circulation of these *assignats* with all their might'.[2] The National Assembly also announced them in a special address on 30 April 1790 as a great means of deliverance from 'all the uncertainty and all the results of a credit continuously abandoned to the caprices of greed; the nation has no further need of anything but union, constancy, and firmness ...'[3] At this stage the *assignats* were intended as a means of retiring debt, but they soon came to serve the Treasury as short-term advances of funds instead of the old *anticipations*. The suppression of the *Caisse de l'extraordinaire*, the special 'treasury' for debt purposes, in January 1793 was in one aspect a frank adoption of *assignats* for regular, normal state payments as well as for debt. A decree of 8 April 1793 ordered all government purchases and payments to soldiers to be in *assignats*. Three days later, the Convention prohibited circulation, sale and purchase of gold and silver coin. All transactions were henceforth to be in *assignats*, now the principal legal currency. Small denominations had already been issued for many months. The issue of *assignats* increased with the needs of the Crown from the original issue of 400 millions decreed on 19 December 1789 and another 800 millions on 29 September 1790 to a ceiling of 1,200 millions imposed by a decree at the end of the Constituent Assembly's term and a new ceiling of 2,400 million livres on 24 October 1792 at the beginning of the Convention. By the time

[1] Camille Bloch, *Bulletin d'histoire économique de la révolution publié par la commission de recherche...* (Paris, 1911), p. 46.
[2] *Ibid.* p. 49.
[3] *Ibid.* pp. 49 and 52.

the printing machines were ceremonially broken on 30 Pluviose, Year IV, about 40 billions had been issued in *assignats*.[1] As this huge figure suggests (being about eight times as large as the original capital debt) the *assignats* had become worthless. As a result many holders of the long-term or funded French debt in Geneva and France had gone bankrupt. But this result had not been intended. The revolutionary government had originally devised *assignats* to rid the debt of the irregular, short-term investments held by bankers and financiers. One of the aims of this policy had been to protect the interests of the *rentiers* whom the government had viewed as more legitimate creditors. By using *assignats* in such large amounts, they had lost the baby with the bathwater but they had saved the republic.

[1] *Ibid.* p. 26.

15

TOWARDS PUBLIC
ADMINISTRATION

'NOT LONG AGO, under the monarchy, the bureaucratic armies did not exist', Balzac wrote in 1836, and he went on to explain that French bureaucracy began in the French revolution.[1] On this point, if not perhaps on all his points concerning the administration, evidence bears out the novelist's thoughts. The system of public finances under the ancien régime was certainly not bureaucratic, and to describe the system as a bureaucracy is to be guilty of an anachronism. Bureaucracy came only in the reign of Louis XVI, as an aspect of the revolution, and it developed as a new system for defending and promoting the general interest of the nation against the private interests which had nearly always dominated the finances of the monarchy. The employees and bureaux which have been too loosely described as a bureaucracy seem, on close inspection, to have been a combination of aristocracy and private business. Most of the bureaux of the old financial administration had worked for venal accountants, for magistrates or for tax farmers, and had been in their pay and served their purposes. The employees were, as Balzac writes, 'learning a science which was supposed to serve them in making a fortune'. People wishing to put their sons into 'les finances', that is, into the service of Receivers General, Treasurers General and other accountants or tax farmers, were invited in a handbook about Paris published in 1760, to send them for instruction to one of six 'maîtres d'écriture et d'arithmétique'.[2] This handbook writes of 'les finances' as of a private enterprise in which fortune, ability and 'protection' will bring success and wealth. Without a trace of irony or disapproval the book links aristocratic patronage and private enterprise as two obvious features of the royal financial services.

Only after Necker had begun to reorganize these services in the public interest, during his first ministry (1776–81), by reducing the power and the numbers of the venal accountants, magistrates and tax farmers, did complaints about bureaucracy become common and only then, too, was the

---

[1] Balzac, La Comédie humaine, Pléiade Edition, vol. VI, p. 872.
[2] Jèze, Etat ou tableau de la ville de Paris (1760), pp. 238–9.

word *bureaucratie* used in its present sense.[1] In the Finance Department itself Necker promoted the bureaux and the common clerks in them, making them directly dependent on the Minister. He thereby threatened the aristocratic character of the Department and inadvertently struck an early blow for revolutionary bureaucracy. One of his enemies then wrote:

We have only to look at the *Almanach Royal* to be convinced that [the *premiers commis*] d'Ailly, Melin, Hamelin and Couturier have the functions which their masters used to have; the [venal magistrates like] de Cotte, de Montaran, Dufour-de-Villeneuve, Valdec de Lessart, de Bonnaire des Forges, are at the level of the sieur Dufresne [a *premier commis*]. If we add to that the formation of the Comité contentieux and the duties given and taken away at will from Councillors of State, we see the very evident indecency of that communion of functions between persons of the highest dignity of the magistracy with persons who have been paid by private individuals. Can the education and talents of these intruders in the most honourable posts in the administration be compared with those of the magistrates who were Intendants of Finance?[2]

These aristocratic lines were written sometime before Necker fell in 1781, and hardly ten years later the class of venal office-holders had nearly disappeared altogether, leaving the bureaux alone to administer government policy. Reformed and rearranged, the old bureaux became part of the new national civil service.

The truth of this general statement is by no means obvious, even though there is much evidence for it in the foregoing chapters; and in particular, the old financial system needs a fresh scrutiny to bring out the reasons for denying it any claim to be described as a bureaucracy. First, by later standards there was nothing collective or unified about the bureau of the ancien régime for there were no uniform salary scales, no formal or abstract positions to be filled, and no idea of a functional organization to be charted in a diagram such as the revolutionary governments began to draw up. Bureaucratic organization—collective, unified, regular, mechanical— necessarily depends upon the systematic application of general laws and regulations. The aristocratic society of the ancien régime inevitably undermined all general laws and regulations because privileges, *grâces*, favours and marks of distinction consisted in personal exemptions and exceptions. We know this best, perhaps, in the field of taxation where any general law merely gave the Crown fresh opportunities for awarding exemptions. But in every other field, too, the personal, the idiosyncratic, or what in America today would be called the 'individualistic', always prevailed over the

---

[1] See above, p. 46.
[2] Coppons, *Examen de la théorie* (Paris, 1785), pp. 85 and 143. The general sense of these lines is clear enough, but for an explanation see above, pp. 55–6.

general law and the general interest. In the Department of Finance the bureau was merely a collection of individuals serving a master and he was more important than the bureau as a whole. The employees were bound by no general regulations but served their master and were utterly dependent upon him. He paid their salaries from a lump sum which he received for the purpose and which he could pay to whomever he wished to hire and in whatever amounts he chose. The case of Guimard, who once challenged the system, shows the dependence of the employees.[1] Throughout the kingdom the King himself set an example, after all, by ruling in a personal way with no obvious distinctions between his private life and his public duties; and so each royal official set himself up as an individual person rather than a member of a bureau. His own relationship with the King was the strongest of his ties as an official, even though it might be indirectly through a superior. So long as he remained a loyal and obedient subject, the individual could set his own career above public principle and above the general interest; the system was therefore one of stark individualism, by later standards a vast hierarchy of corruption, each official making his way in a struggle for social advancement.

Secondly, the status of the old royal officials was not bureaucratic except at the lowest levels. The characteristic higher official, having purchased his office, enjoyed a measure of independence unknown to his successors of the revolutionary period and claimed the honour due to a nobleman, as the above-quoted passage innocently reveals. Contrasting 'persons of the highest dignity of the magistracy with persons who have been paid by private individuals', the writer shows that the respectable higher official would not usually accept emoluments in the form of a salary because that would damage his dignity by making him dependent upon whoever paid it. For example, to protect his aristocratic status, an Indendant of Finance whom Necker allowed to keep certain duties even after suppressing the Intendancies of Finance in 1777 refused in advance any salary and hoped that Necker would not offer him one because it would be beneath his dignity to accept it from such a low-born person as Necker. 'If he wished to force me to accept some *grâce pécuniaire*, he would cause me the most real pain which would certainly hurt me more than the suppression of my office.'[2] Other Intendants of Finance and even well-born clerks refused to take the Minister's shilling if the Minister were a commoner like Necker. A salary being a mark of subordination might safely come only from a social

---

[1] See above, p. 72.
[2] A.N., 144 AP 145, Lefèvre d'Ormesson papers, d'Ormesson to d'Ailly, 10 July 1777. For other examples see above, pp. 56 and 60.

278

superior, as in the case of salaries which the King paid to his Secretaries of State and other officers. Otherwise, the dignity of a higher official would allow him to accept payment only in the form of fees, royal pensions or other favours, interest payments on the capital finance of a venal office (*gages*) or some other, because none of these were marks of dependence except on the King. To work with the King and for him was a coveted honour, but to work in an organized and integrated department, like the one Necker seemed to be planning, was to work for the Minister, not for the King.

One of the most characteristic features of the old administration was payments in the form of gifts, bonuses and gratuities. Following the example set by the King himself, who was always ready to reward faithful or special service with presents, all branches of the royal administration made such payments in money or in kind. To quote, for instance, the Administrative Committee of the *Régie générale* in December 1781, 'The salary of the Directors of the Aides has always consisted more in the eventual *gratifications*, resulting either from the duties on products or from the portion of fines allotted to them, than in the fixed emoluments attached to their places, and this arrangement, which gives them a personal interest in their takings, ought to be maintained...'[1] In this case, and in many others, *gratifications* were a normal and substantial part of a royal servant's income. The highest Treasurers General received, in 1781, gratuities larger than the highest clerical salaries: 24,000 livres for the War Treasurer, Mégret de Sérilly; 20,000 livres for the Marine Treasurer, Boutin; 15,000 livres for the Receiver General of the *Revenus casuels*, Bertin; 30,000 livres for the Treasurer of the Royal Households, Randon de la Tour; and 10,000 livres for the Treasurer of *dépenses diverses*, Rouillé de l'Etang.[2] Such payments to accountants were sometimes justified as incentives, but even clerks in the Finance Department, who neither collected nor spent any funds, drew salaries fixed by nothing but official approval of their personal requests. Administrative records show that clerks wrote obsequious letters begging for salary increases, pensions or offices and the ministerial or royal 'bon' at the bottom of the letter sufficed to grant the request. The King or Minister might be scrupulous and just in judging such letters but the method shows even salaries to have been a sort of royal gift or *grâce*. The salary was a personal arrangement and not a function of any policy or general law or regulation.

---

[1] A.N., G² 109, Régie générale; *Etat de frais de régie faits et arrêtés au comité de l'administration le 19 décembre 1781.*

[2] A.N., F⁴ 2680, Gratification des trésoriers généraux.

A slightly different form of gratuity were the *étrennes* of candles, wax, wine and tobacco distributed annually among the many high financial officials by the General Farm. Judges, Intendants and others in the provinces were accustomed to receiving such gifts from towns, guilds and private individuals. When clerks of the Royal Treasury endorsed bills or coupons for the royal service, thereby guaranteeing them with their personal credit, custom entitled them to a gratuity, and Dufresne told the Finance Committee in 1791 that twenty clerks who had each endorsed bills to the value of 30,000 livres would normally have been entitled to an official gratuity of 400 livres.[1] That service, at least, was beyond the normal call of clerical duty, though it was characteristic of the Crown to transform it into a profitable opportunity. A more flagrant example is the customary payment of thirty-two purses (*bourses*) each worth 400 livres, whenever the Royal Council approved one of the annual financial statements of the Royal Treasury: twelve purses to the Keepers and others connected with the Treasury and the Ministry of Finance, and the remaining twenty purses to the higher members of the Paris Chamber of Accounts.[2] The list of such payments would be difficult to compile and very long; suffice it to remark that honour, favour and social influence played so large a part in the royal administration, and notions of social utility so small a part, that few if any employees received their entire emoluments in the form of regular salaries fixed according to some evaluation of the work done.

Another unbureaucratic feature of the ancien régime, just as generally hated by the revolutionaries, was the practice of making appointments by patronage and personal influence. All posts, whether for sale or not, went to the relations, friends or clients of someone in a position to influence the appointment. This was so normally and frankly done that personnel records show it, as for instance on a printed form of 1777 for listing captains and other employees of the General Farm in the district of Lyon. This form is divided into columns headed, 'Leurs mœurs', 'Leurs capacités, s'ils savent écrire et verbaliser', 'Leurs nominations', and—curiously brazen to our eyes—'Leurs protecteurs'.[3] Employees in the Department of Finance, too, owed their appointments to the influence of people at court or to relations already in the royal service; for example, Anson, later so active in reforming the Department, made his career by the personal intervention of Lefèvre d'Ormesson whose father he had first served as a secretary. Anson

---

[1] A.N., AB XIX 327, 22e conférence, 8 March 1791.
[2] A.N., AB XIX 327, 32e conférence, 7 June 1791. Whenever the Chamber of Accounts approved a naval account, ten magistrates were entitled to purses. (First conf., 23 Sept. 1790.)
[3] A.N., G¹ 73.

had reached the rank of *premier commis* when Lefèvre d'Ormesson became Controller General in 1783, and we find the patron then writing to Louis XVI on Anson's behalf:

The Sieur Barbault de Glatigny, Receiver General of Finance for Grenoble, died yesterday without leaving a son or a nephew in a position to succeed him...The Queen who had at first desired this place for a Sieur Thibault, *Régisseur des étapes*, has deigned to put off her plans for the Sieur Thibault until another occasion. The Controller General has the honour to propose in consequence to Your Majesty to grant the Sieur Anson his *bon* for the charge of Receiver General of Finance.[1]

The letter bears the royal *bon* at the bottom. Not all clerks were sufficiently well patronized to reach the eminence of a Receiver Generalship. There were a number of clerical dynasties, such as that of a *premier commis*, Charles Hersemulle de la Roche, who explained on the departmental personnel list of 1793 that he had been appointed in 1788 by virtue of the services of his father, grandfather and great-grandfather going back to 1712.[2] When we turn from clerks to the men who patronized them, we find families sustained in official posts by relationships ramifying in many directions, and all making their way by mutual assistance, like ivy up a wall.

To describe this system as corrupt is to judge it by the harsh alien standards of the French revolution and after, for appointment by patronage was the normal, standard procedure of the Bourbon monarchy, indeed, of European monarchies generally. In the minds of the King's loyal subjects, employment in the service of the Crown was a reward and a mark of personal distinction. So traditional a writer as Réal de Curban in his ponderous book, *La Science du gouvernement* (1760–5), showed hardly a trace of the new notion of social utility, so common in the works of d'Holbach and other writers of the Enlightenment. His sections entitled 'De la distribution des emplois' and 'Des récompenses' revealed a belief that employment was part of a system of government by royal rewards and punishments; and he urged Kings to distribute benefices, pensions, posts (*charges*) and employment (*emplois*) in such a way as to create lasting feelings of gratitude and dependence in those rewarded. Réal de Curban saw no difference between hiring a man for a salary and giving him a title, a decoration or anything else in the royal gift. Offering advice to the penurious Bourbons on cheap methods for binding men to them with gratitude, he argued that the royal coffers would stretch further in salaries (*emplois*) than in pensions and went on to suggest that another 'just means which Princes have for doing good to men worthy of the state's gratitude is to use their good offices to have

[1] A.N., F⁴ 1946, Anson's personal dossier; letter dated 5 Oct. 1783.
[2] A.N., F⁴ 1015.

these deserving men marry rich girls, whose dowries would be infinitely useful rewards to these individuals without costing the state anything'.[1] Réal de Curban was describing the system he knew. The King himself set an example in the realm by finding places for favourites and by personally choosing ministers and councillors according to his own preferences and the advice of the Queen, the queen-mother, a mistress or some trusted friend. All these advisers themselves had advisers and all used their influence to place friends and relations, using royal appointments as stepping stones in the social climb, just as they used marriages, titles, military decorations, wealth and friendships. How could men lower in the social scale behave any differently? When Cochereau, a *premier commis* in the Finance Department, changed jobs 'to facilitate the establishment of his children', and struggled to place his son-in-law, he was merely trying to do much what all magistrates did and what Louis XVI himself had done in 1773 by establishing an *apanage* for his younger brother, the comte d'Artois.[2]

Social influence in the ancien régime, as in other countries at the time, was a kind of power which ruled openly over the royal administration and other institutions, unchecked by the restrictions which the revolutionary governments were to devise against it. Social influence did not end in the French revolution, of course; far from it. Yet the revolution propounded certain principles by which social influence in the administration stood condemned, and devised machinery which went some way in stopping it. The ancien régime on the contrary embraced social influence in principle. The theory of it was dignified with a bland explanation by one of the royal press censors, Robinet, in his *Dictionnaire universel des sciences morales, économiques, politiques et diplomatiques* under the title, 'Crédit', sub-title, 'Du crédit auprès des grands'.[3] Robinet defined this sort of credit as the use of other people's power to obtain a service or a place, not for oneself, which he defined differently as 'faveur', but for someone else. The various reasons why a man in high office would respond to the requests of one person on behalf of another did not include friendship, according to Robinet, because powerful people have little regard and less opportunity for friendship. Esteem he took to be the best reason, and argued that credit based on esteem might be regarded as a justice rendered to merit, though we should observe that the merit in such a case would necessarily be that of the supplicant rather than the supplicant's candidate for office. Fear, too, Robinet believed to be a common reason for men's credit with the high and mighty;

---

[1] Réal de Curban, *La Science du gouvernement*, vol. III, p. 202.
[2] A.N., F⁴ 1032², memorandum by Cochereau.
[3] Vol. XIV (1780), p. 451. This was Jean-Baptiste-René Robinet (1735–1820).

for all men, however well placed, needed the goodwill or the dependence of lesser men and would even answer the requests of domestic servants lest they do harm through their intimate connections with their great masters. Robinet, imbued with the practices of the aristocracy in which he lived, saw nothing wrong with social influence. Very few men did. The highest standards of social morality required members of the same family, even distant relations, to assist one another and to promote the family fortunes by placing as many members as possible in office.[1] The Crown was often served by families rather than by mere individuals—the Colberts, Turgots and Lefèvre d'Ormessons—and these in turn were served by families of clerks such as the Costers and the de Villiers. No fundamental change was necessary to extend this system of social influence to friends and acquaintances.

In such an aristocratic social hierarchy, a bureaucratic hierarchy could hardly exist. From his first appointment every official was known by his social or financial standing and influence, to which he owed his place. 'One of the Directors of the Domains Administration, protected by the Queen and by Monsieur [the King's brother]', Joly de Fleury wrote of Jean-Louis Delagarde, in assessing him for a post of Receiver General of Finance. 'He has had the promise of a high financial place because of his project of marriage with Mademoiselle de Montluzon.'[2] Joly de Fleury was considering the man's social position as a primary qualification for an office. An official's place was in turn a social asset, but none was sufficient by itself to command the obedience of social superiors who might happen to hold posts lower in the administrative hierarchy, as Necker found to his cost. That difficulty seldom arose, however, because in the normal course of events a man could not get a post in which he might have authority over his social superiors. At all events a venal office-holder necessarily stood outside the administrative hierarchy like any professional or businessman, and took orders only from the King or the royal councils, that is to say, the orders of his business clients and social superiors. In the financial system of the ancien régime the beginnings of bureaucratic structure, in which the individual would be subservient to the bureau he served, might be seen only in the individual bureaux working for ministers, venal officials and financial companies. But these bureaux were usually scattered in an unbureaucratic way. When Necker tried to integrate the bureaux of his Department by abolishing the venal Intendants of Finance, he was taking a revolutionary step as well as a bureaucratic one, and his successors, especially Calonne, soon restored the

---

[1] This view of the family is nicely explained by Georges Snyders, *La Pédogogie en France aux XVIIe et XVIIIe siècles* (Paris, 1964), p. 235.
[2] B.N., Joly de Fleury papers 1437, fol. 283, 17 Feb. 1782.

old aristocratic disorganization of the Department by dividing the bureaux among many semi-independent magistrates.[1] The revolutionary assemblies took up Necker's work, and in 1791, Anson prevented the creation of a group of independent 'directeurs-généraux' in the new Ministry of the Interior by pointing out that they would be much like the old Intendants of Finance.[2] This was an example of the bureaucratic accomplishments of the revolutionary governments: the destruction of that class of official who had long intervened between the Minister and the common clerk.

The financial services of the ancien régime employed, then, a number of highly paid, powerful officials whom the revolutionary governments either removed or reduced in salary and status. These high officials were of two principal types: on the one hand the venal magistrates, accountants and tax farmers, and on the other hand the commissioned *premiers commis* and *directeurs* who were on the threshold of the former group and hoping to acquire venal offices for their sons if not for themselves. For centuries these two groups had existed side by side, or rather, the one slightly beneath the other, in uneasy cooperation; but in Necker's first ministry (1776–81) a certain rivalry developed between them because Necker tended to prefer the *premiers commis* to the venal magistrates and accountants.[3] The finance ministers of the next six years favoured the latter group, which became very numerous under Calonne; but from May 1787 Loménie de Brienne and Necker once more reversed the trend in favour of the commissioned *premiers commis*, and abolished many venal offices. The National Assembly completed this process by suppressing all venal offices and reorganizing all the bureaux in six ministries, the Treasury and other accessory agencies with no intermediaries between the Ministers and the *premiers commis*. All the great aristocratic officials and nearly all the powerful corps of independent accountants were swept away by the National Assembly, leaving only the *premiers commis*, part of the triumphant Third Estate, for whom the revolutionary events seemed in the early years to be a victory. In the limited monarchy of 1789 and 1790 the twenty-one *premiers commis* of the Finance Department and the five *premiers commis* and fourteen highly-paid *liquidateurs*, *caissiers* and *chefs* of the Royal Treasury stood, indeed, near the top of the administrative pyramid immediately under the Minister.

This early phase was soon followed, however, by a second phase in which the democratic-republican forces drastically reduced the status and salaries of these remaining high employees. Naturally, a good many individuals had

---

[1] See above, p. 56.
[2] Pierre-Hubert Anson, *Discours sur l'organisation du ministère* (10 April 1791), B.N., 8° L²⁷ 10.   [3] See above, p. 58.

better fortune by getting other posts in the earlier years: Tarbé became the first Minister of Public Contributions in 1791, and Gaudin and Cornus de la Fontaine became Treasury Commissioners in the summer of that year; but the majority of them remained in the financial administration and suffered a decline in prestige and in salary. Their fall was all the greater because many of them had been high and mighty personages in the ancien régime, wielding some of the power of their masters the magistrates and accountants, hoping to acquire offices themselves, already gathering pensions and other royal gifts, hurrying back and forth from Versailles, and sometimes even beginning to live nobly with carriages and houses and high-sounding names. Apart from pensions, *acquits-patents* and other royal favours, their regular salaries had been high, averaging about 10,000 a year in 1788 for each of the thirty-two *premiers commis* then in the Finance Department, and rising to an average of 13,000 livres for the twenty-one still in that Department in 1790. Bertrand Dufresne, indeed, received 60,000 as Treasury Director from August 1788 and his second-in-command, the *Premier commis des finances*, drew 30,000, as also did Joseph Coster, the *premier commis* of the bureau charged with making arrangements for the Estates General and the Provincial Estates.[1] All these were naturally identified with the King and the royal ministers, whose servants they were, and as this executive part of the government became more and more suspect to the left wing of the Constituent Assembly and then of the Legislative Assembly (1791–2), the *premiers commis* suffered accordingly.

To begin with, the *premiers commis* were undermined by the committees of the Constituent Assembly which very early took over much of the policy-making and executive work of government. We have seen how Dufresne became the servant of the Finance Committee in Autumn 1790; the same fate overtook other officials.[2] Then a certain deputy very active on the Pensions Committee, Armand-Gaston Camus, academician and former *parlementaire*, made it his business to gather information about the *premiers commis*, their salaries, pensions, property and pretensions, through the efforts of a spy in one of Dufresne's bureaux. This was a clerk named Vitry, with a small job if we may judge from his modest salary of 2,800 livres, and he informed on many *premiers commis* with bitter sarcasm. Camus used his information and also adopted a similarly bitter tone in reports to the Assembly on pensions, including pensions of *premiers commis*, reports 'of a wickedness so black', a *premier commis* wrote of one report,

---

[1] At this stage, the Treasury Director and the *Premier commis des finances* were still part of the Finance Department. Most of the information about these salaries is in A.N., D x 3; F^{IA} 565; and the printed *Bureaux de l'administration générale* (Paris, 1790) (B.N., Lf^{99} 6).   [2] See above, p. 222.

'that I cannot conceive how anyone but Monsieur Camus could have drawn it up'.[1] The Constituent Assembly abolished many pensions and also effected a modest economy by adopting a maximum salary of 12,000 livres a year for *premiers commis*.[2]

This was only a beginning, and the Legislative Assembly reduced that maximum to a mere 8,000 livres in the course of a budgetary debate on 1 June 1792. The debate began with a proposal of the Finance Committee to reduce the salaries of Ministers from 100,000 livres to 70,000 and to fix those of bureau chiefs at 10,000 livres. The committee spokesman argued that these reductions might be even more severe except that inflation had already raised prices by more than one-third. Cambon, the future Finance Minister of the Committee of Public Safety, stood up and declared 25,000 livres to be quite enough for a Minister: 'there are fine people living in furnished rooms (*chambres garnies*)...honour and public applause are the only proper recompense in a time of liberty and equality' etc.[3] The Assembly adopted the figure of 50,000 livres for all Ministers except the one for Foreign Affairs who was awarded 75,000 livres because, as Cambon put it, 'he has to feed diplomats'. When the debate turned to the Minister's servants, the *premiers commis* or bureau heads, one zealous republican thought 4,000 livres enough. A former *premier commis* of the Finance Department sensibly proposed a salary scale rising from 3,000 to 6,000 and finally to 10,000, but this time Cambon carried the Assembly with him in suggesting a maximum of 8,000 livres. When this ruling took effect on 1 June 1792, there was an immediate saving of 36,000 livres in the budget of the Ministry of Public Contributions alone.[4]

This and other such saving due to budgetary debate in the legislature was a triumph of parliamentary control over the executive part of the government, but it also marked the end of aristocratic influence in administration. In the monarchy the *premiers commis* with 10,000 or 15,000 livres a year had been well above their clerks but still only mid-way up the social and administrative ladder to the offices of Master of Requests, Treasurer General or Payer of the rentes.[5] Their association with these higher officials, their

---

[1] Claude-Charles Coster, *Journal manuscrit* (1790), entry for 30 June 1790; Vitry was born at Versailles, 16 Dec. 1742, and worked in the *Contrôle général* for twenty-seven years until discharged in Oct. 1791 by de Lessart 'dont les principes alors ne quadraient pas avec les siens', Vitry tells us (A.N., AF III 28, dossier 97, 27 Brumaire An IV). Some of his reports to Camus are in A.N., D X 3.
[2] *Arch. Parl.*, vol. XXXI, p. 595, decree of 29 Sept. 1791, art. 7.
[3] *Arch. Parl.*, vol. XLIV, pp. 435 ff.
[4] A.N., H 1448, *Etat de la composition des bureaux du ministère des contributions publiques*.
[5] Their emoluments came from many sources, varied greatly, and I have discussed their complexities elsewhere (see above, chapters 4 and 5). Some idea of the scale of their in-

imitation of the aristocratic example, and their hopes for the future had all reinforced the tendency, natural in an aristocracy, to emphasize social differences between them and their common clerks. Like their superiors, the *premiers commis* had been personages each with an individual identity affirmed by still higher persons who chose to patronize them. No common standard of usefulness permitted an assessment of a man's work rather than his person and social standing. No standard grades of salary, no statement of executive functions, no underlying principle of social utility, and no budgetary debate of costs had interfered with the social hierarchy rising from the lowest office-boy, paid less than 1,000 livres, to the Master of Requests drawing anything from 30,000 livres and up. By the time the Convention met in October 1792, however, salaries of more than 10,000 livres had all but disappeared in the civil service and the upper ranks had either dropped out altogether or else sunk to a level only slightly above the *chefs* and *commis* whom they once would have scorned to associate with. Some Masters of Requests, Intendants in the old Finance Ministry, continued out of condescension or perhaps a patriotic concern for the public service, to work as surveillants without salary until 1792 and then disappeared.[1] There was no room for them in a bureaucracy. And the time had passed when the *premiers commis*, such as Anson and Hamelin, could obtain salaries of 12,000 livres, several thousand livres more in gratuities and pensions, and then go on to win offices as Receivers General of Finance, thus opening the possibility of noble title for their sons if not for themselves.[2] Henceforth the *premier commis* was merely in the highest administrative grade and no longer a personage of importance. 'He grows old in the bureaux, he dies a *premier commis*', Cambon remarked in June 1792.[3] In the financial services of the republic, the bureau was to be much more important than the individual officials in it.

In the ancien régime, the aristocratic standing of higher officials had contrasted sharply with the standing of most of the clerks kept as salaried employees. These, in ascending order of rank, the *garçons de bureau*, *commis*, *chefs*, might be thought of as having bureaucratic status, except that they were more like the domestic servants of the men they served. They

comes may be gleaned from the decision to pay each of the new Treasury Administrators, formerly Treasurers General and Keepers, 50,000 livres a year from the organization of the Treasury in 1788.

[1] Chaumont de la Millière, Michau de Montaran, Tolozan and Chardon were all listed as such in the new Ministry of the Interior to which their bureaux had been transferred (A.N., F^1b 1–2, *Etat des bureaux du ministère de l'intérieur en exécution de décret du 14 jan. 1792*).

[2] On Anson and Hamelin, see A.N., F^4 1032^2; F^4 2680; F^4 1957; V^1 518; F^4 1946 etc.

[3] *Arch. Parl.*, vol. XLIV, p. 444.

were hardly royal servants. They depended entirely upon their masters and even those whose names appeared in the *Almanach Royal* were listed for the most part under their masters' names. The royal accountants and tax farmers hired and fired them at will as if they had been household servants. The long, rambling memorandum of Charles-Nicolas Roland, published in 1784 to protest against his arbitrary arrest and imprisonment, reveals in great detail how personal the services of a clerk might be.[1] For several years Roland lived with his employer, a Receiver General of Finance named Watelet, better known as an art collector and critic, and did much private business for him as well as assisting in the management of royal finances. It appears from these pages that Roland believed himself arbitrarily imprisoned entirely on Watelet's personal initiative, Watelet having wasted royal funds on his personal pleasures and then blamed the fraud on Roland, his clerk. Whatever the rights in this case, it shows that the relationship of clerk and superior was entirely personal. As a journalist of the time wrote for the amusement of his readers, an employer had to watch his clerks closely lest a change of fortune reverse their positions. 'How I would like to be a painter to catch the glance which a superior throws when crossing his bureaux!'[2]

The subordinate employees were freed during the French revolution from this personal dependence on their masters, who became merely their superiors. The difference was subtle but unmistakable. Their salaries had hitherto come from a lump sum paid to the higher official for all his office employees and expenses and the salary of any individual depended upon his master's generosity. In the revolutionary civil service the clerks became 'clerks of the Department', as a deputy explained to the National Assembly, and they had a status independent of their superiors.[3] Although superiors still had decisive influence over their fate in the bureaux, that influence had to be exercised in formal procedures, for the clerk was now in some measure a national civil servant. There was to be an ambiguity in the meaning of the term 'fonctionnaire' for many years, some people understanding by the term only elected public representatives, but even the lowest customs employees began to think of themselves as deserving of the term also.[4] In any event the venal, independent, aristocratic senior officials were disappearing, leaving at all levels only salaried civil servants paid from the central

---

[1] Roland, *Mémoire au Roi Louis XVI en dénonciation d'abus d'autorité...* (London, April 1784), 283 pp. and two folding tables. (B.M., 10660 C 15.)

[2] L. S. Mercier, *Tableau de Paris*, vol. VII, p. 106.

[3] Lamy, *Opinion sur l'importance de décréter la responsabilité des chefs de bureaux* (Paris, 1790) (B.M., F. R. 112 (20)), p. 7.

[4] J. F. Bosher, *The Single Duty Project* (London, 1964), p. 159.

Treasury. This was deliberately done. 'Let us replace the General Farm', a deputy urged the Constituent Assembly in a typical speech, 'by a new organization in which the only agents necessary will be the employees, and in which their salaries...will be regulated according to their utility.'[1]

The change necessarily included a great deal more than the mere removal of the old higher ranks, important though that was, because the intrinsic vices of the ancien régime—or what the revolutionaries saw as vices—had formed the minds of the common clerks. Those vices of patronage, grace and favour, the sycophantic attitude of the domestic servant, came under heavy attack in the revolution, notably in various institutional changes. The National Assembly debated the matter of gifts and gratuities as early as 27 November 1789 when a member of the Finance Committee put forward a motion to forbid all gifts and *dons d'étrennes* in the royal administration. The committee member, Lebrun, acknowledged Necker as the source of the idea, Necker having condemned all *étrennes* in his own Department and so stimulated the Committee to make this condemnation legal and general throughout all administrative services. Immediately an ecclesiastical deputy stood up in the Assembly and suggested that judges ought to be included in the new restriction and forbidden to receive their customary presents of wax and candles. 'You are a professor of canon law', another shouted. 'Why don't you include professors?' (*On rit beaucoup*, says the minutes of the meeting.)[2] D'Ailly then reported that Necker had told him the King was planning to abolish all *étrennes*, especially those of Intendants, Governors, Commanders and others accustomed to receive them from the towns, provinces, guilds and corporations. And finally the committee's motion, amended to include not only executive agents but everyone exercising any public function, was re-read and decreed. It stated:

The National Assembly considering that every public function is a duty; that all the agents of the administration, salaried by the nation, owe to the state their work and their care; that ministers being necessary they should grant neither favour nor preference and consequently have no right to special gratitude; again, considering that it is vital to the regeneration of *mœurs*, as well as to the economy of finances and of the special revenues of the provinces, cities, guilds and communities, to eliminate the traffic of corruption and venality formerly carried on under the name of *étrennes*, *vins-de-ville*, *gratifications*, etc., has decreed and decrees that from 1 December next no administrative agent, nor any of those who ...exercise some public function, shall be permitted to receive anything in the nature of *étrennes*, *gratifications*, *vins-de-ville* or under any other denomination

---

[1] François-Antoine-Joseph de Hell, *Arch. Parl.*, vol. XVIII, p. 414.
[2] *Arch. Parl.*, vol. X, p. 269.

whatever, from corps, provincial administrations, towns, communities, guilds or private individuals, on pain of [being charged with fraud]; that no expense of that nature will be allowed in the accounts of the said corps, administrations, towns, and guilds.[1]

This law appears to have been carried out, at least during the next few years, though it was not intended to stop the payment of regular annual gratuities to zealous civil servants at Christmas, and the Assembly allowed for such payments in its calculation of the new departmental budgets.

Patronage, personal influence and the resulting fragmentation of administrative services all fell victim to the bureaucratic tendencies of the revolutionary governments. First, patronage and social influence in the administration came directly under attack in the revolution and standards of qualification for officials developed, rudimentary though they were. A decree on the naval administration read, 'There may not be in the civil administration of a port more than two individuals from the same family, even second cousins, brothers-in-law and nephews.'[2] A decree of 20 March 1791 ordered that for three years, all appointments of employees to the new and surviving branches of the financial administration had to be made from among the unemployed of the suppressed branches, and the Ministers set about enforcing this law.[3] Secondly, a measure of social equality removed one of the obstacles to proper organization, and when complaints against the authority of officials reached the National Assembly, a member of it offered a lesson in modern bureaucracy: 'Men are equal, administrations are not; subordination and inequality are not synonymous; the superiority is in the thing and not in the person...'[4] A man wields the power of a high government post in the general interest rather than his own (ran the argument) and if he puts his personal interests first, as under the ancien régime, then he is corrupt. During the republican era the Minister of Public Contributions, then a social equal and addressed in the familiar 'tu' and 'toi' by his employees, exercised his authority by appealing to late and lazy employees to avoid 'affecting an aristocratic appearance and insulting both the public and the good conduct of their colleagues, older and wiser than they, on whom they have shifted some of their work', and by appealing to their obligation to the republic and to the general interest. He concluded,

---

[1] *Loc. cit.* This was reiterated in different words in a decree of the Convention, 10 Oct. 1792 (*Arch. Parl.*, vol. LII, p. 436).
[2] Decree of the Convention, 14 Pluv. An II, art. 3 (B.M., R 679 (10)).
[3] A.N., G¹ 63, ministerial circulars.
[4] René-Gaston Baco de la Chapelle, *Réponse de Monsieur Baco, député de la Loire inférieure...* 20 pp. (B.M., F. R. 112(23)), p. 12.

'I shall use republican severity towards all those who do not do their work as true Republicans.'[1]

Thus did the principles of social and civil equality begin to make room for powerful systems of bureaucratic inequality which the ancien régime would not have tolerated. Of course the removal of patronage and personal influence from the administration was very imperfect, even in those revolutionary years—but so was the social revolution. Then as now, patronage and social inequality went hand in hand.

Another feature of the ancien régime had been the surety bond (*cautionnement*) posted by every cashier or other official who regularly handled large sums of money but held no venal office which the Crown might regard as security against fraud. From one point of view this was a cash deposit, a type of loan really, on which the Crown had paid interest, but from another point of view it had established the 'official' as merely a sort of business agent of the crown. The revolutionary governments changed this business relationship in two steps, the first of which was a law requiring the official to pledge real estate as security rather than a cash deposit. Intended to remove that kind of government debt, to discriminate against financiers, to make up for a scarcity of money capital, and to encourage the purchase of nationalized property, this system in turn came under attack in the demo-

---

[1] A.N., H 1448, Destournelles to Bert, 22 Frimaire An II. The letter reads, J'ai reçu l'avis, Citoyen, que plusieurs Employés des Bureaux des Contributions publiques se montrent négligens à remplir les devoirs de leurs places; *que les uns arrivent fort tard,* que d'autres s'absentent plusieurs jours de suite, soit en supposant des maladies, sois sous d'autres prétextes. Et enfin que quelques uns affectant l'extérieur de l'aristocratie semblent insulter et au public et à la bonne conduite de ceux de leurs Camarades, plus âgés ou plus sages qu'eux, sur lesquels ils se débarrassent d'une partie de leur besogne. J'ai peine à croire que des hommes qui doivent être des Républicains et qui sans doute prétendent à ce titre, puissent mériter de si graves reproches. Il m'est plus satisfaisant de penser qu'il y a de l'exagération ou peut-être même de la malveillance dans les inculpations qui leur sont faites.

Comment se persuader que ceux qui, sous le rapport de l'intérêt général, et de l'intérêt particulier, ont contracté une double obligation envers la République soient assez ingrats pour la trahir (car c'est la trahir que de la tromper) et assez peu délicats pour recevoir d'elle le prix d'un travail qu'ils lui refusent? Quoi qu'il en soit, Je t'invite, Citoyen, à surveiller de près les employés de la division à la tête de laquelle tu es placé, et de rappeller rigoureusement à leurs devoirs ceux qui s'en écartent. Je n'ai pas besoin de t'engager à leur prêcher d'exemple: à ces égards, je suis à porté de te juger moi-même par ton travail, et personne ne peut m'en imposer pour ou contre toi et les autres premiers commis. Je voudrais que mes occupations multiples me laissassent le temps de parcourir quelques fois vos Bureaux pour apprécier aussi moi-même les travaux des employés qui sont sous votre inspection. C'est à toi, Citoyen, de me suppléer dans ce soin pour ce qui te concerne. Je me propose cependant de la remplir personnellement de tems à autre. Préviens les employés, tes coopérateurs, et avertir les, que j'userai de la sévérité républicaine envers tous ceux qui n'exerceront pas leurs places en vrais Républicains.

Salut et fraternité
(Destournelles)

cratic-republican phase of the revolution because any kind of surety bond tended to reserve official posts for the rich and because the system appeared to the revolutionaries to embody a cynical acquiescence in the old exploitation of public finances by public servants. In 1793 there was a popular suspicion, amply supported by recent events, that financiers often robbed the state under the cover of bonds, even pledges of land. 'I ask therefore,' said one orator in the Convention, 'that there be no more bonds of money, but only bonds of patriotism.'[1] The nation's best guarantees of honest service are virtue and talent in the officials it chooses, and continuous inspection by the nation. 'Le véritable cautionnement, c'est la guillotine',[2] was a view expressed by various deputies, including Danton who soon afterwards lost his own head on that principle. When he uttered those words, however, it was to challenge the ancient business contract of government and official. During the years of virtue and terror, an oath of loyalty replaced all surety bonds.

In contrast to all the changes at the upper levels of the administration and all the rearrangements of the bureaux, the mass of common clerks remained extraordinarily stable as a social group through the revolutionary years. Their lives, work and most of all their social composition, changed very little, for each successive government retained their services and there was no decimation of their ranks to make room for others. Every new agency, such as the *Caisse de l'extraordinaire* or the *Direction de la liquidation*, hired most of its clerks from among those discharged from the suppressed bureaux of the General Farm, *Régie générale* and others; even unemployed clerks of the venal Receivers General found work in the swelling bureaux of the new financial services. The Committee of Public Safety and the Directory each scrutinized the bureaux to purge them of political enemies, and a very few clerks lost their jobs because they could not produce *certificats de civisme* in 1793–4 or were so politically active in the following years that they suffered the displeasure of the Directory.[3] A few went off to the war: nine out of 219 employees listed for the *Direction de la liquidation* in May 1793;[4] but most remained at home by virtue of various laws exempting civil servants from military duty. Probably the greatest loss of personnel in the Treasury, the Finance Department and other central financial services was owing to a decline in real wages when salaries remained stable in a period of

---

[1] Léonard Bourdon, 3 Nov. 1793 (*Ancien Moniteur*, vol. XVIII, pp. 341 ff.). Louis-Etienne Beffroy de Beauvoir, *Rapport sur la cautionnement des comptables* (1793) (B.N., Le³⁸ 470).
[2] Danton, 2 Feb. 1794 (*Ancien Moniteur*, vol. XIX, p. 377).
[3] Decrees of 4 Frimaire and 5 Ventôse, An III.
[4] *Etat des citoyens* (B.N., Lf¹⁵⁷ 10).

rapid inflation. From 1787 to 1791 approximately half of the men in these agencies earned less than 2,000 livres a year, and only a handful of their superiors, the *premiers commis* and *chefs*, earned more than 5,000 livres. True, there were adjustments for inflation, so that by April 1796, for example, the Treasury employees were receiving *assignats* with a face value of half their annual salaries—every fortnight![1] Yet their nominal salaries did not rise, and as early as 1792 many clerks were leaving the civil services in order to go into banks and commercial firms.[2] Whatever the reasons for the losses of personnel, they had their greatest effect under the Directory, when large numbers of men of the ancien régime quit the financial services. A list of employees in the Ministry of Public Contributions in April 1794 shows that more than two-thirds of them (111/162) had joined their bureaux before 1789, 30 of these even before 1770, and of the 51 men hired in the five years since 1789, no more than 20 had come in 1793 and 1794.[3] During the next three years, however, the Ministry hired at least 91 new men, possibly more, and lost 63 of the pre-revolutionary men, leaving only 48 of them, less than one-fifth of the total personnel listed in Spring 1797.[4] Whatever precautions we take in interpreting these figures, we are obliged to conclude that the Finance Department lost fewer of its pre-revolutionary men during the five years of revolution ending in April 1794 than it lost during the next three years, mainly under the régimes of the Thermidorians and the Directory.

A study of the *premiers commis* in that Department leads to the same general conclusion. In April 1794 there were 16 of these, 12 of whom had remained in the same posts since before the Revolution.[5] Another had rejoined the Department after only a brief interruption in a career going back into the ancien régime.[6] Of the 3 new men, one had had a previous career in the bureaux of the War Ministry.[7] Three years later, however, only 4 of the 12 old hands remained in their posts;[8] another 4 had sunk to the rank of

[1] A.N., AF III 29.
[2] Marbot, 1 June 1792, *Arch. Parl.*, vol. XLIV, p. 444.
[3] A.N., AF II 163.
[4] Lists in A.N., AF III 29. The Ministry then had a total of 276 men, about one-third of whom had been hired since the beginning of Year III. These lists show forty-eight hired in Year II, but these probably came in with bureaux transferred to the Ministry in the process of reorganization.
[5] Jacques-Etienne de Villiers, Edmé-Louis Henry, Michel-François Hocquet, Claude Armenault, Joseph-Gabriel Le Peintre, Michel-François Moreau, Albert-Joseph Ulpien Hennet, Louis Legrand, Charles Hersemulle de la Roche, Anne-Etienne Boizot, Joseph-Alexandre Bergon, Edmé-François Anthoine.
[6] Jean-Baptiste-Pierre Angebault.
[7] Jean-Nicolas James. The others were Jean Boutin and Pierre Couret.
[8] Louis Legrand, Hennet, Anthoine and Armenault.

chef with much lower salaries;[1] and no less than 8 new *premiers commis* had joined the Department.[2] Some of these new men had come from outside the ranks of the civil service, and so broken a tradition which the Finance Department had maintained throughout the five years of revolution: one had been a deputy elected to the Constituent Assembly in 1789;[3] two had been engaged in foreign trade;[4] and two others had been lawyers.[5] In the Finance Department the revolutionary régimes had made profound changes in organization but not in personnel, except at the highest levels, and it was the Directory which began to bring in new men on a large scale.

Still more evidence tends to show that the social composition of the Department remained stable during the hectic revolutionary years. Under the ancien régime clerks, *chefs* and even *premiers commis* had lived mainly in the north-western quarters of central Paris, north of the Louvre and the Tuileries. As the lists of 1793 and 1794 show, about two-thirds of the 168 employees still lived in those quarters, west of what was then the rue Saint Denis, but they were scattered widely among the various Paris *sections* there, even the greatest concentrations of employees amounting to only a score in each of the three *sections* named Pîques or Place Vendôme, Bibliothèque or Le Pelletier, and La Montagne or Butte des Moulins.[6] About one-third of the Departmental employees lived outside the north-western quarters of Paris and these were widely scattered throughout the city, no more than 3 or 4 in each *section*. Probably the only effect of the revolution on the residence of clerks was to disperse them a little by reducing their real wages and so forcing them to move away from the expensive centre quarters of the city, and by driving them out of the government buildings where many had been in the habit of residing near their bureaux.

Turning from residence to place of birth, we find signs of a gradual increase in the numbers of provincial men, not so much in the Finance

[1] James (5,600 livres instead of 8,000), Le Peintre, Moreau and Angebault.
[2] Marie-Alexandre Dupré, Pierre Lenormand, Giles-Jean Paterson, Abraham-Isaac Dutertre, François-Nicolas Legrand, Pierre-Jean-Baptiste Montaiglon, Jacques Cyalis de Lavaud, Raison.
[3] Dupré.
[4] Lanormand and Paterson, mostly at Cadiz.
[5] Raison, 'Clerc de procureur et homme de loi'; François-Nicolas Legrand, 'procureur au Châtelet'. Of the remaining three, Cyalis de Lavaud had served for many years as a *premier commis* in the Department and been temporarily removed in 1793; Dutertre had been a secretary at the Intendancy of Burgundy before the revolution and then a *premier commis* in the Caisse de l'extraordinaire; and Montaiglon had been in the bureaux of the General Farm from 1776 until the suppression when he had joined the Caisse de l'extraordinaire also.
[6] See the map appended to G. Rudé, *The Crowd in the French Revolution*, showing the forty-eight sections of Paris.

Department itself, where the lists for 1793 and 1794 both show two-thirds born in the provinces, but in comparing this Department with the newly reorganized *Direction générale de la liquidation* in which three-fifths of the 224 employees were provincial in origin.[1] Analyse the personnel lists as we will, however, we shall find a remarkable stability in social composition of the Finance Department throughout the revolutionary years, and there is little reason to suspect much change in the composition of the Treasury and other financial services, at least until the Directory period.

To compare the structure of the entire financial system in 1787 with its new structure in 1794 is to discover that a vast system of private enterprise had been converted into a bureaucracy. The various managing groups, for whom the finances of the monarchy had been a field of opportunity for profit and social advancement, had disappeared leaving only the common clerks in their bureaux, now integrated in ministries and subsidiary services. The logical integration of the bureaux had been revolutionary, for the ancien régime had maintained them as a mere collection without uniformity or total plan, in much the same spirit as it had maintained the collection of old provinces which the revolution reformed as uniform *départements*. Within each ministry or other agency—the Customs Service, the *Régie* of Domains and Property Registration, the Treasury—the employees had come to have graded salaries where they had once negotiated their pay more or less individually, and the legislature, for its budget debates, could rapidly sum up a ministry in terms of the numbers of employees at each salary level. To make sure that officials obeyed legislation on matters of organization and personnel, the legislatures quickly adopted the practice of sending for charts and tables of each ministry, notably by decrees of 29 September 1791 (art. 10), 14 January 1792, 20 March, 8 April and 14 May 1793.

In creating this bureaucracy the men of the revolutionary assemblies, whatever their differences, appear to have been tacitly agreed on a number of fundamental things. Whatever sides they took in the political struggle between the Crown and the legislature for the control of the financial administration and in the argument over the constitutional nature of the Treasury, most men shared a vision of a new system of public finance that would be mechanically efficient, proof against disorder and corruption, and divorced from private enterprise and from politics. Rarely a subject of speeches or pamphlets, this vision was manifested in incidental comments and in the assumptions and the vocabulary to be found in nearly everything said or written by these reformers. The fragmentary ideas composing their

---

[1] *Etat des citoyens* (1793) (B.N., Lf 157 10).

vision were not in themselves revolutionary, but once assembled the ideas illuminate one another and form an intellectual and moral foundation for the administrative revolution of the time.

One of the main ideas was that the administration of finances could be rendered mechanically efficient. In the age of the Watt steam-engine and the Jacquard loom, of the *Encyclopédie* with its volumes of engravings of machines, of Newton's triumph over continental rivals, of La Mettrie's *L'Homme machine* (1747)—the age of the Enlightenment, in short—the word 'machine' had been increasingly used to describe administrative organizations. By the end of the eighteenth century the machine had become an obsessive image. Anson used it to describe the projected Ministry of the Interior, Camus to describe the entire administration, Marat to represent municipal administrations, and to sum up, the machine image in the writings of Lebrun, Roederer, Laffon de Ladébat and many others seems to show that this generation thought of administrative and political agencies as analogous to machines.[1] The other possible analogy, comparing the organization to the human body as Hobbes for instance had done, seldom appears in the writings of the late eighteenth-century French reformers and revolutionaries.[2] De Vaine chose to explain that the executive power of government was suspended because 'on ne perfectionne pas un ressort sans en arrêter le mouvement', and he went on to advise the *Constituante* to organize the executive 'assez énergiquement pour qu'il soit efficace'.[3] A growing range of mechanical virtues were invoked. Condorcet's plan for the Treasury was to achieve 'une marche égale et constante'.[4] Guyton-Morveau reported of a certain new treasury bureau that the 'new organization will have attained the regularity and the uniformity which should assure the service'.[5] One of Cambon's maxims was 'the uniformity

---

[1] Camus, *Réponse à Necker* (1790), p. 29; Anson, *Discours sur l'organisation du ministère* (10 April 1791), p. 2; Briois-Beaumetz, *Projet sur l'organisation du trésor public* (21 July 1790), *passim*; Lebrun, *Rapport et projet de décret sur l'organisation du trésor public* (11 Dec. 1790) (*Arch. Parl.*, vol. XXI, pp. 370–91, *passim*); Marat, *L'Ami du peuple*, no. XIV, 24 September 1789, p. 122; Roederer, *Rapport* (10 Dec. 1790) (*Arch. Parl.*, vol. XXI, pp. 579–87); Laffon de Ladébat, *Rapport du comité de l'ordinaire* (10 Feb, 1792); *Mémoires sur les rentes et sur les offices*, (B.N., Lf⁸⁰ 85, second memoir (1789), p. 4); Dubu de Longchamps, *Mémoire pour Messieurs les Maîtres de Postes sur le fait des messageries...* (1790) (B.N. Lf⁹² 26), p. 6.

[2] Barbé-Marbois used it in a mixed metaphor, referring to the Treasury as the heart of the body politic, but going on to refer to its mechanical properties. (Letter dated 9 August 1796 in A.N., AF III 130, dossier 611.)

[3] De Vaines, *Des moyens d'assurer le succès et la durée de la constitution* (Paris, 1790), pp. 27–8.

[4] Condorcet, *Sur la constitution du pouvoir...* p. 35.

[5] Guyton-Morveau, *Rapport sur l'établissement d'un bureau dans la trésorerie nationale...* (26 Nov. 1791), p. 9.

which is the principal basis of a good administration'.[1] Lebrun urged the *Constituante* at one point to 'simplify the wheels of the administration'.[2] Inseparable from the mechanical image was a sharper concept of function. Whereas the posts of official during the ancien régime had been *offices*, *charges* or *places*, they now began to be called *emplois* or *fonctions* and the officials themselves were for the first time described as *fonctionnaires*.[3] Even priests were so called under the civil constitution of the clergy, and decrees began to refer to the King as the 'premier fonctionnaire public'.[4] When the General Farm disappeared, some customs officials proudly described themselves as 'fonctionnaires publics'.[5] This utilitarian vocabulary was used to describe organizations with quasi-mechanical virtues: 'A free nation must create functionaries', runs a typical statement, 'only in strict proportion to its need, and after having carefully studied the necessity for each place in a complete plan of administration in order to remove those places with no utility (*sans utilité*).'[6] In part this idea concerned the choice of men, and Antoine Burté was thus arguing for a selection according to ability when he publicly reviewed the list of candidates for the new Bureau of Accounts, rejecting the duc de Survilliers as inept, a certain Boucher because 'he himself agrees that he has not the first notion of accounting', and several others because they were chosen only for their influential relations.[7] In the application which interests us now, however, the idea of function became a principle of quasi-mechanical organization and this application is clearly visible in an influential speech of Pierre-Hubert Anson which will serve as an example.

The Constituent Assembly was debating the structure of the projected ministries, proposed by the Constitution Committee, when Anson rose on 10 April 1791 to plead for organization according to 'fonctions analogues'.[8] Demeunier had already expressed the views of the Constitution Committee on the illogical character of ancien régime ministries.[9] Again and again Anson stressed the importance of grouping similar administrative subjects and tasks. 'It is on that classification [*des matières et des fonctions*] that I place the greatest emphasis; it is the ancient confusion of heterogeneous

---

[1] Cambon, Dec. 1792 (B.N., Le³⁸ 1912).   [2] *Arch. Parl.*, vol. XXI, p. 374.
[3] Bernardin, *Roland et le ministère de l'intérieur*, p. 199.
[4] *Proc. verb. de l'ass. nat.*, vol. XVIII, session 4 Jan. 1791 and session 28 March 1791, decrees on residence rules.
[5] J. F. Bosher, *The Single Duty Project* (London, 1964), p. 159.
[6] Etienne Clavière, *Réflexions sur les formes et les principes* (1791), p. 22.
[7] A. Burté, *Observations sur la nomination des commissaires de la comptabilité* (27 Nov. 1791).
[8] Anson, *Discours sur l'organisation du ministère* (10 April 1791), p. 3.
[9] Bernardin, *Roland et le ministère de l'intérieur*, p. 188.

matters which used to make the ministers so dependent on their bureaux. Overburdened with occupations which did not have analogous principles, the ministers were led to decide everything precipitously and superficially.' So saying, Anson proceeded to argue that all matters of revenue and finance ought to be separated from matters of general internal administration. 'It is an old error', he said, 'to believe that there is a similarity between the functions of the executive power in these respects...' This was a blow aimed at the Department of Finance which had defects in organization apparent to Anson during his many years as a *premier commis*. He was not the only one to make this observation. Another former *premier commis*, Michel Dailly, also rose in the Assembly to make the same point.[1] The immediate effect of these speeches was that the projected Ministry of the Interior was stripped of revenue functions which had made it seem like an imitation of the old Department of Finance, and these functions were grouped in a new Department of Public Contributions. France was not yet ready to accept a Department of Public Instruction which Anson put forward that day as more useful to the nation than even the Department of Foreign Affairs. But all six of the Departments established by the Assembly —for War, Marine, Justice, Foreign Affairs, Interior and Public Contributions—met the utilitarian standards of the Assembly except in one respect. They were in the hands of ministers who might not have the interests of the nation at heart, and through the ministers they were open to the corruption of financial and other private interests.

One of the very earliest administrative ideas current in the Assembly, associated with the taking of the Bastille and other revolutionary events, was that the executive agents of the nation, 'le despotisme ministériel abattu', in Jean de Vaine's colourful phrase, needed careful supervision lest they use national funds to restore their lost powers in the nation.[2] This was at first the ancient idea that the King, forever good, was inevitably surrounded by faulty ministers; but after the flight of the royal family to Varennes (21 June 1791) this respectable idea began to give way to a republican sequel in which the King was held to be no less corrupt than his ministers. Of course the Constituent Assembly divided into many conflicting groups over issues such as whether the King as the executive head, or the Assembly as the legislature, ought to choose ministers, whether ministers should be responsible to the King or to the Assembly, and what forms the legislative supervision of ministers should take. Yet even conservative

---

[1] *Ancien Moniteur*, réimpr., vol. VII, p. 575 (9 March 1791). Claude-Charles Coster remarked in his *Journal Manuscrit*, entry for 25 Nov. 1790, on 'le grand principe d'uniformité qu'il faut établir dans le Ministère comme partout ailleurs'.

[2] De Vaines, *Des moyens d'assurer le succès...* (1790), p. 11.

groups assumed that executive ministers could not be allowed a free hand in the management of funds.[1] The example of British political patronage, with the ministers of George III dipping into public funds to reward their supporters, stood like a warning beacon to the Constituent Assembly. Furthermore it was not only the corruption of ministerial influence but also the mere arbitrariness of it which the Assembly abhorred. On the list of faults in the administration of the ancien régime, faults to be guarded against, *l'arbitraire* ranked with *désordre* and *confusion*. The supervision of revenue-collection could be put in the hands of a Minister of Public Contributions, but once collected the revenue could not be entrusted to a minister or indeed to the executive at all. Reformers and revolutionaries all envisaged a system of mechanical functions as the best guarantee of public funds against ministerial faults, and the Treasury was at the heart of that system.

It would be difficult to exaggerate the role of the Treasury in the revolutionary theory of public finance. All those interested in the financial problems that had baffled the ancien régime, all who were engaged in reforming the financial administration, whether members of the assemblies or public functionaries, all saw the Treasury in one form or another as the instrument of financial regeneration. In Condorcet's plan for the Treasury, to take a good example, we find an elaborate system of checks and balances to prevent the abuses of the ancien régime and to render the financing of the state public, incorruptible and efficient. In Condorcet's plan and most others the Treasury appeared as a mechanism for processing public funds without the intervention of private financial interests. The Treasury was partly a product of the universal hatred of financiers, and it had to be made proof against the conspiracies of syndicates, 'compagnies de financiers, espèce parasite', to quote Cornus de la Fontaine. But who were the financiers? They were first and foremost the accountants who had managed public funds for profit rather than for salaries, the 'Treasurers whose fate was to be either continually going bankrupt or rapidly building up immense fortunes', the Payers of the rentes whose work might be just as well done by 'one Treasurer with a well-organized bureau', and the Farmers General, *Régisseurs* and Receivers General.[2] The Receivers General claimed in vain

[1] Bernardin, *Roland et le ministère de l'intérieur*, pp. 23–30; *Ancien Moniteur*, réimpr. vol. v, p. 726; Condorcet, *Sur la constitution du pouvoir*... (1790), p. 30; Guyton-Morveau, *Rapport sur l'établissement* (1791), p. 8; Rougier-Labergerie, *Opinion* (9 April 1792), p. 1.
[2] Cornus de la Fontaine, *Idées sur l'administration des finances*, An VIII, p. 24; Condorcet, *Sur la constitution du pouvoir*... p. 21; Rougier-Labergerie, *Opinion* (9 April 1792), p. 1; Briois-Beaumetz, *Projet sur l'organisation du trésor public*.

to be administrators rather than financiers; it mattered little that some of the most active reformers were former accountants: Anson, Dufresne, Laborde de Méréville, Jean de Vaine, Lecouteulx de Canteleu and others. All seem to have shared a vision of 'the immense counting house'[1] which they called the *Trésor public* and then, at the request of the six commissioners, the *Trésorerie nationale*. 'This name will always remind you', said the commissioners, 'that nothing must come out of it except for the public good.'[2]

The Assembly gave close attention to the organization of the Treasury and to its place in the whole scheme of government. Whereas the ancien régime had been concerned only with accountants and their offices and caisses which had cumulated pell-mell, unrelated to any charted or abstract plan of functions, this revolutionary generation was finding Newton's universe in the working of the state, plotting out a galaxy of articulated processes by making divisions and definitions that have been remembered principally in the famous division of powers—legislative, executive and judicial—but which affected everything they touched including the financial system. They separated the administration of revenues, in the Ministry of Public Contributions, from that of expenditures, in the Treasury. They separated the administration of past finances, 'l'extraordinaire', from that of present and future finances, 'l'ordinaire'.[3] They separated public finance from private finance with increasing rigour. They separated the administration of finance from politics by putting the Treasury under an appointed Crown commission. And after much argument, they decided to have six commissioners who, while directing the whole together, could each direct the work of a different part of the Treasury and separately watch or 'contrôle' one another. All this was consciously done. 'You will observe', the Treasury Commissioners wrote to the Legislative Assembly in 1792, 'that the great principle of the separation of powers can be applied to all parts of the political economy, to the administrative order as to the constitutional order, doubtless because it is founded on human weakness and corruptibility which is only too evident.'[4] The vast administrative revolution in which the Treasury developed was founded on a belief in the perfectibility, not of man, but of organization. This principle was not altogether strange to the ancien régime: 'La politique ne change pas les

[1] The phrase is by Montesquiou-Fezensac, speech of 10 March 1791 (B.M., F. R. 502).
[2] *Ancien Moniteur*, réimpr. (14 April 1791), vol. VIII, p. 130.
[3] Braesch, *Finances et monnaies révolutionnaires*, premier fasc., p. 89.
[4] *Mémoire sur les principes et les avantages de l'établissement des payeurs-généraux* (Paris, 1792) (B.N., Le³³, 3 H (8)), p. 6.

cœurs,' Réal de Curban had written, 'mais elle met à profit les passions.'[1] What was new was the systematic application of this principle to the public administration. By careful administrative arrangements, by cunning devices like double-entry book-keeping, by building carefully regulated machines of men and paper, that generation of reformers hoped to prevent the corruption which had undermined the ancien régime. This reproach of the ancien régime and this hope for the future were both expressed in one of the favourite sayings of the time: 'it is better to prevent abuses than to punish them'.[2] In the realm of public finance, the Treasury and the rest of the bureaucracy were the instruments by which the revolutionary committees intended to prevent abuses.

It is not too far-fetched, I think, to compare this bureaucratic tendency in government with the organization beginning about the same time in industry. Where the royal finances had once been managed by individual magistrates and accountants in their own residences with their small bureaux gathered around them, like small workshop masters with their journeymen and apprentices, the French revolution gathered all the clerks into large buildings like factories, organized them in functional departments with proper division of labour and so transformed public finance into a large-scale modern industry. There was, of course, no steam engine in a ministry to draw all the employees together, but the systems of central records and financial accounts rapidly acquired the characteristics of machines. Many bureaux became dependent on them. Perhaps the most striking change in the structure of the Treasury during the few years after its founding in 1788 was the growth of a central accounting section which had not been included in the original plan. In the ancien régime, there had been small accounting centres attached to separate bureaux but no central accounts. By 1793 the central accounting section had thirty-one employees, and there was a separate director of final accounts. Here was a machine in the service of the state, and certain observers in this and the next generation wrote almost lyrical passages about the effects of double-entry book-keeping in public accounts. The mechanization of public finances was different from the mechanization of industry, of course, and in particular the administrative revolution occurred much more deliberately and rapidly than the industrial revolution and was done by the governments of the French revolution in the general interest rather than by private enterprise for individual profit. It might not, indeed, be too fanciful to imagine that the financial

---

[1] Réal de Curban, *La Science du gouvernement*, vol. III, p. 8.
[2] Anson, *Discours* (10 April 1791), p. 3; Cornus de la Fontaine, *Idées sur l'administration des finances*, An VIII, p. 14; Roederer, *Rapport* (20 Dec. 1790); Sabien Flori, *Le Comité de trésorerie*, p. 63.

aristocracy of the ancien régime had gripped the finances of the monarchy and exploited them in a system of private social enterprise until the revolutionaries nationalized public finances much as later governments nationalized public utilities and railways. At any rate, in the realm of government finance, the French revolution seems to have brought to an end an era of private capitalism and inaugurated an age of public administration.

16

CONCLUSION

I

THE FINANCIAL difficulties facing Louis XVI, which more than anything else first brought his government low, may appear on casual inspection to be only the budgetary difficulties familiar to many governments: insufficient revenue, burdensome expenditure and debt. These difficulties were in the forefront of the debates in the 1780s. Even the most careful study of the eighteenth-century discussions will usually conclude that if the Parlements were wrong in blaming the financial trouble on the waste of funds in war and court spending, then Calonne was probably correct in pointing to the unequal and irrational system of taxation. Calonne's view is the one most historians adopt, but others prefer to go by Turgot's interpretation. He saw the financial problems as being fundamentally economic ones calling for an encouragement of agriculture and trade, and by so doing he revived old Colbertist ideas in the quaint physiocratic form so dear to liberal hearts in the nineteenth century. A free and prosperous economy, ran the argument, will furnish the revenues necessary for those few services which private enterprise may leave to the government. In one form or another, then, a budgetary view of the Crown's financial difficulties—annual deficits cumulating as a debt—dominated the policies of Turgot, Calonne and many of the others of that time, with the result that it also prevails in our history books.

The more we study the monarchical institutions of government finance, however, the more superficial the budgetary view appears. In the first place, we look in vain for the budget which is supposed to have needed balancing: no such thing existed, nor anything like it, until after the revolution, and the very word was foreign, not imported from England until the 1780s. Even the financial accounts required for a modern budgetary control were lacking. The Chamber of Accounts was interested only in the honesty and accuracy of the individual accountant, not in statements of national business. Nor can we find the famous Royal Treasury, forever empty in the history books and in the eighteenth-century memoirs; the two Keepers of the Royal Treasury, one for even-numbered years and the other for odd-numbered years, kept only two caisses (funds) which never received much more than about half of the government's revenues and never made the expenditures which would have appeared in a budget. Hundreds of other caisses received and spent royal funds beyond either the knowledge or the control of the Keepers. As for the Controller General of Finance, his bureaux managed no money themselves but endeavoured to meet all the Crown's commitments by assigning payments to the various caisses of the accountants, tax farms and other agencies. He could exercise no budgetary control over the whole revenue and expenditure because there was no central consolidated revenue fund. The Minister never knew on any particular day, or even in any particular year, exactly how much revenue there was to spend. Much less did he follow the budgetary procedure of planning expenditures for each year, and then finding the ways and means to carry out the plan. Finally, the debt did not in fact accumulate in the form of annual deficits, and the very concept of a deficit, like that of a budget, was a revolutionary idea. The debt merely trickled into the system as did the revenues, half-known, eternal like poverty itself, posing only such problems as government and nation chose to see in it. The ministers and other subjects of Louis XVI gradually came to regard the financial difficulties as major problems of state, dramatized them and even endeavoured to solve them.

Most Bourbon kings had survived debt and bankruptcy; the financial difficulties in the later years of Louis XIII, Louis XIV and Louis XV were probably as bad as those on the eve of the French revolution. Why did the financial troubles of Louis XVI develop into a major crisis? Leaving aside the important economic and political circumstances of depression and rampant sovereign courts, known to every student of the French revolution, we may deduce additional circumstances from our study of financial institutions. Every other financial crisis in the Bourbon monarchy had culminated in a Chamber of Justice, directing public attention towards the accountants, tax farmers and other financiers—not without justification—as profiteers and therefore responsible for the trouble. At the same time Chambers of Justice had provided a convenient legal means for cancelling debts to the financiers and forcibly recovering large sums from them. On the occasion of these Chambers the Crown had taken advantage of the financiers' momentary weakness to make reforms in the financial institutions. Colbert had done this while his Chamber of Justice did its work in the 1660s; the Chamber of 1716–17 had assisted the regent Duke of Orléans to do the same. But during the eighteenth century the Farmers General, Receivers General, Treasurers General, Payers of the rentes and other high accountants had become noble in such large numbers, and merged with the ruling classes to such an extent, that the Crown was in no position to establish a Chamber of Justice against them. The long series of Chambers of Justice came to an end in 1717. True, the debts incurred in New France were drastically reduced after the Seven Years War by means of criminal proceedings against the Intendant Bigot and many others from the colony, but anything of that kind for France itself was politically impossible in view of the social position of the financiers as a class. 'All is lost', Montesquieu wrote prophetically, 'when the lucrative profession of the *traitants* succeeds in becoming an honoured profession by means of its wealth.'[1] Those Finance Ministers who attempted anything in the nature of an attack on the financiers, especially Terray, Turgot and Necker, suffered political defeat and were obliged to retire. It was in these circumstances that the financial trouble ripened into a major crisis.

'La Finance se croyait en possession d'état, comme la noblesse et la magistrature...'[2] In this comment on the ancien régime, Mollien, Napoleon's Treasury Minister, summed up one of the characteristics of the financial administration in which he had served as a *premier commis*. The higher offices had become the private property of accountants and were fast becoming the patrimony of noble families. Accountable only to the Chambers of Accounts, these high financial figures were not part of an administrative hierarchy and not subject to ministerial inspection or command. Most of their income did not come from salaries but from profits on their activities as the Crown's bankers, collecting and spending revenues, lending the government more and more money, and engaging in their own business activities. Loosely organized in professional corps or *compagnies* with committees to review their corporate interests, the financiers exercised a profitable monopoly over the collecting and spending of royal revenues and over the short-term credit business in the system. The short-term advances were in the form of notes, rescriptions, *assignations* and other negotiable instruments which the individual financiers or the corporate body of Farmers General issued on their own private credit. Of course their credit rested ultimately on their official positions, but the Crown nevertheless depended upon their notes for the operations of a system in which most payments could only be made by anticipating future revenue. It was not so much the discounting of expected revenues which put the Crown at the mercy of the financiers, for after all the British government also anticipated revenues by means of short-term credit notes. The trouble in France lay in

---

[1] *L'Esprit des lois*, Livre XIII, ch. XX, 'Des traitants'.
[2] Mollien, *Mémoires* (1898), vol. I, p. 69.

the monopoly which enabled the financiers to exploit the system for their own profit. So powerful was their monopoly that they successfully resisted or perverted all attempts of bankers to move into this field, excluding even two discount banks (*caisses d'escompte*) which might have developed into semi-public institutions discounting credit notes at low rates of interest, as the Bank of England did.

The class of financiers, their upper ranks moving in noble circles, engaged in collecting, spending and lending for the royal government as private entrepreneurs, not as salaried officials. Finance Ministers and others who observed the system recognized the profit motive as the principal incentive in it. Even in their very positions as venal accountants and tax farmers, the financiers were private businessmen because they customarily borrowed the capital purchase-price (*finance*) of their offices and paid interest on it to their creditors. Their royal offices were often only part of their total business assets. Nothing prevented them from also investing in profitable real-estate schemes or in industry, as some of them did, and like private businessmen they sometimes went bankrupt. In that event they customarily suffered prosecution by a *Cour des aides* on behalf of their creditors, by a Chamber of Accounts on the Crown's behalf, and sometimes by the Châtelet or criminal court as well. In the operations of this financial system we can find no clear distinction between private funds and public funds, between private businessmen and government officials, or between personal and public affairs. Those distinctions were first drawn in the French revolution.

But at least ten years before the revolution, even if we date it from 1787, informed observers could see that unless the royal government recovered the control of its own financial processes by subjecting them to a system of public administration, then no basic reforms could be carried out and no real improvements in the Crown's financial position established. In 1770, about the same time that the Chancellor, Maupeou, launched his attack on the sovereign courts, the Finance Minister, Terray, inaugurated a decade of ministerial endeavours to wrest control of the financial system from the accountants and tax farmers. He suppressed a number of offices, beginning with the Payers of the defunct sovereign courts, and tried to rationalize the receiving system by making the lower *Receveurs particuliers* responsible to the Receivers General instead of to the Chambers of Accounts. His successor in office, Turgot, seems to have been sympathetic with this work, but he accomplished very little, and the most determined and successful of the reformers turned out to be Jacques Necker. Necker's complicated and intelligent work has too often appeared in the history books as petty economizing. One of his purposes was to 'nationalize' the management of Crown funds by replacing the independent, venal financiers with salaried and dependent financial officers organized in *régies*.[1] He actually got as far as to suppress most of the fifty powerful Receivers General before he was politically defeated and forced to retire in 1781. Another of Necker's policies was to establish more rigorous ministerial control over the financial system by requiring more and better financial statements to the Department of Finance and by rationalizing that Department in a bureaucratic manner.

The famous *Contrôle général des finances*, or Finance Department, was not bureaucratic, and only after Necker had tried to make it so did his critics begin to complain about *bureaucratie* in the modern sense of the term. The word *bureau* was ambiguous in the ancien régime, for it could mean both a royal commission or minor council, such as the *Almanach royal* listed in large numbers, and also a minister's or magistrate's group of clerks, which is the meaning more familiar to us. We must therefore be careful to recognize that when a jurist such as Charles Loyseau used the term *bureaucratie*, he had in mind the rule of royal commissions or councils rather than that of executive bureaux in ministerial departments.[2] It is the more modern sense of the word, however, which applies to the influence of Necker and the revolutionary National Assembly upon the financial administration. For Necker deliberately dismissed the powerful, venal Intendants of Finance in his Department and began to work directly with the *premiers commis* of the bureaux. By removing the independent, venal magistrates in favour of dependent, salaried administrators he was at the same time integrating the Department and giving the bureaux more power. Furthermore, to remove the Intendants of Finance from their positions at the head of the bureaux was to carry out a tiny social revolution, for most of them were noblemen. The Department of Finance was normally a little aristocracy. When Necker put the *premiers commis*, merely successful clerks like himself, at the head of some of the bureaux he was taking steps to make the Department of Finance bureaucratic, and ten years later the National Assembly completed this process. So far as the system was bureaucratic, it was able to deny the financiers their profits, at least for a few years. Many financiers hated Necker as a banker, and banker he was, but they also hated him as the first organizer of the revolutionary bureaucracy which was later to assume control of the financial system in the name of the nation. Before

---

[1] For an explanation of the *régie*, see above, p. 121.
[2] This confusion is apparent in, for instance, Pierre Legendre, 'Evolution des systèmes d'administration et histoire des idées: l'exemple de la pensée française', *Annali della Fondazione Italiana per la Storia amministrativa* (Milan), vol. III (1966), p. 256.

the National Assembly took up Necker's work, however, there were to be six years of reactionary efforts after his fall in 1781.

The Finance Ministers of those reactionary years, Joly de Fleury, Lefèvre d'Ormesson (one of the former Intendants of Finance whom Necker had dismissed) and especially Calonne, restored the noble, venal magistrates to their commanding positions as heads of divisions in the Department of Finance and even increased their numbers. The reaction went much further, however, than departmental reorganization. The Receivers General of Finance and a number of other venal accountants recovered their lost offices. Necker's new bureaucratic arrangements largely disintegrated. Whereas Necker had supervised the Crown's financial business with the aid of his *Premier commis des finances*, Bertrand Dufresne, and for the purpose of reducing the freedom and private profit of the financiers, the reactionary Ministers worked instead with various financiers as advisers. The common policy of Joly de Fleury and Calonne was to restore the private-enterprise system of caisses and accountants and to make it work successfully. Calonne, indeed, had deep personal commitments to the system and to the social group of aristocratic financiers to which both of his wives and many of his friends and relatives belonged. He therefore endeavoured to draw public attention away from the financial administration, and in the famous reforms he prepared for the Assembly of Notables (1787) he dealt mainly with questions of tax reform. Desirable though it was to rationalize the various taxes, Calonne's plan, if adopted and implemented, would almost certainly have had the effect of strengthening the system of caisses and accountants with its pernicious private management of public funds. This did not happen because the Notables did not adopt Calonne's programme. Calonne suffered political defeat and retired, and a financial crisis drew public attention to the shortcomings of the system of caisses and accountants.

The crisis consisted mainly of five notorious bankruptcies among the major accountants, including a Treasurer General for War, a Treasurer General for the Marine, a Receiver General of Finance and two others only slightly less prominent. Of course these were by no means the first bankruptcies, but they occurred at the worst possible time for Calonne, during the first six months of the year 1787, before, during and after the meeting of the Assembly of Notables in which he revealed more of the Crown's debts and difficulties than the public had hitherto suspected. We now believe we recognize the financial crisis, in which other accountants, too, tottered on the brink of failure, as an event in the economic recession of those troubled years, but the observing public and the sovereign courts who prosecuted the unfortunate financiers did not doubt that the bankruptcies were entirely fraudulent. The Crown certainly lost a good deal of money in them. Even before the last of them had occurred, the Archbishop of Aix, Boisgelin de Cucé, had induced the Assembly of Notables to endorse a memorandum on the need for reform in the system of caisses and accountants and in particular a consolidation of caisses or, as we might say, an amalgamation of the revenue funds. If this memorandum excited little comment among the pamphleteers of the time (and less among the historians since), it nevertheless expressed one of the policies of that trio of archbishops which helped to bring down Calonne in May 1787 and to replace him soon afterwards with one of their own number, Loménie de Brienne.[1]

He is probably the most misunderstood Finance Minister of the reign, for much the same reasons that Necker is misunderstood, because it was Necker's work which he took up after the six years of reaction against it. To say nothing of Brienne's personal admiration for Necker, three policies marked him as Necker's successor in the field of administrative reform. First, he suppressed many financial offices, notably that of the Receiver General of the *Revenus casuels*, at the very heart of the venal system, the accountant who actually sold the royal offices. Secondly, in March 1788, Brienne accomplished the extraordinary feat of combining the two Keepers of the Royal Treasury with the two Treasurers General for the major spending departments for War and Marine, and another Treasurer General for miscellaneous and debt payments, these five accountants henceforth to be the administrators of an organized Royal Treasury. This was a logical step following Necker's earlier consolidation of many other Treasurers' posts to make the larger posts of Treasurer General, and this organized Treasury soon became the greatest instrument of the revolution in public finance. Thirdly, Loménie de Brienne tried unsuccessfully to issue public credit notes to circulate in place of the private notes he was obliged to suspend in August 1788. His suspension of payments was interpreted at the time simply as a royal 'bankruptcy'; in fact it was a precocious attempt to replace private short-term credit with national or public credit. As Brienne himself remarked later, the National Assembly finally accomplished much the same reform less than three years afterwards.

The National Assembly, in large majority, did not like the financial system precisely because it was in the hands of profit-seeking capitalists—they used that word—and in this respect the debt seemed to them to be the worst feature of a bad system. The parts of the debt which stood condemned in their eyes were those owing to financiers: short-term credit notes of all

---

[1] The third member of the group was Champion de Cicé.

kinds, private capital investments in venal offices, and in fact, all except the rentes. The better to protect and to pay the rentes, the Assembly set out to do away with all the Crown's obligations to venal office-holders, especially financiers. But the very credit system itself, not merely those particular debts, became the object of reform. When the Assembly realized that paper credit notes of some kind were a necessity and that the rescriptions, *assignations* and accountant's notes could not be abolished without being replaced, the majority refused to make the capitalistic *Caisse d'escompte* into a national bank with the privilege of renting its private credit to the government. Instead the Assembly created a national agency, the *Caisse de l'extraordinaire*, to issue notes—the *assignats*—backed by a national guarantee rather than by private credit. On the same principles the Assembly kept under public control the sale of clerical and royal property confiscated to pay the national debts. Calonne, Dupont de Nemours and other conservative defenders of the old financial system were voted down by a majority determined to free the national finances from private financial exploitation. The parliamentary forces imbued with the new principles of nationalism were composed of provincial representatives brought into the Assembly in the elections of 1789. They were only too anxious, once Mirabeau, Custine and others had made the issues clear, to exert the crushing weight of their numbers to thwart the ambitions of Parisian financial interests, whether of bankers or financiers. Until the end of 1789 and perhaps even longer, the bankers Lecouteulx, Delessert, Boscary, Laborde and many others who had assisted in the capture of the Bastille and other such early revolutionary activities, appeared to have won a great victory over the accountants and Farmers General.[1] It was a Pyrrhic victory. The Assembly snatched the spoils from them by voting again and again for national management of public finances. There were still fortunes to be made at public expense, especially after war broke out in April 1792, but no longer by lodging in the very fibre of the administration, as the accountants and tax farmers had done under the ancien régime.

The National Assembly planned to guard the public finances by bureaucratic organization. With a vision of mechanical efficiency and articulation, systems of clock-like checks and balances such as eighteenth-century Frenchmen found everywhere, even in nature itself, the revolutionary planners hoped to prevent corruption, putting their faith in the virtues of

---

[1] For their connection with the capture of the Bastille, Albert Mathiez, 'Les capitalistes et la prise de la Bastille', *La Révolution française* (1926), pp. 578–82; and Edouard Vellay, 'Les agents de change et la prise de la Bastille', *L'Intermédiaire des chercheurs et curieux* (Jan. 1956), pp. 26–30; (1955), pp. 103, 289, 408 and 623.

organization to offset the vices of individual men. This hope was at the very heart of the financial revolution. Instead of several hundred separate caisses (funds) in the hands of independent, profit-seeking accountants and tax farmers, France was to have a consolidated central fund in a bureaucratic Treasury composed only of salaried officials performing their duties according to a rational plan of functions. The Treasury grew and grew over the revolutionary years, absorbing the other caisses one after another. The Assembly demanded lists of employees, salaries and operating expenses, and arranged for full annual accounts such as the monarchy never had. Meanwhile the old Department of Finance disintegrated—if such a term may be applied to the dissolution of so incoherent a Department—and most of its bureaux were incorporated in the Treasury and the new Ministries for the Interior and for Public Contributions. In addition there soon appeared a temporary administration for retiring irregular debts and winding up all the business of the ancien régime. All these new agencies took over whole bureaux from the ancien régime and whenever necessary organized new bureaux with the clerks from the defunct tax farms, Receiver Generalships and the like. In the financial administration, at least, it seems clear that the mass of lowly clerks moved successfully from the old régime to the new. But not so their noble, venal superiors, the magistrates and accountants. Some of them moved successfully upward into ministerial ranks, but most of them dropped out of the administration altogether. What they had known as an aristocratic system, based on personal position in a social hierarchy, became a bureaucracy with an administrative hierarchy in which the organization of public functions took precedence over the claims of individual officials.

These administrative changes occurred together with social changes. Which of them, if any, were fundamental? The prevailing view of the French revolution is that it was fundamentally a struggle between two social classes, a capitalistic bourgeoisie defeating a feudal nobility. In this view, it would be respectable to conclude that the administrative changes were wrought by a triumphant bourgeois class.[1] We might make a *prima facie* argument for this conclusion by citing the role of Necker, the Third Estate and other commoners in the revolutionary work of administrative

---

[1] This is the general interpretation of that great school of historians inspired by the ideas and the personality of Georges Lefebvre, and it is the most scholarly and convincing general interpretation which we have. The late Professor Alfred Cobban, in his book *The Social Interpretation of the French Revolution* (Cambridge, 1964) and subsequent articles, has identified the social interpretation as an orthodoxy holding sway in the scholarly world and has shown it to have many inconsistencies and weaknesses. He did not make the mistake, however, of supposing this interpretation to be a house of cards, or a system of errors, which would collapse easily. Neither, I hope, do I.

reform. Were they perhaps imposing the standards of a modern business firm upon the system of government finance? This line of argument is plausible enough, so far as it goes, but to establish it firmly we should have to ignore or explain away too many awkward facts: the explicitly anti-capitalist decisions of the National Assembly, inspired by a desire to drive the capitalists out of the sphere of national public finance; the royalist and socially conservative views of so many reformers who were hoping to regenerate the royal administration more or less on the English model; and the widely held principle of protecting the general interest against private interests, a principle which royalists like Bertrand Dufresne shared with Jacobins like Pierre-Joseph Cambon. None of these facts will fit properly into the social interpretation which has become standard.

The most awkward fact is that the French revolutionaries transformed the system of government finances from a capitalism into a bureaucracy. Contrary to the standard view, groups of private entrepreneurs gave way to groups of officials. The old accountants and tax farmers were not officials at all; in eighteenth-century terms they were capitalists as much as the bankers were. Commonly referred to as *financiers, traitants* or *gens d'affaires*, they had for centuries engaged in private enterprise in the realm of public finance. How could we fit them into our present-day social interpretation? To which of the classes would they belong if the French revolution were indeed a victory of a capitalistic bourgeoisie over a feudal nobility? We could hardly count these defeated and dispersed *financiers* among the triumphant bourgeoisie. There were less than a dozen of them in the National Assembly. The Assembly deliberately trampled on their interests. However, still less could we see them as part of a defeated 'feudal' class because the government finances which they exploited were certainly not part of a 'feudal' landed economy. To regard the *financiers* as merely the lackeys of the landed nobility would be to contradict the foregoing chapters in which I have tried to show that they often became noblemen themselves and at the same time they borrowed and invested, bought and sold, like modern businessmen. Their royal offices were business assets as well as rungs on the social ladder into the noble class. Furthermore, this capitalistic system of government finances became bureaucratic in the French revolution— the very opposite of what would have been necessary to satisfy the standard social interpretation. In short, we can hardly see the subject of this book as part of a class struggle, as it is usually defined, unless we stand well away from the facts and equip ourselves with a dogmatic belief that political and administrative changes are necessarily only functions of social events. The standard social interpretation finds little support in this book, after all, and could only be brought into it as a *deus ex machina* forcing artificial conclusions by an act of intellectual imperialism.

This is only to say that I have come to different conclusions. And these last remarks are intended only as a defence against the social interpretation, not as an attack on it. Without pretending to challenge that reigning view on such frail evidence as these chapters contain, I think that in the transformation of the financial system something happened that was more fundamental than the victory of one social class over another. This was the invention of an administrative weapon for social and political domination. Nearly every régime in the quarter century from 1770 to 1795—and many régimes thereafter—assisted in perfecting the financial bureaucracy, which was an invention, like the highly organized army, that no government could afford to ignore. With its flexible hierarchy of command, its division of labour, its central records, its double-entry book-keeping systems, and its mechanical efficiency, the new bureaucratic administration was capable of mobilizing the financial resources of the nation to a degree Louis XIV could hardly have imagined. The French revolution built a national business machine out of men and paper, not the first in Europe, certainly, yet so far improved that it furnished the wealth necessary for twenty years of war against nearly the whole of Europe.[1] The analogous process in the realm of manufacturing has been described as part of an 'industrial revolution'. In France, the industry of government underwent a revolution much earlier, more suddenly, more completely and on a larger scale than any branch of manufacturing at the time. Only changes in the industry of war could compare with it.[2]

II

No one will suppose even for a moment that the French revolution resolved all the financial problems of the Bourbon monarchy or that by 1795 the central administration of finances had reached a stage of impeccable efficiency. Neither in the parliamentary speeches nor in the records of institutions are there any grounds for such conclusions. If the foregoing chapters seem to have a whiggish air of progress onward and upward, this is not because their subject lacks the complexity and ambiguity to be found in the lives of men and in the usual course of public affairs. It is because, in trying

[1] Very probably the English and Prussian methods of mobilizing the wealth of the nation for the purposes of the government were well in advance of the French except during the revolution.

[2] The 'industries' of government and war are obviously closely associated but the connection between them, and indeed this whole line of speculation, can have little place in this volume.

to make my thesis clear, I have said both less and more than would be necessary in a full history of French finances during that age: less of what is in other books with other interpretations, and more of those themes which seem to me both fundamental and widely misunderstood. To René Stourm, Marcel Marion and others, financial history was mainly about adjusting taxes and balancing budgets.[1] Consequently, their books are full of the efforts of each succeeding régime to overcome fiscal and budgetary difficulties. I have been trying to show that those efforts had their place within a framework of administrative arrangements and that seen in this light the financial history of France is mainly the story of a struggle between private or personal interests, on the one hand, and on the other hand, the general or public interest. In this light, furthermore, the French revolution was a triumph of the general interest over selfish private ones; the revolutionary governments imposed a national bureaucracy upon a financial system hitherto dominated by private financiers and other businessmen.

To show the twenty years of the reign of Louis XVI and the revolution to best advantage in this field, the historian ought perhaps to write the financial history of the next twenty years as well. He would find, I suspect, that the Directory, the Consulate and the Empire were slowly reverting to the administrative arrangements of the ancien régime. In the winds of those troubled years many straws blow in the same direction. The First Republic had fought its wars by government or public enterprise, and by patriotism, as Camille Richard has shown in the sphere of war supplies and equipment.[2] But after Thermidor, he writes, 'patriotic enthusiasm and the revolutionary spirit declined simultaneously. The progressive ruin of institutions born during the Terror deprived the government of the means for action and for constraint which had permitted it to overcome the resistance of private egotism.' It was Barras, the thermidorean, who first brought the great capitalist, Ouvrard, into the service of the government.[3] Ouvrard tells how the Directory invited him to debate the question of whether the Navy could be more efficiently supplied by a government *régie* or by a private enterprise. As late as 1797, naval supplies were still being managed by a revolutionary *régie*, but then the Directory decided to let Ouvrard manage the system privately under the title of *munitionnaire général* in the manner of the ancien régime.[4] The Directory period saw, in the words of a modern historian:

[1] Stourm, *Les Finances de l'ancien régime* (1885); and Marion, *Histoire financière* (1914). These are the standard works on the subject.
[2] Richard, *Le Comité de salut public et les fabrications de guerre* (1922); the quotation is on p. 798.   [3] Gabriel-Julien Ouvrard, *Mémoires sur sa vie*, vol. I, p. 24.
[4] Ouvrard, *Mémoires*, vol. I, p. 256.

the interests of the state and private interests confront one another, combine inextricably with corruption, fraud, unreasonable profits...Under the Directory and even under the Consulate the couple government–supply merchants evokes another couple: that of the monarchy at the end of the ancien régime and of its financiers and *rentiers*. This recourse to supply merchants was a scarcely disguised form of borrowing.[1]

Military supplies were, however, less of an encroachment on the public sector than, say, the collection of taxes or the paying of the rentes. Under the Empire, the biggest supply-merchants such as Ouvrard, Vanderberghe and Michel the elder, were moving towards that field, or so it seems, when they extended credit and other financial services to the government on such a scale and with such profits to themselves that their story reads like a chapter from the reign of Louis XIV.

This disastrous result (a minister reported to the Council in 1806), stems from a cumulation of business and public functions: we see them [Ouvrard etc.] at the same time figure as acknowledged agents of the Spanish government engaged in supplying naval food and munitions and as *faiseurs de services* to that same government; as *faiseurs de services* for the Public Treasury and as suppliers to the armies and navies of France. Unhappy assemblage! Incompatible functions! Frightful ramification of business![2]

Bonaparte went much further still in restoring the ancien régime. He enlarged the sphere of cooperation with bankers and relied upon their private credit. His Council of Finance, like those of the Bourbons, was in great measure a ways and means committee, seeking expedients. Napoleon and his ministers used and abused businessmen just as the Bourbons had done, and they even had the classic Bourbon contempt for the *faiseurs d'affaires* on whom they depended.[3] Like the Bourbons before him, Bonaparte mortgaged a whole range of public assets.

The *rentes foncières*, payments to the government for the purchase of nationalized property, served him as security for paper rescriptions with which he paid supply merchants.[4] The revolution had done away with that form of government debt and it had also abolished short-term debt in the form of venal offices and surety bonds (*cautionnements*). The receivers and spenders of public funds therefore had no claims on the revolutionary

---

[1] Louis Bergeron, 'Profits et risques dans les affaires parisiennes à l'époque du directoire et du consulat', *Annales historiques de la révolution française*, vol. 38 (1966), p. 370.

[2] Napoléon I, *Lettres au Comte Mollien, ministre du trésor public* (Havana, Cuba, 1959), p. 393: Mollien to the Conseil, 17 Feb. 1806.

[3] Stourm, *Les Finances du Consulat* (1902), p. 61.

[4] *Ibid.* p. 69.

government, their employer, except for their salaries. This was a triumph of revolution. It was, indeed, a revolution in itself. To have maintained such a salutary independence of the managers of public funds would have accorded well with Bonaparte's hope to preserve all that was best in the revolution, but instead he began to revert to the methods of the ancien régime from the moment he took power.[1] On 24 Brumaire, An VIII, only a matter of days after the famous *coup d'état* bringing the Consulate to power, Bonaparte proposed to create *soumissions des Receveurs généraux*, obligatory subscriptions of about 10% of the sums which the Receivers General collected. This was very roughly equivalent to the purchase-price of an office of Receiver General under Louis XVI, and these subscriptions formed a total capital debt of nearly 11 million francs. Each Receiver General was also ordered at this time to give the government a number of signed rescriptions redeemable in a fixed period of months, just as under the ancien régime. Finally, to guarantee the redemption of these rescriptions, Napoleon set up a central fund, the *Caisse de garantie et d'amortissement* independently of the Treasury. As René Stourm observes, this was nothing but a restoration of the old Bourbon system, stopping short of the full venal system by which the Receivers General would have actually possessed their offices.[2] The results, too, were much the same, because the Receivers General became state bankers much as before, and for their advances the imperial government began to pay very heavily.[3] Going on to further reactionary steps in the same direction, the Consulate demanded surety bonds from all *régisseurs*, administrators, payers and *caissiers* and even from notaries and common employees. By the end of the Consulate the capital fund of this debt to government employees had reached a total value of about 40 million francs and in 1814 it stood at no less than 100 millions.[4]

As under the Bourbon monarchy, private interests seem to have begun to sap the very fibre of public institutions. Marion tells us, under the head, 'Napoléon capitaliste', how Bonaparte accumulated large sums personally in the manner of the Bourbons and their ministers, and like Louis XV he felt no obligation to invest in the loans opened by his own government. In 1810 Bonaparte put nearly a million francs into a Prussian state loan and fretted about getting the highest possible return on this investment. In 1811 he put over three millions in a Saxon loan. True, the latter was indirectly for the purpose of furthering Polish preparations to invade Russia. But Bonaparte's objectives are not the point at issue: he, like the

---

[1] *Ibid.*, p. 95.
[2] *Ibid.*, p. 195.
[3] *Ibid.*, pp. 206 and 211.
[4] *Ibid.*, pp. 96–101.

Bourbons, could be expected to identify his private interests with those of his empire. The point is that he was creating a financial system more and more at the mercy of private interests. Like the Bourbons, he tended to confuse public funds with private. His system, like the Bourbon system, sustained a class of rich capitalist-noblemen. From time to time he could bully these *notables* to the profit of the government, as the Bourbons had done, but the system as a whole seems to have been moving back towards the primitive arrangements of the ancien régime. René Stourm tells us that the Restoration governments had to begin all over again to fashion a system of public administration.[1]

That said, we need only glance through the *Almanach national* and the *Almanach impérial* to see that a very large bureaucracy continuously served the Directory, the Consulate and the Empire. At no stage after the revolution, even in the years 1795–1815, did the Treasury and the Finance Department lose their virtue as public agencies to such an extent as to sink to the condition they had been in during the ancien régime. Tycoons like Ouvrard never won such a total and intimate command of the finances as the accountants and tax farmers of the eighteenth century had held, and indeed never developed into such a class. The spectre of venality and other forms of personal power seem to have threatened the public bureaucracy under the imperial régime; yet even with its new aristocratic hierarchy crowned with the Emperor's new dynasty, France nevertheless continued to maintain the consolidated revenue fund which the revolution had made. Bonaparte even created a new post of minister for the Treasury; the first Minister was Bertrand Dufresne, Necker's *Premier commis des finances* in the years 1776–81, and when he died in 1801, he was replaced by Nicolas-François Mollien who in the 1780s had served as a *premier commis* in the *Bureaux des impositions*. True, their task was to find money to pay for their master's imperial projects, a task familiar enough to the Finance Ministers of the ancien régime only twenty years before and odious to the National Assembly of 1789. Bonaparte no doubt perverted the revolutionary bureaucracy to his own personal ambitions. But at least he maintained the bureaucracy. Furthermore, he departed from the ancien régime as well as from the revolution in creating a central bank, the Bank of France, which he was free to do since there was no class of venal accountants and tax farmers standing in the way. Again, war and other imperial commitments sowed confusion in the processes of collecting and spending, yet the machinery for public accounts and control never ceased to work at producing statements of public business and final accounts. No Chamber of Accounts and no venal

[1] *Ibid.*, p. 338.

317

tax farmers or accountants prevented the imperial government from supervising its own financial processes. When the administrative reformers of the Restoration, Baron Louis and Villèle, began their work, enough of the revolutionary bureaucracy remained so that they did not need another revolution to found a system of public finance.

A LIST OF TREASURERS, TREASURERS GENERAL AND RECEIVERS GENERAL

Throughout this book I have continually referred to the accountants as a group. I could not encumber the text and notes with their names, offices and relationships, however, except for the few needed as examples in the course of description and argument. Most of them, even those holding major offices, do not appear by name. This list of 276 men is intended to identify two of the most important groups of accountants and in an elementary way to give substance to my general references to them. At the same time, for those names which do appear in the foregoing chapters, the reader may find it convenient to refer to an alphabetical catalogue such as this one.

This is by no means a complete list. More than one volume would be needed to identify all the *Payeurs des rentes*, *Receveurs des tailles*, *Receveurs des domaines et bois*, *Payeurs* of the various sovereign courts, *Contrôleurs* and others engaged in the system. Besides, information about accountants is not easy to find. For this list I have drawn on a variety of sources, mainly the manuscript registers of the 'V' and 'P' series in the Archives Nationales, Paris. Most of the dates come from the official *lettres de provision*. The reader may also refer to the splendid lists of magistrates edited by François Bluche; many families of accountants appear in them.

Key to Symbols

(date–date)	dates of birth or baptism and death	FG	Farmer General
		f.	father
RG	Receiver General of Finance	m.	mother
R	Receiver	s.	son
TG	Treasurer General of Finance	d.	daughter
T	Treasurer	w.	wife
Secr.	Secretary		

Anson, Pierre-Hubert (11 June 1744–1810): *commis* and *premier commis* in Dept. of Finance from 1767; RG Grenoble from 17 Dec. 1784 after Barbault de Glatigny; elected to National Assembly 1789.

Auguié, Pierre-César (25 Dec. 1738–?): RG Lorraine & Barrois from 12 Dec. 1781.

Auzillon de Berville, François-Louis (20 March 1734–?): TG Ligues Suisses, Grisons & Alliés from 23 June 1762; his f., Louis-Claude held the office for twenty-nine years and died 21 Jan. 1754.

Bailly, Jean-Claude: TG Ligues Suisses, Grisons & Alliés; Secr. at Dept. of Foreign Affairs; Secr. du Roi from 20 March 1783.

Barbaut (or Barbault) de Glatigny, Louis-Claude-Marthe (27 Jan. 1725– 4 Oct. 1783): RG Bourges from 15 June 1768; RG Grenoble from 1 May 1782; simultaneously régisseur for Poudres & Salpêtres; his w., Adrienne-Félicité Couet, was d. of Pierre-Antoine Couet and Anne-Félicité Barbaut.

Barjac de Renneville, Honoré-Joseph (26 Dec. 1726–?): TG Maison du Roi from 17 Feb. 1756 after Augustine-Bouret de Villaumont.

Baron, Louis-Jacques (7 March 1732–?): RG Burgundy from 14 Nov. 1781, 'Ecuyer, nôtre Conseiller receveur en la Chancellerie près notre cour de Parlement de Bezançon et Notaire honoraire à Paris.'

Batailhe de Francès, Jean-Fauste: RG Soissons from 3 June 1741 after Etienne-Charles-Félix Lallemant de Nantouillet; Secr. du Roi.

Batailhe de Francès, Jean (28 May 1722–1784): avocat au Parlement; écuyer; RG Soissons from 10 Dec. 1778 after his f., Jean-Fauste; his heirs (listed A.N., P. 2841) included Jacques, ambassador to London, Louis-François Bat. de Fr. de Montval, écuyer, Jean-Joseph Bat. de Fr. d'Aville, écuyer, Elisabèthe-Sabine-Josèphe married to Louis-Augustin Blondel (écuyer, Councillor of State), Marie-Claude married to Jean-Claude Douet (écuyer, FG), Jeanne-Marguerite widow of Nicolas Durand de Villegagnon, and Charlotte-Françoise Bat. de Fr. Précy.

Batailhe de Françès d'Aville, Jean-Joseph (2 March 1738–?): écuyer; RG Soissons from 7 July 1784 after his f., Jean.

Baudard de Saint James, Claude (7 May 1738–3 July 1787): T for Colonies de l'Amérique from 31 Jan. 1758 by letters of dispense d'âge after his f., Georges-Nicolas Baud. de Vaudesir; TG de la Marine from 1 Jan. 1783; went bankrupt Feb. 1787; his s., Alphonse.

Baudard de Vaudesir, Georges-Nicolas (?–20 Jan. 1771): T for Colonies de l'Amérique from 8 Jan. 1753 after Jean-Baptiste-Jacques Boucher; concurrently R des Tailles at Angers; his w., Marguerite-Catherine Baudry; d., Marie married Jean-Maurice de Faventines, écuyer and FG; s., Claude Baud. de Saint James.

Beaugéard, Pierre-Martin: T des Etats de Bretagne from 1777.

Beaujon, Nicolas (1 March 1718–1786): RG La Rochelle from 5 March 1756 after Gratien Drouilhet; RG Rouen from 12 Dec. 1781; court banker; brother of Jean-Nicolas Beaujon du Seilhon; uncle of Jacques-Bernard de Balan and Catherine de Balan.

Begon, Jean-Baptiste (21 Dec. 1706–?): R des Tailles at Vendôme; RG Montauban from 23 Dec. 1746 after Pierre Duquesnoy; sold the office in 1771 to Mel de Saint Céran for 770,000 livres.

Beranger, Jean-Louis-Loiseau (?–1785): T 'de feu Philippe Orléans'; FG.

Bergeret, Pierre-Jacques-Onesime (8 June 1715–21 Feb. 1785): RG Montauban from 26 Aug. 1741 after Charles-François-Michel Damblerieux; w., Jeanne Viguier; s., Pierre-Jacques; s., Jean-Marie Bergeret de Talmont; d., Josephe-Claudine-Pierette; his f. was a FG for over twenty years.

Bergeret, Pierre-Jacques (24 Oct. 1742–?): RG Montauban from 6 April 1785 after his f.

Bernard de Marville, Charles-Claude (?–17 Feb. 1782): RG Amiens from 1754; two sisters: Anne-Charlotte, w. of Gaspard-Louis Rouillé d'Orfeuille and Marguerite-Félicité, w. of Louis-Agathon de Flavigny.

Bernard de Montigny, Charles: RG Amiens from 4 Aug. 1741 after Jean-Simon Mouffle, *Conseiller secr. maison couronne et finances.*

Bertin, Pierre-Vincent: RG des Revenus Casuels; f. of Louis-Charles and Pierre-Nicolas.

Bertin, Pierre-Nicolas: RG des Revenus Casuels until 1730; s. of Pierre-Vincent; brother of Louis-Charles.

Bertin de Blagny, Louis-Charles (1695–1742): Master of Requests; RG des Revenus Casuels from 1730 to 1742; s. of Pierre-Vincent; f. of Auguste-Louis.

Bertin, Auguste-Louis (7 July 1725–?): RG des Revenus Casuels from 23 Nov. 1742 after his f., Louis-Charles; *lettres de dispense d'âge* 15 Nov. 1742; *arrêt du Conseil* of 24 Oct. 1742 authorized *lettres de commission* of 31 Oct. 1742 for him to finish his father's *exercices*; his *lettres de provision* say that his uncle, Pierre-Nicolas, and his grandfather, Pierre-Vincent, held the office for fifty-two years between them and that his f., Louis-Charles, held it for thirteen years; *lettres de survivance* for the office 31 Dec. 1786 for Joseph-François-Xavier de Prestre de Seneste; did Auguste-Louis hold the office at the time of suppression in Nov. 1787, or did a certain Simon Bertin from the War bureaux hold it, as we are told in A.N., F⁴ 1038?

Blondel de Gagny, Augustin (?–1776): T de la Caisse générale des Amortissements 1749 to 10 July 1776; his s. Barthélemy-Augustin Blondel d'Azaincourt married Catherine-Charlotte Edmée de la Haye; his d., Anne-Henriette; owned a great collection of paintings.

Boisneuf, Pierre-Adrien (1726–?): R des Capitations de la Cour until 1 Jan. 1776.

Boissière, Isaac-Pierre: T des Finances de Bretagne.

Bollioud, François-David, seigneur de Saint Jullien: R du Clergé de France from 1739.

Bonneval, Louis-Charles-Michel de: T de la Maison 'de la feu Reine' until 1779.

Borde, Jean-Benjamin de la (5 Sept. 1734–?): RG Poitiers from 28 Dec. 1757 after Philippes-Guillaume Tavernier de Boullongne.

Boubée de Broquens, Gabriel-Joseph (12 Sept. 1747–?): RG for Châlons from 28 Aug. 1776 after François-Abraham-Marie Mouchard.

Boucher, Jean-Baptiste-Jacques: T des Colonies françaises de l'Amérique from 4 Jan. 1750.

Boula de Charny, François-Gaillot (?–4 May 1778): T Ecuries et Livrées du Roi for the provinces of Normandy, Limousin and Auvergne.

Boula d'Orville, Augustin-Marie (11 March 1757–?): T Ecuries et Livrées du Roi from 27 May 1778 after his uncle (above).

Bourboulon, Antoine (3 May 1737–?): TG des Maisons et Finances de la comtesse d'Artois from 16 Sept. 1773; *Intendant et Contrôleur général de l'Argenterie, Menus plaisirs*, etc. from 17 Aug. 1775; TG de la comtesse d'Artois by letters patent from the comte d'Artois 19 Feb. 1780 confirmed by royal letters patent 15 March 1780, at a *finance* of 300,000 livres; went bankrupt from 5 March 1787 and fled to England.

Bourdeille, Paul Fayard du: RG Grenoble from 1759 to 1780; RG Amiens from 1782.

Bouret de Valleroche, Antoine-François (29 Nov. 1711–?): RG Riom from 24 April 1752 after Paul Delpeche who died 22 Nov. 1751.

Bouret de Vezelay, Jacques-Louis-Guillaume (2 Oct. 1733–1777): T de l'Artillerie et du Génie from 15 Jan. 1766 after Gabriel Michel.

Bourgault Ducoudray, Jacques-Etienne: R des fonds des pauvres communautés de filles religieuses; went bankrupt 1779 and replaced by Labé de Morambert; his w., Marie-Anne-Charlotte L'Herbette.

Bourgevin de Norville, Louis-Paul (5 March 1717–29 Dec. 1769): T de la Police de Paris from 14 Aug. 1752 after Jacques-François L'Artois; went bankrupt 1769 and his office passed to Rouillé de l'Etang; his f. a T de la Maréchaussée; two sons, Charles-Louis and Charles-Pierre.

Boutin, Simon-Charles (8 Oct. 1719–?): RG Tours from 19 Aug. 1746; TG de la Marine from 31 Dec. 1780 after Baudard de Saint James; his f., Simon, was RG from 1722.

Brodelet, Jean-Louis: T de la Guerre and *Administrateur Général de la Caisse de Poissy*; Secr. du Roi 17 Nov. 1787.

Bureau de Serandey, Philippe-Alexis: RG Châlons until his death when the office passed to Gigot d'Orcy on 23 June 1773.

Cadeau, Jacques-Paul (8 Jan. 1724–?): *Payeur des Secrétaires du Roi* from 24 March 1779; went bankrupt 23 June 1773.

Cahouet de Villers, Pierre-Louis-René: T de la Maison du Roi from 18 Dec. 1771 until July 1779 when the office suppressed.

Caron, Jean-François: T du Marc d'Or; went bankrupt 13 Jan. 1779; replaced by Le Normand de Flaghac 28 Dec. 1779; his f., Jean-François; his w., Jean-Antoinette Clouet; his s., Antoine-Louis; sister, Catherine-Gabrielle Caron.

Chanorier, Hughes-Eustache (18 Feb. 1704–1771): RG Auch from Dec. 1761 after Bénigne-André Le Gendre de Villemorin.

Chanorier, Jean (16 Nov. 1746–?): RG Auch from 30 Jan. 1771 after his f., Hughes-Eustache.

Chastel, Charles (30 July 1714–?): T de l'Artillerie et Génie from 23 Feb. 1774; one s., Claude-François.

Chastel, Claude-François: RG Moulins; ceded the office to Chastel de Boinville.

Chastel de Boinville, Jean-Baptiste (16 July 1756–?): RG Moulins from 16 Jan. 1788; godfather to sons of Mégret de Sérilly.

Chazet, René-Balthazard-Alissande de (6 Jan. 1729–?): Payer of the rentes; father-in-law of Baron de MacKau; RG Paris from Oct. 1784.

Choart, Louis (7 Sept. 1715–?): RG Bordeaux from 10 March 1741.

Chrisostome de Gresillement, Charles-Jean: T des Troupes du Roi; T des Ponts et Chaussées from 23 Nov. 1742.

Colin, Charles-Jacques (15 Jan. 1707–July 1775): T de la Vennerie, Fauconnerie et Toiles de Chasse du Roi from 16 Nov. 1763 after Adrien-François-Wayines de Launay; the office passed at his death to Michel-Joseph Leduc.

Conte, Pierre de; T des Turcies et Levées from 19 Jan. 1742 after Nicolas-Henry Cressac de la Bachellerie.

Coste de Champeron, Joseph-Alexandre: RG Flanders and Hainaut from 6 Nov. 1745 after Pierre-Charles de Villette; Payer of the rentes for 3 years.

Couet, Pierre-Antoine: T payeur des gages assignés sur les fermes du Roi; his d. married Barbaut de Glatigny.

Coullaud, François: T des Ponts et Chaussées at Poitier from 27 Oct. 1755 after his f., Pierre-Catherine.

Dangé de Bagneaux, Louis-Baltazar (10 Dec. 1738–?): TG de l'Hôtel royal des Invalides from 16 March 1758 after Noel-Mathieu-Etienne Périchon.

Darjuzon, Gabriel-Thomas-Marie (1 Feb. 1761–?): RG Amiens from 19 May 1784 for a *finance* of 480,000 livres after his f., Jean-Marie.

Darjuson, Jean-Marie (26 Sept. 1713–1784): FG; RG Amiens from 28 Nov. 1781 after Le Normant for 480,000 livres of which he borrowed 300,000 from Joseph Duruey.

Darnay, Jean-Baptiste (4 Sept. 1719–?): R des Tailles for Paris from 3 April 1750; RG Lyon from 10 Dec. 1755 after Louis Marquet.

Darras, Claude (?–1788): T de la Caisse des Arrérages and also the Caisse des Amortissements; *Secr. du Roi* from 1767.

De la Faye, Julien-Pierre: TG des Gratifications des Troupes.

Delagarde, Jean-Louis (17 June 1733–?): *Directeur de l'Administration des Domaines*; RG Lyon from 26 Sept. 1783.

De la Haye, Antoine-Philippe (4 Aug. 1763–?): RG Alençon from Nov. 1789 for a *finance* of 560,000 livres.

Delaunay, Alexandre-Louis (25 Aug. 1753–?): RG Flandres, Hainaut et Artois from 30 Jan. 1782; his f., Pierre.

Delaunay, Denis-Joseph (1733–?): *Commissaire-général des ports et arsenaux de la Marine*; RG du duc d'Orléans.

Delaunay, Pierre (?–1780): RG Flandres, Hainaut et Artois; *Secr. du Roi*; *Directeur de la Manufacture royale des Glaces*; his w., Anne-Marie-Sophie Le Noir; three sons, Auguste-Jean Delaunay de Tillière, Alexandre-Louis, and Pierre-Paul Delaunay Bourdetot.

Delpech de Chaumont, Paul (?–22 Nov. 1751): RG Riom.

Delpont, Jean (31 March 1711–?): RG Montpellier from 12 June 1754 after Pierre-Joseph La Garde.

Denis, Jean-François: T des Bâtiments du Roi in 1770.

Desbrets, Claude (12 Dec. 1719–1785): R des Tailles for Gannat from 1747; RG Poitiers from 30 March 1763 after Jean-Benjamin de la Borde; gave up the office 17 Dec. 1783 to Joseph Duruey; his w., Marie Parseval; d., Marie-Elisabeth married Pierre-Louis-Paul Randon de Lucenay; d., Claudine-Julie married Pierre-Nicolas de Delay de Blancmesnil and then Louis-Charles-Pierre de Labaig de Viella, 'tuteur'.

Deschamps, Joseph-Antoine (?–21 Oct. 1788): TG des Monnaies until his death; a bastard according to notes in A.N., P 2845.

Desvaux, Jacques-Philippes (?–21 Aug. 1784): RG Burgundy from 27 Jan. 1785; d., Angélique-Marie married Antoine de Flandres de Brunville, *parlementaire*.

D'Haucourt, Claude-Godard (17 Dec. 1716–?); FG; RG Alençon from 14 Nov. 1781.

Drouet de Santerre, Barthélemy-Pierre (1734–1818): *commis* in Finance Dept. until 1787; TG for the *Maison du comte d'Artois* from 6 March 1787 after Bourboulon and until 1818 when his s., Anselem-Barthélemy, held it until 1824 when the comte d'Artois became Charles X. This 'trésor' temporarily closed by government order on 28 May 1792. The original office cost 300,000 livres.

Drouilhet, Gratien (27 Jan. 1702–31 Jan. 1756): RG La Rochelle from 2 March 1742 after François-Penot de Tournières de la Cossière, his father-in-law.

Dubu de Longchamp, Pierre-Michel: T de la Caisse générale des Amortissements established by Edict of Dec. 1764.

Du Chauffour, Edouard-Amédé (4 Sept. 1713–?): RG des Boëtes des Monnayes de France et T payeur des gages des officiers de la Cour des Monnayes from 10 Feb. 1741 after Claude Buisson.

Ducluzeau, Jean-Lafon (30 March 1745–?): RG La Rochelle from 11 July 1787 after sixteen years as R des Tailles for Périgueux. He bought the office from Simon-Emmanuel Julien Le Normant for 400,000 livres; his s., Alexis-Lafon Ducluzeau de Maréal (14 May 1748–?) was made R des Tailles for Périgueux in 1789.

Dumas, Gabriel-Olivier-Benoist (3 June 1707–19 May 1777): RG Orléans from 6 June 1744 after Jean-Hyacinthe Davarse de Saint Amarand; resigned in 1777 in favour of Jean-François Le Gendre de Laferrière; *Secr. du Roi*; *Conseiller au Conseil de l'Isle de Bourbon*; *Directeur de la Cie. des Indes*; Commandant on the island of Moka; his brother, Benoin Benoist Dumas, was Governor and Commander 'aux Indes', *Directeur de la Cie. des Indes* and *Chevalier de l'Ordre de Saint Michel*.

Dupille de Saint-Séverin, Louis (1 March 1718–?): TG des Troupes de la Maison du Roi from 23 March 1748 after his brother, Jacques-Louis; *seigneur de Flée*, near Semur; former Cavalry Captain and *Chevalier de l'Ordre Militaire de Saint Louis*; his w., Marie-Catherine-Adelaide de Massol de Rebetz; went bankrupt after Necker abolished his office in 1778; imprisoned by the Chamber of Accounts 5 June 1786 but released by the Crown etc.

Dupin de Francœuil, Louis-Claude: RG Metz from 1738 after his f., Claude Dupin; ceded the office on 3 Feb. 1768 to Pierre-Armand Vallet de Villeneuve; *Secr. du Roi*; his second w., Louis-Marie-Madeleine Guillaume de Fontaine, an illegitimate d. of Samuel Bernard.

Duquesnoy, Pierre: RG Montauban in 1740.

Durieux, Jean-Baptiste (29 July 1712–?): T des Ponts et Chaussées at Amiens from 8 March 1753 after Paul-Joseph Joly.

Durey de Morsan, Joseph-Marie-Anne (14 Aug. 1717–?): RG Franche Comté from 5 March 1756 after his f., Pierre Durey d'Hannencourt who had held it for twenty-six years.

Duruey, Joseph (23 Dec. 1741–1793): RG Poitiers from 17 Dec. 1783 after Claude Desbrets; *agent de change*; Court Banker in 1788 and 1789; famous creditor and financial agent of the Crown; Councillor of State; Administrator of the Caisse d'Escompte; his d., Angélique-Josèphe (1770–1851) married Antoine-Pierre, comte de Chaumont, s. of Chaumont de la Galaizière.

Dutartre, Antoine-Jean-Baptiste (21 Sept. 1714–?): TG des Bâtiments du Roi from 18 May 1768 after Anne-Joseph Peilhon; his office suppressed March 1788 and evaluated at 600,000 livres; his brother, Etienne-Nicolas Dutartre de Bourdonné (?–1782) was Payer of the rentes; three sisters, Marie-Geneviève married Guillaume-Claude de Lalac, Marie-Geneviève [sic] married Claude Aleaume and Nicole-Elizabeth married Jean-Jacques Le Sièvre des Brières.

Echenerry de Montauzer, Jean de (14 June 1682–?): TG des Ponts et Chaussées from 13 Nov. 1742 after Claude-Bonaventure de la Rue de Beaumont.

Fabus, Michel-Henry: RG des Domaines et Bois for Paris; TG de l'Hôtel royal des Invalides from 1 Dec. 1752 after Denis Le Riche; went bankrupt on 26 March 1765 and his property, including the Château de Montgeron, was inventoried on 2 Aug. 1765; his w., Anne-Jeanne Mocquet, heiress of Le Riche.

Fayard de Bourdeilles, Paul (25 Oct. 1730–?): RG Dauphiné from 24 Feb. 1749 after Gautier de Beauvoir, his great-uncle; his f., Laurent Fayard de Champagneux.

Fillion de Villemur, Marie-Camille: RG Rouen from 1732; RG Paris from 19 Nov. 1745 after his f., Nicolas-François Fillion de Villemur who became Garde du Trésor royal.

Fleuriau de Touchelonge, Aimé-Paul (28 May 1757–?): RG Moulins from 11 Feb. 1789 after Henry-François Lamouroux; *Secr. du Roi.*

Foissy, Pierre de (5 May 1718–?): RG Metz from 5 Feb. 1745 after his f., Jacques de Foissy.

Fontaine, Louis (17 June 1706–?): RG Limôges from 22 April 1755 after Etienne Le Texier de Mennetou; resigned the office to Jean-Louis Tourteau on 3 May 1775; *Maître d'Hôtel Ordinaire.*

Fontaine de Biré, Marie-Sébastien-Charles-François (6 April 1727–?): T des Guerres for Lille and Artois during the Seven Years War; TG des Dépenses de la Guerre from 8 Aug. 1782 for *finance* of 1,600,000 livres: '...issû d'une famille noble et ancienne d'Anjou' says the *lettres de provision* (A.N., P 2523); his w., Philippine-Louis Cardon de Garsignies (or Garcigny); one of his two daughters married Antoine-Léon Amelot de Chaillou, son of the marquis de Chaillou, minister, and the King signed the marriage contract; two sons, Marie-Pierre Joseph (1767–?), and Marie-Géry (10 May 1769–?).

Fougeret, Jean (17 March 1734–?): RG Burgundy from 5 Oct. 1762 after Joseph-Marie-Anne Durey de Morsan.

Fremin, Claude-René (30 June 1716–?): TG des Ponts et Chaussées from 26 May 1746 after Chrisostome de Grésillent; his f. was *Secr. du Roi*; his brother a *maître ordinaire* in the Paris Chamber of Accounts.

Gaillard de Beaumanoir, Jean-Baptiste (14 Feb. 1704–?): TG des Maréchaussées des pays d'élections de Metz et d'Alsace from 11 May 1759 after his brother, Emmanuel-Jacques Gaillard de Gagny, who held it since 1729 and died March 1759; Captain of Dragoons and *Chevalier de l'Ordre Royal et Militaire de Saint Louis*.

Gaillard de Gagny, Emmanuel-Jacques (?–March 1759): RG Dauphiné from 30 Oct. 1741 after Louis-Michel Scruy de Saint Rémy; TG des Maréchaussées de France.

Gaultier, André-René (3 Dec. 1733–?): *Payeur des Officiers de la Maison du Roi* from 30 Dec. 1752 after Pierre Thirou de Montgrand; his f. was *Secr. du Roi*; his brother, Guillaume-René Gaultier de Montgéroult.

Gaultier de Montgéroult, Guillaume-René (1 June 1735–?): *Payeur des Officiers de la Maison du Roi* from 29 Aug. 1754 after his brother, André-René Gaultier.

Gautier de Beauvoir, Paul: RG Dauphiné for thirty-two years, resigned in 1759 for Fayard de Bourdeilles, his great-nephew.

Geoffroy de Montjoy, Claude-Gilbert: R of the six sols per livre of the capitation from 26 July 1776; the collection was to rebuild the justice palace burned in Jan. 1776; RG des Domaines et Bois for Paris from 10 Aug. 1756.

Gerac, Blaise (24 Dec. 1718–?): T for the pays de Nebouzan from 27 July 1748 after his f., Bertrand Gerac.

Gigot d'Orcy, Jean-Baptiste-François (8 Feb. 1737–?): RG Châlons from 23 June 1773; his f., Pierre-Simphorien Gigot, *Secr. du Roi*.

Gojard, Achille-Joseph (12 Jan. 1740–?): *commis* and *premier commis* in the Dept. of Finance from about 1759 to 29 Aug. 1788; RG Paris from

20 Dec. 1786 after Thiroux de Montsange; *Surintendant des Finances de la Maison d'Artois* from 29 Oct. 1788 at a *finance* of 300,000 livres and annual salary of 38,400; his w., Marie-Françoise-Lucie Gardel (8 April 1755–8 Dec. 1828) drew 1,800 livres pension from the Maison d'Artois until her death.

Gueffier, Etienne-Christophe (6 May 1705–?): RG Poitiers from 18 March 1740 after his f., Louis.

Guillot Delorme, Jean-Baptiste-Hilaire (14 Jan. 1721–?): RG Lorraine and Barrois from 1756; RG Paris from 12 Dec. 1781 for a *finance* of 1,280,000 livres.

Guillot de Montgrand, Jacques (19 Dec. 1723–?): R des Tailles for Cahors; RG Limôges from 20 Dec. 1781 at a *finance* of 480,000 livres; went bankrupt Sept. 1790.

Hamelin, Marie-Romain (4 Dec. 1734–?): *premier commis* in the Finance Dept. until 1783; RG Bourges from 6 Oct. 1784, the letters of provision praising twenty-four years of service in the Finance Department (A.N., V^1 518); his w., Marie-Jeanne Puissant.

Haran de Borda, Jean de: TG des Ponts et Chaussées, resigned the office on 23 May 1771.

Harvoin, François-Joseph (18 Sept. 1715–?): *Contrôleur ordinaire des Guerres* 1744; R des Tailles for Paris from 10 Feb. 1751; RG Alençon from 9 Nov. 1761 at *finance* of 500,000 livres after Charles-François Pajot; RG Tours from 12 Dec. 1781 at a *finance* of 1,070,000 livres; TG for Mesdames de France, Adelaide and Victoire; salary of 24,000 livres a year, 1767–87 for drawing up the *Etats du Roi*; *Secr. du Roi* from 30 Dec. 1749; went bankrupt and fled to Holland 20 Jan. 1787; his s. (1746–?) married (1) d. of Louis Choart RG and (2) d. of Brunet, *avocat au Conseil* and widow of comte de Rochard, Cavalry Captain.

Hébert, Antoine-François (1709–?): TG de l'Argenterie, Menus Plaisirs et Affaires de la Chambre du Roi; Necker suppressed his office.

Hocquart, Antoine-Louis-Hyacinthe (23 Jan. 1739–?): RG Bourges from 18 March 1760 after Marandon de la Maisonfort; his f., Louis Jacques-Charles, was TG de l'Artillerie et du Génie for thirty years.

Huet de Toriny, Guillaume (7 March 1708–1781): RG Limôges from 27 July 1774 after Renard de Roussiac; his w., Adelaide-Françoise-Geneviève Garnier.

Imbert, Joseph: RG Principauté de Dombes with his f. from 1763 and recognized by the Chamber of Accounts from 19 March 1779. The tax farmer for Dombes was Joseph Le Rat.

Joubert, Laurent-Nicolas: TG des Etats de Languedoc until he died 30 March 1792.

Julien, Jean-Louis (17 Aug. 1748–1792): RG Limôges from 14 Nov. 1781; s. of a well-known banker and *Secr. du Roi*.

Laborde, Jean-Joseph, marquis de (1724–94); court banker; f. of François-Louis-Joseph; held *survivance* of his son's office of *Garde du Trésor royal* from 26 Jan. 1785; brother-in-law of Micault d'Harvelay.

Laborde de Méréville, François-Louis-Joseph (1761–1802): *Garde du Trésor royal* from 13 Dec. 1776 as *survivant* and *adjoint* to Micault d'Harvelay and from 26 Jan. 1785 fully; *lettres de dispense d'âge* of 26 Jan. 1785; elected to the National Assembly 1789; emigrated 1793 and died in London.

La Freté, Jean-Jacques (9 July 1728–?): postal administrator; RG Lorraine and Barrois from 14 Nov. 1781; shareholder in the *caisse d'escompte*.

Lamouroux, Henri-François (7 July 1741–?): RG Moulins from 5 July 1769 after his uncle, Pierre Lamouroux de Saint Jullien; resigned the office to Fleuriau de Touchelonge in 1789; owned much land and in 1781 owed the Royal Treasury 130 millions (B.N., Joly de Fleury Papers 1435).

Lamouroux de Saint Jullien, Pierre (22 July 1695–?): RG Moulins from 30 June 1741 after his brother, François Lamouroux.

Landry, Clair-Louis (30 April 1691–?): RG Riom from 27 July 1742 after Pierre-Louis Nicolas Meulan; f. of Etienne-Nicolas.

Landry, Etienne-Nicolas: RG Riom from 1752 to 1790.

Lartois, Jacques-François (6 Sept. 1714–?): TG de la Police de Paris from 12 June 1749 after Hilaire Tripperet.

Lasvernhes, Pierre (20 March 1709–?): T des Ponts et Chaussées for Tours from 16 June 1758.

Laussat, Jean-Gratien de (10 April 1728–?): *Secr. du Roi*; TG de la Couronne de Navarre et Béarn from 23 April 1766; his s., Pierre-Clément; his f., Pierre de Laussat a *parlementaire* at Pau.

Laussat, Pierre-Clément de (23 Nov. 1756–?): RG Pau and Bayonne from March 1784, the first to hold this office; s. of Jean-Gratien.

Le Brest, Nicolas-François (?–21 Jan. 1767): TG des Fortifications de France; *écuyer, Secr. du Roi*; his f., Barthélemy Le Brest; his m., Marie-Nicole Tardif and these parents married 9 April 1697.

Le Clerc, Nicolas-Armand (22 June 1745–?): RG Orléans from 22 Feb. 1786 after Claude-Henry Watelet; his f., Armand, was Terray's *Premier commis des finances* and ennobled by letters in Aug. 1770; *Secr. des Commandements de la Reine* from 1774.

Le Couteulx de Canteleu, Jean-Barthélemy (5 March 1746–18 Sept. 1818): TG de la Caisse de l'Extraordinaire from 20 Jan. 1790 but had to give up the post to his elder brother because of his functions as deputy for the Third Estate of Rouen in the National Assembly; banker; member of the *Conseil des Anciens* Sept. 1795; *secr. du Conseil* 27 Jan. 1796; various honours in the Consulate, Empire and Restoration.

Lecouteulx du Molay, Jean-Jacques (18 July 1740–?): administrator of the *Caisse d'Escompte*, April 1778; administrator of the *Compagnie des Indes* 1785–8; RG et Payeur de la Caisse de l'Extraordinaire from 7 March 1790 for which he deposited a *cautionnement* of 800,000 livres in real estate.

Leduc de Survilliers, Michel-Joseph (5 May 1748–?): *avocat au Parlement*; TG de la Vennerie, Fauconnerie et Toilles de Chasse from 31 Dec. 1775 after Charles-Jacques Collin; *premier commis de la Trésorerie de la Maison du Roi*; TG des Monnaies de France en survivance.

Legendre de la Ferrière, Antoine-Jean-François (12 March 1751–?): RG Orléans from 29 Jan. 1777 after Dumas; removed from office in 1780, his affairs in disorder; his f., Jean-Jacques Le Gendre Dammeville was *Trésorier de France* at Caen.

Le Gendre de Villemorien, Bénigne-André (5 Feb. 1687–?): RG Auch from 26 April 1748 after Martin d'Artaguiette; his s., Philippe-Charles Legendre de Villemorien (27 Jan. 1718–?) was a parlementaire in Paris and RG of Domaines et Bois at Soissons from 5 Jan. 1748.

Léger, André-Marie (14 Jan. 1723–?): RG La Rochelle from 30 June 1758 after David-Pierre Perrinet du Pezeau.

Le Maître de la Martinière, Jean (15 Jan. 1715–?): TG des Fortifications from 1 Feb. 1749 to 1 Jan. 1756; TG de l'Artillerie et du Génie from 15 Feb. 1760; resigned in 1774 to Chastel; *lettres de légitimation* Aug. 1781 for Jean-Maurice Le Maître, bastard son of Le Maître and of Marie-Cécile Maurice Ellebo (not married).

Le Marchand, Philippe (2 May 1721–?): TG de la Prévôté de l'Hôtel from 8 Feb. 1755; took another such office by letters of 24 Feb. 1759 after Olivier Hardy.

Le Noir, Jacques-Joseph (14 June 1712–?): TG des Offrandes, Aumônes, Dévotions et Bonnes Œuvres du Roi from 18 Jan. 1760 after Jules-Nicolas-Duvancel; this office suppressed July 1779, restored March 1784.

Le Normand, Hervé-Guillaume: TG de la Régie générale des Monnaies before Deschamps.

Le Normand de Champflé, Louis-Henry-Auguste (16 Feb. 1702–?): RG Amiens from 30 Nov. 1757 after Etienne-Pierre Masson de Maison Rouge.

Le Normand, Louis-Jean (26 Jan. 1735–?): RG Amiens from 17 Nov. 1768 after his f., Louis-Henry-Auguste Le Normand de Champflé.

Le Normant, François-Nicolas, sieur de Flaghac (13 Sept. 1725–April 1783): RG des Vingtièmes et Capitation de Paris from 9 Dec. 1772 at a *finance* of 600,000 livres; TG du Marc d'Or from 28 Dec. 1779 after Jean-François Caron; RG Paris; *Maître d'Hôtel ordinaire du comte d'Artois*; his w., Marie-Louis O'Murphy de Boisfailly; she had been married before to Jacques de Beaufranchet Dayat by whom she had a son, Jean-Jacques; one d., Marie-Victoire.

Le Normant, Simon-Emmanuel-Jullien (de Cadiz) (24 Feb. 1740–?): *Secr. du Roi* 1 Aug. 1777 after Antoine Le Couteulx; RG La Rochelle from 14 Nov. 1781 and resigned it to Jean-Lafon Ducluzeau on 3 July 1787; RG Tours from 28 Feb. 1787 after Harvoin; administrator of the *Caisse d'Escompte* 1783–8; went bankrupt March 1792.

Le Pot de la Fontaine, Denis-Paul (8 Oct. 1731–?): *avocat au Parlement*; *Secr. du Roi* from 31 March 1784; RG Orléans from 23 Sept. 1778 after Watelet.

Le Prestre, Louis-Joseph-Edmond: RG Caen from 1729 to 1748; TG de l'Ordinaire des Guerres de la Maison du Roi in 1770; his nephew, Michel-Edmond Le Prestre de Neubourg.

Le Prestre de Neubourg, Michel-Edmond (21 Dec. 1722–?): RG Caen from 20 Dec. 1748 after his uncle, Louis-Joseph-Edmond Le Prestre.

Le Roy de Joinville, Joseph (21 May 1729–?): T des Ponts et Chaussées at Bordeaux from 29 Sept. 1758 after Nicolas Thomas; RG of Domaines et Bois.

Le Seurre, Arnould-Philippe (12 Jan. 1723–?): T of Fortifications in Champagne and Brie from 10 April 1750 after Christophe Alyot de Luçay.

Le Texier de Mennetou, Etienne; RG Rouen from 22 April 1755 after Jean Guyot de Villers.

Magon de la Balue, Jean-Baptiste (1713–19 July 1794): *Banquier de la Cour* 1769; Director of the Compagnie des Indes 1764; on an advisory committee for treasury reform 15 March 1788; eldest son, Andrien-Dominique; four other children, Laurent Magon de Terlaye, Raphael Magon de la Balue, Madame de Saint Pern and Madame de Meslay; one bastard d., Marie de la Mercede Jeanne, dite Magon de la Balue, by the widow of a Spanish naval commander, Jean de Madariaga, and this d. died 22 Nov. 1781 aged eleven; from a noble family of merchant-bankers of Saint Malo.

Mallet, Daniel-Joseph (12 Jan. 1691–?): RG des Etats de Cambrai from 22 June 1740.

Marendon de Maisonfort, Louis-François (28 Nov. 1715–?): RG Bourges from 6 Aug. 1745 after his f., Louis; gave up the office 1760.

Marchal de Sainscy, Louis-Pierre-Sébastien (31 Oct. 1714–?): RG of Domaines et Bois from 13 Jan. 1747 to 30 Sept. 1772; *Œconome du Clergé de France* from 1749 (?) to 1782; received these offices from elder brother, Pierre Marchal Dandrimont, chevalier; gave them in turn to his s., Louis-René; his f., Sébastien, died 1748 or 1749; chevalier of the Order of Saint Louis; Cavalry Captain; Governor of Abbeville.

Marchal de Sainscy, Louis-René (26 Sept. 1749–?): RG of Domaines et Bois from 30 Sept. 1772 after his f., Louis-Pierre-Sébastien; *Œconome du Clergé* from 1782; went bankrupt in 1787.

Marchal Dandrimont, Pierre (?–13 Dec. 1783): eldest s. of Sébastien Marchal and Anne Mercier; elder brother of Louis-Pierre-Sébastien; RG of Domaines et Bois de Metz until 13 Jan. 1747; on 25 Aug. 1745 married Charlotte-Emilie Penot de Tournière La Cossière, d. of François Penot de Tournière La Cossière, who was RG La Rochelle and related to many other accountants.

Maréchaux des Entelles, Charles (26 May 1748–?): TG du Marc d'Or from 21 July 1784 after François-Louis Tronchin.

Marianne, Antoine (9 Feb. 1700–?): TG Ligues Suisses, Grisons et Alliés from 27 May 1754 after Louis-Claude Auzillon de Berville who died 21 Jan. 1754 and after François-Charles Sonnet de la Tour.

Marigner (or Mareigner), René-Augustin (21 Oct. 1731–?): *premier commis* in the Royal Treasury (Grand Comptant) for eighteen years; TG for the Maison de Madame la comtesse de Provence; RG Paris from 30 Sept. 1789 after Charles-Jacques-Louis Meulan.

Marquet de Bourgade, Jacques (1718–12 April 1784): Postal administrator from 3 Aug. 1783; army supplier in the War of Austrian Succession and the Seven Years War; uncle to Calonne's first wife; adviser to Joly de Fleury.

Marquet de Mont Saint Père, Louis (15 Aug. 1715–?): RG Lyon from 1750; RG Bordeaux from 22 Nov. 1755 after Charles-François Michel de Roissy; his w., Louise-Michèle Paris-Duverney, d. of famous financier; brother of Marquet de Bourgade; Calonne married one of their seven children.

Marquet de Montbreton, Jean-Daniel (25 June 1724–?): RG Dauphiné from 18 March 1760 after Emmanuel-Jacques Gaillard de Gagny who died 17 March 1759; RG Rouen from 12 Dec. 1781; brother of Marquet de Bourgade and Marquet de Mont Saint Père; married d. of Dumas, RG.

Marquet Desgrèves, Maurice-Alexandre (3 Feb. 1748–?): RG Bordeaux from 21 April 1773 after his father, Louis Marquet de Mont Saint Père; went bankrupt and fled 11 May 1789; his sister, Jacqueline-Henriette, married François-Nicolas de la Guillaumye, Intendant of Corsica.

Martin, Joseph (12 May 1686–?): RG Provence, Forcalquier, etc., from 26 Aug. 1740 after Jean-Armand Ragueneau de Villemont.

Maussion de la Courtjay, Etienne-Charles (?–15 Oct. 1773): RG Alençon until death; succeeded by Antoine-Pierre Maussion who died 18 March 1778; the office passed to André de Trenonay.

Mégret de Sérilly, Antoine-Jean-François (14 Sept. 1746–10 May 1794): TG for War from 31 March 1770 concurrently with his uncle, Thomas de Pange; TG for War from 24 March 1779 at *finance* of a million livres; went bankrupt June 1787 and ruined; his f., Antoine Mégret d'Etigny, Intendant of Auch and Pau, etc.; his uncle Mégret de Sérilly was Intendant of Alsace; his w., Marie-Louise-Thomas de Domangeville.

Mel de Saint Ceran, Pierre-Nicolas (28 Sept. 1722–?): RG Montauban from 7 Aug. 1771 after Jean-Baptiste Begon; R des Tailles for Bordeaux until them; went bankrupt 16 June 1790; owned a house at Sucy-en-Brie.

Melin, Isaac: T des Ordres du Saint Esprit et de Saint Michel in 1780s; was he related to Antoine-Jean Melin (1726–?), *premier commis* Finance Dept. and the War Dept., *Secr. général de l'Ordre de Saint Louis*?

Meulan, Charles-Jacques-Louis (17 Aug. 1738–?): RG Paris from 24 Feb. 1759 after his f., Pierre-Louis-Nicolas; *avocat au Parlement*; for the new office of RG Paris in 1781, he borrowed 500,000 livres of the *finance* of 1,280,000 livres from four 'bourgeois de Paris': Louis-Hypolite-Jean-François Blanchin, Henry-Ollivier Charpentier de la Boullaye, Nicolas Dupuy and Jacques-Edmé Berthier by contracts of 30 Dec. 1781; two uncles, Guy-Martin Terré Du Petitval (RG des Domaines et Bois) and Meulan de la Sourdière (Payer of the rentes).

Meulan, Pierre-Louis-Nicolas (25 Jan. 1709–30 Oct. 1777): RG Paris from 5 Oct. 1762 after Marie-Camille-Fillion de Villemur; RG Riom from 27 July 1742 after François Prat; his w., Marie-Catherine Terré; his brother, Marie-Pierre-Charles Meulan d'Ablois; his s., Charles-Jacques-Louis.

Micault d'Harvelay, Joseph (?–1786): Keeper of the Royal Treasury from 1775 after his great-uncle, Pâris de Montmartel, until 1785; brother of Jean-Vivant Micault de Courbeton, *régisseur des poudres et salpêtres*; brother-in-law of Jean-Joseph de Laborde; his w., Anne-Josèphe de Nettine, later became Calonne's second wife.

Michel, Gabriel (23 Jan. 1702–1765): *Secr. du Roi*; TG Artillerie et Génie from 14 April 1758 at a *finance* of 600,000 livres, after his f., Charles Michel de Roissy.

Michel de Roissy, Charles-François (22 July 1726–?): RG Bordeaux from 19 Nov. 1745 after his f., Charles Michel de Roissy.

Millet, Charles-Simon (10 June 1724–?): RG Moulins from 6 June 1744 after his f., Charles-François, who had held it twenty-two years; his m., Anne-Claude Le Texier.

Millin Du Perreux, Jerosme-Robert (13 Jan. 1733–?): RG Rouen from 10 Dec. 1766 after Etienne Le Texier de Mennetou; *écuyer*; his f., Philippe-Robert Millin de Montgirard, married on 27 April 1732; administrator of the royal lottery; his w., Mlle Le Grand, he married 22 Oct. 1763; owned château du Perreux near Nogent; went bankrupt 31 May 1786 and ruined; in 1781 already owed 364 millions to the Royal Treasury.

Millon d'Ainval, Jean-Louis (2 Jan. 1740–?): RG Lyon from 21 June 1769 after his uncle, Pierre-Louis-Paul Randon de Boisset; through his w., Antoinette-Maurice Bureau de Serandey, he inherited office of RG Châlons in 1773 and disposed of it to Gigot d'Orcy.

Montbrun, Jean-Marie de (7 April 1727–?): T Ponts et Chaussées at Auch from 15 July 1754 after Jean-Etienne de la Borde.

Moret de Parzy, Jean-Baptiste (21 June 1724–?): T Ponts et Chaussées in Moulins from 20 Oct. 1757 after Pierre-René-Tirot de Saint Martin.

Moron, Antoine (15 Aug. 1715–?): RG Lyon from 14 Feb. 1750; resigned to Louis Marquet.

Mouchard, François-Abraham-Marie (18 Jan. 1712–19 Oct. 1782): RG Châlons from 2 Sept. 1740 after Jean-Claude-Prosper Héron de Villefosse; in 1781 he borrowed for this *finance* 195,000 livres from Jean-Baptiste Deheppe, procureur en la prévôté royale de Montfaucon en Champagne, and 60,000 livres from Jean Golzard, notary and bailiff of the comté de Grandpré; his d., Marie-Anne-Françoise, married Claude, comte de Beauharnois; his d., Anne-Louis, married François-Philippes-Amédée Mouchard de Chabans.

Mouffle de Géorville, Jean-Baptiste-René (?–1783): TG de la Marine from 1743.

Mouffle de Géorville, Louis-Barthélemy (?–20 Jan. 1764): TG de la Marine; went bankrupt when he died; his sister, Françoise-Louise married Louis-Toussaint Duraget de Champlionin, Governor of Vassey; Radix de Sainte Foy took the office.

Nogaret, Armand-Frédéric-Ernest (1734–?): *premier commis* to the duc de la Vrillière; TG des Maisons, Finances et Domaines du comte d'Artois from 1776 to 1780 at a *finance* of 300,000 livres; lost the office in a re-organization in 1780.

Noguier de Malijai, Louis-Maximilien-Toussaint (12 Oct. 1743–?): RG Provence, Forqualquier, etc., from 31 Aug. 1785 after his f., Pierre-Vincent Noguier, at a *finance* of 260,000 livres.

Nugues de la Peratière, Claude (16 Feb. 1707–?): RG Rouen from 27 Nov. 1745 after Fillion de Villemur.

Ollivier, Jacques-David (30 May 1713–3 May 1777): RG Lyon from 17 April 1739 after his f., David Ollivier, who held it for eighteen years; his w., Anne-Marguerite Lamouroux; his s. inherited the office in 1777.

Oursin de Digoville, Pierre: RG Caen for thirty-nine years until 27 Feb. 1771; f. of Pierre-Etienne Oursin de Montchevreuil.

Oursin de Montchevreuil, Pierre-Etienne (10 Oct. 1745–?): RG Caen from 27 Feb. 1771; s. of Pierre Oursin de Digoville.

Pajot de Marcheval, Charles-François (9 Sept. 1728–?): RG Alençon from 29 Aug. 1754 after his f., François Pajot de Marcheval who died 27 Aug. 1754.

Pajot de Marcheval, François (25 March 1692–?): RG Alençon from 26 April 1742 after Jean-Baptiste Racine du Jouquay; R in the General Farm in Orléans for twenty-six years; f. of Charles-François.

Parat de Chalandray, Louis-Pierre (15 Nov. 1746–?): RG Lorraine from 1768 to 1780; RG Orléans from 10 Dec. 1781.

Pâris de Bollardière, Eustache (3 Sept. 1722–?): R des Impositions for the Election of Montevilliers; RG Grenoble from 28 Nov. 1781; related to d'Harvelay, Keeper of the Royal Treasury.

Pâris de Montmartel, Jean (1690–1766): *marquis de Brunoy, terre érigée en marquisat par lettres du Roi, octobre 1757; Garde du Trésor royal* until 1755; great-uncle of Micault d'Harvelay who succeeded him in the office; member of large famous family.

Pâris de Treffond, Louis (22 June 1713–?): RG Rouen from 31 Dec. 1760 after Claude Nugnes de la Seraltière; *Secr. du Roi* from 10 March 1764.

335

Pâris de Trefond des Gayères, Armand-Joseph-Louis: RG Rouen from 1776 to 1780 as a very young man so Jean-Louis Le Boeuf was commissioned to supervise the work until he reached his majority.

Parseval Deschênes, Alexandre: *lettres de survivance* 19 Dec. 1775 for office of RG Limôges; RG Metz and Alsace 1786 to 1790.

Pavée de Provenchères, Guillaume: *mâitre ancien de la Chambre aux Deniers du Roi* at the suppression, July 1779.

Peilhon, Anne-Joseph (14 Jan. 1729–?): *avocat au Parlement*; TG des Bâtiments du Roi from 11 May 1754 after Jacques-Mathurin Taboureau d'Orval who died 31 Dec. 1753; his f., Pierre-Gabriel was *Secr. du Roi*.

Penot de Tournière, Charles: *Conseiller du Roi*; R du Barage et Pavé de Paris from 26 April 1757; Payer of the rentes; related to Marchal de Sainscy.

Périchon, Noel-Mathurin-Etienne (25 Dec. 1698–1764): TG des Colonies Française de l'Amérique from 31 Jan. 1758 after Guillaume-Pierre Tavernier de Boullogne.

Périchon de Vaudreuil, Etienne-Guillaume (27 April 1705–?): RG des Domaines et Bois for Moulins from 1767 after Jacques-Mathieu Augéard.

Pernon, Louis (6 Jan. 1711–?): TG des Troupes de la Maison du Roi from 22 Oct. 1757 after Louis-Joseph-Edmond Le Prestre; his s., Louis-Aimé Pernon, had *lettres de survivance* of 4 Jan. 1778; deputy for Lyon on the *Conseil royal du Commerce*.

Perrinet de Faugnes, Pierre: RG Flandres, Hainaut & Artois.

Perrinet de Faugnes de Tauvenay, Athenase-Etienne-Louis: RG Flandres, Hainaut & Artois from 1773 to 12 Dec. 1785 when he resigned it to Thibault; 'particulièrement protégé de la Reine par entremise de M. l'abbé de Vermont,' Dailly wrote on 28 Sept. 1781 (B.N., Joly de Fleury 1435); his w., Suzanne-Jacqueline Poupardin.

Perrinet du Pezeau, David-Pierre (16 June 1697–?): RG Flandres, Hainaut & Artois from 30 June 1758 after Joseph-Alexandre Cosie de Champeron who died 5 April 1758; RG La Rochelle for twenty-nine years from 8 July 1729; *Secr. du Roi*.

Personne de la Chapelle, Daniel-Louis (10 Oct. 1715–?): TG des Maréchaussées de France from 7 Feb. 1770 after Bourgevin de Norville; resigned the office to his s., Louis-Marie; *écuyer*.

Pillon, Claude (15 March 1731–1789); R des Impositions for Paris from 21 June 1775 at *finance* of 112,000 livres; went bankrupt 1789.

Préaudeau de Chemilly, Eugène-Claude (24 March 1738–?): TG des Maréchaussées de France from 5 June 1765 after Jean-Baptiste Gaillard de Beaumanoir, his brother-in-law.

Préaudeau de Monchamps, Louis-Etienne (14 Sept. 1733–?): TG Artillerie et Génie from 16 Sept. 1772 after Jacques-Louis-Guillaume Bouret de Vezelay; went bankrupt on 11 Aug. 1778 and ruined; the office passed to Veytard by letters of 26 Aug. 1778; Nicolas Bellinger commissioned to complete earlier accounts; owned château de Bourneville near Villers-Cotteret.

Prévost, Gabriel: TG Ponts et Chaussées; *Secr. du Roi*; went bankrupt Feb. 1779 and ruined after thirty years service; owned property near Montargis and Bordeaux.

Prouveur de Pont, Bertrand-August-Florent (3 July 1734–?): T Ponts et Chaussées at Hainaut after Richard Balthazar Fouillet.

Quinson, François-Roch de: RG du Clergé.

Radix de Chevillon, Claude-Mathieu (24 Jan. 1728–?): *Payeur du Parlement de Paris* from 19 Nov. 1759 after Victor Chardon; concurrently *Payeur des rentes*; T du Département de Paris in 1792.

Radix de Sainte Foy, Claude-Pierre-Maximilien (1736–?): TG de la Marine after Mouffle de Géorville; *surintendant des finances* to the comte d'Artois from 1776 to 1781; went bankrupt 8 Aug. 1781; diplomat and ambassador; his f., Claude-Mathieu Radix, payer of the rentes, died 15 April 1773; his brother, Claude-Mathieu Radix de Chevillon; his sister, Marie-Geneviève married Nicolas-Augustin de Malbec de Montjoy de Briges, *premier écuyer de la Grande écurie du Roi*.

Randon de Boisset, Pierre-Louis-Paul (25 Oct. 1709–?): RG Lyon from 30 Jan. 1758 after Jean-Baptiste Darnay; FG; his nephew, Millon d'Ainval.

Randon de Hanencourt, Jean-Antoine: RG Poitiers for twenty years until he ceded it to his s., Jean-Ferdinand-Elie, by act of 7 Jan. 1788.

Randon de Hanencourt, Jean-Ferdinand-Elie (2 Sept. 1761–?): RG Poitiers from 13 Feb. 1788.

Randon de la Tour, Marc-Antoine-François-Marie (30 June 1736–?): TG de la Maison et Finance de la Reine from 1 Jan. 1777 after his uncle, Pierre Randon de Pommery; commissioned by letters of 15 Feb. 1777 to finish his uncle's *exercices*; rewarded for his father-in-law's services as doctor to the Queen (de Lanvue); TG de la Maison du Roi et de la Reine from 11 Oct. 1779, new office created July 1779 at *finance* of a million livres; Administrator of the Royal Treasury from March 1788.

Randon de Massanne, Elie: RG Poitiers from 30 Oct. 1741 after Etienne-Christophle Gueffier; his f. was a *capitoul* of Toulouse.

Randon de Pommery, Charles-Nicolas (15 Sept. 1766–?): RG Soissons from 28 Jan. 1784 after his f., Pierre; *lettres de dispense d'âge.*

Randon de Pommery, Pierre (19 Nov. 1714–?): TG de la Maison de la Reine and Garde général des Meubles de la Couronne; RG Soissons from 15 June 1768 after Nicolas Durant de Belleguise.

Raviot, Guillaume (11 Oct. 1739–?): *Conseiller au Parlement de Bourgogne* for seven years; *vicomte* 'mayeur' of Dijon for fourteen years; *président de la chambre du Tiers Etat des Etats généraux de Bourgogne*; RG Bourgogne, Bresse, Bugey, Valromey and Dombes from 27 Jan. 1785 after Jacques-Philippes Desvaux who died 21 Aug. 1784.

Renard de Roussiac, Jean-Baptiste-Antoine; RG Limôges from 1737 to 15 July 1771 when he resigned the office to Huet de Toriny.

Ribes, Jean (31 Aug. 1750–?): RG Languedoc, Roussillon & Pays de Foix from 1783 to 1790; concurrently RG Orléans from 13 May 1789 after Nicolas-Armand Le Clerc who resigned it to him 15 April 1789; 'lettres de dispense d'apurement de comptes quant à présent des offices dont il est pourvu.'

Richard, Jean-Marie (?–Aug. 1783); RG Tours from 1747 to 1783; 'cette office a passé de père en fils depuis si longtemps,' wrote Joly de Fleury in 1781 (B.N., Joly de Fleury 1438, fol. 16); heirs at his death: two brothers, Louis Richard de la Bretêche and Jean-Claude Richard de Saint Nom, three nephews, Jean-Marie Roslin (son of Marie-Jeanne Richard), Pierre-Jacques Bergeret de Talmont and Jean-Marie Bergeret (sons of Josèphe-Marguerite Richard).

Richard de la Bretêche, Louis: Postal administrator from 1772; RG Tours from 10 Oct. 1783 after his brother, Jean-Marie Richard, the *finance* at 1,070,000 livres; went bankrupt 1790 (?).

Rocher, Olivier (12 Feb. 1708–?): T Turcies et Levées from 18 June 1745 after Pierre de Coste; *finance* 177,000 livres; office suppressed Jan. 1772.

Roissy, Charles-François-Michel de (?–29 Aug. 1755): RG Bordeaux succeeded by Louis Marquet.

Rolland de Tremeville, Louis (9 Sept. 1702–?): RG Riom from 15 May 1756 after Antoine-François Bouret de Valroche; his s., Rolland de Villarceaux.

Rolland de Villarceaux, Barthélemy-Louis (16 Aug. 1733–?): RG Riom from 5 Oct. 1762 after his f., Louis Rolland de Tremeville; his brother-in-law was Jean-André Vassal.

Rouillé de l'Etang, David-Etienne (20 Jan. 1731–?): TG Police de Paris from 25 April 1770 after Bourgevin de Norville who died 29 Dec.

1769; TG des Dépenses Diverses from 1778 to 1788; Commissioner of the Public Treasury from July 1791; his nephew, Piscatory, a *chef* in the Finance Dept. from 1778 to 1791.

Roulleau, Marie-Louis-César: *Commissaire, Receveur et Contrôleur aux Saisies réelles près les Cours et Juridictions de Paris* from 17 Aug. 1775 at a *finance* of 300,000 livres; went bankrupt and fled Sept. 1784; succeeded by Nicolas Coulon from 21 June 1785.

Rousseau, Jacques: T des Garnisons et Mortes Pays in Burgundy and Bresse from 27 July 1748 after Etienne Rossignol.

Rousseau, Pierre (18 June 1729–? 1785): RG Domaines et Bois at Orléans; RG Domaines et Bois for Lorraine and Barrois from 1773; RG Paris 21 April 1784; T and RG des octrois for Paris; his w., Marie-Anne-Julie de Kessel.

Rousseau de Pantigny, Louis (26 Oct. 1710–1777): RG Bourges from 30 Dec. 1748 after Pierre Pougin de Nomion, his father-in-law, who held it for eighteen years; his s., Jean-Louis Rousseau de Pantigny.

Rousseau de Patigny, Jean-Louis (22 July 1753–?): RG Bourges from 31 Dec. 1777 after his f., Louis; *lettres de dispense d'âge* of 30 Oct. 1777; *avocat au Parlement*; *caissier des Recettes générales*.

Roustain, Pierre: T and R de la Bourse Commune des Banquiers expéditionnaires de la Cour de Rome à Paris from 6 Sept. 1760 after Philippe-Masot du Buissons who died 30 April 1731.

Saint Laurent, Joseph de (18 Aug. 1707–?): TG Colonies Françaises de l'Amérique from 11 April 1764 after Noel-Mathurin-Etienne Périchon.

Saint Séverin, Louis Dupille de: TG de l'Ordinaire des Guerres de la Gendarmerie et des Troupes de la Maison du Roi.

Savalette de Langes, Charles-Pierre-Paul de (1746–98): *Garde du Trésor royal* together with his f., Savalette de Magnanville, from 14 Feb. 1773, and alone from 7 Feb. 1782, confirmed by *lettres patentes* of 19 Nov. 1785; one of the Treasury Commissioners during the revolution; *Conseiller au Parlement de Paris*, 1766–71.

Savalette de Magnanville, Charles-Pierre (1713–?): parlementaire, Master of Requests (1738), Intendant of Tours (1745), Keeper of the Royal Treasury (1756), noble; f. of Savalette de Langes.

Selle, César-Luc-Marie de (19 Oct. 1723–16 Jan. 1781): TG Marine from 20 April 1763; *Conseiller du Roi*; his heirs were Jean-François de Selle (Master of Requests), Jean-Baptiste de Selle du Réal (Captain in the Lille Regiment) and Joseph-Maurice de Selle de Beauchamp (former T of the Marine at Toulon); Antoine Lalbin continued his *exercices* by letters of 31 Jan. 1781.

Sonnet des Fontenelles, Etienne-Jean (14 Feb. 1723–?): TG Ligues Suisses & Grisons from 17 Aug. 1763 after François-Charles Sonnet de la Tour, his brother; *Chevalier de l'Ordre de Saint Louis*; the family served the Crown for more than a century.

Stocard, Jean-Marie (13 Oct. 1732–?): Banquier expéditionnaire en Cour de Rome et de la Leghorn from 1762 after Pierre Lancesserer who died 1 Oct. 1760.

Taboureau d'Orval, Jacques-Mathurin (25 July 1692–?): TG Bâtiments du Roi from 16 Oct. 1741 after Antoine-Henry Pérard.

Taillepied de Bondy, Jean-Baptiste-Marie-Adeobat (30 April 1741–?): RG Auch from 5 Oct. 1762 after Robert-Jean-Baptiste Taillepied, his f.

Tavernier de Boullongne, Guillaume: TG de l'Extraordinaire des Guerres; two sons, Guillaume-Pierre and Philippe-Guillaume; *Secr. du Roi*; FG; *Payer des Gages des Officiers du Bureau de Finance d'Orléans*; *Secr. Contrôleur en la Chancellerie près la Cour des Comptes, Aides et Finances de Franche-comté*.

Tavernier de Boullongne, Guillaume-Pierre (17 June 1710–?): TG Colonies Françaises de l'Amérique from 4 Jan. 1750, in recognition of services of his f. and his brother, Philippe-Guillaume.

Tavernier de Boullongne de Magnanville, Jean-Baptiste (9 Sept. 1749–?): TG de l'Extraordinaire des Guerres; nephew of Guillaume-Pierre Tavernier de Boullongne.

Tavernier de Boullongne de Preninville, Philippe-Guillaume (5 Feb. 1712–?): RG Poitiers from 18 Oct. 1749 after François-Christophle Lalive; s. of Guillaume and younger brother of Guillaume-Pierre.

Terrède, Jean-Joseph (13 Feb. 1697–?): RG Toulouse from 19 May 1741 after Jean-Pierre Colomar.

Thibault, Jean-Pierre (1 July 1747–?): RG Flandres, Hainaut & Artois from 21 Dec. 1785 after Pierre-Perrinet de Faugnes de Thauvenay whose s., Athenase-Etienne-Louis Perrinet ceded it to him.

Thierrion, Louis-Niçaise-Théodore (29 Sept. 1741–?): RG Auch from 30 Sept. 1789 after Jean Chanorier at a *finance* of 450,000 livres.

Thiroux de Montsange, Denis-Philibert, sieur de la Bretèche Saint Nom (9 Jan. 1715-1786): Postal administrator; RG Paris from 28 Jan. 1778 after Pierre-Louis-Nicolas Meulan; office suppressed in 1780 and restored 1785; RG Paris from 27 Jan. 1785; his heirs: w., Thérèse-Antoinette Bourette and his s., Narcisse-Etienne de Durfort; went bankrupt at his death.

Thomas de Pange, Jean-Baptiste (?–1780): TG de l'Extraordinaire des Guerres from 1753 after his f., Jean-Baptiste-Louis-Thomas who had held it since 1742; from 31 March 1770 his nephew, Mégret de Sérilly, exercised the office 'conjointement et concurremment'; his heirs were three young sons, Marie-Louis, Marie-Denis and Marie-Jacques and two grandchildren, Louis-Jacques-Philippe-Hypolite de Saint Simon and Françoise-Régis-Marie-Josèphe-Balbine de Saint Simon, both children of his deceased daughter, Françoise-Louise and of her husband, Claude-Anne, marquis de Saint Simon, Grand d'Espagne.

Thoynet, François (19 June 1736–?): TG Ponts et Chaussées from 23 May 1771 after Haran de Borda.

Touchy, François (20 April 1719–?): RG Montpellier from 20 Sept. 1755 after Guillaume Mazade de Saint Bresson and on refusal of his brother, Pierre-Antoine Touchy.

Tourteau de Septeuil, Jean-Baptiste (7 Oct. 1753–?): RG Châlons from 15 Sept. 1784 after his f., Jean-Louis; T of the Royal Civil List in 1791 and 1792; fled and emigrated on 10 August 1792; still alive in 1826 and collecting indemnities for property in many *départements*.

Tourteau de Septeuil, Jean-Louis (28 Oct. 1725–?): RG Limôges from 3 May 1775 after Louis Fontaine; his f., Jean-Baptiste was 'Conseiller secr. en la Chancellerie près la Cour de Parlement de Pau'; RG Lyon from 28 Nov. 1781 to Sept. 1783; RG Châlons from 1783 to 1784; his s., Jean-Baptiste.

Trenonay, André de (17 Nov. 1732–?): RG Alençon from 11 June 1778 on recommendation of the duc d'Anjou, the duc d'Alençon and the comte du Maine; held the office until 1789.

Tronchin, François-Louis (?–29 May 1784): TG du Marc d'Or by commission of his f., and *lettres patentes* 8 Dec. 1770 and *lettres de commission* 16 Feb. 1780; he had replaced Hardouin de Beaumois; *Secr. des commandements du duc d'Orléans*; after his death, Jean-Louis Carnot commissioned to finish his *exercices*; his brother, Jean-Robert, was FG adjoint.

Turmenys, Jean de (?–31 March 1727): *marquis de Nointel; Garde du Trésor royal* until his death; the office then went to his brother, Edmé-François de Turmenys de Montigny by *lettres* of 4 Sept. 1727; 'membre du Conseil de Direction de l'Ordre de Notre Dame du Mont Carmel et de Saint-Lazare.'

Ugla, Jean-Augustin (8 Aug. 1732–?): RG Montpellier from 20 Nov. 1747 after Jean Raynaud.

341   22-3

Vallet de Villeneuve, Pierre-Armand (28 July 1731–?): RG Metz from 3 Feb. 1768 after Dupin de Francœuil, his father-in-law; his w., Madeleine-Suzanne Dupin de Francœuil, brought the office as part of her dowry.

Varenne, Jacques (7 Jan. 1700–?): RG Brittany from 29 Oct. 1766 after Jean-Baptiste Simon de Boyer de la Boissière; held the office together with his s., Claude Varenne de Beost; *Chevalier de l'Ordre de Saint Michel*; former *Secr. en chef des Etats de Bourgogne*.

Varenne de Beost, Claude (Dec. 1722–?): RG Brittany from 29 Oct. 1766 concurrently with his f., Jacques; complex affair in A.N., F^{30} 199; one member of the family held the office at the revolution.

Vassal, Jean-André (10 May 1738–?): RG Languedoc, Roussillon and the pays de Foix from 10 May 1757 with *lettres de dispense d'âge*; RG Riom from 20 Dec. 1781; of the *finance* of 750,000 livres, he borrowed 400,000 livres from Blaise-Louis Robinson, bourgeois de Paris by contract 14 Dec. 1781; brother-in-law of Rolland de Villarceaux, of Mesnard de Chousy and of a certain Séguier.

Véron, Louis-Grégoire (8 Feb. 1721–15 June 1780): *Secr. du Roi*; RG Franche-Comté from 5 Oct. 1762 after Joseph-Marie-Anne Durey de Mortans; his f., Louis-Henry Véron, *Secr. du Roi*, died 21 March 1770; his w., Jeanne-Marguerite de Niquet; his s., Aimé-Louis Véron de Seranne; his d., Antoinette-Josephine-Gabrielle Véron.

Veytard, François-Joseph (28 Nov. 1727–?): TG de l'Artillerie et du Génie from 26 Aug. 1778 after Préaudeau.

Villette, Pierre-Charles de: T de l'Extraordinaire des Guerres.

Watelet, Claude-Henri (30 Aug. 1718–1785): RG Orléans from 10 March 1741 after his f., Nicolas-Robert Watelet; when he died, his *caissier*, François Thuaut, took over the business and went bankrupt Jan. 1786, but Watelet had been in debt for years; writer and artist who lived in the Louvre; employer of Charles-Nicolas Roland.

A LIST OF SOURCES AND
WORKS CITED

(Books were published in Paris unless otherwise
listed. The code numbers in brackets are those
of the copy I used.)

MANUSCRIPT SOURCES

Archives nationales (AN)

AB xix 327. Bertrand Dufresne's record of meetings with the Finance Committee
in 1790–91

AF ii 8 (dossiers 49 and 50); AF ii 21ᴬ (dossier 162); AF ii 21ᴮ (dossier 163);
AF ii 163; AF iii 28 (dossier 94). Lists of employees, salaries and other
payments

4 AP 190. Revenues for 1776

144 AP 102, 108, 129, 130, 131, 132, 156, etc. Papers of Lefèvre d'Ormesson

C 224, 260, 356 National Assembly

D vi 1 to 8. Lists of personnel, salaries and other payments

D x 1 to 3. Lists of personnel, salaries, etc., correspondence on financial
arrangements

Fᴵᴬ 1, 2; Fᴵᴬ 565 and 568; Fᴵᴮ 1, 2. Tables of the Finance Department employees and bureaux

F4 1015, 1032², 1045, 1076, 1079, 1082, 1083, 1086, 1087, 1236, 1935, 1936, 1957,
2021, 2022, 2680. Accounts, lists, statistics and tables from the financial
administration

F³⁰ 106. A thick register of information on the Treasury, July 1796

F³⁰ 199. Accounts of the Receivers General 1790–1

F³⁰ 110ᴬ. Papers on financial administration

Gᴵ and G². Papers concerning the *Régie générale*, the General Farm and the
Domains Administration

H 1448. Organization tables of the Ministry of Public Contributions in 1792 and
other financial tables

P series. Hundreds of registers of the Paris Chamber of Accounts divided into
three concurrent series which supplement one another: the *plumitif*, the
memoriaux and the *journal*

Vᴵ series. Lettres de provision d'office, not complete but very full.

T 200⁷, 200¹², 165¹⁵, 594. Confiscated papers and official files concerning individuals in the French revolution

Bibliothèque nationale (BN)

MS fr. 11012. Chamber of Accounts

MS fr. 11696. Corresp. of Bailly with Necker, Dufresne and others, 1789–92

Nouv. acq. fr. 23617. Assembly of Notables
Joly de Fleury Papers. Hundreds of registers etc., on finances in the years 1781–3 in particular.
Reserve LC² 2225. Nouvelles à la Main, 1788

Archives du département de la Seine
DQ series of records on births, marriages and deaths

Archives de l'assistance publique, Paris
Papers of Auget de Montyon

Public Record Office, London (P.C. 1/124, 1/125, 1/128, etc.)
Papers of Calonne, mostly about his affairs as an *emigré*

Cornell University Library
Papers of Drouet de Santerre, 1770–1850
Charles-Claude Coster, *Journal manuscrit*, 1790–1, 2 vols

PRINTED WORKS

Collections of Laws and Tracts

Duvergier, *Collection complète des lois, décrets, ordonnances, règlements*...1788–1830, 2nd ed. (1834)
Collection des édits, déclarations et arrêts du Conseil d'état (B.N., F 23.664 etc.)
Collection générale des décrets rendus par l'Assemblée nationale, 15 vols. up to June 1791.
Collection Rondonneau, archives nationales, AD IX 431, 491, etc.
Isambert, Taillandier and Decrusy, *Recueil général des anciennes lois françaises*, 29 vols., 1822–7
Collections of French Revolutionary Pamphlets at the British Museum (The Croker Collection); at Cornell University Library; at the library of the University of British Columbia (on Necker and Calonne and by them); at the John Rylands Library, Manchester; and at the Bibliothèque nationale, Paris.

Books and Articles

Administration des domaines, Etat général des différens emplois de l'Administration des domaines tant à Paris que dans les provinces, avec les émoluments de chacun de ces emplois, tant en fixe que casuel, 35 pp., 9 July 1790 (B.N., Lf⁹⁰ 17).
Adresse à l'Assemblée nationale par les anciens employés des Receveurs généraux des finances supprimés, 4 pp. (Lf⁷⁶ 29).
Almanach de Versailles, 1770s and 1780s.
Amelot de Chaillou, Antoine-Léon-Anne, *Mémoire sur l'organisation des bureaux de l'administration de la Caisse de l'extraordinaire*, 1791 (MS A.N., D VII 1).
Antoine, Michel, 'Les comités de ministres sous le règne de Louis XV', *Revue d'histoire de droit français et étranger*, 1951, pp. 193–230.

Le Fonds du Conseil d'état du Roi aux Archives nationales, 1955.
'Les conseils des finances sous le règne de Louis XV', *Revue d'histoire moderne et contemporaine*, 1958, pp. 161–200.
Aperçu du travail auquel se sont appliqués les commis des divers bureaux de l'administration de la Caisse de l'extraordinaire, 1792 (B.N., Lf [157] 8).
Archives parlementaires de 1787 à 1860, recueil complet des débats législatifs et politiques des chambres françaises.
Arnould, Ambroise-Marie, *Rapports fait par Arnould au nom d'une commission spéciale sur les cautionnements à exiger des payeurs et caissiers du Trésor public*, 3 Germinal, An VIII (B.N., Le[51] 120).
Ashton, Robert, *The Crown and the Money Market, 1603–1640*, Oxford, 1960.
Assemblée nationale, procès-verbaux, 1789–91.
Audiffret, Charles-Louis-Gaston d', marquis, *Ministère des finances. Ordonnance du Roi du 31 Mai 1838, portant règlement sur la comptabilité publique*, 1838, 351 pp.
Système financier de la France, 2 e ed., 1854, 5 vols.
Augéard, J.-M., *Mémoires secrets*, 1866.
Aylmer, George, *The King's Servants: The Civil Serivce of Charles I*, London, 1961.
Babel, Antony, 'Jacques Necker et les origines de l'interventionisme', *Mélanges Edgar Milhaud*, 1934, pp. 25–44.
Baco de la Chapelle, René-Gaston, *Réponse à l'adresse à l'Assemblée nationale du Directoire de Nantes*, 20 pp. (B.M. FR 122 (23)).
Bailly, Antoine, *Histoire finançière de la France depuis l'origine de la monarchie jusqu'à la fin de 1786*, 1830, 2 vols.
Balzac, Honoré de, *La Comédie humaine*, Pléiade Ed., vol. VI (*Les Employés*, 1836).
Barnave, Antoine-Pierre-Joseph-Marie, *Œuvres*, 1843, 5 vols.
Baugh, Daniel, *British Naval Administration in the Age of Walpole*, Princeton, N.J., 1965, 577 pp.
Belin, Jean, *La Logique d'une idée-force: l'idée d'utilité sociale et la révolution française (1789–92)*, 1939, 628 pp.
Béranger, *Essai sur le contrôle*, 1790, 30 pp. (B.N., Lf[80] 87).
Bergeron, Louis, 'Profits et risques dans les affaires parisiennes à l'époque du Directoire et du Consulat', *Annales historiques de la révolution française*, vol. 38 (1966), pp. 359–89.
Bernardin, Edith, *Jean-Marie Roland et le Ministère de l'Intérieur, 1792–93*, 1964, 667 pp.
Bernot, *La Comptabilité des finances et la liquidation des dettes de l'état*, 1790, 72 pp. (B.N., Lb[39] 8285).
Besenval, Pierre-Joseph-Victor de (baron), *Mémoires*, 1821, 2 vols.
Binney, J. E. D., *British Public Finance and Administration, 1774–92*, Oxford, 1958.
Bloch, Camille, *Bulletin d'histoire économique de la révolution*, 1911 (concerning the *assignats*).
Procès-verbaux du comité des finances de l'Assemblée constituante, Rennes, 1922, 2 vols.

Blondel, Jean, *Introduction à l'ouvrage intitulé De l'administration des finances par M. Necker*, 1785.

Bluche, François, *L'Origine des magistrats du parlement de Paris au XVIIIe siècle*, 1956, 412 pp.

Les Magistrats du Grand conseil au XVIIIe siècle, 1690–1791, 1966, 189 pp.

Les Magistrats de la Cour des monnaies 1715–1790, 1966, 80 pp.

Boislisle, A. M. de, *Chambre des comptes de Paris, pièces justificatives pour servir à l'histoire des premiers présidents, 1506–1791*, 1873, 789 pp.

Correspondance des Contrôleurs généraux des finances avec les Intendants des provinces, 1874, 3 vols.

Boiteau, Paul, *L'Etat de la France en 1789*, 1861, 535 pp.

Bonvalet des Brosses, Simon-Joseph-Louis, *Etat des finances et des ressources de la France au 1 Janvier 1792*, 1792.

Situation actuelle de la France, 1791, 487 pp.

Richesses et ressources de la France, 1791, 271 pp.

Moyen de simplifier la perception et la comptabilité des deniers royaux, 1789, 116 pp. (B.N., Lb³⁹ 7248).

Bornarel, Frédéric, *Cambon et la révolution française*, 1905, 412 pp.

Bosher, J. F., *The Single Duty Project: A Study of the Movement for a French Customs Union in the Eighteenth Century*, London, 1964, 215 pp.

'Jacques Necker et la réforme de l'état', *Rapport annuel de la Société historique du Canada*, 1963, pp. 162–75.

'The *Premier Commis des finances* in the reign of Louis XVI', *French Historical Studies*, 1964, pp. 475–95.

'Guillaume-François Mahy de Cormeré et la réforme officielle sous l'ancien régime', *Annali della fondazione per la storia amministrativa*, Milan, 1966, pp. 236–53.

'Government and Private Interests in New France', *Canadian Public Administration*, 1967, pp. 244–57.

Bouchary, Jean, *Les manieurs d'argent à Paris à la fin du XVIIIe siècle*, 1939–43, 3 vols.

Bourgoin, Jean, *La Chasse aux larrons*, 1618.

L'Anti-péculat, 1620.

Le Pressoir des éponges, 1624.

Bournisien, Charles, 'La vente des biens nationaux', *Revue historique*, vol. 99 (1908), pp. 244–66; vol. 100 (1909), pp. 15–46.

Bowring, John, *Report on the public accounts of France to the Right Honourable the Lords Commissioners of His Majesty's Treasury*, 1831, 161 pp. and 189 pp. (B.M., P 78, 1831 XIV 339 and 501).

Braesch, Frédéric, *Finances et monnaies révolutionnaires. Recherches études et documents*, Nancy, 1934, 3 vols.

Brette, Armand, *Les Constituants, liste des deputés*, 1897.

Briffaud, Fernand, *Un receveur des finances sous la révolution*, Caen, 1909, 405 pp.

Brissot de Warville, Jacques-Pierre, *Point de banqueroute ou lettre à un créancier de l'état*, London, 1787, 32 pp.

Courrier de Provence, 1789–90.

Lettre à Monsieur Camus...sur différents abus de l'administration actuelle des finances, 21 Jan. 1791, 22 pp.

Buisseret, David, *Sully*, London, 1968.

Burté, Antoine, *Pour l'Assemblée nationale. Observations rapides sur les conditions d'éligibilité des commissaires de la comptabilité*, 1792 (B.N., Lf¹⁶⁰ 38).

Observations sur la nomination des commissaires de la comptabilité, lues à la société des amis de la constitution, 27 Nov. 1791, 15 pp. (B.N., Lb⁴⁰ 2248).

Pour la Convention nationale. Des moyens de rectifier l'organisation du département des contributions publiques, de la caisse de l'extraordinaire et de la Trésorerie nationale, 1792, 60 pp. (B.N., Lf¹⁹¹ 3).

Mémoire à consulter sur la question de savoir s'il est convenable de demander le rapport de l'article X du titre 1er de la loi du 22 août 1790 qui défend de cumuler pension et traitement (B.N., Lb⁴² 340).

Observations sur la fixation à 6000 livres du maximum des traitements dans les administrations publiques, 8 pp. (B.N., Lf⁹⁷ 33).

Calonne, Charles Alexandre de, *Réponse de Monsieur Calonne à l'écrit de Monsieur Necker*, London, Jan. 1788.

Cambon, Pierre-Joseph, *Rapport sur la situation des finances à la date du 1 Avril 1792*, 155 pp.

Camus, Armand-Gaston, *Réponse de Monsieur Camus au mémoire adressé par Monsieur Necker à l'Assemblée nationale le 1 août 1790*, 35 pp. (Lb³⁹ 3863).

Rapport au nom des commissaires de l'extraordinaire sur l'organisation et la dépense des bureaux de la Trésorerie et de la Caisse de l'extraordinaire, 1791, 23 pp. (B.M., R 623).

Carant, Nicolas-Thérèse, *Rapport sur les comptabilité et remplacement des Receveurs généraux et particuliers des finances*, July 1792, 24 pp. (B.N., Le³³ 3 G (7)).

Carra, Jean-Louis, *Un petit mot de réponse*, 1787.

Centre de recherches sur l'histoire des entreprises, 'Types de capitalistes parisiens à la fin du XVIIIe siècle: le probleme des investissements', *Bulletin* no. 2, Oct. 1953, pp. 25–31.

Chambre des Comptes de Paris, *Remontrances de la Chambre des Comptes*, 11 Feb. 1787, 16 pp. (B.N., Lf²⁷ 33).

Chamberland, Albert and Henri Hauser, 'La banque et les changes au temps de Henri II', *Revue historique*, vol. 160 (1929), pp. 268–93.

Chapuisat, Edouard, *Necker (1732–1804)*, 1938, 327 pp.

Charmeil, Jean-Paul, *Les Trésoriers de France à l'époque de la Fronde*, 1964.

Chauleur, Andrée, 'Le rôle des traitants dans l'Administration financière de la France de 1643 à 1653', *Le XVIIe siècle*, no. 65 (1964), pp. 16–49.

Cherest, Aime, *La chute de l'ancien régime, 1787–89*, 1884, 2 vols.

Chevallier, Pierre, ed., *Journal de l'Assemblée des Notables de 1787 par le Comte de Brienne et Etienne-Charles de Loménie de Brienne, Archevêque de Toulouse*, 1960, 144 pp.

Cilleuls, Alfred des, 'Henri IV et la Chambre de Justice de 1607', *Séances et Travaux de l'Académie des Sciences morales et politiques*, vol. 165 (1906), pp. 276–91.

Chronologie des lois, décrets, ordonnances et arrêtés rélatifs à l'organisation et aux attributions du ministère de l'intérieur, et aux nominations des ministres et fonctionnaires de département depuis sa création (7 août 1790) jusqu'au 31 dec. 1835, 143 pp. (B.N., Lf¹³¹ 1).

Claude de Ferrière, *Corps et compilation de tous les commentateurs anciens et modernes sur la coûtume de Paris*, 1745, 4 vols.

Clavière, Etienne, *Mémoire sur la liquidation de la ferme générale et de la Régie générale*, 1793, 30 pp. (B.N., Le³⁸ 80).

Examen du mémoire de Monsieur Amelot sur l'organisation de la Caisse de l'extraordinaire, 1790, 24 pp. (B.N., Lf¹⁵⁷ 2).

Lettres de Monsieur Clavière à Monsieur Beaumetz sur l'organisation du Trésor public (B.N., Lf⁷⁶ 143).

Réflexions sur les formes et les principes auxquels une nation libre doit assujetir l'administration des finances, 1791, 54 and 38 pp. (B.N., Lb³⁹ 9893).

Clément, Pierre, ed., *Lettres, instructions et mémoires de Colbert*, 1861, 9 vols.

Cobban, Alfred, *The Social Interpretation of the French Revolution*, Cambridge, 1964.

Commission de recherche et de publication des documents rélatifs à la vie économique de la révolution, *Recueil des textes législatifs et administratifs concernant les biens nationaux*, 1926, 2 vols.

Compte rendu au Roi au mois de mars 1788 et publié par ses ordres, 1788, 183 pp. (B.M., B 480 (4)).

Compte rendu à la Convention par les commissaires de la Trésorerie de leur administration, depuis 1 juillet 1791 (28 pp.) followed by, *Mémoire sur les opérations rélatives au numéraire depuis 1 juillet 1791 jusqu'au 15 sept. 1792* (80 pp.), 1793 (B.N., Lf¹⁵⁸ 19).

Condorcet, Marie-Jean-Antoine-Nicolas Caritat, marquis de, *Sur la constitution du pouvoir chargé d'administrer le Trésor national*, 36 pp., 1790.

Coppons, le président de, *Examen de la théorie et pratique de Monsieur Necker dans l'administration des finances de la France*, 1785, 536 pp. (B.N., Lb³⁹ 6290).

Coquereau, Jean-Baptiste-Louis, *Mémoires concernant l'administration des finances sous le ministère de Monsieur l'abbé Terray*, 1776.

Cornus de la Fontaine, François-Pierre, *Lettres à l'auteur de l'écrit anonyme intitulé: De la comptabilité des dépenses publiques*, 1822, 178 pp. (B.N., Lf¹⁶⁰ 8).

Idées sur l'administration des finances, Year VIII, 40 pp. (Lb⁴³ 387).

Correspondance du comité des pensions avec les ministres et ordonnateurs relativement aux demandes d'éclaircissements sur les pensions et autres grâces pécuniares, 1790, 128 pp. (B.N., Le²⁷ 20).

Coustant d'Yanville, H., *Chambre des comptes de Paris, essais historiques et chronologiques*, 1866–75, 1022 pp.

Dardel, Pierre, 'Crises et faillites à Rouen et dans la Haute-Normandie de 1740 à l'an v', *Revue d'histoire économique et sociale*, vol. XXVII (1948), pp. 53–71.

Darest de la Chavanne, C., *Histoire de l'administration en France*, 1848, 2 vols.

Daudet, E., 'La conspiration Magon, récit des temps révolutionnaires', *Revue des Deux Mondes*, 1911, pp. 356–90 and 624–55.

Delaby, Raymond, *Le Rôle du Comité d'aliénation dans la vente des biens nationaux d'après la correspondance inédite du constituant Camus avec le Directoire du département de la Côte d'Or, 1790–91*, Dijon, 1928.

De l'acquittement de la dette publique... 1792 (B.N., Lb³⁹ 5931).

Delafont-Braman, C., *Rapport et projet de décret sur le mode de comptabilité de l'ancienne administration des domaines*, 1792, 18 pp. (Le³³ 3 G (8)).

Denormandie, Louis-Valentin, *Convention nationale. Rapport du Directeur-général provisoire de la liquidation en conséquence du décret du 21 dec. 1792*, 1793, 74 pp., (B.M., F 219 (6)).

Dent, Julien, 'An Aspect of the Crisis of the Seventeenth Century: the Collapse of the Financial Administration of the French Monarchy 1653–61', *Economic History Review*, August 1967, pp. 241–56.

Des employés, des réformes et du régime intérieur des bureaux, 1817, 29 pp. (B.N., Lf⁹⁷ 1).

(Deuxième) Compte rendu par les commissaires de la Trésorerie nationale, de leur administration, dans lequel on trouve les principaux détails de l'organisation de cet établissement, 50 pp., 20 Dec. 1794 (B.N., Lf¹⁵⁸ 20).

Dickson, P. G. M., *The Financial Revolution in England*, London, 1967.

Doucet, Roger, 'Le grand parti de Lyon au XVIe siècle', *Revue historique*, vol. 171 (1933), pp. 473–513 and vol. 172 (1933), pp, 1–41.

Etudes sur le gouvernement de François I en relation avec le parlement de Paris, 1925.

Dictionnaire des institutions de la France au XVIe siècle, 1948.

Dubu de Longchamps, Pierre-Michel, *Mémoire pour Messieurs les maîtres de postes sur le fait des messageries à l'assemblée nationale historique des compagnies de messageries de 1775 à 1790*, 1790, 84 pp. (B.N., Lf⁹² 26).

Duchesne, Louis-Henri, *Observations sur un projet d'administration présenté en 1787*, Nov. 1791 (B.N., Rp 7613).

Dufort, J. N., *Mémoires sur les règnes de Louis XV et Louis XVI et sur la révolution*, 1886, 2 vols.

Dufresne, Bertrand, (A dozen reports and speeches under the Directory; letters and memoranda in A.N., C 224, dossier 160; a register in A.N., AB XIX 327).

Dufresne de Saint Léon, Louis-César-Alexandre, *Etudes sur le crédit public*, 1784, 376 pp. (B.N., Res. *E 593).

Mémoire sur la liquidation, ses progrès, son état actuel, ses engagements et ses besoins, Nov. 1791, 48 pp. (B.M., FR 562).

Duguit, L., H. Monnier and R. Bonnard, *Les Constitutions*, 7e éd., 1952.

Dupont-Ferrier, Gustave, *Etudes sur les institutions financières de la France à la fin du moyen âge*, 1930, 3 vols.

Durand, Charles, *Etudes sur le Conseil d'état napoléonien*, 1949.

Durban, Jean-Baptiste-Bertrand, *Essai sur les principes des finances*, London, 1769, 194 pp.

Eclaircissements sur l'organisation du Trésor public, ouvrage dans lequel on démontre les avantages du système de la Reunion des caisses, Nov. 1790, 41 pp. (B.M., FR 502).

Egret, Jean, *La Pré-Révolution française, 1787–88*, 1962, 400 pp.

'Un conseiller d'état à la fin de l'ancien régime, 1775–1789', *Revue historique*, vol. 198 (1947), pp. 189–202.

Encyclopédie méthodique. Finance (Panckoucke), 1783–4, 3 vols.

Encyclopédie méthodique. Jurisprudence (Panckouke).

Etat des citoyens employés dans les bureaux de la Direction générale de la liquidation, May 1793, 23 pp. (B.N., Lf[157] 10).

Etat des ordonnances de comptant, année 1779, 1790, 114 pp. (B.M., R 623).

Etat général des emplois des bureaux de la Régie générale à Paris, et du traitement annuel dont a joui chaque employé, à compter du premier janvier 1787 (B.N., Lf[88] 16).

Etat nominatif des pensions sur le Trésor public, 1789–91, 4 vols. (B.N., Lf[81] 5).

Etat nomimatif des pensions, traitements conservés, dons, gratifications qui se payent sur d'autres caisses que celle du Trésor royal, 1 vol. (B.N., Lf[81] 3).

Etats de comptant de l'année et des restes de l'année 1783; avec la table alphabétique des personnes qui y sont employées, May 1790, 63 and 108 pp. (B.M., FR 551).

Faure, Edgar, *La Disgrâce de Turgot (12 mai 1776)*, 1961, 610 pp.

Flori, Sabien, *Le Comité de trésorerie (1791)*, 1939, 122 pp. (U.B.C., Hj 1093 F 55).

Flour de Saint-Genis, Henri-Alexandre, *Essai sur les pensions de retraite*, 1833, 36 pp. (B.N., Lf[164] 20).

Forbonnais, Francois Veron de, *Recherches et considérations sur les finances de la France depuis l'année 1595 jusqu'à l'année 1721*, Basle, 1758, 2 vols.

Frégault, Guy, 'Essai sur les finances canadiennes (1700–1750)', *Revue d'histoire de l'Amérique française*, vol. 12 (1958–9), pp. 307–23, 459–85; vol. 13 (1959), pp. 30–45, 157–83.

Gaudin, Martin-Michel-Charles, duc de Gaete, *Mémoires, souvenirs, opinions et écrits (1826)*, reprinted 1926, 3 vols.

Gelée, Vincent, *Annotation de Vincent Gelée...sur le Guidon général des finances*, 1594.

Gillet, Pierre-Mathurin, *Rapport et projet de décret sur la comptabilité des anciens receveurs des finances*, Dec. 1792, 10 pp. (B.N., Le[38] 2610).

Godechot, Jacques, *Les institutions de la France sous la révolution*, 1951, 687 pp.

Gomel, Charles, *Histoire financière de l'Assemblée constituante*, 1896, 2 vols.

Gottschalk, Louis, *Jean-Paul Marat, A Study in Radicalism*, 1927, 221 pp.

Goubert, Pierre, *Beauvais et le Beauvaisis de 1660 à 1730*, 1960.

Grosclaude, Pierre, *Malesherbes, témoin et interprète de son temps*, 1961, 806 pp.

Guyot, Pierre-Jean-Jacques-Guillaume, *Traité des droits, fonctions, franchises, exemptions, prérogatives, etc.*, 1786–8, 4 vols. (B.N., 4° Lf[3] 14).

Guyton-Morveau, M.-L.-B., *Rapport sur l'établissement d'un bureau dans la trésorerie nationale pour la liquidation des offices supprimés avant le premier mai 1789...26 nov. 1791*, 1792, 17 pp. (B.N., L[33] 3z).

Hanotaux, Gabriel-Albert-Auguste, ed., *Histoire de la nation française*, 1920, 15 vols.

Harris, Seymour, *The Assignats*, Harvard, 1930.

Harrisson, Jean-Pierre, *Précis et observations sur la nouvelle organisation de la Trésorerie nationale*... 1791, 4 pp. (B.N., Lf¹⁵⁷ 12).

Hauser, Henri, 'The European Financial Crisis of 1559', *Journal of Economic and Business History*, vol. 2 (1929–30), pp. 241–55.

Hennequin, Jean, *Le Guidon général des financiers*, 1585, 334 pp.

Hennet, A.-J.-U., *Théorie du crédit public*, 1816, 587 pp. (B.N., *E 1143).

Essai d'un plan de finance, 1816, 36 pp. (B.N., Rp. 12859).

Herlaut, Colonel, 'Projets de création d'une banque royale en France à la fin du regne de Louis XIV (1702–1712)', *Revue d'histoire moderne*, N.S., no. 6, 1933, pp. 143–60.

Huber, Barthélemy, *Mémoire à consulter et consultation pour le sieur Huber nommé à l'une des places de commissaire de la Trésorerie nationale*, 1791, 23 pp. (B.N., Ln²⁷ 9912).

Hubrecht, G., *Les assignats dans le Haut-Rhin*, Strasbourg, 1932, 255 pp.

Ille, François, *Rapport et projet de décret sur la comptabilité du sieur Bertin, ci-devant Receveur général des parties casuelles*, 11 Aug. 1792, 7 pp. (B.N., L³³ 3 G (15)).

Jacqueton, G., *Documents rélatifs à l'administration financière en France de Charles VII à François I (1443–1523)*, 1891, 324 pp.

Jassemin, Henri, 'La Chambre des Comptes et la gestion des deniers publics au XVe siécle', *Bibliothèque de l'école des Chartes*, vol. 93 (1932), pp. 111–21.

Jèze, avocat au Parlement, *Etat ou tableau de la ville de Paris considerée relativement au nécessaire, à l'utile, à l'agréable et à l'administration*, 1760, cvi pp. and 379 pp. and 134 pp. (B.M., 1486 B 17).

Johnson, J. A., 'Calonne and the Counter-revolution, 1787–92', unpublished London Ph.D. thesis, 1955, 375 pp.

Jouvencel, Henri de, *Le Contrôleur général des finances sous l'ancien régime*, 1901, 430 pp.

Labrousse, C.-E., *La Crise de l'économie française à la fin de l'ancien régime, et au début de la Rèvolution*, 1944, 664 pp.

Laffon de Ladebat, André-Daniel, *Rapport du comité de l'ordinaire des finances sur une motion faite rélativement aux payeurs-généraux des dèpartements*, 10 Feb., 1792, 28 pp. (B.N., Le³³ 3 H (6)).

Lafrêté, *Plan de travail sur les finances*, 15 Oct. 1791, 23 pp. (B.N., Lb³⁹ 10985)

Lalouette, Claude-Joseph, *Eléments de l'administration pratique*, 1812, 757 pp. (B.N., R 6342).

Lamy, Michel-Louis, *Opinion sur l'importance de décréter la responsabilité des chefs de bureaux de l'administration*, 1790, 11 pp. (B.M., FR 112 (20)).

Laplatte, C., 'L'Administration des évêchés vacants et la régie des économats', *La Révue d'histoire de l'Eglise de France*, vol. 23 (1937), pp. 161–225.

Lavisse, Ernest, ed., *Histoire de France depuis les origines jusqu'à la révolution*, 1900–11, 9 vols.

Law, John, *Œuvres complètes* (ed. Harsin), 1934, 3 vols.

Le Bihan, Alain, *Francs-maçons parisiens du grand orient de France (fin du XVIIIe siècle)*, 1966, 489 pp.

Lebrun, Charles-François, duc de Plaisance, *Opinions, rapports et choix d'écrits politiques, recueillies et mis en ordre par son fils aîné*, 1829, 463 pp.

Rapport fait sur la résolution, 17 April 1796.

Legendre, Pierre, 'Evolution des systèmes d'administration et histoire des idées: l'exemple de la pensée française', *Annali della fondazione italiana per la storia amministrativa* (Milan), vol. 3, 1966, pp. 254–74.

Legohérel, Henri, *Les Trésoriers généraux de la Marine, 1517–1788*, 1965.

Le grand bilan du Trésor national pour l'année MDCCXCI extrait du dernier compte de Monsieur Dufresne, 1791, 19 pp. (B.M., F 199 (1)).

Le Roy Ladurie, Emmanuel, *Les paysans de Languedoc*, 1966, 2 vols.

Les quarante payeurs des rentes, financiers héréditaires (B.N., Lf⁸⁰ 90).

Linguet, Simon-Nicolas-Henri, *Annales politiques, civiles et littéraires du dix-huitieme siècle, ouvrage périodique*, 1771–90.

Logette, Aline, *Le comité contentieux des finances près le Conseil du roi (1777–91)*, Nancy, 1964, 324 pp.

Loménie de Brienne, (Memorandum quoted at length in Jean-Louis Soulavie, *Mémoires historiques et politiques du règne de Louis XVI*, 1801, 6 vols., vol. VI, pp. 237–54).

Lot, Ferdinand and Robert Fautier, *Histoire des institutions française au moyen âge*, 1958, vol. 2.

Loyseau, Charles, *Les Œuvres de Maistre Charles Loyseau*, Lyon, 1701.

Lublinskaya, A. D., *French Absolutism: The Crucial Phase, 1620–1629*, Cambridge, 1968.

Luethy, Herbert, *La Banque protestante en France de la révocation de l'édit de Nantes jusqu'à la révolution française*, 1958–63, 2 vols.

Mallet, Jean-Roland, *Comptes rendus de l'administration des finances du royaume de France*, 1789, 431 pp. (B.M., 179 c 11).

Malpart, P. J., *Plan d'administration des finances*, London, 1787, 101 pp. (B.N., R 42795).

Marat, Jean-Paul, *L'Ami du peuple, 1789–93* (Cornell: DC 140 A 514).

Marcé, Victor, *La comptabilité publique pendant la révolution*, 1893, 94 pp.

Marion, Marcel, *Histoire financière de la France*, 1914, 6 vols.

Martin, Germain-Louis, *Histoire économique et financière*, 1920.

Martin, Germain-Louis and Marcel Besançon, *L'Histoire du crédit en France sous le règne de Louis XIV*, 1913.

Martin, Marie-Joseph-Desiré, *Etrennes financières ou recueil des matières les plus importantes en finance, banque et commerce*, 31 Jan. 1789 and 1790, 2 vols. (B.N., Lc²⁵ 137).

Massac, Raymond de, *Manuel des rentes ou tableau général...* 1777, 150 pp. (B.N., Lf⁸⁰ 5).

Traité des immatriculés ou instructions générales sur les formalités qu'il faut observer...pour recevoir les rentes et les pensions royales, 1779, 88 pp. (B.N., F 25541).

Masson, André, *Un mécène bordelais, Nicolas Beaujon, 1718–1786*, Bordeaux, 1937, 218 pp.

Mathiez, Albert, 'Les capitalistes et la prise de la bastille', *La Révolution française*, 1926, pp. 578–82.

Mathon de la Cour, Charles-Joseph, *Collection de comptes-rendus, pièces authentiques, états et tableaux concernant les finances de France depuis 1758 jusqu'en 1787*, 1788, 231 pp. (B.M., 804 e 11).

Matthews, George T., *The Royal General Farms in Eighteenth-Century France*, New York, 1958.

May, Louis-Philippe, *L'Ancien régime devant le mur d'argent*, 1935.

Mémoire concernant les offices de contrôleur des rentes de l'hôtel de ville, Dec. 1789 (B.N., Lf⁸⁰ 85).

Mémoire pour les anciens receveurs-généraux au sujet du décret du cinq juin, qui ordonne l'apposition des scellés chez les anciens comptables, 1793, 4 pp. (B.N., Lf⁷⁶ 32).

Mémoire pour le sieur de Sainte-Foy au surintendant de Monsieur le Comte d'Artois, 1783 (B.N., F³ 35391).

Mémoire sur les principes et les avantages de l'établissement des payeurs-généraux, envoyé par les commissaires de la Trésorerie à l'Assemblée nationale et imprimé par son ordre, 1792, 15 pp. (B.N., Le³³ 3 H (8)).

Mémoire sur les rentes et sur les offices de payeurs et contrôleur, 1789 (B.N., Lf⁸⁰ 85).

Mercier, Louis-Sebastien, *Tableau de Paris*, Amsterdam, 1783–9, 12 vols.

Mirabeau, Honoré-Gabriel Riquetti, comte de, *Courrier de Provence*, 1789–90.

Dénonciation de l'agiotage au Roi et à l'assemblée des notables, 1787, 143 pp. (Cornell 4191 C 407).

Mittié, Stanislas C., *Plan de suppression des Fermiers généraux, des Receveurs généraux des finances, etc.*, 1789, 8 pp. (A.N., D VI I).

Mollien, François-Nicolas, *Mémoires d'un ministre du Trésor public, 1780–1815*, 1898, 2 vols.

Morellet, abbé André, *Lettres de l'abbé Morellet à Lord Shelburne, 1772–1803*, 1898, 342 pp.

Morini-Comby, Jean, *Les Assignats*, 1925, 165 pp.

Morizot, Edmé-Etienne, *Dénonciation contre le sieur Necker, et contre le sieur Lambert*, 1790, 50 pp. (Cornell, DC 141 F 87 V 564).

Mousnier, Roland, *La venalité des offices sous Henri IV et Louis XIII*, Rouen, 1946, 629 pp.

Napoléon I, *Lettres au comte Mollien, Ministre du Trésor public*, Havana, Cuba, 1959.

Necker, Jacques, *Œuvres complètes*, 1820, 7 vols.

De l'administration des finances de la France, 1784, 3 vols.

Sur le Compte rendu...nouveaux éclaircissements, 1787.

Norris, John, *Shelburne and Reform*, London, 1963.

Observations rapides concernant les Receveurs généraux des finances, 1791, 16 pp. (B.N., Lf⁷⁶ 28).

Observations sur la comptabilité et sur la juridiction de la Chambre des Comptes, 1789, 75 pp. (B.N., Lf²⁷ 36).

Observations sur l'arrangement concerté de rendre aux administrateurs leurs charges de Trésoriers généraux, et de leur laisser les fonds sous la responsabilité des Ministres, à commencer du 1 juillet 1790, 1790, 7 pp. (B.M., FR 502).

Ouvrard, Gabriel-Julien, *Mémoires sur sa vie et ses diverses opérations financières*, 1826, 3 vols.

Pares, Richard, *Limited Monarchy in Great Britain in the Eighteenth Century* (Historical Association Pamphlet), London, 1957.

Perroud, Claude, 'Aventures d'un chef de bureau (A.-F. Le Tellier) sous la révolution', *La Révolution française*, vol. 53 (1907), pp. 255–68.

Phytilis, Jacques etc., *Questions administratives au dix-huitième siècle*, 1965.

Pièces à produire par les Receveurs des finances, 1792, 2 pp. (B.N., Lf⁷⁶ 31).

Poisard, Léon, 'Le crédit public pendant la révolution française', *La Révolution française*, vol. 15 (1888), pp. 227–54 and 312–33.

Radix de Sainte Foy, *Mémoire à Monseigneur le comte d'Artois sur l'administration de ses finances*, 1781, 111 pp. (B.N., Lf¹⁵ 8).

Ranum, Orest, *Richelieu and the Councillors of Louis XIII*, Oxford, 1963.

Ravel, Pierre, *La Chambre de justice de 1716*, 1928.

Réal de Curban, Gaspard de, *La science du gouvernement, ouvrage de morale, de droit et de politique*, 1761–5, 8 vols.

Rébillon, Armand, *Les Etats de Bretagne, 1661 à 1789*, 1932.

Receveurs généraux, *Pétition des ci-devant Receveurs généraux à la Convention nationale*, 10 pp. (B.N., Lf ⁷⁶ 33).

Réflexions sur la partie du projet d'organisation du Trésor public de Monsieur Beaumetz, 12 pp. (B.M., F* 26).

Répertoire national ou memorial chronologique de tous les actes authentiques rélatifs à la révolution, 1788–92, 7 vols.

Rey, Maurice, *Le Domaine du Roi et les finances extraordinaires sous Charles VI, 1388–1413*, 1965.

Reymondin, G., *Bibliographie méthodique des ouvrages en langue française parus de 1543 à 1908 sur la science des comptes*, 1909, 330 pp.

Richard, Camille, *Le Comité de Salut public et les fabrications de guerre*, 1922.

Richelieu, *Mémoires du Cardinal de Richelieu* (Société de l'histoire de France), 1920.

Robinet, Jean-Baptiste-René, *Dictionnaire universel des sciences morales, économiques, politiques et diplomatiques ou bibliothèque de l'homme d'état et du citoyen*, London, 1777–83, 30 vols.

Roederer, Pierre-Louis, *Œuvres*, 1853–9, 8 vols.

Roland, Charles-Nicolas, *Mémoire au Roi Louis XVI en dénonciation d'abus d'autorité et de mépris des loix exercés contre moi, Roland*, London, April 1784, 283 pp. Reprinted 1789 (B.M., 10660 C 15).

Le financier patriote; ou la nation éclairée sur ses vrais intérêts, London, 1789, 172 and 222 pp. (B.M., F 31 (1)).

Recueil d'idées patriotiques remises successivement à messieurs du comité des finances et du comité des recherches, 1789, 152 pp. (B.M., F 662 (13)).

Romier, Lucien, *Le Royaume de Catherine de Médicis*, 1922, 2 vols.

Roton, Robert de, *Les Arrêts du Grand Conseil portant dispense du marc d'or de noblesse*, 1951, 538 pp.

Rougier-Labergerie, *Opinion et projet de décret sur les 87 Payeurs-généraux*, 9 April 1792, 23 pp. (B.N., L³³ 3z).

Sagnac, Philippe, 'Le crédit de l'état et les banquiers à la fin du XVIIe et au commencement du XVIIIe siècle', *Revue d'histoire moderne et contemporaine*, vol. IX (1908), pp. 257–72.

Schnapper, Bernard, *Les rentes au XVIe siècle*, 1957.

Seligmann, *La première tentative d'émission fiduciaire en France*, 1925.

Shortt, Adam, ed., *Documents Relating to Canadian Currency, Exchange and Finance during the French Period*, Ottawa, 1925.

Signorel, Jean, *Etude historique sur la législation révolutionnaire relative aux biens des émigrés*, 1915.

Snyders, Georges, *La Pédagogie en France au XVIIe et XVIIIe siècles*, 1964.

Soufflot de Merey, Pierre, *Précis sur la Banque territorial*, 15 ventose, An XII, 35 pp.

Considérations sur le rétablissement des jurandes et maîtrises, 1805, 187 pp. (B.N., Res. F 1840).

Considérations sur l'utilité des corporations, l'hérédité des offices et le rétablissement etc., May 1814, 83 pp. (B.N., V 53068).

Soulavie, Jean-Louis, *Mémoires historiques et politiques du règne de Louis XVI*, 1801.

Stourm, René, *Bibliographie historique des finances de la France au dix-huitième siècle*, 1895, 341 pp.

Les Finances de l'ancien régime, 1885.

Les Finances du Consulat, 1902.

Taylor, George, 'The Paris Bourse on the Eve of the Revolution, 1781–89', *American Historical Review*, vol. 67 (1962), pp. 951–77.

Turgot, Anne-Robert, *Œuvres*, ed. Gustave Schelle, 1913–23, 5 vols.

Turpin, Gerard-Maurice, *Mémoire concernant la comptabilité des finances rédigé par l'agent du Trésor public*, 1790, 24 pp. (B.M., R 479).

Vaillé, Eugène, *Histoire général des postes françaises*, 1947, 6 vols.

Un scandale financier au XVIIIe siècle. L'affaire Billard d'après des documents inédits, 1934 (B.M., 010665 f 11).

Vaines, Jean de, *Des moyens d'assurer le succès et la durée de la constitution*, 1790, 32 pp. (B.N., Lb³⁹ 2964).

Recueil de quelques articles tirés de différents ouvrages périodiques, 1799, 220 pp. (B.N., Res. Z 1311).

Vellay, Edouard, 'Les agents de change et la prise de la bastille', *L'Intermédiaire des chercheurs et curieux* (Jan. 1956), pp. 26–30; (1955), pp. 103, 289, 408, 623.

Vernier, Théodore, *Rapport du comité des finances sur l'organisation de la Trésorerie nationale*, 1791, 56 pp. (B.M., FR 502).

Elémens de finances, 1789, 158 pp. (B.N., R 53432).

Vilar-Berrogain, Gabrielle, *Guide des recherches dans les fonds d'enregistrement sous l'ancien régime*, 1958.

Walter, Gerard, *Robespierre* (1936), 2 vols.

Watson, J. Steven, *The Reign of George III*, Oxford, 1960.

Zeller, Gaston, *Les institutions de la France au XVIe siècle*, 1948.

INDEX

Names mentioned only in the alphabetical appendix are not in this index. Page numbers set in bold type refer to the more substantial statements about the subject.